The Invisible Web

The Invisible Web

Uncovering Information Sources
Search Engines Can't See

Chris Sherman

and

Gary Price

CyberAge Books

Information Today, Inc.
Medford, New Jersey

Seventh printing, December 2007

The Invisible Web: Uncovering Information Sources
Search Engines Can't See

Library of Congress Cataloging-in-Publication Data

Sherman, Chris
    The invisible Web : uncovering information sources search engines can't see / Chris Sherman and Gary Price.
        p. cm.
    Includes bibliographical references and index.
    ISBN 0-910965-51-X
    1. Online databases--Directories. 2. Database searching. 3.
Internet searching. I. Price, Gary, 1965-   . II. Title.
    ZA4450 .S54 2001
    025.04--dc21

                                                                2001028818

Printed and bound in the United States of America

Publisher: Thomas H. Hogan, Sr.
Editor-in-Chief: John B. Bryans
Managing Editor: Deborah R. Poulson
Copy Editors: Pat Hadley-Miller, Dorothy Pike
Production Manager: M. Heide Dengler
Book Designer: Kara Mia Jalkowski
Cover Designer: Jeremy Pellegrin
Proofreader: Susan Muaddi Darraj
Indexer: Sharon Hughes

Dedication

To my children, Skylar Javin Sherman and Sonya Aubrey Sherman.

The world is full of mostly invisible things,
And there is no way but putting the mind's eye,
Or its nose, in a book, to find them out.
—Howard Nemerov

– C.S.

To my mother and father, I love you!
– G.P.

Table of Contents

Figures and Tables xiii

Foreword xv

Acknowledgments xix

Introduction xxi
    The Invisible Web in a Nutshell xxii
    What to Expect from This Book xxiii
    Boldly Go Where No Search Engine Has Gone Before xxvi

About www.invisible-web.net xxix

Chapter 1 - The Internet and the Visible Web 1
    How the Internet Came to Be 2
    Early Net Search Tools 3
    Enquire Within Upon Everything 8
    Weaving the Web 10
    Early Web Navigation 12
    The First Search Engines 13

Chapter 2 - Information Seeking on the Visible Web 17
    Browsing vs. Searching 19
    Web Directories 22
        How Web Directories Work 22
        Issues with Web Directories 24
    Search Engines 26
        How Search Engines Work 26
        Issues with Search Engines 32
    Search Engines vs. Directories 36

Chapter 3 - Specialized and Hybrid Search Tools 37

Targeted Directories and Focused Crawlers 38
    Targeted Directories 39
    Focused Crawlers 41
Vertical Portals (Vortals) 43
    How to Find Vortals 44
Metasearch Engines 44
    Issues with Metasearch Engines 45
Value-Added Search Services 46
Alternative Search Tools 48
    Browser Agents 48
    Client-Based Search Tools 50
    Web Rings 51
    Fee-Based Web-Accessible Services 52
Next Stop: The Invisible Web 52

Chapter 4 - The Invisible Web 55

Invisible Web Defined 56
Why Search Engines Can't See the Invisible Web 62
Four Types of Invisibility 70
    The Opaque Web 70
    The Private Web 73
    The Proprietary Web 73
    The Truly Invisible Web 74

Chapter 5 - Visible or Invisible? 77

Navigation vs. Content Sites 78
Direct vs. Indirect URLs 79
    The URL Test 80
Specialized vs. Invisible 82
Visible vs. Invisible 83
    The Library of Congress Web Site:
    Both Visible and Invisible 86
The Robots Exclusion Protocol 89

Chapter 6 - Using the Invisible Web 91

Why Use the Invisible Web? 92
    When to Use the Invisible Web 95
Top 25 Invisible Web Categories 96
What's NOT on the Web—Visible or Invisible 103
Spider Traps, Damned Lies, and Other Chicanery 105
Keeping Current with the Invisible Web 109
Build Your Own Toolkit 111

Chapter 7 - Case Studies 115
  Case 1 - Historical Stock Quotes 115
  Case 2 - Patent Information 117
  Case 3 - Real-Time Tracking 119
  Case 4 - Locating an Out of Print Book 120
  Case 5 - Telephone Numbers and Zip Codes 121
  Case 6 - Finding Online Images 122
  Case 7 - Investment Research 123
  Case 8 - The Invisible Web Fails to Deliver! 124

Chapter 8 - The Future: Revealing the Invisible Web . . .127
  Smarter Crawlers 128
  The Promise and Pitfalls of Metadata 129
  Beyond Text 130
  Delving into Databases 130
  Hypertext Query Languages 132
  Real-Time Crawling 132
  Long Live the Invisible Web 133

Chapter 9 - The Best of the Invisible Web 135
  Invisible Web Pathfinders 135
  An Invisible Web Directory 137
  Frequently Asked Questions about the Directory 138
  In Summary: The Top 10 Concepts to Understand
            about the Invisible Web 142

Chapter 10 - Art and Architecture 145
  Architecture 146
  Artists 147
  Galleries on the Web 148
  Gateways to Art and Architecture Resources 151
  Reference 152

Chapter 11 - Bibliographies and Library Catalogs 153
  Bibliographies 154
  Library Catalogs 160

Chapter 12 - Business and Investing 163
  Company Information and Research 164
  Consumer Resources 169
  Economics—United States 169
  Economics—World 173
  Financial Institutions 175
  General Business Resources 176
  Government Contracts 177
  Industry-Specific Resources 178
  Investment Resources 182

Jobs and Career Information 185
Lookup Services 187
Marketing Resources 188
Pension Resources 189
Personal Finances 190
Philanthropy and Non-Profit Resources 190
Research and Development 192
Real Estate 193
Tariffs and Trade 194
Trade Shows and Conventions 196

Chapter 13 - Computers and Internet 199
Computers and Computing 200
Internet Resources 203

Chapter 14 - Education 207
Classroom and Teacher Support 208
Directories and Locators 209
Financial Information and Scholarships 212
General Education Resources 213
Statistics 215

Chapter 15 - Entertainment 217
Amusements 218
General Entertainment Resources 218
Movies and Cinema 219
Music 221
Performances and Events 224

Chapter 16 - Government Information and Data 227
Directories and Locators 228
General Government Resources 230
Government Documents 231
Government Officials 234
Government Programs 235
Politics, Policy, and International Relations 236
Statistics 238

Chapter 17 - Health and Medical Information 241
Diseases and Conditions 242
Images 246
Healthcare and Medical Information .247
Healthcare Professional Resources 249
Locators 251
Nutrition 253
Patient Information and Consumer Resources 254
Pharmaceutical Drugs 256
Research 257
Workplace Health and Safety 259

Chapter 18 - U.S. and World History 261
United States History 262
World History 267

Chapter 19 - Legal and Criminal Resources 271
Attorney and Law Firm Locators 272
Crime and Criminals 273
Decisions 273
Documents and Records 274
General Legal Resources 274
Intellectual Property 276
Laws, Codes, and Treaties 278

Chapter 20 - News and Current Events 283
Audio 284
Directories 284
News Search Resources 285
Video 288

Chapter 21 - Searching for People 291
Famous and Historical People 292
Genealogy Resources 293
Group and Affiliation Directories 294
Online White Pages and Lookup Tools 297
Veterans and Currently Serving Military 299

Chapter 22 - Public Records 301
General Public Records Resources 302
Location-Specific Public Records 303

Chapter 23 - Real-Time Information 311
Environment 312
Government 313
Miscellaneous Tracking 314
Space and Satellite 314
Stock Quotes 315
Transportation 315
Weather 317

Chapter 24 - Reference 319
Associations 320
Awards 321
Books 322
Calculators 323
Consumer Resources 324
Dictionaries, Glossaries, and Translation Resources 325
Food and Beverages 327
General Reference Resources 328
Journals and Periodicals 331

Library/Online Searching 332
Locators 333
Maps and Geography 335
Sports 338
Travel 339
Weather 341

Chapter 25 - Science 343
Agriculture 344
Biology 345
Botany 347
Chemistry 348
Earth Sciences 350
Energy 353
Engineering 355
Environment 356
General Science Resources 361
Mathematics and Physics 362
Oceanography 362
Research and Development 363
Space and Astronomy 365
Weather and Meteorology 367

Chapter 26 - Social Sciences 369
Anthropology 370
Archaeology 370
Demographics 371
Development Resources 373
General Resources.................................374
Gender Studies and Data..........................375
Latin America 376
Military Resources 377
Psychology 377
Research and Development 378
Religion 378

Chapter 27 - Transportation 381
Air 382
Automobile 384
General Transportation Resources 384
Maritime 386
Railroad 387

Glossary 389

References 397

About the Authors 401

Index 403

Figures

Figure 2.1 Hierarchichal Graph vs. Inverted Index Structures 20

Figure 5.1 The Library of Congress Home Page 87
Figure 5.2 The Library of Congress Collection Finder 88

Tables

Table 1.1   A Timeline of Internet Search Technologies 15

Table 2.1   Open vs. Closed Model Web Directories 23
Table 2.2   A Typical Inverted Index Data Structure 30
Table 2.3   Directories vs. Search Engines 36

Table 3.1   Specialized and Hybrid Search Tools 43

Table 4.1   On the Web vs. Via the Web 60
Table 4.2   Types of Invisible Web Content 61

Table 5.1   The Gateway to Educational Materials vs. AskERIC 83
Table 5.2   INTA Trademark Checklist vs. Delphion Intellectual
            Property Network 84
Table 5.3   Hoover's vs. Thomas Register of American
            Manufacturers 85
Table 5.4   WebMD vs. National Health Information Center
            Health Information Resource Database 86

Foreword

Internet search engines, not readily available to the general public until the mid-1990s, have in a few short years made themselves part of our everyday lives. It's hard to imagine going about our daily routines without them. Indeed, one study from the Fall of 2000 on how people seek answers found that search engines were the top information resource consulted, used nearly 1/3 of the time.

Of course, it's common to hear gripes about search engines. Almost like bad weather, our failures in locating information with them provide a common experience that everyone can commiserate with. Such complaints overlook the fact that we do indeed tend to find what we are looking for most of the time with search engines. If not, they would have long been consigned to the Internet's recycle bin and replaced with something better. Nevertheless, it is the search failures that live in our memories, not the successes. "What a stupid search engine! How could it not have found that?" we ask ourselves.

The reasons why are multifold. Sometimes we don't ask correctly, and the search engine cannot interrogate us to better understand what we want. Sometimes we use the wrong search tool, for example, looking for current news headlines on a general-purpose Web-wide search engine. It's the cyberspace equivalent of trying to drive a nail into a board with a screwdriver. Use the right tool, and the job is much easier.

Sometimes the information isn't out there at all, and so a search engine simply cannot find it. Despite the vast resources of the World Wide Web, it does not contain the answers to everything. During such times, turning to information resources such as books and libraries, which have served us valiantly for hundreds of years, may continue to be the best course of action.

Of course, sometimes the information is out there but simply hasn't been accessed by search engines. Web site owners may not want their information to be found. Web technologies may pose barriers to search engine access. Some information simply cannot be retrieved until the right forms are processed. These are all examples of information that is essentially "invisible" to search engines, and if we had a means to access this "Invisible Web," then we might more readily find the answers we are looking for.

The good news is that the Invisible Web is indeed accessible to us, though we might need to look harder to find it. Chris Sherman and Gary Price have put together a unique guide to the Web's hidden information resources—a must-read for every serious online searcher, and a book that makes our transition from the visible Web to the netherworld of the invisible Web easier. Though we can't see it easily, there's nothing to fear from the Invisible Web and plenty to gain from discovering it.

Danny Sullivan
Editor, SearchEngineWatch.com
May 2001

O world invisible, we view thee,
O world intangible, we touch thee,
O world unknowable, we know thee,
inapprehensible, we clutch thee!

—Francis Thompson
In No Strange Land

Acknowledgments

*I write the way women have babies. You don't know it's going to
be like that. If you did, there's no way you'd go through with it.*
                                                    —Toni Morrison

When I first proposed this book to CyberAge Books' Editor-in-Chief
John Bryans, we were sitting outdoors in San Diego, enjoying a wonderful Thai lunch in a decidedly offline environment. In the warmth of
that late autumn day, writing a book on the Invisible Web seemed like a
straightforward project, a book that could be dispatched with ease and
aplomb, and John welcomed the idea enthusiastically.

John's enthusiasm remains but, like Toni Morrison, I "didn't know it
was going to be like that." The Invisible Web is a fascinating, but very
elusive, phenomenon, and writing about it has proven to be one of the
major challenges of my professional life. Gary and I spent countless
hours simply trying to wrap our brains around the concept of the
Invisible Web, let alone giving birth to this book. We owe a huge debt of
gratitude to dozens of information professionals who took the time to
talk with us and patiently help us clarify and crystallize our ideas into
what we hope is a coherent portrait of this tremendously valuable but
largely unknown wealth of information on the Web.

Special thanks to Tara Calishain, Sean Dreilinger, Sue Feldman, Ran
Hock, Sundar Kadayam, Matt Koll, Bill Mickey, Greg Notess, Jeff
Pemberton, Marshall Simmonds, Danny Sullivan, and Mahendra Vora,

and many others too numerous to name. I'd also like to thank About.com for providing such a wonderful environment for me to learn and write about search—and especially to my editor, Avram Piltch, for his generous support and 24/7 availability. And many thanks to Steve Lawrence, C. Lee Giles, and Kurt Bollacker of the NEC Research Institute for creating ResearchIndex, an indispensable Invisible Web research tool.

We're grateful to have the opportunity to work with Tom Hogan, John Bryans, Deborah Poulson, and the staff of consummate professionals at CyberAge Books and Information Today, Inc.

To Gary Price: I've never met a more skilled, persistent, and curious searcher. The number and breadth of the resources you've discovered for this book astonishes me—and the hits just keep on coming!

To my children, Skylar and Sonya: I'm looking forward to spending weekends and evenings with you again!

And to my wife, Janice, my best friend and companion for life: Thank you. It's a hopeless cliché, but it's true—I couldn't have done this without you. I'm grateful every day that you ultimately said "yes."

—Chris Sherman

To my friends and colleagues at the Gelman and Virginia Campus Libraries of George Washington University: Thanks for everything including several wonderful ideas for compilations.

To the staff and faculty of the Library and Information Science Program at Wayne State University: Thanks for teaching me about our wonderful profession.

Special thanks and kudos to library/info pals, mentors, and friends: Tara Calishain, Doug Carroll, Judy Field, Susan Fingerman, Bob Fraser, Bob Holley, Helene Kassler, Laura Kazmierczak, Sheri Lanza, Rachelle Linner, Carole Leita, Greg Notess, Chris Paschen, Barbara Quint, Barbara Semonche, and Genie Tyburski.

To the many visitors of "direct search" and the other sites I compile: I am thrilled that you find my work of value.

To the Zussman Family: You can have my help searching the Web whenever you need it.

To Chris Sherman: My colleague and friend who teaches me something new about the search world just about every day.

Finally, to Lisa Beth Cohen: Trying to type just a few words about how much and how important you are in my life is simply impossible. Simple and direct, I LOVE YOU LISA!!!

—Gary Price

Introduction

If you're like most people, you have a love-hate relationship with search engines and Web directories. You love them, because the Web has become an integral part of daily life, and these pathfinders are crucial guides that help you navigate through an exploding universe of constantly changing information. Yet you also hate them, because all too often they fail miserably at answering even the most basic questions or satisfying the simplest queries. They waste your time, they exasperate and frustrate, even provoking an extreme reaction, known as "Web rage," in some people. It's fair to ask, "What's the problem here? Why is it so difficult to find the information I'm looking for?"

The problem is that vast expanses of the Web are completely invisible to general-purpose search engines like AltaVista, HotBot, and Google. Even worse, this "Invisible Web" is in all likelihood growing significantly faster than the visible Web that you're familiar with. It's not that the search engines and Web directories are "stupid" or even badly engineered. Rather, they simply can't "see" millions of high-quality resources that are available exclusively on the Invisible Web.

So what is this Invisible Web and why aren't search engines doing anything about making it visible? Good question.

There is no dictionary definition for the Invisible Web. Several studies have attempted to map the entire Web, including parts of what we call the Invisible Web. To our knowledge, however, this book represents the first comprehensive effort to define and map the Invisible Web. We have consulted with numerous Web search experts and developers of major search engines, and have found little consensus among the professional Web search community regarding the cartography of the Invisible Web. Nonetheless, during the course of our research for this book, a relatively clear picture of the properties and boundaries of the Invisible Web has gradually emerged. The picture is constantly shifting in the currents of new and improved technology, but nonetheless paints a portrait that we feel serves as an accurate snapshot of the Invisible Web today.

The Invisible Web in a Nutshell

The first challenge for the Web searcher is to understand that the Invisible Web exists in the first place. Your interest in this book puts you well on the way. If your searching experience has been limited to the general-purpose Web search tools like Yahoo! and Google, you will soon see that you have been accessing only a small fraction of "Web accessible" information. Many people—even those "in the know" about Web searching—make many assumptions about the scope and thoroughness of the coverage by Web search engines that are simply untrue.

In a nutshell, the Invisible Web consists of material that general-purpose search engines either cannot or, perhaps more importantly, *will not* include in their collections of Web pages (called *indexes* or *indices*). The Invisible Web contains vast amounts of authoritative and current information that's accessible to you, using your Web browser or add-on utility software—but you have to know where to find it ahead of time, since you simply cannot locate it using a search engine like HotBot or Lycos.

Why? There are several reasons. One is technical—search engine technology is actually quite limited in its capabilities, despite its tremendous usefulness in helping searchers locate text documents on the Web. Another reason relates to the costs involved in operating a comprehensive search engine. It's expensive for search engines to locate Web resources and maintain up-to-date indices. Search engines must also cope with unethical Web page authors who seek to subvert their indexes with millions of bogus "spam" pages—pages that, like their unsavory e-mail kin, are either junk or offer deceptive or misleading information. Most of the major engines have developed strict guidelines for dealing with spam, which sometimes has the unfortunate effect of excluding legitimate content.

These are just a few of the reasons the Invisible Web exists. This book takes a detailed look at the nature and extent of the Invisible Web, and offers pathfinders for accessing the valuable information it contains. The bottom line for the searcher is that understanding the Invisible Web and knowing how to access its treasures can save both time and frustration, often yielding high-quality results that aren't easily found any other way.

What to Expect from This Book

To truly understand what the Invisible Web is, and why it exists, it's important to have a clear understanding of the visible Web and how general-purpose search engines work.

We've designed this book to fit the needs of both novice and advanced Web searchers. If you're new to Web searching, Part I provides essential background information on the design and structure of the Internet, its history and evolution, and the various tools available to help information seekers find what they're looking for. Throughout Part I, we gradually reveal the Invisible Web by describing the structure and operation of the visible Web, and by illustrating the limitations of Web search tools and their gaps in coverage.

If you're a relatively skilled searcher who's already familiar with the nuances of the Web, you can cut to the chase and start with Chapter 3, which begins a detailed exploration of the Invisible Web. Part II, beginning with Chapter 9, is an annotated guide to the best of the Invisible Web. We've selected resources for this section from a broad range of categories that illustrate the high quality of information available on the Invisible Web.

In Chapter 1, *The Internet and the Visible Web*, we trace the development of the Internet and many of the early tools used to locate and share information via the Net. We show how the limitations of these relatively primitive tools ultimately spurred the popular acceptance of the Web. As Tim Berners-Lee, creator of the Web, has written, "To understand the Web in the broadest and deepest sense, to fully partake of the vision that I and my colleagues share, one must understand how the Web came to be." This historical background, while fascinating in its own right, lays the foundation for understanding why the Invisible Web could arise in the first place.

Chapter 2, *Information Seeking on the Visible Web*, offers a detailed look at the two predominant Web search services: search engines and Web directories. We examine their strengths and weaknesses, and show how, even though they are useful for finding information on the visible Web, they cannot fully access the riches of the Invisible Web. This chapter discusses the challenges faced by the builders of search engines and directories, and the compromises and tradeoffs they must make that have a direct bearing on what's ultimately included—and excluded—from your search results.

Several prominent studies have determined that search engines simply perform an inadequate job of finding and indexing Web pages. While it is true that search engines do not have comprehensive coverage of the Web, the material they miss is not necessarily part of the Invisible Web. In Chapter 3, *Specialized and Hybrid Search Tools*, we discuss alternative search tools that can help the searcher locate information that, while not part of the Invisible Web, is still difficult if not impossible to find using general-purpose search engines and directories. These specialized and hybrid search tools include targeted directories and crawlers, metasearch engines, value-added search services, "alternative" search tools, and fee-based Web services. We describe and provide examples of all of these types of tools, omitting traditional proprietary database services, which are beyond the scope of the book.

The paradox of the Invisible Web is that it's easy to understand why it exists, but it's very hard to actually define or describe in concrete, specific terms. Nonetheless, that's exactly what we attempt to do in Chapter 4, *The Invisible Web*. In this chapter, we define the Invisible Web, and delve into the reasons why search engines can't "see" its content. We also discuss the four different "types" of invisibility, ranging from the "opaque" Web, which is relatively easy to access, to the truly invisible Web, which requires both determination and specialized finding aids to access its treasures.

In Chapter 5, *Visible or Invisible?*, we get down to the brass-tacks of how to recognize Invisible Web content on your own. We'll show you how to identify Invisible Web pages by looking for telltale signs that signal problems for search engines. We'll also show you how to differentiate between Invisible Web resources and specialized search engines and directories by using a number of comparative case studies.

Although the focus of this book is on the valuable resources found on the Invisible Web, we are not advocating that you abandon the general-purpose search tools you now use. Quite the opposite! In Chapter 6, *Using the Invisible Web*, we discuss why and when to use the Invisible Web to make your Web searching time more efficient by selecting the best available search tool for each particular task. In many respects, searching with a general-purpose search engine is like using a shotgun, whereas searching with an Invisible Web resource is more akin to a taking a highly precise rifle-shot approach. It's only by thinking carefully about your quarry that you'll be able to select your appropriate search "weapon."

Though there are many technical reasons why major search engines don't index the Invisible Web, there are also "social" reasons having to do with the validity, authority, and quality of online information. Because the Web is open to everybody and anybody, a good deal of its content is published by non-experts—or even worse, by people with a strong bias that they seek to conceal from readers. As mentioned earlier, search engines must also cope with millions of bogus "spam" pages. No matter whether you're searching the visible or Invisible Web, it's important to always maintain a critical view of the information you're accessing. Chapter 6 covers some important techniques for assessing the validity and quality of online information. We also present some excellent resources for keeping current with the rapid growth of the Invisible Web.

Chapter 7, *Case Studies*, presents eight scenarios that demonstrate both the power of Invisible Web resources, and why general-purpose search tools simply fail miserably at finding the materials used in the examples. In each case study, we attempt not only to show how search tools function, but also to illustrate the problem-solving approach the searcher uses to satisfy an information need.

The Invisible Web's value and rapid growth have attracted the attention of some skilled researchers who are working to make it more accessible by general search tools. In Chapter 8, *The Future: Revealing the Invisible Web*, we take a brief look at some of the more interesting approaches and projects likely to illuminate portions of the Invisible Web in coming years.

The directory section of the book begins with Chapter 9, *The Best of the Invisible Web*. This chapter describes a number of exceptional pathfinder sites that provide links to high-quality Invisible Web content. The remaining chapters make up a directory of more than 1,000

Invisible Web sites hand-selected by the authors. Each chapter focuses on a specific topic or subject to help you quickly pinpoint the resources you need for a wide range of information needs. The directory includes resources that are informative, of high quality, and contain worthy information from reliable information providers that are not visible to general-purpose search engines. We give precedence to resources that are freely available to anyone with Web access.

As an added bonus, we have made this directory available online at the companion Web site for this book, www.invisible-web.net. The online directory includes the most up-to-date annotations and links for each resource, and is continually updated to include new Invisible Web resources as we locate them.

Throughout the book, we include sidebars debunking commonly held beliefs about search engines and searching the Web that are simply untrue. These "Web Search Myths" can lead to poor or even disastrous results for the unwary searcher. They also can lead to false assumptions about what is—and is not—part of the Invisible Web.

Although the Invisible Web is a relatively complex subject, our style is informal, seeking to demystify our topic rather than impress the reader with our erudition. By necessity, there are a fair number of technical terms used in the book. Whenever we introduce a technical term that's particularly important, we also provide an accompanying definition box nearby. The glossary contains complete definitions of all of these important terms, as well as all other technical terms used in the book.

Boldly Go Where No Search Engine Has Gone Before

By now, you're probably convinced that the Invisible Web is an incredibly valuable resource for serious searchers. It is, but there are a number of things you should keep in mind as you set out to explore the Web's hidden reaches.

The Invisible Web is huge, vaguely defined, and incorporates databases with a wide variety of interfaces. This means that there is a fairly significant learning curve for getting comfortable with what's available. Don't despair if it seems overwhelming at first! Learning to use

Invisible Web resources is just like learning any new and valuable resource. Though it may seem like second nature now, when you first learned how to look a word up in the dictionary or find a number in the telephone book, it took time, patience, and practice, too.

And remember—there are numerous exceptions to the rules. In this book we have done our best to generalize in a way that does not make incorrect assumptions. We understand and acknowledge that there are inconsistencies in some aspects of the book. We don't view these as "gotchas"—rather, we feel exceptions to the rules illustrate the richness inherent in the Web as a whole.

The Invisible Web holds incredibly valuable resources for the searcher. Journeys into the Invisible Web lead not only to treasures that aren't easily located, but often provide the pleasure and satisfaction experienced by early explorers who led expeditions into regions of the world marked *Terra Incognito* on early maps. In *The Invisible Web*, our goal is to provide you with a detailed map of a vast expanse of cyberspace that is still relatively uncharted territory, allowing you to boldly go where no search engine has gone before.

About
www.invisible-web.net
A Web Site for Readers

The Invisible Web is in a state of constant change, and will continue to transform over time. To help you keep up with the changes, and to make it easy for you to access and use Invisible Web resources, the authors have created www.invisible-web.net. The site features updates to material included in the book, links to the Invisible Web resources listed in Chapters 9–27, and more.

www.invisible-web.net was created for you as a valued reader of *The Invisible Web*. To access it, go to http://www.invisible-web.net. We hope you will bookmark the site and utilize it whenever your research is likely to benefit from the use of Invisible Web resources.

Please send any comments or suggestions by e-mail to feedback@invisible-web.net.

CHAPTER 1

The Internet and the Visible Web

To understand the Web in the broadest and deepest sense, to fully partake of the vision that I and my colleagues share, one must understand how the Web came to be.
— Tim Berners-Lee, *Weaving the Web*

Most people tend to use the words "Internet" and "Web" interchangeably, but they're not synonyms. The Internet is a networking protocol (set of rules) that allows computers of all types to connect to and communicate with other computers on the Internet. The Internet's origins trace back to a project sponsored by the U.S. Defense Advanced Research Agency (DARPA) in 1969 as a means for researchers and defense contractors to share information (Kahn, 2000).

The World Wide Web (Web), on the other hand, is a software protocol that runs on top of the Internet, allowing users to easily access files stored on Internet computers. The Web was created in 1990 by Tim Berners-Lee, a computer programmer working for the European Organization for Nuclear Research (CERN). Prior to the Web, accessing files on the Internet was a challenging task, requiring specialized knowledge and skills. The Web made it easy to retrieve a wide variety of files, including text, images, audio, and video by the simple mechanism of clicking a hypertext link.

1

DEFINITION

Hypertext

A system that allows computerized objects (text, images, sounds, etc.) to be linked together. A hypertext link points to a specific object, or a specific place with a text; clicking the link opens the file associated with the object.

The primary focus of this book is on the Web—and more specifically, the parts of the Web that search engines can't see. To fully understand the phenomenon called the Invisible Web, it's important to first understand the fundamental differences between the Internet and the Web.

In this chapter, we'll trace the development of some of the early Internet search tools, and show how their limitations ultimately spurred the popular acceptance of the Web. This historical background, while fascinating in its own right, lays the foundation for understanding why the Invisible Web could arise in the first place.

How the Internet Came to Be

Up until the mid-1960s, most computers were stand-alone machines that did not connect to or communicate with other computers. In 1962 J.C.R. Licklider, a professor at MIT, wrote a paper envisioning a globally connected "Galactic Network" of computers (Leiner, 2000). The idea was far-out at the time, but it caught the attention of Larry Roberts, a project manager at the U.S. Defense Department's Advanced Research Projects Agency (ARPA). In 1966 Roberts submitted a proposal to ARPA that would allow the agency's numerous and disparate computers to be connected in a network similar to Licklider's Galactic Network.

Roberts' proposal was accepted, and work began on the "ARPANET," which would in time become what we know as today's Internet. The first "node" on the ARPANET was installed at UCLA in 1969 and gradually, throughout the 1970s, universities and defense contractors working on ARPA projects began to connect to the ARPANET.

In 1973 the U.S. Defense Advanced Research Projects Agency (DARPA) initiated another research program to allow networked computers to communicate transparently across multiple linked networks. Whereas the ARPANET was just one network, the new project was designed to be a "network of networks." According to Vint Cerf, widely regarded as one of the "fathers" of the Internet, "This was called the Internetting project and the system of networks which emerged from the research was known as the 'Internet'" (Cerf, 2000).

It wasn't until the mid 1980s, with the simultaneous explosion in use of personal computers, and the widespread adoption of a universal standard of Internet communication called Transmission Control Protocol/Internet Protocol (TCP/IP), that the Internet became widely available to anyone desiring to connect to it. Other government agencies fostered the growth of the Internet by contributing communications "backbones" that were specifically designed to carry Internet traffic. By the late 1980s, the Internet had grown from its initial network of a few computers to a robust communications network supported by governments and commercial enterprises around the world.

Despite this increased accessibility, the Internet was still primarily a tool for academics and government contractors well into the early 1990s. As more and more computers connected to the Internet, users began to demand tools that would allow them to search for and locate text and other files on computers anywhere on the Net.

Early Net Search Tools

Although sophisticated search and information retrieval techniques date back to the late 1950s and early '60s, these techniques were used primarily in closed or proprietary systems. Early Internet search and retrieval tools lacked even the most basic capabilities, primarily because it was thought that traditional information retrieval techniques would not work well on an open, unstructured information universe like the Internet.

Accessing a file on the Internet was a two-part process. First, you needed to establish direct connection to the remote computer where the file was located using a terminal emulation program called Telnet. Then you needed to use another program, called a File Transfer Protocol (FTP) client, to fetch the file itself. For many years, to access a file it was necessary to know both the address of the computer and the exact location and name of the file you were looking for—there were no search engines or other file-finding tools like the ones we're familiar with today.

DEFINITIONS

File Transfer Protocol (FTP)
A set of rules for sending and receiving files of all types between computers connected to the Internet.

Telnet
A terminal emulation program that runs on your computer, allowing you to access a remote computer via a TCP/IP network and execute commands on that computer as if you were directly connected to it. Many libraries offered telnet access to their catalogs.

Thus, "search" often meant sending a request for help to an e-mail message list or discussion forum and hoping some kind soul would respond with the details you needed to fetch the file you were looking for. The situation improved somewhat with the introduction of "anonymous" FTP servers, which were centralized file-servers specifically intended for enabling the easy sharing of files. The servers were anonymous because they were not password protected—anyone could simply log on and request any file on the system.

Files on FTP servers were organized in hierarchical directories, much like files are organized in hierarchical folders on personal computer systems today. The hierarchical structure made it easy for the FTP server to display a directory listing of all the files stored on the server, but you still needed good knowledge of the contents of the FTP server. If the file you were looking for didn't exist on the FTP server you were logged into, you were out of luck.

The first true search tool for files stored on FTP servers was called Archie, created in 1990 by a small team of systems administrators and graduate students at McGill University in Montreal. Archie was the proto-type of today's search engines, but it was primitive and extremely limited compared to what we have today. Archie roamed the Internet searching for files available on anonymous FTP servers, downloading directory list-ings of every anonymous FTP server it could find. These listings were stored in a central, searchable database called the Internet Archives Database at McGill University, and were updated monthly.

Although it represented a major step forward, the Archie database was still extremely primitive, limiting searches to a specific file name, or for computer programs that performed specific functions. Nonetheless, it proved extremely popular—nearly 50 percent of Internet traffic to Montreal in the early '90s was Archie related, according to Peter Deutsch, who headed up the McGill University Archie team.

"In the brief period following the release of Archie, there was an explosion of Internet-based research projects, including WWW, Gopher, WAIS, and others" (Deutsch, 2000).

"Each explored a different area of the Internet information problem space, and each offered its own insights into how to build and deploy Internet-based services," wrote Deutsch. The team licensed Archie to others, with the first shadow sites launched in Australia and Finland in 1992. The Archie network reached a peak of 63 installations around the world by 1995.

Gopher, an alternative to Archie, was created by Mark McCahill and his team at the University of Minnesota in 1991 and was named for the university's mascot, the Golden Gopher. Gopher essentially combined the Telnet and FTP protocols, allowing users to click hyperlinked menus to access information on demand without resorting to addi-tional commands. Using a series of menus that allowed the user to drill down through successively more specific categories, users could ulti-mately access the full text of documents, graphics, and even music files, though not integrated in a single format. Gopher made it easy to browse for information on the Internet.

According to Gopher creator McCahill, "Before Gopher there wasn't an easy way of having the sort of big distributed system where there were seamless pointers between stuff on one machine and another machine. You had to know the name of this machine and if you wanted to go over here you had to know its name.

"Gopher takes care of all that stuff for you. So navigating around Gopher is easy. It's point and click typically. So it's something that anybody could use to find things. It's also very easy to put informa-tion up so a lot of people started running servers themselves and it was the first of the easy-to-use, no muss, no fuss, you can just crawl around and look for information tools. It was the one that wasn't written for techies."

Gopher's "no muss, no fuss" interface was an early precursor of what later evolved into popular Web directories like Yahoo!. "Typically you set this up so that you can start out with [a] sort of overview or general structure of a bunch of information, choose the items that you're interested in to move into a more specialized area and then either look at items by browsing around and finding some documents or submitting searches," said McCahill.

A problem with Gopher was that it was designed to provide a listing of files available on computers in a specific location—the University of Minnesota, for example. While Gopher servers were searchable, there was no centralized directory for searching all other computers that were both using Gopher and connected to the Internet, or "Gopherspace" as it was called. In November 1992, Fred Barrie and Steven Foster of the University of Nevada System Computing Services group solved this problem, creating a program called Veronica, a centralized Archie-like search tool for Gopher files. In 1993 another program called Jughead added keyword search and Boolean operator capabilities to Gopher search.

DEFINITIONS

Keyword
A word or phrase entered in a query form that a search system attempts to match in text documents in its database.

Boolean
A system of logical operators (AND, OR, NOT) that allows true-false operations to be performed on search queries, potentially narrowing or expanding results when used with keywords.

Popular legend has it that Archie, Veronica and Jughead were named after cartoon characters. Archie in fact is shorthand for "Archives." Veronica was likely named after the cartoon character (she was Archie's girlfriend), though it's officially an acronym for "Very Easy Rodent-Oriented Net-Wide Index to Computerized Archives." And Jughead (Archie and Veronica's cartoon pal) is an acronym for "Jonzy's Universal Gopher Hierarchy Excavation and Display," after its creator, Rhett "Jonzy" Jones, who developed the program while at the University of Utah Computer Center.

Myth: The Web and the Internet Are the Same

The Internet is the world's largest computer network, made up of millions of computers. It's really nothing more than the "plumbing" that allows information of various kinds to flow from computer to computer around the world.

The Web is one of many interfaces to the Internet, making it easy to retrieve text, pictures, and multimedia files from computers without having to know complicated commands. You just click a link and voila: You miraculously see a page displayed on your browser screen.

The Web is only about 10 years old, whereas the Internet is 30-something. Prior to the Web, computers could communicate with one another, but the interfaces weren't as slick or easy to use as the Web. Many of these older interfaces, or "protocols," are still around and offer many different, unique ways of communicating with other computers (and other people).

Other Internet protocols and interfaces include:

- E-mail
- Forums & Bulletin Boards
- Internet Mailing Lists
- Newsgroups
- Peer-to-Peer file sharing systems, such as Napster and Gnutella
- Databases accessed via Web interfaces

As you see, the Internet is much more than the Web. In fact, the last item on the list above, databases accessed via Web interfaces, make up a significant portion of the Invisible Web. Later chapters will delve deeply into the fascinating and tremendously useful world of Web accessible databases.

A third major search protocol developed around this time was Wide Area Information Servers (WAIS). Developed by Brewster Kahle and his colleagues at Thinking Machines, WAIS worked much like today's metasearch engines. The WAIS client resided on your local machine, and allowed you to search for information on other Internet servers using natural language, rather than using computer commands. The servers themselves were responsible for interpreting the query and returning appropriate results, freeing the user from the necessity of learning the specific query language of each server.

WAIS used an extension to a standard protocol called Z39.50 that was in wide use at the time. In essence, WAIS provided a single computer-to-computer protocol for searching for information. This information could be text, pictures, voice, or formatted documents. The quality of the search results was a direct result of how effectively each server interpreted the WAIS query.

All of the early Internet search protocols represented a giant leap over the awkward access tools provided by Telnet and FTP. Nonetheless, they still dealt with information as discrete data objects. And these protocols lacked the ability to make connections between disparate types of information—text, sounds, images, and so on—to form the conceptual links that transformed raw data into useful information. Although search was becoming more sophisticated, information on the Internet lacked popular appeal. In the late 1980s, the Internet was still primarily a playground for scientists, academics, government agencies, and their contractors.

Fortunately, at about the same time, a software engineer in Switzerland was tinkering with a program that eventually gave rise to the World Wide Web. He called his program Enquire Within Upon Everything, borrowing the title from a book of Victorian advice that provided helpful information on everything from removing stains to investing money.

Enquire Within Upon Everything

"Suppose all the information stored on computers everywhere were linked, I thought. Suppose I could program my computer to create a space in which anything could be linked to anything. All the bits of information in every computer at CERN, and on the planet, would be available to me and to anyone else. There would be a single, global information space.

"Once a bit of information in that space was labeled with an address, I could tell my computer to get it. By being able to reference anything with equal ease, a computer could represent associations between things that might seem unrelated but somehow did, in fact, share a relationship. A Web of information would form."

— Tim Berners-Lee, *Weaving the Web*

The Web was created in 1990 by Tim Berners-Lee, who at the time was a contract programmer at the Organization for Nuclear Research (CERN) high-energy physics laboratory in Geneva, Switzerland. The Web was a side project Berners-Lee took on to help him keep track of the mind-boggling diversity of people, computers, research equipment, and other resources that are de rigueur at a massive research institution like CERN. One of the primary challenges faced by CERN scientists was the very diversity that gave it strength. The lab hosted thousands of researchers every year, arriving from countries all over the world, each speaking different languages and working with unique computing systems. And since high-energy physics research projects tend to spawn huge amounts of experimental data, a program that could simplify access to information and foster collaboration was something of a Holy Grail.

Berners-Lee had been tinkering with programs that allowed relatively easy, decentralized linking capabilities for nearly a decade before he created the Web. He had been influenced by the work of Vannevar Bush, who served as Director of the Office of Scientific Research and Development during World War II. In a landmark paper called "As We May Think," Bush proposed a system he called MEMEX, "a device in which an individual stores all his books, records, and communications, and which is mechanized so that it may be consulted with exceeding speed and flexibility" (Bush, 1945).

The materials stored in the MEMEX would be indexed, of course, but Bush aspired to go beyond simple search and retrieval. The MEMEX would allow the user to build conceptual "trails" as he moved from document to document, creating lasting associations between different components of the MEMEX that could be recalled at a later time. Bush called this "associative indexing … the basic idea of which is a provision whereby any item may be caused at will to select immediately and automatically another. This is the essential feature of the MEMEX. The process of tying two items together is the important thing."

In Bush's visionary writings, it's easy for us to see the seeds of what we now call hypertext. But it wasn't until 1965 that Ted Nelson actually described a computerized system that would operate in a manner similar to what Bush envisioned. Nelson called his system "hypertext" and described the next-generation MEMEX in a system he called Xanadu.

Nelson's project never achieved enough momentum to have a significant impact on the world. Another twenty years would pass before Xerox implemented the first mainstream hypertext program, called NoteCards, in 1985. A year later, Owl Ltd. created a program called Guide, which functioned in many respects like a contemporary Web browser, but lacked Internet connectivity.

Bill Atkinson, an Apple Computer programmer best known for creating MacPaint, the first bitmap painting program, created the first truly popular hypertext program in 1987. His HyperCard program was specifically for the Macintosh, and it also lacked Net connectivity. Nonetheless, the program proved popular, and the basic functionality and concepts of hypertext were assimilated by Microsoft, appearing first in standard help systems for Windows software.

Weaving the Web

The foundations and pieces necessary to build a system like the World Wide Web were in place well before Tim Berners-Lee began his tinkering. But unlike others before him, Berners-Lee's brilliant insight was that a simple form of hypertext, integrated with the universal communication protocols offered by the Internet, would create a platform-independent system with a uniform interface for any computer connected to the Internet. He tried to persuade many of the key players in the hypertext industry to adopt his ideas for connecting to the Net, but none were able to grasp his vision of simple, universal connectivity.

So Berners-Lee set out to do the job himself, creating a set of tools that collectively became the prototype for the World Wide Web (Connolly, 2000). In a remarkable burst of energy, Berners-Lee began work in October 1990 on the first Web client—the program that allowed the creation, editing, and browsing of hypertext pages. He called the client WorldWideWeb, after the mathematical term used to describe a collection of nodes and links in which any node can be linked to any other. "Friends at CERN gave me a hard time, saying it would never take off—especially since it yielded an acronym that was nine syllables long when spoken," he wrote in *Weaving the Web*.

To make the client simple and platform independent, Berners-Lee created HTML, or HyperText Markup Language, which was a dramatically simplified version of a text formatting language called SGML (Standard Generalized Markup Language). All Web documents formatted with HTML tags would display identically on any computer in the world.

Next, he created the HyperText Transfer Protocol (HTTP), the set of rules that computers would use to communicate over the Internet and allow hypertext links to automatically retrieve documents regardless of their location. He also devised the Universal Resource Identifier, a standard way of giving documents on the Internet a unique address (what we call URLs today). Finally, he brought all of the pieces together in the form of a Web server, which stored HTML documents and served them to other computers making HTTP requests for documents with URLs.

Berners-Lee completed his work on the initial Web tools by Christmas 1990. In little more than two months he had created a system that had been envisioned for decades. Building the tools was the easy part. The hard part was to get the world to embrace the Web.

Berners-Lee wrote the original programs for the Web on the NeXT system, but thanks to his tireless efforts to persuade others to use the system, there were soon Web clients and servers available in a variety of different operating systems. As more and more people within CERN began to use the Web, the initial skepticism began to wear away.

Berners-Lee began actively to promote the Web outside of the lab, attending conferences and participating in Internet mailing and discussion lists. Slowly, the Web began to grow as more and more people implemented clients and servers around the world. There were really two seminal events that sparked the explosion in popular use of the Web. The first was the development of graphical Web browsers, including Voila, Mosaic, and others that integrated text and images into a single browser window. For the first time, Internet information could be displayed in a visually appealing format previously limited to CD-ROM-based multimedia systems. This set off a wave of creativity among Web users, establishing a new publishing medium that was freely available to anyone with Internet access and the basic skills required to design a Web page.

Then in 1995, the U.S. National Science Foundation ceased being the central manager of the core Internet communications backbone, and transferred both funds and control to the private sector. Companies were free to register "dot-com" domain names and establish an online presence. It didn't take long for business and industry to realize that the Web was a powerful new avenue for online commerce, triggering the dot-com gold rush of the late 1990s.

Early Web Navigation

The Web succeeded where other early systems failed to catch on largely because of its decentralized nature. Despite the fact that the first servers were at CERN, neither Berners-Lee nor the lab exercised control over who put up a new server anywhere on the Internet. Anyone could establish his or her own Web server. The only requirement was to link to other servers, and inform other Web users about the new server so they could in turn create links back to it.

But this decentralized nature also created a problem. Despite the ease with which users could navigate from server to server on the Web simply by clicking links, navigation was ironically becoming more difficult as the Web grew. No one was "in charge" of the Web; there was no central authority to create and maintain an index of the growing number of available documents. To facilitate communication and cross-linkage between early adopters of the Web, Berners-Lee established a list Web of servers that could be accessed via hyperlinks. This was the first Web directory. This early Web guide is still online, though most of the links are broken (http:// www.w3.org/History/19921103-hypertext/hypertext/DataSources/ bySubject/Overview. html).

Beyond the list of servers at CERN, there were few centralized directories, and no global Web search services. People notified the world about new Web pages in much the same way they had previously announced new Net resources, via e-mail lists or online discussions. Eventually, some enterprising observers of the Web began creating lists of links to their favorite sites. John Makulowich, Joel Jones, Justin Hall, and the people at O'Reilly & Associates publishing company were among the most noted authors maintaining popular link lists.

Eventually, many of these link lists started "What's New" or "What's Cool" pages, serving as de facto announcement services for new Web pages. But they relied on Web page authors to submit information, and the Web's relentless growth rate ultimately made it impossible to keep the lists either current or comprehensive.

What was needed was an automated approach to Web page discovery and indexing. The Web had now grown large enough that information scientists became interested in creating search services specifically for the Web. Sophisticated information retrieval techniques had been available since the early 1960s, but they were only effective when searching closed, relatively structured databases. The open, laissez-faire nature of the Web made it too messy to easily adapt traditional information retrieval techniques. New, Web-centric approaches were needed.

But how best to approach the problem? Web search would clearly have to be more sophisticated than a simple Archie-type service. But should these new "search engines" attempt to index the full text of Web documents, much as earlier Gopher tools had done, or simply broker requests to local Web search services on individual computers, following the WAIS model?

The First Search Engines

Tim Berners-Lee's vision of the Web was of an information space where data of all types could be freely accessed. But in the early days of the Web, the reality was that most of the Web consisted of simple HTML text documents. Since few servers offered local site search services, developers of the first Web search engines opted for the model of indexing the full text of pages stored on Web servers. To adapt traditional information retrieval techniques to Web search, they built huge databases that attempted to replicate the Web, searching over these relatively controlled, closed archives of pages rather than trying to search the Web itself in real time. With this fateful architectural decision, limiting search engines to HTML text documents and essentially ignoring all other types of data available via the Web, the Invisible Web was born.

The biggest challenge search engines faced was simply locating all of the pages on the Web. Since the Web lacked a centralized structure, the only way for a search engine to find Web pages to index was by following links to pages and gathering new links from those pages to add to the queue to visit for indexing. This was a task that required computer assistance, simply to keep up with all of the new pages being added to the Web each day.

But there was a subtler problem that needed solving. Search engines wanted to fetch and index all pages on the Web, but the search engines frequently revisited popular pages at the expense of new or obscure pages, because popular pages had the most links pointing to them—which the crawlers naturally followed. What was needed was an auto-mated program that had a certain amount of intelligence, able to recognize when a link pointed to a previously indexed page and ignor-ing it in favor of finding new pages.

These programs became known as Web robots—"autonomous agents" that could find their way around the Web discovering new Web pages. Autonomous is simply a fancy way of saying that the agent pro-grams can do things on their own without a person directly controlling them, and that they have some degree of intelligence, meaning they can make decisions and take action based on these decisions.

In June 1993 Mathew Gray, a physics student at MIT, created the first widely recognized Web robot, dubbed the "World Wide Web Wanderer." Gray's interest was limited to determining the size of the Web and track-ing its continuing growth. The Wanderer simply visited Web pages and reported on their existence, but didn't actually fetch or store pages in a database. Nonetheless, Gray's robot led the way for more sophisticated programs that would both visit and fetch Web pages for storage and indexing in search engine databases.

The year 1994 was a watershed one for Web search engines. Brian Pinkerton, a graduate student in Computer Sciences at the University of Washington, created a robot called WebCrawler in January 1994. Pinkerton created his robot because his school friends were always sending him e-mails about the cool sites they had found on the Web, and Pinkerton didn't have time to surf to find sites on his own—he wanted to "cut to the chase" by searching for them directly. WebCrawler went beyond Gray's Wanderer by actually retrieving the full text of Web documents and storing them in a keyword-searchable database. Pinkerton made WebCrawler public in April 1994 via a Web interface. The database contained entries from about 6,000 different servers, and after a week was handling 100+ queries per day. The first Web search engine was born.

The image evoked by Pinkerton's robot "crawling" the Web caught the imagination of programmers working on automatic indexing of the Web. Specialized search engine robots soon became known generically as "crawlers" or "spiders," and their page-gathering activity was called "crawling" or "spidering" the Web.

Crawler-based search engines proliferated in 1994. Many of the early search engines were the result of academic or corporate research projects. Two popular engines were the World Wide Web Worm, created by Oliver McBryan at the University of Colorado, and WWW JumpStation, by Jonathon Fletcher at the University of Stirling in the U.K. Neither lasted long: Idealab purchased WWWWorm and transformed it into the first version of the GoTo search engine. JumpStation simply faded out of favor as two other search services launched in 1994 gained popularity: Lycos and Yahoo!.

Michael Mauldin and his team at the Center for Machine Translation at Carnegie Mellon University created Lycos (named for the wolf spider, Lycosidae lycosa, which catches its prey by pursuit, rather than in a web). Lycos quickly gained acclaim and prominence in the Web community, for the sheer number of pages it included in its index (1.5 million documents by January 1995) and the quality of its search results. Lycos also pioneered the use of automated abstracts of documents in search results, something not offered by WWW Worm or JumpStation.

Also in 1994, two graduate students at Stanford University created "Jerry's Guide to the Internet," built with the help of search spiders, but consisting of editorially selected links compiled by hand into a hierarchically organized directory. In a whimsical acknowledgment of this structure, Jerry Wang and David Filo renamed their service "Yet Another Hierarchical Officious Oracle," commonly known today as Yahoo!.

Table 1.1 A Timeline of Internet Search Technologies

Year	Search Service
1945	Vannevar Bush Proposes "MEMEX"
1965	Hypertext Coined by Ted Nelson
1972	Dialog—First Commercial Proprietary System
1986	OWL Guide Hypermedia Browser
1990	Archie for FTP Search, Tim Berners-Lee creates the Web
1991	Gopher: WAIS Distributed Search
1993	ALIWEB (Archie Linking), WWWWander, JumpStation, WWWWorm
1994	ElNet Galaxy, WebCrawler, Lycos, Yahoo!
1995	Infoseek, SavvySearch, AltaVista, MetCrawler, Excite
1996	HotBot, LookSmart
1997	NorthernLight
1998	Google, InvisibleWeb.com
1999	FAST
2000+	Hundreds of search tools

In 1995 Infoseek, AltaVista, and Excite made their debuts, each offering different capabilities for the searcher. Metasearch engines—programs that searched several search engines simultaneously—also made an appearance this year (see Chapter 3 for more information about metasearch engines). SavvySearch, created by Daniel Dreilinger at Colorado State University, was the first metasearch engine, and MetaCrawler, from the University of Washington, soon followed.

From this point on, search engines began appearing almost every day. As useful and necessary as they were for finding documents, Web search engines all shared a common weakness: They were designed for one specific task—to find and index Web documents, and to point users to the most relevant documents in response to keyword queries. During the Web's early years, when most of its content consisted of simple HTML pages, search engines performed their tasks admirably. But the Internet continued to evolve, with information being made available in many formats other than simple text documents. For a wide variety of reasons, Web search services began to fall behind in keeping up with both the growth of the Web and in their ability to recognize and index non-text information—what we refer to as the Invisible Web.

To become an expert searcher, you need to have a thorough understanding of the tools at your disposal and, even more importantly, when to use them. Now that you have a sense of the history of the Web and the design philosophy that led to its universal adoption, let's take a closer look at contemporary search services, focusing on their strengths but also illuminating their weaknesses.

CHAPTER 2

Information Seeking on the Visible Web

The creators of the Internet were fundamentally interested in solving a single problem: how to connect isolated computers in a universal network, allowing any machine to communicate with any other regardless of type or location. The network protocol they developed proved to be an elegant and robust solution to this problem, so much so that a myth emerged that the Internet was designed to survive a nuclear attack (Hafner and Lyon, 1998).

In solving the connectivity problem, however, the Net's pioneers largely ignored three other major problems—problems that made using the Internet significantly challenging to all but the most skilled computer users. The first problem was one of incompatible hardware. Although the TCP/IP network protocol allows hardware of virtually any type to establish basic communications, once a system is connected to the network it may not be able to meaningfully *interact* with other systems. Programs called "emulators" that mimic other types of hardware are often required for successful communication.

The second problem was one of incompatible software. A computer running the UNIX operating system is completely different from one running a Windows or Macintosh operating system. Again, translation programs were often necessary to establish communication. Finally, even if computers with compatible hardware and software connected over the Internet, they still often encountered the third major problem:

incompatible data structures. Information can be stored in a wide variety of data structures on a computer, ranging from a simple text file to a complex "relational" database consisting of a wide range of data types.

In creating the Web, Tim Berners-Lee sought to solve all three of these problems. To a large extent, he succeeded in solving the problems of hardware and software incompatibilities. Like the TCP/IP network protocol, the Web's HTML language was designed to function almost identically on computers using any type of hardware or software. The goal was to allow users to access information with a simple point and click interface that required no other knowledge of how a system functioned. HTML would also display documents in virtually identical format regardless of the type of hardware or software running on either the computer serving the page or the client computer viewing the document.

To meet this goal, HTML was engineered as a very simple, bare-bones language. Although Berners-Lee foresaw Web documents *linking* to a wide range of disparate data types, the primary focus was on text documents. Thus the third problem—the ability to access a wide range of data types—was only partially solved.

The simplicity of the point and click interface also has an Achilles' heel. It's an excellent method for *browsing* through a collection of related documents—simply click, click, click, and documents are displayed with little other effort. Browsing is completely unsuitable and inefficient, however, for *searching* through a large information space. To understand the essential differences between browsing and searching, think of how you use a library. If you're familiar with a subject, it's often most useful to *browse* in the section where books about the subject are shelved. Because of the way the library is organized, often using either the Dewey Decimal or Library of Congress Classification system, you know that all of the titles in the section are related, and serendipity often leads to unexpected discoveries that prove quite valuable.

If you're unfamiliar with a subject, however, browsing is both inefficient and potentially futile if you fail to locate the section of the library where the material you're interested in is shelved. *Searching*, using the specialized tools offered by a library's catalog, is far more likely to provide satisfactory results.

Using the Web to find information has much in common with using the library. Sometimes browsing provides the best results, while other information needs require nothing less than sophisticated, powerful searching to achieve the best results. In this chapter, we take a closer look at browsing and searching—the two predominant methods for finding information on the Web. In examining the strengths and weaknesses of each approach, you'll understand how general-purpose information-seeking tools work—an essential foundation for later understanding why they cannot fully access the riches of the Invisible Web.

Browsing vs. Searching

There are two fundamental methods for finding information on the Web: browsing and searching. Browsing is the process of following a hypertext trail of links created by other Web users. A hypertext link is a pointer to another document, image, or other object on the Web. The words making up the link are the title or description of the document that you will retrieve by clicking the link. By its very nature, browsing the Web is both easy and intuitive.

Searching, on the other hand, relies on powerful software that seeks to match the keywords you specify with the most relevant documents on the Web. Effective searching, unlike browsing, requires learning how to use the search software as well as lots of practice to develop skills to achieve satisfactory results.

When the Web was still relatively new and small, browsing was an adequate method for locating relevant information. Just as books in a particular section of a library are related, links from one document tend to point to other documents that are related in some way. However, as the Web grew in size and diversity, the manual, time-intensive nature of browsing from page to page made locating relevant information quickly and efficiently all but impossible. Web users were crying out for tools that could help satisfy their information needs.

Search tools using two very different methods emerged to help users locate information on the Web. One method, called a *Web directory*, was modeled on early Internet search tools like Archie and Gopher. The other method, called a *search engine*, drew on classic information retrieval techniques that had been widely used in closed, proprietary databases but hardly at all in the open universe of the Internet. In general, Web directories provide a context-based framework for structured browsing, while search engines, as their name implies, provide no context but allow searching for specific keywords or phrases. Web directories are similar to a table of contents in a book; search engines are more akin to an index.

Like a table of contents, a Web directory uses a hierarchical structure to provide a high level overview of major topics. Browsing the table of contents allows the reader to quickly turn to interesting sections of a book by examining the titles of chapters and subchapters. Browsing the subject-oriented categories and subcategories in a Web directory likewise leads to categories pointing to relevant Web documents. In both cases, however, since the information is limited to brief descriptions of what you'll find, you have no assurance that what you're looking for is contained in either the section of the book or on a specific Web page. You must ultimately go directly to the source and read the information yourself to decide.

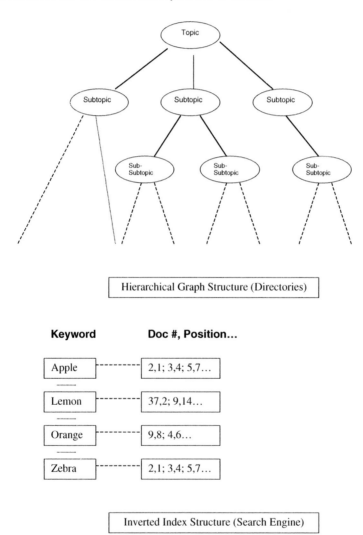

Figure 2.1 **Hierarchical Graph vs. Inverted Index Structures**

A book's index offers a much finer level of granularity, providing explicit pointers to specific keywords or phrases regardless of where they appear in the book. Search engines are essentially full-text indexes of Web pages, and will locate keywords or phrases in any matching documents regardless of where they are physically located on the Web.

From a structural standpoint, a directory has the form of a hierarchical graph, with generic top-level categories leading to increasingly more specific subcategories as the user drills down the hierarchy by clicking hypertext links. Ultimately, at the bottom-most node for a branch of the hierarchical graph, the user is presented with a list of document titles hand-selected by humans as the most appropriate for the subcategory.

Search engines have no such hierarchical structure. Rather, they are full-text indexes of millions of Web pages, organized in an inverted index structure. Whenever a searcher enters a query, the entire index is searched, and a variety of algorithms are used to find relationships and compute statistical correlations between keywords and documents. Documents judged to have the most "relevance" are presented first in a result list.

DEFINITION

Relevance

The degree to which a retrieved Web document matches a user's query or information need. Relevance is often a complex calculation that weighs many factors, ultimately resulting in a score that's expressed as a percentage value.

Browsing and searching both play important roles for the searcher. By design, browsing is the most efficient way to use a directory, and searching with keywords or phrases is the best way to use a search engine. Unfortunately, the boundaries between what might be considered a "pure" directory or search engine are often blurred. For example, most directories offer a search form that allows you to quickly locate relevant categories or links without browsing. Similarly, most search engines offer access to directory data provided by a business partner that's independent of the actual search engine database. Muddying the waters further, when you enter keywords into a search engine, results are presented in a browsable list.

These ambiguities notwithstanding, it's reasonably easy to tell the difference between a Web directory and a search engine—and it's an important distinction to make when deciding what kind of search tool to use for a particular information need. Let's take a closer look at Web directories and search engines, examining how they're compiled and how they work to provide results to a searcher.

Web Directories

Web directories, such as Yahoo!, LookSmart, and the Open Directory Project (ODP) are collections of links to Web pages and sites that are arranged by subject. They are typically hierarchical in nature, organized into a structure that classifies human knowledge by topic, technically known as ontology. These ontologies often resemble the structure used by traditional library catalog systems, with major subject areas divided into smaller, more specific subcategories.

Directories take advantage of the power of hypertext, creating a clickable link for each topic, subtopic, and ultimate end document, allowing the user to successively drill down from a broad subject category to a narrow subcategory or specific document. This extensively linked structure makes Web directories ideal tools for browsing for information. To use another real-world metaphor, directories are similar to telephone yellow pages, because they are organized by category or topic, and often contain more information than bare-bones white pages listings.

How Web Directories Work

The context and structure provided by a directory's ontology allows its builders to be very precise in how they categorize pages. Many directories annotate their links with descriptions or comments, so you can get an idea of what a Web site or page is about before clicking through and examining the actual page a hyperlink points to.

There are two general approaches to building directories. The closed model used by Yahoo!, LookSmart, and NBCi relies on a small group of employees, usually called editors, to select and annotate links for each category in the directory's ontology. The expertise of directory editors varies, but they are usually subject to some sort of quality-control mechanism that assures consistency throughout the directory.

The open model, as epitomized by the Open Directory Project, Wherewithal, and other less well known services, relies on a cadre of volunteer editors to compile the directory. Open projects tend to have more problems with quality control over time, but since they cost so little to compile and are often made freely available to anyone wishing to use their data, they have proven popular with the Web community at large.

Table 2.1 Open vs. Closed Model Web Directories

Open Model Directories	Closed Model Directories
Open Directory Project (ODP) Used by: • AOL • Google, HotBot, Lycos • More than 100 smaller search services	LookSmart Used by: • MSN • Time Warner • More than 220 ISPs
Wherewithal	Yahoo!
Zeal	About.com
Go Guides	NBCi

Most Web directories offer some type of internal search that allows the user to bypass browsing and get results from deep within the directory by using a keyword query. Remember, however, that directories consist only of links and annotations. Using a directory's search function searches the words making up these links and annotations, *not* the full-text of Web documents they point to, so it's possible that your results will be incomplete or omit potentially good matches.

Since most directories tend to be small, rarely larger than one to two million links, internal results are often supplemented with additional results from a general-purpose search engine. These supplemental results are called "fall-through" or "fall-over" results. Usually, supplemental results are differentiated from directory results in some way. For example, a search on Yahoo! typically returns results labeled "Web Sites" since Yahoo! entries almost always point to the main page of a Web site. Fall-through results are labeled "Web Pages" and are provided by Yahoo!'s search partner, which was Google at the time of writing. Different search engines power fall-through results for other popular Web directories. For example, MSN and About.com use fall-through results provided by Inktomi, while LookSmart uses AltaVista results. When a directory search fails to return any results, fall-through results from a search engine partner are often presented as primary results.

In general, Web directories are excellent resources for getting a high-level overview of a subject, since *all* entries in a particular category are "exposed" on the page (rather than limited to an arbitrary number, such as 10 to 20, per page).

Issues with Web Directories

Because their scope is limited and links have been hand-selected, directories are very powerful tools for certain types of searches. However, no directory can provide the comprehensive coverage of the Web that a search engine can. Here are some of the important issues to consider when deciding whether to use a Web directory for a particular type of search.

Directories are inherently small. It takes time for an editor to find appropriate resources to include in a directory, and to create meaningful annotations. Because they are hand compiled, directories are by nature much smaller than most search engines. This size limitation has both positives and negatives for the searcher. On the positive side, directories typically have a narrow or selective focus. A narrow or selective focus makes the searcher's job easier by limiting the number of possible options. Most directories have a policy that requires editors to perform at least a cursory evaluation of a Web page or site before including a link to it in the directory, in theory assuring that only hyperlinks to the highest quality content are included.

Directories also generally feature detailed, objective, succinct annotations, written by a person who has taken the time to evaluate and understand a resource, so they often convey a lot of detail. Search engine annotations, on the other hand, are often arbitrarily assembled by software from parts of the page that may convey little information about the page.

On the negative side, Web directories are often arbitrarily limited, either by design or by extraneous factors such as a lack of time, knowledge, or skill on the part of the editorial staff.

Unseen Editorial Policies. Although many Web directories publish editorial standards and selection criteria, other factors may influence the contents of a directory. Ordinary "office politics" may favor one editor's work over another's, for example. With open model directories, which rely on the efforts of volunteers, a number of cases have been reported where some editors took advantage of their position to remove or block competitors' listings. Though most directories strive to provide objective coverage of the Web, it's important to be vigilant for any signs of bias and the quality of resources covered.

Timeliness. Directory links are typically maintained by hand, so upkeep and maintenance is a very large issue. The constantly changing, dynamic nature of the Web means that sites are removed, URLs are changed, companies merge—all of these events effectively "break" links in a directory. Link checking is an important part of keeping a directory up to date, but not all directories do a good job of frequently verifying the links in the collection.

Directories are also vulnerable to "bait and switch" tactics by Webmasters. Such tactics are generally used only when a site stands no chance of being included in a directory because its content violates the directory's editorial policy. Adult sites often use this tactic, for example, by submitting a bogus "family friendly" site, which is evaluated by editors. Once the URL for the site is included in the directory, the "bait" site is taken down and replaced with risqué content that wouldn't have passed muster in the first place. The link to the site (and its underlying URL) remains the same, but the site's content is entirely different from what was originally submitted by the Webmaster and approved by the directory editor. It's a risky tactic, since many directories permanently ban sites that they catch trying to fool them in this manner. Unfortunately, it can be effective, as the chicanery is unlikely to be discovered unless users complain.

Lopsided coverage. Directory ontologies may not accurately reflect a balanced view of what's available on the Web. For the specialized directories that we discuss in the next chapter, this isn't necessarily a bad thing. However, lopsided coverage in a general-purpose directory is a serious disservice to the searcher.

Some directories have editorial policies that mandate a site being listed in a particular category even if hundreds or thousands of other sites are included in the category. This can make it difficult to find resources in these "overloaded" categories. Examples of huge, lopsided categories include Yahoo!'s "Business" category and the Open Directory Project's "Society" category.

The opposite side of this problem occurs when some categories receive little or no coverage, whether due to editorial neglect or simply a lack of resources to assure comprehensive coverage of the Web.

Charging for listings. There has been a notable trend toward charging Webmasters a listing fee to be included in many directories. While most businesses consider this a reasonable expense, other organizations or individuals may find the cost to be too great. This "pay to play" trend almost certainly excludes countless valuable sites from the directories that abide by this policy.

Search Engines

Search engines are databases containing full-text indexes of Web pages. When you use a search engine, you are actually searching this database of retrieved Web pages, *not* the Web itself. Search engine databases are finely tuned to provide rapid results, which is impossible if the engines were to attempt to search the billions of pages on the Web in real time.

Search engines are similar to telephone white pages, which contain simple listings of names and addresses. Unlike yellow pages, which are organized by category and often include a lot of descriptive information about businesses, white pages provide minimal, bare bones information. However, they're organized in a way that makes it very easy to look up an address simply by using a name like "Smith" or "Veerhoven."

Search engines are compiled by software "robots" that voraciously suck millions of pages into their indices every day. When you search an index, you're trying to coax it to find a good match between the keywords you type in and all of the words contained in the search engine's database. In essence, you're relying on a computer to essentially do simple pattern-matching between your search terms and the words in the index. AltaVista, HotBot, and Google are examples of search engines.

How Search Engines Work

Search engines are complex programs. In a nutshell, they consist of several distinct parts:

- The Web crawler (or spider), which finds and fetches Web pages

- The indexer, which as its name implies, indexes every word on every page and stores the resulting index of words in a huge database

- The query processor, which compares your search query to the index and recommends the best possible matching documents

Let's take a closer look at each part.

Myth: All Search Engines Are Alike

Search engines vary widely in their comprehensiveness, currency, and coverage of the Web. Even beyond those factors, search engines, like people, have "personalities," with strengths and weaknesses, admirable traits, and irritating flaws. By turns search engines can be stolidly reliable and exasperatingly flaky. And just like people, if you ask for something outside their area of expertise, you'll get the electronic equivalent of a blank stare and a resounding "huh?"

A huge issue is the lack of commonality between interfaces, syntax, and capabilities. Although they share superficial similarities, all search engines are unique both in terms of the part of the Web they have indexed, and how they process search queries and rank results. Many searchers make the mistake of continually using their "favorite" engine for all searches. Even if they fail to get useful results, they'll keep banging away, trying different keywords or otherwise trying to coax an answer from a system that simply may not be able to provide it.

A far better approach is to spend time with all of the major search engines and get to know how they work, what types of queries they handle better than others, and generally what kind of "personality" they have. If one search engine doesn't provide the results you're looking for, switch to another. And most important of all, if none of the engines seem to provide reasonable results, you've just got a good clue that what you're seeking is likely to be located on the Invisible Web—if, in fact, it's available online at all.

WEB CRAWLERS

Web crawlers are the "scouts" for search engines, with the sole mission of finding and retrieving pages on the Web and handing them off to the search engine's indexers, which we discuss in the next section. It's easy to imagine a Web crawler as a little sprite scuttling across the luminous strands of cyberspace, but in reality Web crawlers do not traverse the Web at all. In fact, crawlers function much like your Web browser, by sending a request to a Web server for a Web page, downloading the entire page, then handing it off to the search engine's indexer.

Crawlers, of course, request and fetch pages much more quickly than you can with a Web browser. In fact most Web crawlers can request hundreds or even thousands of unique pages simultaneously. Given this power, most crawlers are programmed to spread out their requests for pages from individual servers over a period of time to avoid over-whelming the server or consuming so much bandwidth that human users are crowded out.

Crawlers find pages in two ways. Most search engines have an "add URL" form, which allows Web authors to notify the search engine of a Web page's address. In the early days of the Web, this method for alert-ing a search engine to the existence of a new Web page worked well—the crawler simply took the list of all URLs submitted and retrieved the underlying pages.

Unfortunately, spammers figured out how to create automated bots that bombarded the add URL form with millions of URLs pointing to spam pages. Most search engines now reject almost 95 percent of all URLs submitted through their add URL forms. It's likely that, over time, most search engines will phase-out their add URL forms in favor of the second method that crawlers can use to discover pages—one that's more easy to control.

This second method of Web page discovery takes advantage of the hypertext links embedded in most Web pages. When a crawler fetches a page, it culls all of the links appearing on the page and adds them to a queue for subsequent crawling. As the crawler works its way through the queue, links found on each new page are also added to the queue. Harvesting links from actual Web pages dramatically decreases the amount of spam a crawler encounters, because most Web authors only link to what they believe are high-quality pages.

By harvesting links from every page it encounters, a crawler can quickly build a list of links that can cover broad reaches of the Web. This technique also allows crawlers to probe deep within individual sites, following internal navigation links. In theory, a crawler can discover and index virtually every page on a site starting from a single URL, if the site is well designed with extensive internal navigation links.

Although their function is simple, crawlers must be programmed to handle several challenges. First, since most crawlers send out simulta-neous requests for thousands of pages, the queue of "visit soon" URLs must be constantly examined and compared with URLs already exist-ing in the search engine's index. Duplicates in the queue must be elim-inated to prevent the crawler from fetching the same page more than once. If a Web page has already been crawled and indexed, the crawler must determine if enough time has passed to justify revisiting the page, to assure that the most up-to-date copy is in the index. And because crawling is a resource-intensive operation that costs money, most search engines limit the number of pages that will be crawled and indexed from any one Web site. This is a crucial point—you can't assume that just because a search engine indexes some pages from a site that it indexes *all* of the site's pages.

Because much of the Web is highly connected via hypertext links, crawling can be surprisingly efficient. A May 2000 study published by researchers at AltaVista, Compaq, and IBM drew several interesting conclusions that demonstrate that crawling can, in theory, discover most pages on the visible Web (Broder et al., 2000). The study found that:

- For any randomly chosen source and destination page, the probability that a direct hyperlink path exists from the source to the destination is only 24 percent.

- If a direct hypertext path does exist between randomly chosen pages, its average length is 16 links. In other words, a Web browser would have to click links on 16 pages to get from random page A to random page B. This finding is less than the 19 degrees of separation postulated in a previous study, but also excludes the 76 percent of pages lacking direct paths.

- If an undirected path exists (meaning that links can be followed forward or backward, a technique available to search engine spiders but not to a person using a Web browser), its average length is about six degrees.

- More than 90 percent of all pages on the Web are reachable from one another by following either forward or backward links. This is good news for search engines attempting to create comprehensive indexes of the Web.

These findings suggest that efficient crawling can uncover much of the visible Web. This is important to keep in mind as we begin to examine the types of content that truly makes up the Invisible Web in later chapters.

SEARCH ENGINE INDEXERS

When a crawler fetches a page, it hands it off to an indexer, which stores the full text of the page in the search engine's database, typically in an inverted index data structure. An inverted index is sorted alphabetically, with each index entry storing the word, a list of the documents in which the word appears, and in some cases the actual locations within the text where the word occurs. This structure is ideally suited to keyword-based queries, providing rapid access to documents containing the desired keywords.

As an example, an inverted index for the phrases "life is good," "bad or good," "good love," and "love of life" would contain identifiers for each phrase (numbered one through four), and the position of the word within the phrase. Table 2.2 shows the structure of this index.

Table 2.2 A Typical Inverted Index Data Structure

bad	(2,1)		
good	(1,3)	(2,3)	(3,1)
is	(1,2)		
life	(1,1)	(4,3)	
love	(3,2)	(4,1)	
of	(4,2)		
or	(2,2)		

To improve search performance, some search engines eliminate common words called *stop words* (such as *is*, *or*, and *of* in the above example). Stop words are so common they provide little or no benefit in narrowing a search so they can safely be discarded. The indexer may also take other performance-enhancing steps like eliminating punctuation and multiple spaces, and may convert all letters to lowercase. Some search engines save space in their indexes by truncating words to their root form, relying on the query processor to expand queries by adding suffixes to the root forms of search terms.

Indexing the full text of Web pages allows a search engine to go beyond simply matching single keywords. If the location of each word is recorded, proximity operators such as NEAR can be used to limit searches. The engine can also match multi-word phrases, sentences, or even larger chunks of text. If a search engine indexes HTML code in addition to the text on the page, searches can also be limited to specific fields on a page, such as the title, URL, body, and so on.

THE QUERY PROCESSOR

The query processor is arguably the most complex part of a search engine. The query processor has several parts, including the primary user interface (the search form), the actual "engine" that evaluates a query and matches it with the most relevant documents in the search engine database of indexed Web pages, and the results-output formatter.

Myth: Search Engine Indexes Are Current

Crawling the Web is an expensive, resource-intensive operation. It costs a search engine a certain amount of money each time it retrieves and indexes a page. Once a page is included in a search engine's index, the engine may not recrawl the page for an extended period of time. This may be because the crawler is smart enough to know that the page doesn't change frequently, but more often it's because limited resources require that the crawler focus on newer or more popular areas of the Web.

A lack of freshness in a search engine index can lead to bizarre or irrelevant results if a Web page has changed since the last time a search spider indexed the page. Let's look at an example.

Say that on June 1, a Web author creates a Web page that has 2,500 words in 10 paragraphs. The author may or may not submit the URL of the page to search engines requesting that they spider the page. Nonetheless, some people on the Web create links to the page, so Web crawlers can find it anyway.

On July 20, a spider from search engine A crawls the page and includes the page in its index.

On August 20, a spider from search engine B crawls the same page. The page is now included in two separate indexes, and a search for keywords on the page will return an accurate result from both engines.

But then on September 20, the Web author decides to make some changes, and eliminates paragraphs 3, 4, and 5 from the document. The author does not notify the engines that he has changed the page (by resubmitting the URL to the "submit URL" form provided by each engine). The copy of the page in the search engines' indexes no longer matches the actual page on the Web.

On October 5, a user of search engine A submits a query that causes the Web page to be displayed in the result list. However, the keywords in the query that caused the engine to include the page in the result list were in the paragraphs removed by the page author on September 20th. In this case, the search engine has returned an accurate result based on the copy of the page in its index, but based its relevance ranking on an old version of the page that no longer contains what the searcher is looking for. If the searcher clicks through and reads the updated page he won't find what he is looking for, leaving the searcher puzzled and confused. The searcher will likely blame the "poor" result on the "dumb" search engine, when in fact the problem was simply that the engine was calculating relevance using a copy of a document that was out of date.

Most of the major search engines have stepped up efforts to recrawl Web pages on a more frequent basis. Many are employing "smart" crawlers that learn to revisit frequently changing pages more often. Others are simply throwing more resources and money at the problem, attempting to keep up with the rapidly changing Web by brute force. Nonetheless, the currency of all search indexes is a problem every searcher should consider.

The search form and the results format vary little from search engine to search engine. All have both basic and advanced search forms, each offering slightly varying limiting, control, and other user-specified functions. And most result formats are equally similar, typically displaying search results and a few additional extras like suggested related searches, most popular searches, and so on.

The major differentiator of one search engine from another lies in the way relevance is calculated. Each engine is unique, emphasizing certain variables and downplaying others to calculate the relevance of a document as it pertains to a query. Some engines rely heavily on statistical analysis of text, performing sophisticated pattern-matching comparisons to find the most relevant documents for a query. Others use link analysis, attempting to capture the collective wisdom of the Web by finding the documents most cited by other Web authors for a particular query.

How an engine calculates relevance is ultimately what forms its "personality" and determines its suitability for handling a particular type of query. Search engine companies closely guard the formulas used to calculate relevance, and change them constantly as algorithms are updated for improved quality or tweaked to outwit the latest technique used by spammers. Nonetheless, over time, a searcher can generally get to know how well a particular engine will perform for a query, and select an engine appropriately.

Issues with Search Engines

Just as Web directories have a set of issues of concern to a searcher, so do search engines. Some of these issues are technical; others have to do with choices made by the architects and engineers who create and maintain the engines.

Cost of crawling. Crawling the Web is a resource-intensive operation. The search engine provider must maintain computers with sufficient power and processing capability to keep up with the explosive growth of the Web, as well as a high-speed connection to the Internet backbone. It costs money every time a page is fetched and stored in the search engine's database. There are also costs associated with query processing, but in general crawling is by far the most expensive part of maintaining a search engine.

Since no search engine's resources are unlimited, decisions must be made to keep the cost of crawling within an acceptable budgetary range. Some engines limit the total number of pages in their index, dumping older pages when newer ones are found. Others limit the frequency of recrawl, so pages in the index may be stale or out of date. Still others limit their crawling to certain portions or domains believed to contain reliable, non-duplicated material.

Whenever an engine decides to limit its crawling, it means pages that potentially could be included in its index are not. It's tempting to think that these unretrieved pages are part of the Invisible Web, but they aren't. They are visible and indexable, but the search engines have made a conscious decision not to index them. Competent searchers must take this into account when planning a research strategy.

Much has been made of these overlooked pages, and many of the major engines are making serious efforts to include them and make their indexes more comprehensive. Unfortunately, the engines have also discovered through their "deep crawls" that there's a tremendous amount of duplication and spam on the Web. The trade-off between excluding bogus material and assuring that all truly relevant material will be found is a difficult one, and virtually assures that no engine will ever have a totally comprehensive index of the Web.

"Dumb" crawlers. At their most basic level, crawlers are uncomplicated programs. Crawlers are designed simply to find and fetch Web pages. To discover unindexed pages, crawlers rely on links they've discovered on other pages. If a Web page has no links pointing to it, a search engine spider cannot retrieve it unless it has been submitted to the search engine's "add URL" form.

Another problem with search engines compiled by crawlers is simply that it takes a lot of time to crawl the entire Web, even when the crawler is hitting millions of pages a day. Crawler *lag time* is a two-fold issue: First, there's typically a gap between when a page is published on the Web and when a crawler discovers it. Second, there's a time lag between when a crawler first finds a page and when it recrawls the page looking for fresh content. Both of these time issues can contribute to incomplete or inaccurate search results.

Current generation crawlers also have little ability to determine the quality or appropriateness of a Web page, or whether it is a page that changes frequently and should be recrawled on a timely basis.

User expectations and skills. Users often have unrealistic expectations of what search engines can do and the data that they contain. Trying to determine the best handful of documents from a corpus of millions or billions of pages, using just a few keywords in

Myth: Search Engines Overlap in Coverage

The Web is commonly described as a huge haystack of information, with searchers looking for the elusive needle. In the words of Dr. Matthew Koll, an early pioneer in recognizing and writing about the Invisible Web, there are many ways that a search engine can address the needle in the haystack problem (Koll, 1998).

It can consider:

- A known needle in a known haystack
- A known needle in an unknown haystack
- An unknown needle in an unknown haystack
- Any needle in a haystack
- The sharpest needle in a haystack
- Most of the sharpest needles in a haystack
- All the needles in a haystack
- Affirmation of no needles in the haystack
- Things like needles in any haystack
- Let me know whenever a new needle shows up
- Where are the haystacks?
- Needles, haystacks—whatever.

In the myth on page 53, we show that the search engines don't index the entire Web. It's tempting to think that if you simply combine results from all of the major search engine indexes you'll get a much more comprehensive map of the Web, but this isn't true. Greg Notess, owner of Search Engine Showdown, regularly tests the major search engines for overlap. His work demonstrates that there is surprisingly little overlap between the major search engines and directories (Notess, 2000).

In one recent analysis, Notess compared the results of five small searches run on 14 different search engines. The five searches found a total of 795 hits, 298 of which represented unique pages. Of those 298 hits, 110 were found by only one of the 14 search engines, while another 79 were found by only two.

Given the increasing use of measures such as clickthrough analysis and link popularity, the major engines will have much more overlap of popular, well-linked pages than on more obscure, less popular pages. If you're searching for something popular or timely, you need be less concerned about the lack of overlap than if you're looking for something unusual or rare. In this case, it's vital to use more than one search engine to assure comprehensive results.

a query is almost an impossible task. Yet most searchers do little more than enter simple two- or three-word queries, and rarely take advantage of the advanced limiting and control functions all search engines offer.

Search engines go to great lengths to successfully cope with these woefully basic queries. One way they cope is to create a set of preprogrammed results for popular queries. For example, if a pop star releases a hit song that generates lots of interest, the engine may be preprogrammed to respond with results pointing to biographical information about the star, discographies, and links to other related music resources. Another method is to adjust results so that the most popular, commonly selected pages rise to the top of a result lists. These are just two techniques search engines apply to help users who can't or won't take advantage of the powerful tools that are available to them. Taking the time to learn how a search engine works, and taking advantage of the full capabilities it offers can improve search results dramatically.

Speedy Response vs. Thorough Results. Now that we live on "Internet time," everyone expects nearly instantaneous results from search engines. To accommodate this demand for speed, search engines rarely do as thorough an analysis as they might if time were not an issue. Shortcuts are taken, total results are truncated, and invariably important documents will be omitted from a result list.

Fortunately, increases in both processing power and bandwidth are providing search engines with the capability to use more computationally intensive techniques without sacrificing the need for speed. Unfortunately, the relentless growth of the Web works against improvements in computing power and bandwidth simply because as the Web grows the search space required to fully evaluate it also increases.

Bias toward text. Most current-generation search engines are highly optimized to index *text*. If there is no text on a page—say it's nothing but a graphic image, or a sound or audio file—there is nothing for the engine to index. For non-text objects such as images, audio, video, or other streaming media files, a search engine can record, in an Archie-like manner, filename and location details but not much more. While researchers are working on techniques for indexing non-text objects, for the time being non-text objects make up a considerable part of the Invisible Web.

Table 2.3   Directories vs. Search Engines

Directories	Search Engines
Inherently small	No inherent or artificial size restrictions
Selected links chosen for quality	Mass quantities of links, no quality control
Poor for exhaustive searches	Good for exhaustive searches
Can include limited Invisible Web content, but don't allow direct searching of it	Can technically include and allow searching of some Invisible Web content but often do not
Often point to Web site top-level or home pages, but no deeper	Typically index the full text of many, if not all, pages on every site

Search Engines vs. Directories

To summarize, search engines and Web directories both have sets of features that can be useful, depending on the searcher's information need. Table 2.3 compares these primary features.

Early search engines did a competent job of keeping pace with the growth of simple text documents on the Web. But as the Web grew, it increasingly shifted from a collection of simple HTML documents to a rich information space filled with a wide variety of data types. More importantly, owners of content stored in databases began offering Web gateways that allowed user access via the Web. This new richness of data was beyond the capability of search engine spiders, designed only to handle simple HTML text pages.

In the next chapter, we discuss specialized and hybrid search tools that bring the searcher closer to the Invisible Web or actually deliver a limited portion of it by using some sophisticated indexing and retrieval techniques.

Chapter 3

Specialized and Hybrid Search Tools

Directories and search engines are the two fundamental tools available to the Web searcher. However, there are also a variety of specialized and hybrid search tools that should be part of any searcher's arsenal. These tools take many forms, and sometimes they are confused with Invisible Web resources. They are not—they simply extend or enhance the capabilities of search engines and directories that focus on material that's part of the visible Web.

These alternative tools have both positives and negatives for the searcher. On the plus side, these tools tend to be smaller, and are focused on specific categories or sources of information. Because they are small relative to the general-purpose search engines and directories, they are often more reliable and stable. These tools tend also to be updated more frequently than the general-purpose tools. Their interfaces are often optimized for maximum utility for the underlying information they search. And, because they are limited to specific categories, they often offer greater depth of coverage for a category than the general-purpose tools.

This flexibility also can be perceived as a minus. The searcher must learn how to use multiple interfaces, the specialized commands and other unique capabilities offered by each tool. These hybrid resources also require an investment in time to understand the scope of the materials they cover. In many ways, they are close kin of the books found in a ready reference section of a library, as they are often focused to answer specific questions, quickly and easily.

In this chapter, we look at a variety of specialized and hybrid search tools, including targeted directories and focused crawlers, vertical portals (vortals), metasearch engines, value-added search services, "alternative" search tools, and fee-based Web services.

Targeted Directories and Focused Crawlers

Targeted directories and focused crawlers, as their names imply, focus on a specific subject area or domain of knowledge. Just as you have always used a subject-specific reference book to answer a specific question, targeted search tools can help you save time and pinpoint specific information quickly on the Web. Why attempt to pull a needle from a large haystack with material from all branches of knowledge when a specialized tool allows you to limit your search in specific ways as it relates to the type of information being searched? Searching a smaller, targeted universe of data can increase your precision because there is potentially less unrelated or irrelevant information to get in the way.

As an example, consider the problem of looking up a friend's phone number. Intuitively, most of us would instantly reach for a phone book rather than an encyclopedia. Why? Because phone books are specialized resources that are designed solely for the purpose of looking up phone numbers. Encyclopedias, on the other hand, are general-purpose reference works containing a wide range of information on a huge variety of subjects—and most people would rightly think it's ridiculous to use an encyclopedia to look up a phone number.

Yet this is exactly what many of those same people do when they use a general-purpose search engine or directory such as AltaVista or Yahoo! when there are far more appropriate search tools available for a specialized task. The problem is partly that many people think search engines and Web directories are somehow all encompassing, able to process any request for information. They may not realize that there are specialized resources that will do a much better job of satisfying their information need.

Targeted directories and crawlers are functionally similar to general-purpose Web directories and search engines, but will often yield much higher quality results for certain types of searches, for a number of reasons. Let's take a closer look at both of these types of specialized Web search tools.

Targeted Directories

Targeted directories are Web guides compiled by humans that focus on a particular specialized topic or area of information. They are generally compiled by subject matter experts whose principal concerns are quality, authority, and reliability of the resources included in the directory. Standards for inclusion in a targeted directory tend to be more rigorous than for general-purpose Web directories. And, quite often, annotations are extensive, almost functioning as an abstract of a Web resource rather than the more common brief descriptions offered by general-purpose directories.

EXAMPLES OF TARGETED DIRECTORIES

EEVL (Edinburgh Engineering Virtual Library)

http://www.eevl.ac.uk/

EEVL is a guide to engineering information on the Internet. It is a free service, created and run by a team of information specialists from Heriot-Watt University, with input from a number of other universities in the U.K. The site features a catalogue of quality engineering resources (selected by subject consultants), targeted engineering search engines, bibliographic and events databases, including the Recent Advances in Manufacturing bibliographic database, a directory of science and technology librarians, an Engineering on the Internet bibliography, and Hot Links to useful sites that offer many specialized ways of limiting your search for very specific types of information.

Classics Resources on the Web

http://www.classics.cam.ac.uk/Faculty/links.html

An extensive directory of literary, linguistic, historical, and philosophical resources developed and maintained by the Humanities faculty at Cambridge University.

The Internet Intelligence Index

http://www.fuld.com/i3/index.html

The Internet Intelligence Index is designed to help you gather competitive intelligence information. It contains links to more than 600 intelligence-related Internet sites, covering everything from macroeconomic data to individual patent and stock quote information. The Internet Intelligence Index is maintained by Fuld & Company, a leading firm in the field of Competitor Intelligence.

Odden's Bookmarks

http://oddens.geog.uu.nl/index.html

Subtitled "The Fascinating World of Maps and Mapping," this "oddly" named directory (after its compiler, Roelof P. Oddens) features more than 11,000 cartographic links in areas including maps and atlases, sellers of cartographic material, map collections, cartographic and geoservers, cartographic and geographical societies, departments of cartography, government cartography, and many more.

Targeted directories offer several advantages over general-purpose Web directories such as Yahoo! or LookSmart. These advantages include:

Comprehensive subject coverage. Many of the pages included in targeted directories are available via general-purpose directories, but targeted directories are more likely to have comprehensive coverage of a particular subject area. In essence, they are "concentrated haystacks" where needles are more likely to be the size of railroad spikes, and much easier to find.

Up-to-date listings. People who compile and maintain targeted directories have a vested interest in keeping the directory up to date, as they are usually closely and personally associated with the directory by colleagues or other professionals in the field. Keeping the directory up to date is often a matter of honor and professional reputation for the compiler.

Listings of new resources. Since the compilers of targeted directories are often subject-matter experts in their field, they closely follow new developments in their fields. They also can rely on a network of other people in the field to monitor new developments and alert them when a new Web resource is available. Site developers are also motivated to inform targeted directories of new resources for the prestige factor of securing a listing. Finally, many focused directories are compiled by non-profit organizations, which are not subject to the occasional subtle pressure of bias from advertisers.

Focused Crawlers

Like targeted directories, focused crawlers center on specific subjects or topics. But just as general-purpose search engines are far more comprehensive than Web directories, focused crawlers attempt to find and index as many pages as possible within a particular subject area by spidering a limited domain of Web sites known to cover a particular topic.

Focused crawlers will often spider sites more thoroughly and frequently than a general-purpose search engine. Because focused crawlers cover a much smaller portion of the Web than general-purpose search engines, the cost of crawling is much less significant. Most focused crawlers are limited to specific sites by editors who supply a list of URLs to be crawled, rather than randomly crawling the Web. Editorial selection of URLs to crawl reduces the "signal to noise" ratio in the resulting index, by limiting the crawler to sites that have been determined to be appropriate for the specialized index. This doesn't mean links to new resources are ignored, however. In fact, focused crawlers can often discover new resources and add them to their indexes more quickly than general-purpose search engines by following newly created links from a trusted relevant Web site.

EXAMPLES OF FOCUSED CRAWLERS

LawCrawler

http://lawcrawler.lp.findlaw.com/

LawCrawler is a legal search tool and database that provide precision by enabling searches to be focused on sites and within specific domains known to feature high-quality legal information. LawCrawler provides the ability to limit your search to certain types of law related resources. These resources include a legal dictionary, legal NewsLaw reviews, U.S. government sites, the U.S. Constitution, the U.S. Legal Code, U.S. Supreme Court opinions, and information published by all federal circuit courts—even worldwide sites with legal information. Because LawCrawler is powered by the AltaVista search engine software, the searcher can also employ any of the advanced search capabilities provided by AltaVista, but the search is usefully restricted to the specific legal information domains indexed by LawCrawler. LawCrawler is part of the FedLaw service, which has numerous other legal resources, including a targeted directory.

PsychCrawler

http://www.psychcrawler.com

This site is sponsored by an organization with knowledge of the topic, the American Psychological Association, which has a vested interest in making sure that high-quality material is crawled.

PoliticalInformation.Com

http://www.politicalinformation.com

This focused search engine contains an index of the contents of more than 5,000 Web sites chosen for the quality of their content. Targeted sites are recrawled every 2-3 weeks to keep the results current. The site features links to over 270,000 documents solely related to politics and the political process.

Some focused crawlers do nothing more than limit searches to specific top-level domains. Most sites on the Web are in the dot-com top-level domain. But other top-level domains are restricted to certain types of organizations or individuals. Dot-mil (.mil) for example, is for U.S. military Web sites. Dot-edu (.edu) is for educational institutions, dot-gov (.gov) for U.S. government, and so on. Some examples follow.

SearchMil.Com

http://www.searchmil.com

SearchMil.com specializes in military focused searches, combining exhaustive coverage of the dot-mil domain with powerful search engine technology that ranks results in order of popularity. SearchMil's index contains over 1 million military-specific pages.

SearchEdu.Com

http://www.searchedu.com

SearchEdu.com is a focused search engine devoted to university- and education-related Web sites. SearchEdu's index contains more than 20 million pages of academic materials from universities, schools, and libraries, and results are ranked in order of popularity.

FirstGov.Gov

http://www.firstgov.gov

FirstGov.Gov is a focused crawler designed to be a "one stop" portal for government information of all kinds in the United States. The site has more than 20 million pages indexed, with more added every day. FirstGov also features a high-quality directory of government sites, so it's actually a hybrid consisting of both a targeted directory and focused crawler.

Table 3.1 Specialized and Hybrid Search Tools

Type of Search Tool	Examples
Targeted Directory	• EEVL (Edinburgh Engineering Virtual Library) • Classic Resources on the Web • Internet Intelligence Index • Odden's Bookmarks
Focused Crawler	• LawCrawler • PsychCrawler • PoliticalInformation.com • SearchMil.com • SearchEdu.com • FirstGov.gov
Vertical Portal (Vortal)	• Covisint • Buildnet.com • GoFish.com
Metasearch Engines	• Metacrawler • Dogpile • Intelliseek Profusion
Value-Added Search Services	• Northern Light • The Electric Library • Edgar Online
Browser Agents	• Flyswat • Kenjin • Zapper
Client-Based Web Search	• Bullseye Pro • Copernic
WebRings	• Webring.org

Vertical Portals (Vortals)

Vertical Portals (also known as "Vortals") are mini-versions of general-purpose search engines and directories that focus on a specific topic or subject area. They are often made up of both a targeted directory and listings compiled by a focused crawler.

Vortals are most often associated with "Business to Business" (B2B) sites, catering to both the information and commerce needs of particular industries or services. While many Vortals provide great information resources for searchers, their primary focus is usually on providing a virtual marketplace for the trade of goods and services. As such, Vortals can be excellent resources for researchers looking for current information on business concerns ranging from manufacturing to global trade. The searcher should beware, however, that Vortals often have an unabashed profit motive that may introduce a degree of bias into the information they provide. We're not suggesting you avoid Vortals; rather, just keep a more vigilant eye out for quality or bias than you normally might with "pure" Web guides.

How to Find Vortals

There are thousands of Vortals on all conceivable subjects. Rather than providing specific examples, here are two focused directories that specialize in Vortals.

VerticalMatter.com

http://www.verticalmatter.com

A directory of vertical portals, defined as sites that are big enough to be considered a "destination," and generally have community interaction, topical news, and various other portal features.

Yahoo! Business to Business Marketplace

http://b2b.yahoo.com/

Yahoo! B2B Marketplace is a product directory of Vortal sites on the Web. Search by keyword or browse through many commerce Web sites for products organized by category.

Metasearch Engines

Metasearch engines submit queries to multiple search engines and Web directories simultaneously. Rather than crawling the Web and building its own index, a metasearch engine relies on the indices created by other search engines. This allows you to quickly get results from more than one general-purpose search engine.

While some searchers swear by metasearch engines, they are somewhat limited because they can only pass through a small set of the advanced search commands to any given engine. Searchers typically take a "least common denominator" approach that favors quantity of results over refined queries that might return higher quality results.

EXAMPLES OF METASEARCH ENGINES

MetaCrawler

http://www.metacrawler.com

MetaCrawler sends your query to most of the major search engines and directories, and then combines the results in a single list, eliminating duplicates. Unlike the other metasearch engines reviewed here, MetaCrawler sums the scores given by each service it uses, and presents them in a "voted" ordering, with the score (from 1 to 1,000) presented in bold type next to each result. You can customize MetaCrawler to use your favorite search engines, increase or decrease the results per page and per source, set the timeout duration you're willing to wait for results to be returned, and limit the domains that are searched.

Dogpile

http://www.dogpile.com

The rather unusually named Dogpile searches more than two dozen major search sites, including Usenet newsgroups, FTP sites for file downloads, newswires for current headlines, and business news from several sources. Unlike MetaCrawler, which post-processes the results using its own relevance algorithms, Dogpile returns the exact results from each engine with the utmost haste. Results are presented as each engine replies to the query. Dogpile searches three sites at a time. Results from each search engine are grouped together, with the descriptions provided by each site. At the bottom of the results list is a button that continues your search with the next three search engines.

Intelliseek Profusion

http://www.intelliseek.com/adv_search.htm

Intelliseek's Profusion offers a metasearch of nine search engines and directories. You can select all nine individually, or the "best three" or "fastest three" as determined by your query. Profusion also allows you to vary the number of results that are displayed, apply limited Boolean operators, and, uniquely, perform a link check on results to assure that pages you see in the results are still live on the Web.

Issues with Metasearch Engines

Metasearch engines attempt to solve the haystack problem by searching several major search engines simultaneously. The idea is to combine haystacks to increase the probability of finding relevant results for a search. The trap many people fall into is thinking that metasearch engines give you much broader coverage of the Web. Searchers reason that since each engine indexes only a portion of the Web, by using a metasearch engine, the probability of finding documents that an individual engine might have missed is increased. In other words, combining partial haystacks should create a much more complete, larger haystack.

In theory, this is true. In practice, however, you don't get significantly broader coverage. Why? Because the metasearch engines run up against the same limitations on total results returned that you encounter searching a single engine. Even if search engines report millions of potential matches on your keywords, for practical reasons, all of the engines limit the total number of results you can see— usually between 200 and 1,000 total results. Results found beyond these arbitrary cutoff points are effectively inaccessible without further query refinement. Quite the opposite of searching whole haystacks with great precision, you're actually searching only portions of partial haystacks with less precision!

While metasearch engines aren't necessarily the best tools for improving the precision of a search, they do provide several other useful functions by "combining haystacks." Use a metasearch engine when you're just beginning a search on an unfamiliar topic, to get a sense of what keywords might be the most effective for specific engines. Use a metasearch engine when you want extremely quick and dirty results for a popular one- or two-word query. And, finally, use these engines when you want to quickly compare and contrast how the major services process a particular query.

Remember that each metasearch engine searches different sources. Be sure to examine the list of engines searched to assure that your results from your favorite engines are included.

Metasearch engines generally do nothing more than submit a simple search to the various engines they query. They aren't able to pass on advanced search queries that use Boolean or other operators to limit or refine results. Put another way, metasearch engines are increasing the potential relevance of search results at the expense of precision. Quite the opposite of searching whole haystacks, you're actually searching only portions of partial haystacks.

Value-Added Search Services

Some Web search services combine a general-purpose search engine or directory with a proprietary collection of material that's only available for a fee. These value-added search services try to combine the best of both worlds: free resources available on the Web, and high-quality information offered by reputable information publishers.

Many of these services evolved from models used by early consumer-oriented services like the Source, CompuServe, Prodigy, and, of course, today's most popular closed information system, America Online (AOL). Unlike the consumer services, which require a subscription to the complete service to gain access to any of its parts, value-added search services on the Web tend to offer varying levels of access based on need and willingness to pay. Most offer at least some free information (sometimes requiring filling out a simple registration form first).

The premium information offered by these services is generally first rate, and well worth the modest fees if the searcher is looking for authoritative, high-quality information.

EXAMPLES OF VALUE-ADDED SEARCH SERVICES

Northern Light

http://www.northernlight.com

The Northern Light Special Collection is an online business library comprising more than 7,000 trusted, full-text journals, books, magazines, newswires, and reference sources. The breadth of information available in the Special Collection is unique to Northern Light, and includes a wide range of diverse sources such as American Banker, ENR: Engineering News Record, The Lancet, PR Newswire, and ABC News Transcripts. This content is fully searchable and results are seamlessly integrated with Web search results.

Most Special Collection documents range in price from $1.00 to $4.00 per article, with a few higher value sources, such as WEFA and Investext reports costing more. Unlike expensive subscription services that require you to commit to pay up front before you can tell how much you will use, Northern Light will only ask you to pay for what you actually read. They also have an automated "return" policy where your money is refunded for documents that don't meet your needs.

The Electric Library

http://www.elibrary.com

The Electric Library offers free searching and provides brief abstracts of results on its Web site, but charges a subscription fee for full access. The service is often compared to Northern Light, though the Electric Library uses a subscription model with no transactional fees. It is licensed to more than 15,000 schools and libraries, and has more than 80,000 individual subscribers. Subscriptions are available on a monthly ($9.95) or annual ($59.95) basis.

The Electric Library Personal Edition is also unique because its database contains only copyrighted content. Licensed content includes material from 400 publishers, with more than 1,000 titles. Segregated into six categories, the Electric Library contains more than 5.5 million newspaper articles, nearly 750,000 magazine articles, 450,000 book chapters, 1,500 maps, 145,000 television and radio transcripts, and 115,000 photos and images. Fully 95 percent of the content in Electric Library isn't available elsewhere on the Web.

EDGAR Online

http://www.edgar-online.com/

Throughout the year, every U.S. public company is required to disclose the critical business, financial, and competitive details of its activities to the Securities and Exchange Commission. EDGAR Online provides fast and easy access to this SEC information. Visitors to the site get limited access to information on individuals mentioned in proxy statements, historical filings back to 1994, today's filings, and full search by any of ten criteria, including company name, ticker symbol, filing type, industries, and sector.

For professionals or others who require more advanced options, EDGAR Online Premium offers subscribers real-time e-mail notification and advanced management tools that can pinpoint the critical business, financial, and competitive information contained in every SEC filing.

Alternative Search Tools

Most people think of searching the Web as firing up a browser and pointing it to a search engine or directory home page, typing keyword queries, and reading the results on the browser screen. While most traditional search engines and directories do indeed operate this way, there are a number of alternative search tools that both transcend limitations and offer additional features not generally available otherwise.

Browser Agents

Browser agents are programs that work in conjunction with a Web browser to enhance and extend the browser's capabilities. While these tools focus on "search," they work differently from traditional keyword-based search services. The tools attempt to automate the search process by analyzing and offering selected resources proactively. Others go beyond simple keyword matching schemes to analyze the context of the entire query, from words, sentences, and even entire paragraphs.

EXAMPLES OF BROWSER AGENTS

Flyswat

http://www.flyswat.com

In a nutshell, Flyswat analyzes the content of any Web page, and instantly transforms it into a rich resource with dozens or even hundreds of links to sources of additional information that would take you hours to find using conventional Web search tools. Flyswat scans the text on a page, and creates links called "flycons" for the major keywords on the page. Clicking on a flycon raises a pop-up menu that lists information link types. Examples of link types are Company Profile, Stock Quote, Related Books, Download Sites, and so on.

Kenjin

http://www.kenjin.com

Kenjin works in the background, examining the contents of your active window, whether it's a browser, e-mail client, or word processing program. Once Kenjin "understands" the document you're working on, it automatically brings information to you, eliminating the need to stop and search. Kenjin examines the concepts, not keywords, in your active window and therefore delivers links to more relevant information. Kenjin takes advantage of the fact that it's run from your desktop, and provides links not only to the Web but also to local content on your PC and relevant encyclopedia entries or books that match the subject.

Zapper

http://www.zapper.com

Zapper resides on your desktop, and using it is a snap. You can enter a query into its search form, but you can also simply highlight text, press the control key and right click with your mouse, and all of the text will automatically be pasted into the search form. Your source text can be anything—a Web page, an e-mail or word processor document.

Like a metasearch engine, Zapper then submits the search to different sources of information on the Web. But going far beyond what most metasearch engines can do, the sources that are searched will be very specific to your query (medical sites for a medical query, for example). It does this either automatically, using "IntelliZap," which analyzes the context and selects the appropriate search sources, or you can limit the search manually using specialized sites that have been clustered into topic-specific "packs." Zapper analyzes the results, selects the best matches, and presents the results with intelligently extracted annotations showing where the information was found. If you don't like the packs provided, or prefer the search functionality from other sources, you can easily create your own custom zap packs that incorporate the search services from almost any site on the Web.

Browser agents can be very handy add-on tools for the Web searcher. The downside to all of these tools is that they are stand-alone pieces of software that must be downloaded, installed, and run in conjunction with other programs. This can quickly lead to desktop clutter, and potential system conflicts because the programs are not designed to work together. The best strategy for the searcher is to sample a number of these programs and select one or two that prove the most useful for day-to-day searching needs.

Client-Based Search Tools

Client-based Web search utilities (sometimes called "agents" or "bots") reside on your own computer or network, not on the Internet. Like other software, they are customizable to meet your personal needs. Because the software resides on your own computer, it can "afford" to be more computationally intensive in processing your search queries.

Client-based Web search utilities have a number of key features generally not found on Web-based search engines and directories.

- They search multiple sites simultaneously, and you can choose which ones are used.

- They can eliminate dead links from results.

- They can download pages to your computer for more extensive analysis and faster browsing.

- Their search refinement tools are often very sophisticated.

- They generate reports that can be saved, repeated, or automatically updated.

- They can, to a limited degree, access Invisible Web sites that general-purpose search engines cannot penetrate.

EXAMPLES OF CLIENT-BASED SEARCH TOOLS

BullsEye Pro

http://info.intelliseek.com/prod/bullseye_pro.htm

BullsEye Pro combines the best features of a metasearch engine, offline browser, bookmark manager, and Web research report manager into a single unified product. Its simple, clean interface is easy enough for a beginner to use, but beneath the surface sophisticated filtering, sorting, and limiting tools provide extensive controls for power searchers. It's the closest thing to a "Swiss army knife" a Web searcher can hope to find.

The program searches more than 700 sources, organized into more than 100 categories. In addition to the major Web search engines, BullsEye 2 Pro searches hundreds of databases and other sources that are part of the Invisible Web, providing you with access to information the search engines can't see.

Copernic

http://www.copernic.com/products/pro/

Copernic is a search agent that can access more than 600 search engines and specialized information sources grouped in 55 categories. Categories include the Web, newsgroups, e-mail addresses, books, business, games, movies, music, newspapers, software, sports news, tech news, and others.

Copernic allows you to schedule search updates and get e-mail alerts when pages you are tracking have changed. Copernic also does a good job at presenting results, removing advertisement banners, and filtering out useless information and dead links. Copernic supports both Boolean searching and natural language queries.

Like browser agents, client-based Web search tools have both pros and cons for the searcher. If you find yourself running the same search repeatedly and would like to track how results change over time, these utilities can be a godsend. Similarly, their ability to access some Invisible Web resources makes them a useful addition to (but not substitute for) your Invisible Web search arsenal.

Web Rings

Simply put, a Web ring is a group of Web pages that are linked to one another, ostensibly because they all share a similar topic or interest. Uniform navigation buttons let you travel from page to page in the ring until you end up back at your starting point. In effect, a Web ring is a "closed circuit" of Web sites, linked together by a common theme.

These themes are what make Web rings interesting from a searching perspective. As part of a Web ring, a Web site is voluntarily linking with other Web sites that have similar characteristics. Unlike the random categorizations generated by search engines, Web rings allow Webmasters to make direct and specific affiliations with other sites that they think are related to their own. And unlike a list of links, which can become outdated or broken over time, Web ring URLs are kept in a central database that keeps the membership—and links to participating sites—fresh and up to date.

For more information on Web Rings, see the Web Ring home page at http://www.webring.org/.

Fee-Based Web-Accessible Services

Finally, there is an entire class of search tools accessible via the Web, but which do not search the Web themselves. Often, these search tools are proprietary systems that have existed for many years prior to the Web, but in recent years have created Web interfaces for easier access by clients. Although these tools fall outside the scope of this book, we feel it's important to mention them to round out our discussion of alternate search tools.

The most significant of these services are provided by the traditional online information companies, which over the years have compiled huge proprietary databases of information. These companies include familiar names such as Thomson's Dialog, LexisNexis, and Dow-Jones. Many of these companies got their start in the very early days of the information-processing industry during the 1970s. Information professionals love these services, because they aggregate data from numerous sources and providers, serving as huge marts of information—many times larger than what is available on the Web. The twin hallmarks of these services are extremely sophisticated querying and reporting tools, and "massaged" databases where information quality is first rate. As you might expect, gaining access to this sort of premium content is quite expensive.

Next Stop: The Invisible Web

By now, you should have a clear idea of the types of search services that can help you locate information on the visible Web. General-purpose search engines and directories, supplemented with specialized tools like focused crawlers and metasearch engines, are absolutely essential parts of every searcher's toolkit. Now it's time to explore the vast region of the Web that is virtually inaccessible using the Web search tools we've described. It's the part of the Web that search engines can't see: The Invisible Web.

Myth: Search Indexes Are Comprehensive

Perhaps the most pervasive myth about search engines is that they provide comprehensive coverage of the Web. In fact, exactly the opposite is true: no search engine knows about every page on the Web, and most include only 20-50 percent of even *visible* Web pages, let alone Invisible Web content. Why?

Part of the problem, of course, is that search crawlers simply can't keep up with the explosive pace of growth on the Web. With millions of new pages added daily, it's too expensive and resource-intensive to attempt to find every new page added to the Web.

A second problem is that crawlers simply can't find all of the pages on the Web. This can be either because there are no links pointing to some pages (and crawlers can only discover pages by following links), or because the crawler simply can't or won't access some types of content. This type of content, as we will see in the next chapter, is genuinely part of the Invisible Web.

A third reason has to do with the individual characteristics of each search engine, and the rules it follows for gathering and indexing Web pages. Each engine is unique, and they all follow different rules in gathering material. For example:

- Each engine re-crawls Web pages on its own unique schedule.
- Some learn about pages via user submissions, while others do not.
- Some types of content, while technically crawlable, pose challenges or difficulties for spiders. These pages may use frames, or consist of code or objects that do not make spiders happy.
- Webmasters may choose to voluntarily exclude pages by using the Robots Exclusion Protocol, which prevents a crawler from accessing and indexing a page.
- Some engines arbitrarily drop pages from their indexes, either deliberately to make room for new pages, or inadvertently, creating a nettlesome situation for both searchers and Webmasters looking for pages that simply have been "booted out" of the index for no apparent reason.

Webmasters themselves are often to blame for broken links by moving or removing pages on a server. Material on the Web can be changed, added, or removed in just a few seconds. URLs are very explicit addresses—they point to specific filenames in specific directories on Web servers. If a file is renamed, or moved to another directory, its indexed URL automatically becomes broken, and the search engine may not be able to find the new location of the page on its own.

The lack of comprehensive coverage may or may not be a problem for a searcher. Popular, heavily trafficked sites are generally well represented in most general-purpose search engines. More obscure or less-frequently visited sites may not be. However, simply being omitted from a search engine index does not make a page or a site invisible. If a Web site consists of simple HTML pages and has no roadblocks in place to block crawlers, it's firmly in the realm of the visible Web, because at any minute a crawler may discover and index the site. Nonetheless, most Web content that falls into this category will be very difficult to find unless the searcher knows exactly where to look. Even though technically visible, content that's not included in search engine indexes is all but invisible to most searchers. We call this the "Opaque" Web—see Chapter 4 for more information.

Chapter 4

The Invisible Web

The paradox of the Invisible Web is that it's easy to understand why it exists, but it's very hard to actually define in concrete, specific terms. In a nutshell, the Invisible Web consists of content that's been excluded from general-purpose search engines and Web directories such as Lycos and LookSmart. There's nothing inherently "invisible" about this content. But since this content is not easily located with the information-seeking tools used by most Web users, it's effectively invisible because it's so difficult to find unless you know exactly where to look.

The visible Web is easy to define. It's made up of HTML Web pages that the search engines have chosen to include in their indices. It's no more complicated than that. The Invisible Web is much harder to define and classify for several reasons.

First, many Invisible Web sites are made up of straightforward Web pages that search engines could easily crawl and add to their indices, but do not, simply because the engines have decided against including them. This is a crucial point—much of the Invisible Web is hidden because search engines have deliberately chosen to exclude some types of Web content. We're not talking about unsavory "adult" sites or blatant spam sites—quite the contrary! Many Invisible Web sites are first-rate content sources. These exceptional resources simply cannot be found by using general-purpose search engines because they have been effectively locked out. There are a number of reasons for these exclusionary policies, many of which we'll discuss in this chapter. But keep in mind that should the engines change their policies in the future, sites that today are part of the Invisible Web will suddenly join the mainstream as part of the visible Web.

Second, it's relatively easy to classify some sites as either visible or Invisible based on the technology they employ. Some sites using database technology, for example, are genuinely difficult for current generation search engines to access and index. These are "true" Invisible Web sites. Other sites, however, use a variety of media and file types, some of which are easily indexed, and others that are incomprehensible to search engine crawlers. Web sites that use a mixture of these media and file types aren't easily classified as either visible or Invisible. Rather, they make up what we call the "opaque" Web.

Finally, search engines could theoretically index some parts of the Invisible Web, but doing so would simply be impractical, either from a cost standpoint, or because data on some sites is ephemeral and not worthy of indexing—for example, current weather information, moment-by-moment stock quotes, airline flight arrival times, and so on.

In this chapter, we define the Invisible Web, and delve into the reasons search engines can't "see" its content. We also discuss the four different "types" of invisibility, ranging from the "opaque" Web, which is relatively accessible to the searcher, to the truly invisible Web, which requires specialized finding aids to access effectively.

Invisible Web Defined

The definition given above is deliberately very general, because the general-purpose search engines are constantly adding features and improvements to their services. What may be invisible today may become visible tomorrow, should the engines decide to add the capability to index things that they cannot or will not currently index.

Let's examine the two parts of our definition in more detail. First, we'll look at the technical reasons search engines can't index certain types of material on the Web. Then we'll talk about some of the other non-technical but very important factors that influence the policies that guide search engine operations.

At their most basic level, search engines are designed to index Web pages. As we discussed in Chapter 2, search engines use programs called crawlers to find and retrieve Web pages stored on servers all over

---

DEFINITION

The Invisible Web

Text pages, files, or other often high-quality authoritative information available via the World Wide Web that general-purpose search engines cannot, due to technical limitations, or will not, due to deliberate choice, add to their indices of Web pages. Sometimes also referred to as the "Deep Web" or "dark matter."

---

the world. From a Web server's standpoint, it doesn't make any difference if a request for a page comes from a person using a Web browser or from an automated search engine crawler. In either case, the server returns the desired Web page to the computer that requested it.

A key difference between a person using a browser and a search engine crawler is that the person is able to manually type a URL into the browser window and retrieve that Web page. Search engine crawlers lack this capability. Instead, they're forced to rely on links they find on Web pages to find other pages. If a Web page has no links pointing to it from any other page on the Web, a search engine crawler can't find it. These "disconnected" pages are the most basic part of the Invisible Web. There's nothing *preventing* a search engine from crawling and indexing disconnected pages—there's simply no way for a crawler to discover and fetch them.

Disconnected pages can easily leave the realm of the Invisible and join the visible Web in one of two ways. First, if a connected Web page links to a disconnected page, a crawler can discover the link and spider the page. Second, the page author can request that the page be crawled by submitting it to search engine "add URL" forms.

Technical problems begin to come into play when a search engine crawler encounters an object or file type that's not a simple text document. Search engines are designed to index text, and are highly optimized to perform search and retrieval operations on text. But they don't do very well with non-textual data, at least in the current generation of tools.

Some engines, like AltaVista and HotBot, can do limited searching for certain kinds of non-text files, including images, audio, or video files. But the way they process requests for this type of material are reminiscent of early Archie searches, typically limited to a filename or the minimal alternative (ALT) text that's sometimes used by page authors in the HTML image tag. Text surrounding an image, sound, or video file can give additional clues about what the file contains. But keyword searching with images and sounds is a far cry from simply telling the search engine to "find me a picture that looks like Picasso's Guernica" or "let me hum a few bars of this song and you tell me what it is." Pages that consist primarily of images, audio, or video, with little or no text, make up another type of Invisible Web content. While the pages may actually be included in a search engine index, they provide few textual clues as to their content, making it highly unlikely that they will ever garner high relevance scores. Researchers are working to overcome these limitations (see Chapter 8 for more details).

While search engines have limited capabilities to index pages that are primarily made up of images, audio, and video, they have serious problems with other types of non-text material. Most of the major general-purpose search engines simply cannot handle certain types of formats. These formats include:

- PDF or Postscript (Google excepted)
- Flash
- Shockwave
- Executables (programs)
- Compressed files (.zip, .tar, etc.)

The problem with indexing these files is that they aren't made up of HTML text. Technically, most of the formats in the list above can be indexed. The search engines choose not to index them for business reasons. For one thing, there's much less user demand for these types of files than for HTML text files. These formats are also "harder" to index, requiring more computing resources. For example, a single PDF file might consist of hundreds or even thousands of pages. Indexing non-HTML text file formats tends to be costly.

Pages consisting largely of these "difficult" file types currently make up a relatively small part of the Invisible Web. However, we're seeing a rapid expansion in the use of many of these file types, particularly for some kinds of high-quality, authoritative information. For example, to comply with federal paperwork reduction legislation, many U.S. government agencies are moving to put all of their official documents on the Web in PDF format. Most scholarly papers are posted to the Web in Postscript or compressed Postscript format. For the searcher, Invisible Web content made up of these file types poses a serious problem. We discuss a partial solution to this problem later in this chapter.

The biggest technical hurdle search engines face lies in accessing information stored in databases. This is a huge problem, because there are thousands—perhaps millions—of databases containing high-quality information that are accessible via the Web. Web content creators favor databases because they offer flexible, easily maintained development environments. And increasingly, content-rich databases from universities, libraries, associations, businesses, and government agencies are being made available online, using Web interfaces as front-ends to what were once closed, proprietary information systems.

Databases pose a problem for search engines because every database is unique in both the design of its data structures, and its search and retrieval tools and capabilities. Unlike simple HTML files, which search engine crawlers can simply fetch and index, content stored in databases is trickier to access, for a number of reasons that we'll describe in detail here.

Search engine crawlers generally have no difficulty finding the interface or gateway pages to databases, because these are typically pages made up of input fields and other controls. These pages are formatted with HTML and look like any other Web page that uses interactive forms. Behind the scenes, however, are the knobs, dials, and switches that provide access to the actual contents of the database, which are literally incomprehensible to a search engine crawler.

Although these interfaces provide powerful tools for a human searcher, they act as roadblocks for a search engine spider. Essentially, when an indexing spider comes across a database, it's as if it has run smack into the entrance of a massive library with securely bolted doors. A crawler can locate and index the library's address, but because the crawler cannot penetrate the gateway it can't tell you anything about the books, magazines, or other documents it contains.

These Web-accessible databases make up the lion's share of the Invisible Web. They are accessible via the Web, but may or may not actually be on the Web (see Table 4.1). To search a database you must use the powerful search and retrieval tools offered by the database itself. The advantage to this direct approach is that you can use search tools that were specifically designed to retrieve the best results from the database. The disadvantage is that you need to find the database in the first place, a task the search engines may or may not be able to help you with.

Table 4.1 On the Web vs. Via the Web

On the Web	Via the Web
Anyone with server access can place just about anything "on" the internet in the form of a Web page	Various databases, various providers, material not directly searchable via Web search tools
Very little bibliographic control, no language control	Typically highly structured and well indexed
Quality of info extremely varied	Uniformly high quality, often professional resources
Cost is low or free	Invisible Web often low-cost or free: proprietary information services cost can vary, often expensive
Examples: Your vacation pictures AltaVista, Google, Northern Light Many Invisible Web sites	Examples: Full-text of peer reviewed journals Full-text of many newspapers Abstracts Dialog, LexisNexis, Dow-Jones News Retrieval

There are several different kinds of databases used for Web content, and it's important to distinguish between them. Just because Web content is stored in a database doesn't automatically make it part of the Invisible Web. Indeed, some Web sites use databases not so much for their sophisticated query tools, but rather because database architecture is more robust and makes it easier to maintain a site than if it were simply a collection of HTML pages.

One type of database is designed to deliver tailored content to individual users. Examples include My Yahoo!, Personal Excite, Quicken.com's personal portfolios, and so on. These sites use databases that generate "on the fly" HTML pages customized for a specific user. Since this content is tailored for each user, there's little need to index it in a general-purpose search engine.

A second type of database is designed to deliver streaming or real-time data—stock quotes, weather information, airline flight arrival information, and so on. This information isn't necessarily customized, but is stored in a database due to the huge, rapidly changing quantities

of information involved. Technically, much of this kind of data is indexable because the information is retrieved from the database and published in a consistent, straight HTML file format. But because it
changes so frequently and has value for such a limited duration (other
than to scholars or archivists), there's no point in indexing it. It's also
problematic for crawlers to keep up with this kind of information. Even
the fastest crawlers revisit most sites monthly or even less frequently.
Staying current with real-time information would consume so many
resources that it is effectively impossible for a crawler.

The third type of Web-accessible database is optimized for the data it
contains, with specialized query tools designed to retrieve the information using the fastest or most effective means possible. These are often
"relational" databases that allow sophisticated querying to find data that
is "related" based on criteria specified by the user. The only way of accessing content in these types of databases is by directly interacting with the
database. It is this content that forms the core of the Invisible Web.

Let's take a closer look at these elements of the Invisible Web, and
demonstrate exactly why search engines can't or won't index them.

Table 4.2 Types of Invisible Web Content

Type of Invisible Web Content	Why It's Invisible
Disconnected page	No links for crawlers to find the page
Page consisting primarily of images, audio, or video	Insufficient text for the search engine to "understand" what the page is about
Pages consisting primarily of PDF or Postscript, Flash, Shockwave, Executables (programs) or Compressed files (.zip, .tar, etc.)	Technically indexable, but usually ignored, primarily for business or policy reasons
Content in relational databases	Crawlers can't fill out required fields in interactive forms
Real-time content	Ephemeral data; huge quantities; rapidly changing information
Dynamically generated content	Customized content is irrelevant for most searchers; fear of "spider traps"

Why Search Engines Can't See the Invisible Web

Text—more specifically hypertext—is the fundamental medium of the Web. The primary function of search engines is to help users locate hypertext documents of interest. Search engines are highly tuned and optimized to deal with text pages, and even more specifically, text pages that have been encoded with the HyperText Markup Language (HTML). As the Web evolves and additional media become commonplace, search engines will undoubtedly offer new ways of searching for this information. But for now, the core function of most Web search engines is to help users locate text documents.

HTML documents are simple. Each page has two parts: a "head" and a "body," which are clearly separated in the source code of an HTML page. The head portion contains a title, which is displayed (logically enough) in the title bar at the very top of a browser's window. The head portion may also contain some additional metadata describing the document, which can be used by a search engine to help classify the document. For the most part, other than the title, the head of a document contains information and data that help the Web browser display the page but is irrelevant to a search engine. The body portion contains the actual document itself. This is the meat that the search engine wants to digest.

The simplicity of this format makes it easy for search engines to retrieve HTML documents, index every word on every page, and store them in huge databases that can be searched on demand. Problems arise when content doesn't conform to this simple Web page model. To understand why, it's helpful to consider the process of crawling and the factors that influence whether a page either can or will be successfully crawled and indexed.

The first determination a crawler attempts to make is whether access to pages on a server it is attempting to crawl is restricted. Webmasters can use three methods to prevent a search engine from indexing a page. Two methods use blocking techniques specified in the Robots Exclusion Protocol (http://info.webcrawler.com/mak/projects/robots.html) that most crawlers voluntarily honor and one creates a technical roadblock that cannot be circumvented.

The Robots Exclusion Protocol is a set of rules that enables a Webmaster to specify which parts of a server are open to search engine crawlers, and which parts are off-limits. The Webmaster simply creates a list of files or directories that should not be crawled or indexed, and saves this list on the server in a file named robots.txt. This optional file, stored by convention at the top level of a Web site, is nothing more than a polite request to the crawler to keep out, but most major search engines respect the protocol and will not index files specified in robots.txt.

The second means of preventing a page from being indexed works in the same way as the robots.txt file, but is page-specific. Webmasters can prevent a page from being crawled by including a "noindex" meta tag instruction in the "head" portion of the document. Either robots.txt or the noindex meta tag can be used to block crawlers. The only difference between the two is that the noindex meta tag is page specific, while the robots.txt file can be used to prevent indexing of individual pages, groups of files, or even entire Web sites.

Password protecting a page is the third means of preventing it from being crawled and indexed by a search engine. This technique is much stronger than the first two because it uses a technical barrier rather than a voluntary standard.

Why would a Webmaster block crawlers from a page using the Robots Exclusion Protocol rather than simply password protecting the pages? Password-protected pages can be accessed only by the select few users who know the password. Pages excluded from engines using the Robots Exclusion Protocol, on the other hand, can be accessed by anyone *except* a search engine crawler. The most common reason Webmasters block pages from indexing is that their content changes so frequently that the engines cannot keep up.

Pages using any of the three methods described here are part of the Invisible Web. In many cases, they contain no technical roadblocks that prevent crawlers from spidering and indexing the page. They are part of the Invisible Web because the Webmaster has opted to keep them out of the search engines.

Once a crawler has determined whether it is permitted to access a page, the next step is to attempt to fetch it and hand it off to the search engine's indexer component. This crucial step determines whether a page is visible or invisible. Let's examine some variations that crawlers encounter as they discover pages on the Web, using the same logic they do to determine whether a page is indexable.

Case 1. The crawler encounters a page that is straightforward HTML text, possibly including basic Web graphics. This is the most common type of Web page. It is visible and can be indexed.

Case 2. The crawler encounters a page made up of HTML, but it's a form consisting of text fields, check boxes, or other components requiring user input. It might be a sign-in page, requiring a user name and password. It might be a form requiring the selection of one or more options. The form itself, since it's made up of simple HTML, can be fetched and indexed. But the content behind the form (what the user sees after clicking the submit button) may be invisible to a search engine. There are two possibilities here:

- The form is used simply to select user preferences. Other pages on the site consist of straightforward HTML that can be crawled and indexed (presuming there are links from other pages elsewhere on the Web pointing to the pages). In this case, the form and the content behind it are visible and can be included in a search engine index. Quite often, sites like this are specialized search sites like the ones we described in Chapter 3. A good example is Hoover's Business Profiles (http://www.hoovers.com), which provides a form to search for a company, but presents company profiles in straightforward HTML that can be indexed.

- The form is used to collect user-specified information that will generate dynamic pages when the information is submitted. In this case, although the form is visible the content "behind" it is invisible. Since the only way to access the content is by using the form, how can a crawler—which is simply designed to request and fetch pages—possibly know what to enter into the form? Since forms can literally have infinite variations, if they function to access dynamic content they are essentially roadblocks for crawlers. A good example of this type of Invisible Web site is The World Bank Group's Economics of Tobacco Control Country Data Report Database, which allows you to select any country and choose a wide range of reports for that country (http://www1. worldbank.org/tobacco/database.asp). It's interesting to note that this database is just one part of a much larger site, the bulk of which is fully visible. So even if the search engines do a comprehensive job of indexing the visible part of the site, this valuable information still remains hidden to all but those searchers who visit the site and discover the database on their own.

In the future, forms will pose less of a challenge to search engines. Several projects are underway aimed at creating more intelligent crawlers that can fill out forms and retrieve information. One approach uses preprogrammed "brokers" designed to interact with the forms of specific databases. Other approaches combine brute force with artificial intelligence to "guess" what to enter into forms, allowing the crawler to "punch through" the form and retrieve information. However, even if general-purpose search engines do acquire the ability to crawl content in databases, it's likely that the native search tools provided by each database will remain the best way to interact with them. We discuss these future approaches to indexing content in databases in Chapter 8.

Case 3. The crawler encounters a dynamically generated page assembled and displayed on demand. The telltale sign of a dynamically generated page is the "?" symbol appearing in its URL. Technically, these pages are part of the visible Web. Crawlers can fetch any page that can be displayed in a Web browser, regardless of whether it's a static page stored on a server or generated dynamically. A good example of this type of Invisible Web site is Compaq's experimental SpeechBot search engine, which indexes audio and video content using speech recognition, and converts the streaming media files to viewable text (http://www.speech bot.com). Somewhat ironically, one could make a good argument that most search engine result pages are themselves Invisible Web content, since they generate dynamic pages on the fly in response to user search terms.

Dynamically generated pages pose a challenge for crawlers. Dynamic pages are created by a script, a computer program that selects from various options to assemble a customized page. Until the script is actually run, a crawler has no way of knowing what it will actually do. The script should simply assemble a customized Web page. Unfortunately, unethical Webmasters have created scripts to generate millions of similar but not quite identical pages in an effort to "spamdex" the search engine with bogus pages. Sloppy programming can also result in a script that puts a spider into an endless loop, repeatedly retrieving the same page.

These "spider traps" can be a real drag on the engines, so most have simply made the decision not to crawl or index URLs that generate dynamic content. They're "apartheid" pages on the Web—separate but equal, making up a big portion of the "opaque" Web that potentially can be indexed but is not. Inktomi's FAQ about its crawler, named "Slurp," offers this explanation:

"Slurp now has the ability to crawl dynamic links or dynamically generated documents. It will not, however, crawl them by default. There are a number of good reasons for this. A couple of reasons are that dynamically generated documents can make up infinite URL spaces, and that dynamically generated links and documents can be different for every retrieval so there is no use in indexing them" (http://www.inktomi.com/slurp.html).

As crawler technology improves, it's likely that one type of dynamically generated content will increasingly be crawled and indexed. This is content that essentially consists of static pages that are stored in databases for production efficiency reasons. As search engines learn which sites providing dynamically generated content can be trusted not to subject crawlers to spider traps, content from these sites will begin to appear in search engine indices. For now, most dynamically generated content is squarely in the realm of the Invisible Web.

Case 4. The crawler encounters an HTML page with nothing to index. There are thousands, if not millions, of pages that have a basic HTML framework, but which contain only Flash, images in the .gif, .jpeg, or other Web graphics format, streaming media, or other non-text content in the body of the page. These types of pages are truly parts of the Invisible Web because there's nothing for the search engine to index. Specialized multimedia search engines, such as ditto.com and WebSeek are able to recognize some of these non-text file types and index minimal information about them, such as file name and size, but these are far from keyword searchable solutions.

Case 5. The crawler encounters a site offering dynamic, real-time data. There are a wide variety of sites providing this kind of information, ranging from real-time stock quotes to airline flight arrival information. These sites are also part of the Invisible Web, because these data streams are, from a practical standpoint, unindexable. While it's technically possible to index many kinds of real-time data streams, the value would only be for historical purposes, and the enormous amount of data captured would quickly strain a search engine's storage capacity, so it's a futile exercise. A good example of this type of Invisible Web site is TheTrip.com's Flight tracker, which provides real-time flight arrival information taken directly from the cockpit of in-flight airplanes (http://www.trip.com/ft/home/0,2096,1-1,00.shmtl).

Case 6. The crawler encounters a PDF or Postscript file. PDF and Postscript are text formats that preserve the look of a document and display it identically regardless of the type of computer used to view it. Technically, it's a straightforward task to convert a PDF or Postscript file to plain text that can be indexed by a search engine. However, most search engines have chosen not to go to the time and expense of indexing files of this type. One reason is that most documents in these formats are technical or academic papers, useful to a small community of scholars but irrelevant to the majority of search engine users, though this is changing as governments increasingly adopt the PDF format for their official documents. Another reason is the expense of conversion to plain text. Search engine companies must make business decisions on how best to allocate resources, and typically they elect not to work with these formats.

An experimental search engine called ResearchIndex, created by computer scientists at the NEC Research Institute, not only indexes PDF and Postscript files, it also takes advantage of the unique features that commonly appear in documents using the format to improve search results (http://www.researchindex.com). For example, academic papers typically cite other documents, and include lists of references to related material. In addition to indexing the full text of documents, ResearchIndex also creates a citation index that makes it easy to locate related documents. It also appears that citation searching has little overlap with keyword searching, so combining the two can greatly enhance the relevance of results.

We hope that the major search engines will follow Google's example and gradually adopt the pioneering work being done by the developers of ResearchIndex. Until then, files in PDF or Postscript format remain firmly in the realm of the Invisible Web.

Case 7. The crawler encounters a database offering a Web interface. There are tens of thousands of databases containing extremely valuable information available via the Web. But search engines cannot index the material in them. Although we present this as a unique case, Web-accessible databases are essentially a combination of Cases 2 and 3. Databases generate Web pages dynamically, responding to commands issued through an HTML form. Though the interface to the database is an HTML form, the database itself may have been created before the development of HTML, and its legacy system is incompatible with protocols used by the engines, or they may require registration to access the data. Finally, they may be proprietary, accessible only to select users, or users who have paid a fee for access.

Ironically, the original HTTP specification developed by Tim Berners-Lee included a feature called format negotiation that allowed a client to say what kinds of data it could handle and allow a server to return data in any acceptable format. Berners-Lee's vision encompassed the information in the Invisible Web, but this vision—at least from a search engine standpoint—has largely been unrealized.

Myth: What You See Is What You Get

In theory, the results displayed in response to a search engine query accurately reflect the pages that are deemed relevant to the query. In practice, however, this isn't always the case. We've already discussed the problem that arises when a search index is out of date. Search results may not match the current content of the page simply because the page has been changed since it was last indexed.

But there's a more insidious problem: spiders can be fooled into crawling one page that's masquerading for another. This technique is called "cloaking" or, more technically, "IP delivery."

By convention, crawlers have unique names, and they identify themselves by name whenever they request pages from a server, allowing servers to deny them access during particularly busy times so that human users won't suffer performance consequences. The crawler's name also provides a means for Webmasters to contact the owners of spiders that put undue stress on servers. But the identification codes also allow Webmasters to serve pages that are created specifically for spiders in place of the actual page the spider is requesting.

This is done by creating a script that monitors the IP (Internet Protocol) addresses making page requests. All entities, whether Web browsers or search engine crawlers, have their own unique IP addresses. IP addresses are effectively "reply to" addresses—the Internet address to which pages should be sent. Cloaking software watches for the unique signature of a search engine crawler (its IP address), and feeds specialized versions of pages to the spider that aren't identical to the ones that will be seen by anyone else.

Cloaking allows Webmasters to "break all the rules" by feeding specific information to the search engine that will cause a page to rank well for specific search keywords. Used legitimately, cloaking can solve the problem of unscrupulous people stealing metatag source code from a high-ranking page. It can also help sites that are required by law to have a "search-unfriendly" disclaimer page as their home page. For example, pharmaceutical companies Eli Lilly and Schering-Plough use IP delivery techniques to assure that their pages rank highly for their specific products, which would be impossible if the spiders were only able to index the legalese on pages required by law.

Unfortunately, cloaking also allows unscrupulous Webmasters to employ a "bait and switch" tactic designed to make the search engine think the page is about one thing when in fact it may be about something completely different. This is done by serving a totally bogus page to a crawler, asserting that it's the actual content of the URL, while in fact the content at the actual URL of the page may be entirely different. This sophisticated trick is favored by spammers seeking to lure unwary searchers to pornographic or other unsavory sites.

IP delivery is difficult for search crawlers to recognize, though a careful searcher can often recognize the telltale signs by comparing the title and description with the URL in a search engine result. For example, look at these two results for the query "child toys":

Dr. Toy's Guide: Information on Toys and Much More

Toy Information! Over 1,000 award winning toys and children's products are fully described with company phone numbers, photos and links to useful resources...

URL: www.drtoy.com/

AAA BEST TOYS

The INTERNET'S LARGEST ULTIMATE TOY STORE for children of all ages.

URL: 196.22.31.6/xxx-toys.htm

In the first result, the title, description, and URL all suggest a reputable resource for children's toys. In the second result, there are several clues that suggest that the indexed page was actually served to the crawler via IP delivery. The use of capital letters and a title beginning with "AAA" (a favorite but largely discredited trick of spammers) are blatant red flags. What really clinches it is the use of a numeric URL, which makes it difficult to know what the destination is, and the actual filename of the page, suggesting something entirely different from wholesome toys for children. The important thing to remember about this method is that the titles and descriptions, and even the content of a page, can be faked using IP delivery, but the underlying URL cannot. If a search result looks dubious, pay close attention to the URL before clicking on it. This type of caution can save you both frustration and potential embarrassment.

These technical limitations give you an idea of the problems encountered by search engines when they attempt to crawl Web pages and compile indices. There are other, non-technical reasons why information isn't included in search engines. We look at those next.

Four Types of Invisibility

Technical reasons aside, there are other reasons that some kinds of material that can be accessed either on or via the Internet are not included in search engines. There are really four "types" of Invisible Web content. We make these distinctions not so much to make hard and fast distinctions between the types, but rather to help illustrate the amorphous boundary of the Invisible Web that makes defining it in concrete terms so difficult.

The four types of invisibility are:

• The Opaque Web

• The Private Web

• The Proprietary Web

• The Truly Invisible Web

The Opaque Web

The Opaque Web consists of files that can be, but are not, included in search engine indices. The Opaque Web is quite large, and presents a unique challenge to a searcher. Whereas the deep content in many truly Invisible Web sites is accessible if you know how to find it, material on the Opaque Web is often much harder to find.

The biggest part of the Opaque Web consists of files that the search engines can crawl and index, but simply do not. There are a variety of reasons for this; let's look at them.

DEPTH OF CRAWL

Crawling a Web site is a resource-intensive operation. It costs money for a search engine to crawl and index every page on a site. In the past, most engines would merely sample a few pages from a site rather than performing a "deep crawl" that indexed every page, reasoning that a sample provided a "good enough" representation of a site that would satisfy the needs of most searchers. Limiting the depth of crawl also reduced the cost of indexing a particular Web site.

In general, search engines don't reveal how they set the depth of crawl for Web sites. Increasingly, there is a trend to crawl more deeply, to index as many pages as possible. As the cost of crawling and indexing goes down, and the size of search engine indices continues to be a competitive issue, the depth of crawl issue is becoming less of a concern for searchers. Nonetheless, simply because one, fifty, or five thousand pages from a site are crawled and made searchable, there is no guarantee that every page from a site will be crawled and indexed. This problem gets little attention and is one of the top reasons why useful material may be all but invisible to those who only use general-purpose search tools to find Web materials.

FREQUENCY OF CRAWL

The Web is in a constant state of dynamic flux. New pages are added constantly, and existing pages are moved or taken off the Web. Even the most powerful crawlers can visit only about 10 million pages per day, a fraction of the entire number of pages on the Web. This means that each search engine must decide how best to deploy its crawlers, creating a schedule that determines how frequently a particular page or site is visited.

Web search researchers Steve Lawrence and Lee Giles, writing in the July 8, 1999, issue of *Nature* state that "indexing of new or modified pages by just one of the major search engines can take months" (Lawrence, 1999). While the situation appears to have improved since their study, most engines only completely "refresh" their indices monthly or even less frequently.

It's not enough for a search engine to simply visit a page once and then assume it's still available thereafter. Crawlers must periodically return to a page to not only verify its existence, but also to download the freshest copy of the page and perhaps fetch new pages that have been added to a site. According to one study, it appears that the half-life of a Web page is somewhat less than two years and the half-life of a Web site is somewhat more than two years. Put differently, this means that if a crawler returned to a site spidered two years ago it would contain the same number of URLs, but only half of the original pages would still exist, having been replaced by new ones (Koehler, 2000).

New sites are the most susceptible to oversight by search engines because relatively few other sites on the Web will have linked to them compared to more established sites. Until search engines index these new sites, they remain part of the Invisible Web.

MAXIMUM NUMBER OF VIEWABLE RESULTS

It's quite common for a search engine to report a very large number of results for any query, sometimes into the millions of documents. However, most engines also restrict the total number of results they will display for a query, typically between 200 and 1,000 documents. For queries that return a huge number of results, this means that the majority of pages the search engine has determined might be relevant are inaccessible, since the result list is arbitrarily truncated. Those pages that don't make the cut are effectively invisible.

Good searchers are aware of this problem, and will take steps to circumvent it by using a more precise search strategy and using the advanced filtering and limiting controls offered by many engines. However, for many inexperienced searchers this limit on the total number of viewable hits can be a problem. What happens if the answer you need is available (with a more carefully crafted search) but cannot be viewed using your current search terms?

DISCONNECTED URLS

For a search engine crawler to access a page, one of two things must take place. Either the Web page author uses the search engine's "Submit URL" feature to request that the crawler visit and index the page, or the crawler discovers the page on its own by finding a link to the page on some other page. Web pages that aren't submitted directly to the search engines, and that don't have links pointing to them from other Web pages, are called "disconnected" URLs and cannot be spidered or indexed simply because the crawler has no way to find them.

Quite often, these pages present no technical barrier for a search engine. But the authors of disconnected pages are clearly unaware of the requirements for having their pages indexed. A May 2000 study by IBM, AltaVista, and Compaq discovered that the total number of disconnected URLs makes up about 20 percent of the potentially indexable Web, so this isn't an insignificant problem (Broder, etc., 2000).

In summary, the Opaque Web is large, but not impenetrable. Determined searchers can often find material on the Opaque Web, and search engines are constantly improving their methods for locating and indexing Opaque Web material.

The three other types of Invisible Webs are more problematic, as we'll see.

The Private Web

The Private Web consists of technically indexable Web pages that have deliberately been excluded from search engines. There are three ways that Webmasters can exclude a page from a search engine:

- Password protect the page. A search engine spider cannot go past the form that requires a username and password.

- Use the robots.txt file to disallow a search spider from accessing the page.

- Use the "noindex" meta tag to prevent the spider from reading past the head portion of the page and indexing the body.

For the most part, the Private Web is of little concern to most searchers. Private Web pages simply use the public Web as an efficient delivery and access medium, but in general are not intended for use beyond the people who have permission to access the pages.

There are other types of pages that have restricted access that may be of interest to searchers, yet they typically aren't included in search engine indices. These pages are part of the Proprietary Web, which we describe next.

The Proprietary Web

Search engines cannot for the most part access pages on the Proprietary Web, because they are only accessible to people who have agreed to special terms in exchange for viewing the content. Proprietary pages may simply be content that's only accessible to users willing to register to view them. Registration in many cases is free, but a search crawler clearly cannot satisfy the requirements of even the simplest registration process.

Examples of free proprietary Web sites include *The New York Times*, Salon's "The Well" community, Infonautics' "Company Sleuth" site, and countless others.

Other types of proprietary content are available only for a fee, whether on a per-page basis or via some sort of subscription mechanism. Examples of proprietary fee-based Web sites include the Electric Library, Northern Light's Special Collection Documents, and *The Wall Street Journal* Interactive Edition.

Proprietary Web services are not the same as traditional online information providers, such as Dialog, LexisNexis, and Dow Jones. These services offer Web access to proprietary information, but use legacy database systems that existed long before the Web came into being. While the content offered by these services is exceptional, they are not considered to be Web or Internet providers.

The Truly Invisible Web

Some Web sites or pages are truly invisible, meaning that there are technical reasons that search engines can't spider or index the material they have to offer. A definition of what constitutes a truly invisible resource must necessarily be somewhat fluid, since the engines are constantly improving and adapting their methods to embrace new types of content. But at the time of writing this book, truly invisible content consisted of several types of resources.

The simplest, and least likely to remain invisible over time, are Web pages that use file formats that current generation Web crawlers aren't programmed to handle. These file formats include PDF, Postscript, Flash, Shockwave, executables (programs), and compressed files. There are two reasons search engines do not currently index these types of files. First, the files have little or no textual context, so it's difficult to categorize them, or compare them for relevance to other text documents. The addition of metadata to the HTML container carrying the file could solve this problem, but it would nonetheless be the metadata description that got indexed rather than the contents of the file itself.

The second reason certain types of files don't appear in search indices is simply because the search engines have chosen to omit them. They can be indexed, but aren't. You can see a great example of this in action with the Research Index engine, which retrieves and indices PDF, postscript, and even compressed files in real time, creating a searchable database that's specific to your query. AltaVista's Search Engine product for creating local site search services is capable of indexing more than 250 file formats, but the flagship public search engine includes only a few of these formats. It's typically lack of willingness, not an ability issue with file formats.

More problematic are dynamically generated Web pages. Again, in some cases, it's not a technical problem but rather unwillingness on the part of the engines to index this type of content. This occurs specifically when a non-interactive script is used to generate a page. These are static pages, and generate static HTML that the engine could spider. The problem is that unscrupulous use of scripts can also lead crawlers into "spider traps" where the spider is literally trapped within a huge site of thousands, if not millions, of pages designed solely to spam the search engine. This is a major problem for the engines, so they've simply opted not to index URLs that contain script commands.

Finally, information stored in relational databases, which cannot be extracted without a specific query to the database, is truly invisible. Crawlers aren't programmed to understand either the database structure or the command language used to extract information.

Now that you know the reasons that some types of content are effectively invisible to search engines, let's move on and see how you can apply this knowledge to actual sites on the Web, and use this understanding to become a better searcher.

CHAPTER 5

Visible or Invisible?

How can you determine whether what you need is found on the visible or Invisible Web? And why is this important?

Learning the difference between visible and Invisible Web resources is important because it will save you time, reduce your frustration, and often provide you with the best possible results for your searching efforts. It's not critical that you immediately learn to determine whether a resource is visible or invisible—as we said in Chapter 4, the boundary between visible and invisible sources isn't always clear, and search services are continuing their efforts to make the invisible visible. Your ultimate goal should be to satisfy your information need in a timely manner using all that the Web has to offer.

The key is to learn the skills that will allow you to determine where you will likely find the best results—before you begin your search. With experience, you'll begin to know ahead of time the types of resources that will likely provide you with best results for a particular type of search.

In this chapter, we'll be focusing exclusively on Invisible Web resources. We'll show you how to identify Invisible Web pages by looking for telltale signs that signal problems for search engines. We'll also show you how to differentiate between Invisible Web resources and specialized search engines and directories using a number of side-by-side comparative case studies.

Navigation vs. Content Sites

Before you even begin to consider whether a site is invisible or not, it's important to determine what kind of site you're viewing. There are two fundamentally different kinds of sites on the Web:

- Sites that provide content

- Sites that facilitate Web navigation and resource discovery

All truly invisible sites are fundamentally providers of content, not portals, directories, or even search engines, though most of the major portal sites offer both content and navigation. Navigation sites may use scripts in the links they create to other sites, which may make them appear invisible at first glance. But if their ultimate purpose is to provide links to visible Web content, they aren't really Invisible Web sites because there's no "there" there. Navigation sites using scripts are simply taking advantage of database technology to facilitate a process of pointing you to other content on the Web, not to store deep wells of content themselves.

On the other hand, true Invisible Web sites are those where the content is stored in a database, and the only way of retrieving it is via a script or database access tool. How the content is made available is key—if the content exists in basic HTML files and is not password protected or restricted by the robots exclusion protocol, it is not invisible content. The content must be *stored* in the database and must only be accessible using the database interface for content to be truly invisible to search engines.

Some sites have both visible and invisible elements, which makes categorizing them all the more challenging. For example, the U.S. Library of Congress maintains one of the largest sites on the Web. Much of its internal navigation relies on sophisticated database query and retrieval tools. Much of its internal content is also contained within databases, making it effectively invisible. Yet the Library of Congress site also features many thousands of basic HTML pages that can be and have been indexed by the engines. Later in this chapter we'll look more closely at the Library of Congress site, pointing out its visible and invisible parts.

Some sites offer duplicate copies of their content, storing pages both in databases and as HTML files. These duplicates are often called "mirror" or "shadow" sites, and may actually serve as alternate content access points that are perfectly visible to search engines. The Education Resource Information Clearinghouse (ERIC) database of educational resource documents on the Web is a good example of a site that does this, with some materials in its database also appearing in online journals, books, or other publications (http://www.accesseric.org).

In cases where visibility or invisibility is ambiguous, there's one key point to remember: where you have a choice between using a general-purpose search engine or query and retrieval tools offered by a particular site you're usually better off using the tools offered by the site. Local site search tools are often finely tuned to the underlying data; they're limited to the underlying data, and won't include "noise" that you'll invariably get in the results from a general search engine.

That said, let's take a closer look at how you tell the difference between visible and Invisible Web sites and pages.

Direct vs. Indirect URLs

The easiest way to determine if a Web page is part of the Invisible Web is to examine its URL. Most URLs are *direct* references to a specific Web page. Clicking a link containing a direct URL causes your browser to explicitly request and retrieve a specific HTML page. A search engine crawler follows exactly the same process, sending a request to a Web server to retrieve a specific HTML page.

Examples of direct URLs:

- http://www.yahoo.com
  (points to Yahoo!'s home page)

- http://www.invisible-web.net/about.htm
  (points to the information page for this book's companion Web site)

- http://www.forbes.com/forbes500/
  (points to the top-level page for the Forbes 500 database. Though this page is visible, the underlying database is an Invisible Web resource)

Indirect URLs, on the other hand, often don't point to a specific physical page on the Web. Instead, they contain information that will be executed by a script on the server—and this script is what generates the page you ultimately end up viewing. Search engine crawlers typically won't follow URLs that appear to have calls to scripts.

The key tip-offs that a page can't or won't be crawled by a search engine are symbols or words that indicate that the page will be dynamically generated by assembling its component parts from a database. The most common symbol used to indicate the presence of dynamic content is the question mark, but be careful: although question marks are used to execute scripts that generate dynamic pages, they are often simply used as "flags" to alert the server that additional information is being passed along using variables that follow the question mark. These variables can be used to track your route through a site, represent items in a shopping cart, and for many other purposes that have nothing to do with Invisible Web content.

Typically, URLs with the words "cgi-bin" or "javascript" included will also execute a script to generate a page, but you can't simply assume that a page is invisible based on this evidence alone. It's important to conduct further investigations.

Examples of indirect URLs:

- http://us.imdb.com/Name?Hitchcock,+Alfred
  (points to the listing for Alfred Hitchcock in the Internet Movie Database)

- http://www.sec.gov/cgi-bin/srch-edgar?cisco+adj+systems
  (points to a page showing results for a search on Cisco Systems in the SEC EDGAR database)

- http://adam.ac.uk/ixbin/hixserv?javascript:go_to('0002', current_level+1)
  (points to a top-level directory in the ADAM Art Resources database)

The URL Test

If a URL appears to be indirect, and looks like it might execute a script, there's a relatively easy test to determine if the URL is likely to be crawled or not. Place the cursor in the address window immediately to the left of the question mark, and erase the question mark and everything to the right of it. Then press your computer's Enter key to force your browser to attempt to fetch this fragment of the URL. Does the page still load as expected? If so, it's a direct URL. The question mark is being used as a flag to pass additional information to the server, not to execute a script. The URL points to a static HTML page that can be crawled by a search engine spider.

If a page other than the one you expected appears, or you see some sort of error message, it likely means that the information after the question mark in the URL is needed by a script in order to dynamically generate the page. Without the information, the server doesn't know what data to fetch from the database to create the page; these types of URLs represent content that is part of the Invisible Web, because the crawler won't read past the question mark. Note carefully: most crawlers *can* read past the question mark and fetch the page, just as your browser can, but they *won't* for fear of spider traps (explained in Chapter 4).

Sometimes it's trickier to determine if a URL points to content that will be generated dynamically. Many browsers save information about a page in variables that are hidden to the user. Clicking "refresh" may simply send the data used to build the page back to the server, recreating the page. Alternately, the page may have been cached on your computer. The best way to test URLs that you suspect are invisible is to start up another instance of your browser, cut and paste the URL into the new browser's address box, and try to load the page. The new instance of the browser won't have the same previously stored information, so you'll likely see a different page or an error message if the page is invisible.

Browsable directories, given their hierarchical layout, may appear at first glance to be part of the visible Web. Test the links in these directories by simply holding your cursor over a link and examining its structure. If the links have question marks indicating that scripts generate the new pages, you have a situation where the top level of the directory, including its links and annotations, may be visible, but the material it links to is invisible. This is a case where the content of the directory itself is invisible, but content that it links to is not. Human Resources Development Canada's Labor Market Information directory is an example of this phenomenon (http://1mi-imt.hrdc-drhc.gc.ca/ owa_1mi/ owa/sp_show_1mi?1=e&i=1).

It's important to do these tests, because to access most material on the Invisible Web you'll need to go directly to the site providing it. Many huge, content-specific sites may at first glance appear to be part of the Invisible Web, when in fact they're nothing more than specialized search sites. Let's look at this issue in more detail.

Specialized vs. Invisible

There are many specialized search directories on the Web that share characteristics of an Invisible Web site, but are perfectly visible to the search engines. These sites often are structured as hierarchical directories, designed as navigation hubs for specific topics or categories of information, and usually offer both sophisticated search tools and the ability to browse a structured directory. But even if these sites consist of hundreds, or even thousands of HTML pages, many aren't part of the Invisible Web, since search engine spiders generally have no problem finding and retrieving the pages. In fact, these sites typically have an extensive internal link structure that makes the spider's job even easier. That said, remember our warning in Chapter 4 about the depth of crawl issue: because a site is easy to index doesn't mean that search engines have spidered it thoroughly or recently.

Many sites that claim to have large collections of invisible or "deep" Web content actually include many specialized search services that are perfectly visible to search spiders. They make the mistake of equating a sophisticated search mechanism with invisibility. Don't get us wrong—we're all in favor of specialized sites that offer powerful search tools and robust interfaces. It's just that many of these specialized sites aren't invisible, and to label them as such is misleading.

For example, we take issue with a highly popularized study performed by Bright Planet claiming that the Invisible Web is currently 400 to 550 times larger than the commonly defined World Wide Web (Bright Planet, 2000). Many of the search resources cited in the study are excellent specialized directories, but they are perfectly visible to search engines. Bright Planet also includes ephemeral data such as weather and astronomy measurements in their estimates that serve no practical purpose for searchers. Excluding specialized search tools and data irrelevant to searchers, we estimate that the Invisible Web is between 2 and 50 times larger than the visible Web.

How can you tell the difference between a specialized vs. Invisible Web resource? Always start by browsing the directory, not searching. Search programs, by their nature, use scripts, and often return results that contain indirect URLs. This does not mean, however, that the site is part of the Invisible Web. It's simply a byproduct of how some search tools function.

As you begin to browse the directory, click on category links and drill down to a destination URL that leads away from the directory itself. As you're clicking, examine the links. Do they appear to be direct or indirect URLs? Do you see the telltale signs of a script being executed? If so, the page is part of the Invisible Web—even if the destination URLs have no question marks. Why? Because crawlers wouldn't have followed the links to the destination URLs in the first place.

But if, as you drill down the directory structure, you notice that all of the links contain direct links, the site is almost certainly part of the visible Web, and can be crawled and indexed by search engines.

This may sound confusing, but it's actually quite straightforward. To illustrate this point, let's look at some examples in several categories. We'll put an Invisible Web site side-by-side with a high-quality specialized directory and compare the differences between them.

Visible vs. Invisible

The Gateway to Educational Materials Project is a directory of collections of high-quality educational resources for teachers, parents, and others involved in education. The Gateway features annotated links to more than 12,000 education resources.

- Structure: Searchable directory, part of the Visible Web. Browsing the categories reveals all links are direct URLs. Although the Gateway's search tool returns indirect URLs, the direct URLs of the directory structure and the resulting offsite links provide clear linkages for search engine spiders to follow.

Table 5.1 The Gateway to Educational Materials vs. AskERIC

Visible	Invisible
The Gateway to Educational Materials http://www.thegateway.org/	AskERIC http://askeric.org/Eric/

AskERIC allows you to search the ERIC database, the world's largest source of education information. ERIC contains more than one million citations and abstracts of documents and journal articles on education research and practice.

- Structure: Database, limited browsing of small subsets of the database available. These limited browsable subsets use direct

URLs; the rest of the ERIC database is only accessible via the AskERIC search interface, making the contents of the database effectively invisible to search engines.

Very important point: Some of the content in the ERIC database also exists in the form of plain HTML files; for example, articles published in the ERIC digest. This illustrates one of the apparent paradoxes of the Invisible Web. Just because a document is located in an Invisible Web database doesn't mean there aren't other copies of the document existing elsewhere on visible Web sites. The key point is that the database containing the original content is the authoritative source, and searching the database will provide the highest probability of retrieving a document. Relying on a general-purpose search engine to find documents that *may* have copies on visible Web sites is unreliable.

Table 5.2 INTA Trademark Checklist vs. Delphion Intellectual Property Network

Visible	Invisible
INTA Trademark Checklist http://www.inta.org/tmcklst.htm	Delphion Intellectual Property Network http://www.delphion.com/

The International Trademark Association (INTA) Trademark Checklist is designed to assist authors, writers, journalists/editors, proofreaders, and fact checkers with proper trademark usage. It includes listings for nearly 3,000 registered trademarks and service marks with their generic terms and indicates capitalization and punctuation.

- Structure: Simple HTML pages, broken into five extensively cross-linked pages of alphabetical listings. The flat structure of the pages combined with the extensive cross-linking make these pages extremely visible to the search engines.

The Delphion Intellectual Property Network allows you to search for, view, and analyze patent documents and many other types of intellectual property records. It provides free access to a wide variety of data collections and patent information including United States patents, European patents and patent applications, PCT application data from the World Intellectual Property Office, Patent Abstracts of Japan, and more.

- Structure: Relational database, browsable, but links are indirect and rely on scripts to access information from the database.

Data contained in the Delphion Intellectual Property Network database is almost completely invisible to Web search engines.

Key point: Patent searching and analysis is a very complex process. The tools provided by the Delphion Intellectual Property Network are finely tuned to help patent researchers home in on only the most relevant information pertaining to their search, excluding all else. Search engines are simply inappropriate tools for searching this kind of information. In addition, new patents are issued weekly or even daily. The Delphion Intellectual Property Network is constantly refreshed. Search engines, with their month or more long gaps between recrawling Web sites, couldn't possibly keep up with this flood of new information.

Table 5.3 Hoover's vs. Thomas Register of American Manufacturers

Visible	Invisible
Hoover's	Thomas Register of America Manufacturers
http://www.hoovers.com/	http://www.thomasregister.com/

Hoover's Online offers in-depth information for businesses about companies, industries, people, and products. It features detailed profiles of hundreds of public and private companies.

- Structure: Browsable directory with powerful search engine. All pages on the site are simple HTML; all links are direct (though the URLs appear complex). Note: some portions of Hoover's are only available to subscribers who pay for premium content.

Thomas Register features profiles of more than 155,000 companies, including American and Canadian companies. The directory also allows searching by brand name, product headings, and even some supplier catalogs. As an added bonus, material on the Thomas Register site is updated constantly, rather than on the fixed update schedules of the printed version.

- Structure: Database access only. Further, access to the search tool is available to registered users only. This combination of database-only access available to registered users puts the Thomas Register squarely in the universe of the Invisible Web.

Table 5.4 WebMD vs. National Health Information Center Health Information Resource Database

Visible	Invisible
WebMD http://my.Webmd.com/	National Health Information Center Health Information Resources Database http://nhic-nt.health.org/

WebMD aggregates health information from many sources, including medical associations, colleges, societies, government agencies, publishers, private and non-profit organizations, and for-profit corporations.

- Structure: MyWebMD site features a browsable table of contents to access its data, using both direct links and javascript relative links to many of the content areas on the site. However, the site also provides a comprehensive site map using direct URLs, allowing search engine spiders to index most of the site.

The National Health Information Center's Health Information Resource Database includes 1,100 organizations and government offices that provide health information upon request. Entries include contact information, short abstracts, and information about publications and services that the organizations provide.

- Structure: You may search the database by keyword, or browse the keyword listing of resources in the database. Each keyword link is an indirect link to a script that searches the database for results. The database is entirely an Invisible Web site.

As these examples show, it's relatively easy to determine whether a resource is part of the Invisible Web or not by taking the time to examine its structure. Some sites, however, can be virtually impossible to classify since they have both visible and invisible elements. Let's look at an example.

The Library of Congress Web Site: Both Visible and Invisible

The U.S. Library of Congress is the largest library in the world, so it's fitting that its site is also one of the largest on the Web. The site provides a treasure trove of resources for the searcher. In fact, it's hard to even call it a single site, since several parts have their own domains or sub-domains.

The library's home page (http://www.loc.gov/) has a simple, elegant design with links to the major sections of the site. Mousing over the links to all of the sections reveals only one link that might be invisible to the America's Library site.

If you follow the link to the American Memory collection, you see a screen that allows you to access more than 80 collections featured on the site. Some of the links, such as those to "Today in History" and the "Learning Page," are direct URLs that branch to simple HTML pages. However, if you select the "Collection Finder" you're presented with a directory-type menu for all of the topics in the collection. Each one of the links on this page is not only an indirect link but contains a large amount of information used to create new dynamic pages. However,

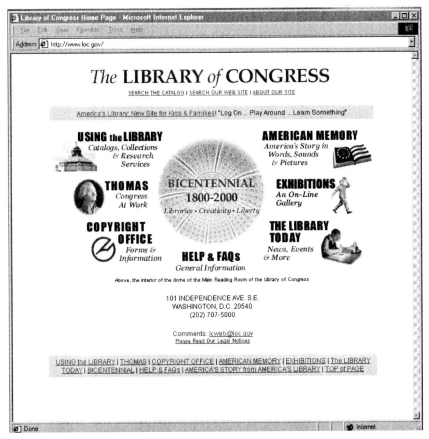

Figure 5.1 The Library of Congress Home Page

once those pages are created, they include mostly direct links to simple HTML pages.

The point of this exercise is to demonstrate that even though the ultimate content available at the American Memory collection consists of content that is crawlable, following the links from the home page leads to a "barrier" in the form of indirect URLs on the Collection Finder directory page. Because they generally don't crawl indirect URLs, most crawlers would simply stop spidering once they encounter those links, even though they lead to perfectly acceptable content.

Though this makes much of the material in the American Memory collection technically invisible, it's also probable that someone *outside* of the Library of Congress has found the content and linked to it, allowing crawlers to access the material despite the apparent roadblocks. In other words, any Web author who likes content deep within the American

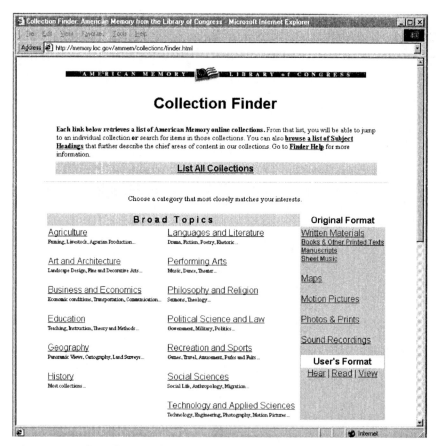

Figure 5.2 The Library of Congress Collection Finder

Memory collection is free to link to it—and if crawlers find those links on the linking author's page, the material may ultimately be crawled, even if the crawler couldn't access it through the "front door." Unfortunately, there's no quick way to confirm that content deep within a major site like the Library of Congress has been crawled in this manner, so the searcher should utilize the Library's own internal search and directory services to be assured of getting the best possible results.

The Robots Exclusion Protocol

Many people assume that all Webmasters want their sites indexed by search engines. This is not the case. Many sites that feature timely content that changes frequently *do not* want search engines to index their pages. If a page changes daily and a crawler only visits the page monthly, the result is essentially a permanently inaccurate page in a search index. Some sites make content available for free for only a short period before moving it into archives that are available to paying customers only—the online versions of many newspaper and media sites are good examples of this.

To block search engine crawlers, Webmasters employ the Robots Exclusion Protocol that we described in Chapter 5. This is simply a set of rules that enable a Webmaster to tell a crawler which parts of a server are off-limits. The Webmaster simply creates a list of files or directories that should not be crawled or indexed, and saves this list in a file called robots.txt. CNN, Canadian Broadcasting Corporation, the *London Times*, and the *Los Angeles Times* all use robots.txt to exclude some or all of their content using the robots.txt file.

Here's an example of the robots.txt file used by the *Los Angeles Times*:

User-agent: *
Disallow: /RealMedia
Disallow: /archives
Disallow: /wires/
Disallow: /HOME/
Disallow: /cgi-bin/
Disallow: /class/realestate/dataquick/dqsearch.cgi
Disallow: /search

The User-agent field specifies which spiders must pay attention to the following instructions. The asterisk (*) is a wildcard, meaning *all* crawlers must read and respect the contents of the file. Each "Disallow" command is followed by the name of a specific directory on the *Los Angeles Times* Web server that spiders are prohibited from accessing and crawling. In this case, the spider is blocked from reading streaming media files, archive files, real estate listings, and so on.

It's also possible to prevent a crawler from indexing a specific page by including a "noindex" meta tag instruction in the "head" portion of the document. Here's an example:

```
<html>
<head>
<title>Keep Out, Search Engines!</title>
<META name="robots" content="noindex, nofollow">
</head>
```

Either the robots.txt file or the noindex meta tag can be used to block crawlers. The only difference between the two is that the noindex meta tag is page specific, while the robots.txt file can be used to prevent indexing of individual pages, groups of files—even entire Web sites.

As you can see, it's important to look closely at a site and its structure to determine whether it's visible or invisible.

One of the wonderful things many Invisible Web resources can do is help you focus your search and allow you to manipulate a "subject oriented" database in ways that would not be possible with a general-purpose search tool. Many resources allow you to organize your results via various criteria or are much more up-to-date than a general search tool or print versions of the same material. For example, lists published by *Forbes* and *Fortune* provide the searcher with all kinds of ways to sort, limit, or filter data that is simply impossible with the print-based versions. Also, you could have a much smaller haystack of "focused" data to search through to find the necessary "needles" of information. In Chapter 6, we'll show you some specific cases where resources on the Invisible Web provide a superior—if not the only—means of locating important and dependable information online.

Chapter 6

Using the Invisible Web

How do you decide when the Invisible Web is likely to be your best source for the information you're seeking? After all, Invisible Web resources aren't always the solution for satisfying an information need. Although we've made a strong case for the value of the resources available on the Invisible Web, we're not suggesting that you abandon the general-purpose search engines like AltaVista, HotBot, and Google. Far from it! Rather, we're advocating that you gain an understanding of what's available on the Invisible Web to make your Web searching time more efficient. By expanding the array of tools available to you, you'll learn to select the best available tool for every particular searching task.

In this chapter, we'll examine the broad issue of *why* you might choose to use Invisible Web resources instead of a general-purpose search engine or Web directory. Then we'll narrow our focus and look at specific instances of *when* to use the Invisible Web. To illustrate these specifics, we've compiled a list of 25 categories of information where you'll likely get the best results from Invisible Web resources. Then we'll look at what's *not* available on the Web, visible or Invisible.

It's easy to get seduced by the ready availability and seeming credibility of online information. But just as you would with print materials, you need to evaluate and assess the quality of the information you find on the Invisible Web. Even more importantly, you need to watch out for bogus or biased information that's put online by charlatans more interested in pushing their own point of view than publishing accurate information.

The Invisible Web, by its very nature, is highly dynamic. What is true on Monday might not be accurate on Thursday. Keeping current with the Invisible Web and its resources is one of the biggest challenges faced by the searcher. We'll show you some of the best sources for keeping up with the rapidly changing dynamics of the Invisible Web.

Finally, as you begin your own exploration of the Invisible Web, you should begin to assemble your own toolkit of trusted resources. As your personal collection of Invisible Web resources grows, your confidence in choosing the appropriate tool for every search task will grow in equal proportions.

Why Use the Invisible Web?

General-purpose search engines and directories are easy to use, and respond rapidly to information queries. Because they are so accessible and seemingly all-powerful, it's tempting to simply fire up your favorite Web search engine, punch in a few keywords that are relevant to your search, and hope for the best. But the general-purpose search engines are essentially mass audience resources, designed to provide something for everyone. Invisible Web resources tend to be more focused, and often provide better results for many information needs. Consider how a publication like *Newsweek* would cover a story on Boeing compared to an aviation industry trade magazine such as *Aviation Week and Space Technology*. Or a how a general newsmagazine like *Time* would cover a story on currency trades vs. a business magazine like *Forbes* or *Fortune*.

In making the decision whether to use an Invisible Web resource, it helps to consider the point of view of both the searcher and the provider of a search resource. The goal for any searcher is relatively simple: to satisfy an information need in a timely manner. Of course, providers of search resources also strive to satisfy the information needs of their users, but they face other issues that complicate the equation. For example, there are always conflicts between speed and accuracy. Searchers demand fast results, but if a search engine has a large, comprehensive index, returning results quickly may not allow for a thorough search of the database.

For general-purpose search engines, there's a constant tension between finding the correct answer vs. finding the best answer vs. finding the easiest answer. Because they try to satisfy virtually any information need, general-purpose search engines resolve these conflicts by making compromises. It costs a significant amount of money to crawl the Web, index pages, and handle search queries. The bottom line is that general-purpose search engines are in business to make a profit, a goal that often works against the mission to provide comprehensive results for searchers with a wide variety of information needs.

On the other hand, governments, academic institutions, and other organizations that aren't constrained by a profit-making motive operate many Invisible Web resources. They don't feel the same pressures to be everything to everybody. And they can often afford to build comprehensive search resources that allow searchers to perform exhaustive research within a specific subject area, and keep up-to-date and current.

Why select an Invisible Web resource over a general-purpose search engine or Web directory? Here are several good reasons:

Specialized content focus = more comprehensive results. Like the focused crawlers and directories we discussed in Chapter 3, Invisible Web resources tend to be focused on specific subject areas. This is particularly true of the many databases made available by government agencies and academic institutions. Your search results from these resources will be more comprehensive than those from most visible Web resources for two reasons. First, there are generally no limits imposed by databases on how quickly a search must be completed—or if there are, you can generally select your own time limit that will be reached before a search is cut off. This means that you have a much better chance of having all relevant results returned, rather than just those results that were found fastest.

Second, people who go to the trouble of creating a database-driven information resource generally try to make the resource as comprehensive as possible, including as many relevant documents as they are able to find. This is in stark contrast to general-purpose search engine crawlers, which often arbitrarily limit the depth of crawl for a particular Web site. With a database, there is no depth of crawl issue—all documents in the database will be searched by default.

Specialized search interface = more control over search input and output. Here's a question to get you thinking. Let's assume that everything on the Web could be located and accessed via a general search tool like Google or HotBot. How easy and efficient would it be to use one of these general-purpose engines when a specialized tool was available? Would you begin a search for a person's phone number with a search of an encyclopaedia? Of course not. Likewise, even if the general-purpose search engines suddenly provided the capability to find specialized information, they still couldn't compete with search services specifically designed to find and easily retrieve specialized information. Put differently, searching with a general-purpose search engine is like using a shotgun, whereas searching with an Invisible Web resource is more akin to a taking a highly precise rifle-shot approach.

As an added bonus, most databases provide customized search fields that are subject-specific. History databases will allow limiting searches to particular eras, for example, and biology databases by species or genomic parameters. Invisible Web databases also often provide extensive control over how results are formatted. Would you like documents to be sorted by relevance, by date, by author, or by some other criteria of your own choosing? Contrast this flexibility with the general-purpose search engines, where what you see is what you get.

Increased precision *and* recall. Consider two informal measures of search engine performance—recall and precision. Recall represents the total number of relevant documents retrieved in response to a search query, divided by the total number of relevant documents in the search engine's entire index. One hundred percent recall means that the search engine was able to retrieve every document in its index that was relevant to the search terms. Measuring recall alone isn't sufficient, however, since the engine could always achieve 100 percent recall simply by returning every document in its index.

Recall is balanced by precision. Precision is the number of relevant documents retrieved divided by the total number of documents retrieved. If 100 pages are found, and only 20 are relevant, the precision is (100/20), or 20 percent. Relevance, unfortunately, is strictly a subjective measure. The searcher ultimately determines relevance after fully examining a document and deciding whether it meets the information need.

To maximize potential relevance, search engines strive to maximize recall and precision simultaneously. In practice, this is difficult to achieve. As the size of a search engine index increases, there are likely to be more relevant documents for any given query, leading to a higher recall percentage. As recall increases, precision tends to decrease, making it harder for the searcher to locate relevant documents.

Because they are often limited to specific topics or subjects, many Invisible Web and specialized search services offer greater precision even while increasing total recall. Narrowing the domain of information means there is less extraneous or irrelevant information for the search engine to process. Because Invisible Web resources tend to have smaller databases, recall can be high while still offering a great deal of precision, leading to the best of all possible worlds: higher relevance and greater value to the searcher.

Invisible Web resources = highest level of authority. Institutions or organizations that have a legitimate claim on being an unquestioned authority on a particular subject maintain many Invisible Web resources. Unlike with many sites on the visible Web, it's relatively easy to determine the authority of most Invisible Web sites. Most offer detailed information about the credentials of the people responsible for maintaining the resource. Others feature awards, citations, or other symbols of recognition from other acknowledged subject authorities. Many Invisible Web resources are produced by book or journal publishers with sterling reputations among libraries and scholars.

The answer may not be available elsewhere. The explosive growth of the Web, combined with the relative ease of finding many things online, has led to the widely held but wildly inaccurate belief that "if it's not on the Web, it's not online." There are a number of reasons this belief simply isn't true. For one thing, there are vast amounts of information available exclusively via Invisible Web resources. Much of this information is in databases, which can't be directly accessed by search engines, but it is definitely online and often freely available.

When to Use the Invisible Web

It's not always easy to know when to use an Invisible Web resource as opposed to a general search tool. As you become more familiar with the landscape of the Invisible Web, there are several rules of thumb you can use when deciding to use an Invisible Web resource.

When you're familiar with a subject. If you know a particular subject well, you've likely already discovered one or more Invisible Web resources that offer the kind of information you need. Familiarity with a subject also offers another advantage: knowledge of which search terms will find the "best" results in a particular search resource, as well as methods for locating new resources.

When you're familiar with specific search tools. Some Invisible Web resources cover multiple subjects, but since they often offer sophisticated interfaces you'll still likely get better results from them compared to general-purpose search tools. Restricting your search through the use of limiters, Boolean logic, or other advanced search functions generally makes it easier to pull a needle from a haystack.

When you're looking for a precise answer. When you're looking for a simple answer to a question, the last thing you want is a list of hundreds of possible results. No matter—an abundance of potential answers is what you'll end up with if you use a general-purpose search engine, and you'll have to spend the time scanning the result list to find what you need. Many Invisible Web resources are designed to perform what are essentially lookup functions, when you need a particular fact, phone number, name, bibliographic record, and so on.

When you want authoritative, exhaustive results. General-purpose search engines will never be able to return the kind of authoritative, comprehensive results that Invisible Web resources can. Depth of crawl, timeliness, and the lack of selective filtering fill any result list from a general-purpose engine with a certain amount of noise. And, because the haystack of the Web is so huge, a certain number of authoritative documents will inevitably be overlooked.

When timeliness of content is an issue. Invisible Web resources are often more up-to-date than general-purpose search engines and directories.

Top 25 Invisible Web Categories

To give you a sense of what's available on the Invisible Web, we've put together a list of categories where, in general, you'll be far better off searching an Invisible Web resource than a general-purpose search engine. Our purpose here is to simply provide a quick overview of each category, noting one or two good Invisible Web resources for each. Detailed descriptions of and annotated links to many more resources for all of these categories can be found in Part II of this book, as well as in the online directory available at http://www.invisible-web.net.

1. **Public Company Filings.** The U.S. Securities and Exchange Commission (SEC) and regulators of equity markets in many other countries require publicly traded companies to file certain documents on a regular schedule or whenever an event may have a material effect on the company. These documents are available in a number of locations, including company Web sites. While many of these filings may be visible and findable by a general-purpose search engine, a number of Invisible Web

services have built comprehensive databases incorporating this information. FreeEDGAR (http://www.freeedgar.com), 10K Wizard (http://www.10kwizard.com), and SEDAR (http://www.sedar. com) are examples of services that offer sophisticated searching and limiting tools as well as the assurance that the database is truly comprehensive. Some also offer free e-mail alert services to notify you that the companies you choose to monitor have just filed reports.

2. **Telephone Numbers.** Just as telephone white pages serve as the quickest and most authoritative offline resource for locating telephone numbers, a number of Invisible Web services exist solely to find telephone numbers. InfoSpace (http://www. infospace.com), Switchboard.com (http://www.switchboard. com), and AnyWho (http://www.anywho.com) offer additional capabilities like reverse-number lookup or correlating a phone number with an e-mail address. Because these databases vary in currency it is often important to search more than one to obtain the most current information.

3. **Customized Maps and Driving Directions**. While some search engines, like Northern Light, have a certain amount of geographical "awareness" built in, none can actually generate a map of a particular street address and its surrounding neighborhood. Nor do they have the capability to take a starting and ending address and generate detailed driving directions, including exact distances between landmarks and estimated driving time. Invisible Web resources such as Mapblast (http://www.mapblast.com) and Mapquest (http://www.map quest.com) are designed specifically to provide these interactive services.

4. **Clinical Trials**. Clinical trials by their very nature generate reams of data, most of which is stored from the outset in databases. For the researcher, sites like the New Medicines in Development (http://phrma.org/searchcures/newmeds/ webdb) database are essential. For patients searching for clinical trials to participate in, ClinicalTrials.gov (http://www.clinicaltrials.gov) and CenterWatch's

(http://www.centerwatch.com) Clinical Trials Listing Service are invaluable.

5. **Patents**. Thoroughness and accuracy are absolutely critical to the patent searcher. Major business decisions involving significant expense or potential litigation often hinge on the details of a patent search, so using a general-purpose search engine for this type of search is effectively out of the question. Many government patent offices maintain Web sites, but Delphion's Intellectual Property Network (http://www.delphion.com/) allows full-text searching of U.S. and European patents and abstracts of Japanese patents simultaneously. Additionally, the United States Patent Office (http://www.uspto.gov) provides patent information dating back to 1790, as well as U.S. Trademark data.

6. **Out of Print Books**. The growth of the Web has proved to be a boon for bibliophiles. Countless out of print booksellers have established Web sites, obliterating the geographical constraints that formerly limited their business to local customers. Simply having a Web presence, however, isn't enough. Problems with depth of crawl issues, combined with a continually changing inventory, make catalog pages from used booksellers obsolete or inaccurate even if they do appear in the result list of a general-purpose search engine. Fortunately, sites like Alibris (http://www.alibris.com) and Bibliofind (http://www.bibliofind.com) allow targeted searching over hundreds of specialty and used bookseller sites.

7. **Library Catalogs**. There are thousands of Online Public Access Catalogs (OPACs) available on the Web, from national libraries like the U.S. Library of Congress and the Bibliothèque Nationale de France, academic libraries, local public libraries, and many other important archives and repositories. OPACs allow searches for books in a library by author, title, subject, keywords, or call number, often providing other advanced search capabilities. webCATS, Library Catalogs on the World Wide Web (http://www.libdex.com/webcats/) is an excellent

directory of OPACs around the world. OPACS are great tools to verify the title or author of a book.

8. **Authoritative Dictionaries**. Need a word definition? Go directly to an authoritative online dictionary. Merriam-Webster's Collegiate (http://www.m-w.com) and the Cambridge International Dictionary of English (http://dictionary.cambridge.org/) are good general dictionaries. Scores of specialized dictionaries also provide definitions of terms from fields ranging from aerospace to zoology. Some Invisible Web dictionary resources even provide metasearch capability, checking for definitions in hundreds of online dictionaries simultaneously. OneLook (http://www.onelook.com) is a good example.

9. **Environmental Information**. Need to know who's a major polluter in your neighborhood? Want details on a specific country's position in the Kyoto Treaty? Try the Envirofacts multiple database search (http://www.epa.gov/enviro/index_java.html).

10. **Historical Stock Quotes**. Many people consider stock quotes to be ephemeral data, useful only for making decisions at a specific point in time. Stock market historians and technical analysts, however, can use historical data to compile charts of trends that some even claim to have a certain amount of predictive value. There are numerous resources available that contain this information. One of our favorites is from BigCharts.com (http://www.bigcharts.com/historical/).

11. **Historical Documents and Images**. You've seen that general-purpose search engines don't handle images well. This can be a problem with historical documents, too, as many historical documents exist on the Web only as scanned images of the original. The U.S. Library of Congress American Memory Project (http://memory.loc.gov) is a wonderful example of a continually expanding digital collection of historical documents and images. The American Memory Project also illustrates that some data in a collection may be "visible" while other portions are "invisible."

12. **Company Directories**. Competitive intelligence has never been easier thanks to the Web. We wrote about Hoover's and the Thomas Register in Chapter 5. There are numerous country or region specific company directories, including the Financial Times' European Companies Premium Research (http://www.globalarchive.ft.com/cb/cb_search.html) and Wright Investors' Services (http://profiles.wisi.com/profiles/comsrch.htm).

13. **Searchable Subject Bibliographies**. Bibliographies are gold mines for scholars and other researchers. Because bibliographies generally conform to rigid formats specified by the MLA or the AP, most are stored in searchable online databases, covering subjects ranging from Architecture to Zoology. The Canadian Music Periodical Index (http://www.nlc-bnc.ca/wapp/cmpi/) provided by the National Library of Canada is a good example as it contains over 25,000 citations.

14. **Economic Information**. Governments and government agencies employ entire armies of statisticians to monitor the pulse of economic conditions. This data is often available online, but rarely in a form visible to most search engines. RECON-Regional Economic Conditions (http://www2.fdic.gov/recon/) is an interactive database from the Federal Deposit Insurance Corporation that illustrates this point.

15. **Award Winners**. Who won the Nobel Peace Prize in 1938? You might be able to learn that it was Viscount Cecil of Chelwood (Lord Edgar Algernon Robert Gascoyne Cecil) via a general-purpose search engine, but the Nobel e-museum (http://www.nobel.se/) site will provide the definitive answer. Other Invisible Web databases have definitive information on major winners of awards ranging from Oscar (http://www.oscars.org/awards_db/) to the Peabody Awards (http://www.peabody.uga.edu/recipients/search.html).

16. **Job Postings**. Looking for work? Or trying to find the best employee for a job opening in your company? Good luck finding what you're looking for using a general-purpose

search engine. You'll be far better off searching one of the many job-posting databases, such as CareerBuilder.Com (http://www.careerbuilder.com), the contents of which are part of the Invisible Web. Better yet, try one of our favorites—the oddly named Flipdog (http://www.flipdog.com). Flipdog is unique in that it scours both company Web sites and other job posting databases to compile what may be the most extensive collection of job postings and employment offers available on the Web.

17. **Philanthropy and Grant Information**. Show me the money! If you're looking to give or get funding, there are literally thousands of clearinghouses on the Invisible Web that exist to match those in need with those willing and able to give. The Foundation Finder (http://lnp.fdncenter .org/finder.html) from the Foundation Center is an excellent place to begin your search.

18. **Translation Tools**. Web-based translation services are not search tools in their own right, but they provide a valuable service when a search has turned up documents in a language you don't understand. Translation tools accept a URL, fetch the underlying page, translate it into the desired language and deliver it as a dynamic document. AltaVista (http://world.altavista.com/) provides such a service. Please note the many limitations and frequent translation issues that often arise. These tools, while far from perfect, will continue to improve with time. Another example of an Invisible Web translation tool is EuroDicAutom (http://eurodic.ip.lu/cgi-bin/edicbin/EuroDicWWW.pl), described as "the multilingual terminological database of the European Commission's Translation Service."

19. **Postal Codes**. Even though e-mail is rapidly overtaking snail mail as the world's preferred method of communication, we all continue to rely on the postal service from time to time. Many postal authorities such as the Royal Mail in the United Kingdom (http://www.royalmail.com/quick_tools/postcodes/default.htm) provide postal code look-up tools.

20. **Basic Demographic Information**. Demographic information from the U.S. Census and other sources can be a boon to marketers or anyone needing details about specific communities. One of many excellent starting points is the American FactFinder (http://factfinder.census.gov/). The utility that this site provides seems to almost never end!

21. **Interactive School Finders**. Before the Web, finding the right university or graduate school often meant a trek to the library and hours scanning course catalogs. Now it's easy to locate a school that meets specific criteria for academic programs, location, tuition costs, and many other variables. Peterson's GradChannel (http://iiswinprd01.petersons.com/Grad Channel/) is an excellent example of this type of search resource for students, offered by a respected provider of school selection data.

22. **Campaign Financing Information**. Who's really buying—or stealing—the election? Now you can find out by accessing the actual forms filed by anyone contributing to a major campaign. The Federal Elections Commission provides several databases (http://www.fec.gov/finance_reports.html) while a private concern called Fecinfo.Com (http://www.fecinfo.com) "massages" government-provided data for greater utility. Fecinfo.com has a great deal of free material available in addition to several fee-based resources. Many states are also making this type of data available.

23. **Weather Data**. If you don't trust your local weatherman, try an Invisible Web resource like AccuWeather (http://www.accuweather.com). This extensive resource offers more than 43,000 U.S. 5-day forecasts, international forecasts, local NEXRAD Doppler radar images, customizable personal pages, and fee-based premium services. Weather information clearly illustrates the vast amount of real-time data available on the Internet that the general search tools do not crawl. Another favorite is Automated Weather Source, found at (http://aws.com/globalwx.html). This site allows you to view local

weather conditions in real-time via instruments placed at various sites (often located at schools) around the country.

24. **Product Catalogs**. It can be tricky to determine whether pages from many product catalogs are visible or invisible. One of the Web's largest retailers, Amazon.com (http://www.amazon.com), is largely a visible Web site. Some general-purpose search engines include product pages from Amazon.com's catalogs in their databases, but even though this information is visible, it may not be relevant for most searches. Therefore, many engines either demote the relevance ranking of product pages or ignore them, effectively rendering them invisible. However, in some cases general search tools have arrangements with major retailers like Amazon to provide a "canned" link for search terms that attempt to match products in a retailer's database.

25. **Art Gallery Holdings**. From major national exhibitions to small co-ops run by artists, countless galleries are digitizing their holdings and putting them online. An excellent way to find these collections is to use ADAM, the Art, Design, Architecture & Media Information Gateway (http://adam.ac.uk/). ADAM is a searchable catalogue of more than 2,500 Internet resources whose entries are all invisible. Specifically, the Van Gogh Museum in Amsterdam (http://www.vangoghmuseum.nl/collection/catalog/alphaMart.asp?LANGID=0&SEL=1) provides a digital version of the museums, collection that is invisible to general search tools.

What's NOT on the Web—Visible or Invisible

There's an entire class of information that's simply not available on the Web, including the following:

Proprietary databases and information services. These include Thomson's Dialog service, LexisNexis, and Dow Jones, which restrict access to their information systems to paid subscribers.

Many government and public records. Although the U.S. government is the most prolific publisher of content both on the Web and in print, there are still major gaps in online coverage. Some proprietary services such as KnowX (http://www.knowx.com) offer limited access to public records for a fee. Coverage of government and public records is similarly spotty in other countries around the world. While there is a definite trend toward moving government information and public records online, the sheer mass of information will prohibit all of it from going online. There are also privacy concerns that may prevent certain types of public records from going digital in a form that might compromise an individual's rights.

Scholarly journals or other "expensive" information. Thanks in part to the "publish or perish" imperative at modern universities, publishers of scholarly journals or other information that's viewed as invaluable for certain professions have succeeded in creating a virtual "lock" on the market for their information products. It's a very profitable business for these publishers, and they wield an enormous amount of control over what information is published and how it's distributed. Despite ongoing, increasingly acrimonious struggles with information users, especially libraries, who often have insufficient funding to acquire all of the resources they need, publishers of premium content see little need to change the status quo. As such, it's highly unlikely that this type of content will be widely available on the Web any time soon.

There are some exceptions. Northern Light's Special Collection, for example, makes available a wide array of reasonably priced content that previously was only available via expensive subscriptions or site licenses from proprietary information services. ResearchIndex, mentioned in Chapter 4, can retrieve copies of scholarly papers posted on researchers' personal Web sites, bypassing the "official" versions appearing in scholarly journals. But this type of semi-subversive "Napster-like" service may come under attack in the future, so it's too early to tell whether it will provide a viable alternative to the official publications or not. For the near future, public libraries are one of the best sources for this information, made available to community patrons and paid for by tax dollars.

Full Text of all newspapers and magazines. Very few newspapers or magazines offer full-text archives. For those publications that do, the content only goes back a limited time—10 or 20 years at the most. There are several reasons for this. Publishers are very aware that the content they have published quite often retains value over time. Few economic models have emerged that allow publishers to unlock that value as yet. Authors' rights are another concern. Many authors retained most re-use rights to the materials printed in magazines and newspapers. For content published more than two decades ago, reprints in digital format were not envisioned or legally accounted for. It will take time for publishers and authors to forge new agreements and for consumers of Web content to become comfortable with the notion that not everything on the Web is free. New micropayment systems, or "all you can eat" subscription services will emerge that should remove some of the current barriers keeping magazine and newspaper content off the Web. Some newspapers are placing archives of their content on the Web. Often the search function is free but retrieval of full text is fee based—for example, the services offered by Newslibrary, at http://www.newslibrary.com.

And finally, perhaps the reason users cannot find what they are looking for on either the visible or Invisible Web is simply because it's just not there. While much of the world's print information has migrated to the Web, there are and always will be millions of documents that will never be placed online. The only way to locate these printed materials will be via traditional methods: using libraries or asking for help from people who have physical access to the information.

Spider Traps, Damned Lies, and Other Chicanery

Though there are many technical reasons the major search engines don't index the Invisible Web, there are also "social" reasons having to do with the validity, authority, and quality of online information. Because the Web is open to everybody and anybody, a good deal of its content is published by non-experts or—even worse—by people with a strong bias that they seek to conceal from readers. Search engines must also cope with unethical Web page authors who seek to subvert their indexes with millions of bogus "spam" pages. Most of the major engines have developed strict guidelines for dealing with spam that sometimes has the unfortunate effect of excluding legitimate content.

No matter whether you're searching the visible or Invisible Web, it's important always to maintain a critical view of the information you're accessing. For some reason, people often lower their guard when it comes to information on the Internet. People who would scoff if asked to participate in an offline chain-mail scheme cast common sense to the wind and willingly forward hoax e-mails to their entire address books. Urban legends and all manner of preposterous stories abound on the Web.

Here are some important questions to ask and techniques to use for assessing the validity and quality of online information, regardless of its source.

Who Maintains the Content? The first question to ask of any Web site is who's responsible for creating and updating it. Just as you would with any offline source of information, you want to be sure that the author and publishers are credible and the information they are providing can be trusted.

Corporate Web sites should provide plenty of information about the company, its products and services. But corporate sites will always seek to portray the company in the best possible light, so you'll need to use other information sources to balance favorable bias. If you're unfamiliar with a company, try searching for information about it using Hoover's. For many companies, AltaVista provides a link to a page with additional "facts about" the company, including a capsule overview, news, details of Web domains owned, and financial information.

Information maintained by government Web sites or academic institutions is inherently more trustworthy than other types of Web content, but it's still important to look at things like the authority of the institution or author. This is especially true in the case of academic institutions, which often make server space available to students who may publish anything they like without worrying about its validity.

If you're reading a page created by an individual, who is the author? Do they provide credentials or some other kind of proof that they write with authority? Is contact information provided, or is the author hiding behind the veil of anonymity? If you can't identify the author or maintainer of the content, it's probably not a good idea to trust the resource, even if it appears to be of high quality in all other respects.

What Is the Content Provider's Authority? Authority is a measure of reputation. When you're looking at a Web site, is the author or producer of the content a familiar name? If not, what does the site provide to assert authority?

For an individual author, look for a biography of the author citing previous work or awards, a link to a resume or other vita that demonstrates experience, or similar relevant facts that prove the author has authority. Sites maintained by companies should provide a corporate profile, and some information about the editorial standards used to select or commission work.

Some search engines provide an easy way to check on the authority of an author or company. Google, for example, tries to identify authorities by examining the link structure of the entire Web to gauge how often a page is cited in the form of a link by other Web page authors. It also checks to see if there are links to these pages from "important" sites of the Web that have authority. Results in Google for a particular query provide an informal gauge of authority. Beware, though, that this is only informal—even a page created by a Nobel laureate may not rank highly on Google if other important pages on the Web don't link to it.

Is There Bias? Bias can be subtle, and can be easily camouflaged in sites that deal with seemingly non-controversial subjects. Bias is easy to spot when it takes the form of a one-sided argument. It's harder to recognize when it dons a Janusian mask of two-sided "argument" where one side consistently (and seemingly reasonably) always prevails. Bias is particularly insidious on so-called "news" sites that exist mainly to promote specific issues or agendas. The key to avoiding bias is to look for balanced writing.

Another form of bias on the Web appears when a page appears to be objective, but is sponsored by a group or organization with a hidden agenda that may not be apparent on the site. It's particularly important to look for this kind of thing in health or consumer product information sites. Some large companies fund information resources for specific health conditions, or advocate a particular lifestyle that incorporates a particular product. While the companies may not exert direct editorial influence over the content, content creators nonetheless can't help but be aware of their patronage, and may not be as objective as they might be. On the opposite side of the coin, the Web is a powerful medium for activist groups with an agenda against a particular company or industry. Many of these groups have set up what appear to be objective Web sites presenting seemingly balanced information when in fact they are extremely one-sided and biased.

There's no need to be paranoid about bias. In fact, recognizing bias can be very useful in helping understand an issue in depth from a particular point of view. The key is to acknowledge the bias and take steps to filter, balance, and otherwise gain perspective on what is likely to be a complex issue.

Examine the URL. URLs can contain a lot of useful clues about the validity and authority of a site. Does the URL seem "appropriate" for the content? Most companies, for example, use their name or a close approximation in their primary URL. A page stored on a free service like Yahoo's GeoCities or Lycos-Terra's Tripod is not likely to be an official company Web site. URLs can also reveal bias.

Deceptive page authors can also feed search engine spiders bogus content using cloaking techniques, but once you've actually retrieved a page in your browser, its URLs cannot be spoofed. If a URL appears to contain suspicious or irrelevant words to the topic it represents, it's likely a spurious source of information.

Examine Outbound Links. The hyperlinks included in a document can also provide clues about the integrity of the information on the page. Hyperlinks were originally created to help authors cite references, and can provide a sort of online "footnote" capability. Does a page link to other credible sources of information? Or are most of the links to other internal content on a Web site?

Well-balanced sites have a good mix of internal and external links. For complex or controversial issues, external links are particularly important. If they point to other authorities on a subject, they allow you to easily access alternative points of view from other authors. If they point to less credible authors, or ones that share the same point of view as the author, you can be reasonably certain you've uncovered bias, whether subtle or blatant.

Is the Information Current? Currency of information is not always important, but for timely news, events, or for subject areas where new research is constantly expanding a field of knowledge, currency is very important.

Look for dates on a page. Be careful—automatic date scripts can be included on a page so that it appears current when in fact it may be quite dated. Many authors include "dateline" or "updated" fields somewhere on the page.

It's also important to distinguish between the date in search results and the date a document was actually published. Some search engines include a date next to each result. These dates often have nothing to do with the document itself—rather, they are the date the search engine's crawler last spidered the page. While this can give you a good idea of the freshness of a search engine's database, it can be misleading to assume that the document's creation date is the same. Always check the document itself if the date is an important part of your evaluation criteria.

Use Common Sense. Apply the same filters to the Web as you do to other sources of information in your life. Ask yourself: "How would I respond to this if I were reading it in a newspaper, or in a piece of junk mail?" Just because something is on the Web doesn't mean you should believe it—quite the contrary, in many cases.

For excellent information about evaluating the quality of Web resources, we recommend Genie Tyburski's excellent *Evaluating The Quality Of Information On The Internet* at http://www.virtualchase.com/quality/index.html.

Keeping Current with the Invisible Web

Just as with the visible Web, new Invisible Web resources are being made available all the time. How do you keep up with potentially useful new additions? One way is to subscribe to the "Invisible Web Newsletter" published by the authors. Visit the companion site to this book for subscription details.

There are also several useful, high-quality current awareness services that publish newsletters that cover Invisible Web resources. These newsletters don't limit themselves to the Invisible Web, but the news and information they provide is exceptionally useful for all serious Web searchers. All of these newsletters are free.

The Scout Report
http://scout.cs.wisc.edu/scout/report/current/
The Scout Report provides the closest thing to an "official" seal of approval for quality Web sites. Published weekly, it provides organized summaries of the most valuable and authoritative Web resources available. The Scout Report Signpost provides the full-text search of nearly 6,000 of these summaries. The Scout Report staff is made up of a group

of librarians and information professionals, and their standards for inclusion in the report are quite high.

Librarians' Index to the Internet (LII)

http://www.lii.org

This searchable, annotated directory of Web resources, maintained by Carole Leita and a volunteer team of more than 70 reference librarians, is organized into categories including "best of," "directories," "databases," and "specific resources." Most of the Invisible Web content reviewed by LII falls in the "databases" and "specific resources" categories. Each entry also includes linked cross-references, making it a browser's delight.

Leita also publishes a weekly newsletter that includes 15-20 of the resources added to the Web site during the previous week.

ResearchBuzz

http://www.researchbuzz.com

ResearchBuzz is designed to cover the world of Internet research. To that end this site provides almost daily updates on search engines, new data-managing software, browser technology, large compendiums of information, Web directories, and Invisible Web databases. If in doubt, the final question is, "Would a reference librarian find it useful?" If the answer's yes, in it goes.

ResearchBuzz's creator, Tara Calishain, is author of numerous Internet research books, including *Official Netscape Guide to Internet Research*. Unlike most of the other current awareness services described here, Calishain often writes in-depth reviews and analyses of new resources, pointing out both useful features and flaws in design or implementation.

Free Pint

http://www.freepint.co.uk/

Free Pint is an e-mail newsletter dedicated to helping you find reliable Web sites and search the Web more effectively. It's written by and for knowledge workers who can't afford to spend valuable time sifting through junk on the Web in search of a few valuable nuggets of e-gold. Each issue of Free Pint has several regular sections. William Hann, Managing Editor, leads off with an overview of the issue and general news announcements, followed by a "Tips and Techniques" section, where professionals share their best searching tips and describe their favorite Web sites.

The Feature Article covers a specific topic in detail. Recent articles have been devoted to competitive intelligence on the Internet, central and eastern European Web sources, chemistry resources, Web sites for senior citizens, and a wide range of other topics. Feature articles are between 1,000-2,000 words long, and are packed with useful background information, in addition to numerous annotated links to vetted sites in the article's subject area. Quite often these are Invisible Web resources. One nice aspect of Free Pint is that it often focuses on European resources that aren't always well known in North America or other parts of the world.

Internet Resources Newsletter
http://www.hw.ac.uk/libwww/irn/

Internet Resources Newsletter's mission is to raise awareness of new sources of information on the Internet, particularly for academics, students, engineers, scientists, and social scientists. Published monthly, Internet Resources Newsletter is edited by Heriot-Watt University Library staff and published by Heriot-Watt University Internet Resource Centre.

Build Your Own Toolkit

As you become more familiar with what's available on the Invisible Web, it's important to build your own collection of resources. Knowing what is available before beginning your search is in many ways the greatest challenge in mastering the Invisible Web. But isn't this a paradox? If Invisible Web resources can't be found using general-purpose search tools, how do you go about finding them?

A great way to become familiar with Invisible Web resources is to do preemptive searching, a process much like the one professional librarians use in collection development. Explore the Invisible Web gateways described in Chapter 9, cherry-picking resources that seem relevant to your information needs, asking yourself what kinds of questions each resource might answer in the future.

As your collection grows, spend time organizing and reorganizing it for easier access. Be selective—choose Invisible Web resources the same way you build your personal collection of reference works. Consider saving your collection of Invisible Web resources with a remote bookmark service such as Backflip (http://www.backflip.com)

Myth: If You Found It Once You'll Find It Again

Search engines can trick you into feeling a false sense of security. It's easy to believe that if you found a page once using a search engine, you needn't bother to bookmark it or mark it as a favorite. Why, just re-enter your search query, and you'll have no problem finding the site again.

Sorry, it doesn't work that way. In fact, you may not get the same results if you repeat a search within an hour, let alone days or weeks later. There are several reasons for this.

First, the Web is in constant flux. Millions of new pages are published to the Web every day, and thousands more are moved to new "addresses," or are removed entirely. This means that the "relevance" of a particular document for a specific search query also changes constantly, as it is compared to other documents added to or removed from the index.

Web page authors can also manipulate relevance rankings, to a certain extent, so pages that once ranked highly can be "bumped" by pages that have been "tweaked" to achieve higher relevance. This is a contact sport for some Web authors, and they spend hours and hours trying to outwit the indexes, occasionally with remarkable—but usually transitory—success.

Second, though they rarely admit it, search engines sometimes misplace parts of their indexes. Sometimes huge parts. During the summer of 1999, for example, both Lycos and HotBot apparently dumped millions of pages, without explanation or warning. Some of those pages are now back in the indexes—others have simply vanished.

The lesson: If you like a Web page enough to want to revisit it, bookmark it, or save it with a page capture utility. Don't leave yourself at the mercy of a search engine that may never be able to locate it for you again.

or Hotlinks (http://www.hotlinks.com). This will give you access to your collection from any Web accessible computer.

Your ultimate goal in building your own toolkit should draw on one of the five laws of library science: to save time. Paradoxically, as you become a better searcher and are able to build your own high-quality toolkit, you'll actually need to spend less time exercising your searching skills, since in many cases you'll already have the resources you need close at hand. With your own collection of the best of the Invisible Web, you'll be able to boldly—and quickly—go where no search engine has gone before.

CHAPTER 7

Case Studies

In Chapter 6 we talked about searching the Invisible Web. In this chapter, we present eight scenarios that demonstrate both the power of Invisible Web resources, and why general-purpose search tools simply cannot find the materials used in the examples. In each case study, we attempt not only to demonstrate how search tools deliver results (or fail to), but to illustrate the problem-solving approach the effective searcher uses to satisfy his or her information need.

Case 1 – Historical Stock Quotes

Steve Smith is doing his income taxes. Last year, he sold some of his holdings of Berkshire Hathaway stock (ticker: BRK.A) that he purchased on November 12, 1996. In going through his records, Steve is unable to locate the confirmation of his purchase that his broker had originally issued. He remembered that he bought the stock just before the close of the market, so he feels that using the closing price for the day will be a safe number to use as his cost basis for calculating the tax on his capital gains.

Steve tries Yahoo!, Excite, and AltaVista, searching for historical stock price quotations for Berkshire Hathaway. The search proves futile. Among his results are links for information on historical Berkshire

County, Massachusetts, the Berkshire Opera company, and even something called *Pigot's 1830 Directories of Oxfordshire, Berkshire and Buckinghamshire counties in the UK*. Interspersed with these false drops are pages ostensibly containing historical information about Berkshire Hathaway. However, when Steve checks them out he finds an interesting story on the Berkshire Cotton Manufacturing Company (historic predecessor of the current Berkshire Hathaway company), an article about CEO Warren Buffett's deep interest in studying the history of business and stocks, and a story about Buffett's son who raises livestock on a farm in the Midwest. But he is unable to find the closing price for BRK.A on November 12, 1996.

Steve is wasting a lot of time and still not finding the answer. In an attempt to get the information directly from the source, he decides to check Berkshire's own Web site. Like many corporate Web sites, it has some useful information for investors, but has no historical quotes for its own stock and doesn't solve Steve's problem. He needs an exact price to use in his tax calculations.

Solution: Steve checks a directory of Invisible Web sites and learns of several services that provide searchable databases of historical quotes. The services differ depending on the date of the stock quote he is searching.   He chooses Bigcharts.com (http://www.bigcharts.com/historical/) and uses its historical quotes search form. Steve enters Berkshire's symbol in the search box with the date he's seeking. In a matter of seconds he learns that the closing price of Berkshire Hathaway Class A shares on November 12, 1996, was $33,500.

The Bigcharts database provides an example of the kind of information that is difficult or impossible to find with a general-purpose search engine for several reasons. First, the information is numeric data that has little meaning without the framework provided by the database. In other words, it's highly unlikely anyone would store page after page of historical stock quotes for the thousands of publicly traded companies on a Web page when a database offers a more efficient means of storing and retrieving that kind of data. Second, since Steve was looking for the price for a specific day, the limiting tools offered by most search engines just aren't precise enough to find that kind of a "needle" in the haystack of the Web, whereas pinpointing specific information in a relational database is a snap. Finally, the Bigcharts database is a known and trusted resource for financial information on the Web. Who knows if some random Web page that might coincidentally have had the information Steve was looking for could be trusted—especially when it comes to finding accurate information for such an important task as calculating taxes?

Although Steve was successful in his quest, the Invisible Web isn't always the answer for this kind of information need. Most of the Invisible Web databases provide quotes only back to the late 1980s. For closing prices prior to that date you will need the help of a proprietary database at your local library.

Case 2 – Patent Information

Wally Wilson is known around his office as the guy to turn to whenever you need to find something on the Internet. His team recently got a contract to help a computer maker "think outside the box" in designing a new input device. The computer company provided the team with the patent number of a previous invention, so Wally's boss gave him the task of finding the full-text (with images) of U.S. Patent number 3541541.

Wally had never done patent searching before, but his success with finding other material on the Web led him to believe that it wouldn't be a problem, so he eagerly tackled the job. Using several general-purpose search tools, Wally found *references* to the patent in the archives of several online message boards, but very little else.

In his searching, Wally also makes a curious and disturbing discovery. Most of the major search engines return a link to a document that appears to be the text of a genuine patent. At first, Wally is fooled into believing that he's found what he's seeking. On closer examination, however, Wally realizes that he's looking at the text of Patent Number 5187468, issued much later than the one he's researching. Yet all of the engines he checked suggested this (incorrect) patent as a useful result. What happened?

Patent applications require references to all previous patents that meaningfully relate to the invention. This statement of "prior art" is used to assert why the current invention is unique and should be granted its own patent protection. The patent Wally is interested in, 3541541, is mentioned as prior art in the document that the search engines suggested. In fact, not only is the patent mentioned, the document contains an exact match for his search terms. To a search engine, that's like hitting pay dirt, even though it constitutes a "false drop" and doesn't satisfy Wally's need. Fortunately, Wally was sharp enough to figure out what was going on before he suffered the embarrassment of showing his boss the wrong patent.

Instead of searching for the patent itself, Wally tried a new strategy—using a search engine to find resources for "patent searching." A search on Excite suggests the United States Patent and Trademark Office as the first link. Wally clicks through and discovers a link for searchable databases. The resulting page offers several searchable databases, *Patent Full-Text Database with Full-Page Images, Patent Bibliographic and Abstract Database*, an Expired Patent Search, and several others. Wally chooses the full-text database http://www.uspto.gov/patft/index.html over a bibliographic database that provides only limited information for each patent.

Clicking the full-text database link brings up further options. After scanning the page, Wally notices a direct link that allows for full-text searching by patent number (http://164.195.100.11/netahtml/srchnum.htm). Wally quickly types in the number and in less than a second has a link to the full-text of patent number 3541541. Wally's job is complete and his boss is very impressed.

This is a case where a general-purpose search engine failed to find the desired end result, but was indispensable in helping Wally locate the "front door" of the Invisible Web database that ultimately provided what he was looking for. This is why both general-purpose search engines and Invisible Web databases should be integral parts of your own Web search toolkit.

Incidentally, U.S. Patent 3541541 is one of the early patents for what evolved into the computer mouse. When the patent was issued to inventor Douglas Engelbart in 1970, he called it an "X and Y Position Indicator." And what about Patent Number 5187468, which turned up in all of the search engine results? That was awarded to the Microsoft Corporation in 1993 for a "Pointing device with adjustable clamp attachable to a keyboard"—essentially a mouse that attaches directly to a computer keyboard.

Note: Searching for patents can be very difficult and time consuming. A great place to learn more is at any one of the Patent and Trademark Depository Library Program libraries. You can learn more about these libraries and find the location of the closest library at http://www.uspto.gov/ Web/offices/ac/ido/ptdl/.

Case 3 – Real-Time Tracking

Barbara Berg's friends tease her by calling her "taxi driver," because she always seems to heading to the airport to pick up friends and family. Though she doesn't mind helping out, Barbara lives in suburban Virginia, 30 miles from the airport, and depending on the time of day and traffic conditions, the drive can take hours. Coupled with many airlines' erratic on-time performance, Barbara has found herself wasting far more time than she can afford. Even though she always calls the airlines for flight arrival information before heading to the airport, she never seems to get accurate information from airline employees.

Barbara saw an ad on television for a search engine that promised, "Simply type in your question and let Hal find the answer." She tried asking this search engine about the arrival time for her husband's flight from Denver, but most of the "answers" were links to sites featuring discount airfares. Other "answers" included an aviation dictionary, and military aircraft information. It wasn't just a problem with Hal—the other general-purpose search engines she tried fared equally poorly.

Barbara is obviously not a sophisticated searcher. But can the Invisible Web help her in her quest to avoid time-wasting delays due to incompetent or less-than-truthful airline employees giving her inaccurate information? Absolutely!

She learns from her local librarian of a service called Flight Tracker available from a Web site called TheTrip.Com (http://www.trip.com/ trs/trip/flighttracker/flight_tracker_home.xsl). This service allows users, at no charge, to track the progress of flights in the air over the U.S. in real time. And Barbara needn't worry about whether the information is accurate or not—it comes directly from the cockpit instruments of the airplanes themselves!

Barbara simply enters the flight number and in just a few seconds she learns the flight's scheduled arrival time. To further allay her concerns over timing, she also sees the airplane's exact location, air speed, and altitude. There's even a graphical version that displays a map of the U.S. with an animated icon of an airplane flying across it.

Flight Tracker is an excellent example of real-time information being made available over the Internet that will likely *never* be included in general-purpose search engines. Why? There are several reasons. First, a lot of real-time information is highly dynamic, constantly changing, and only useful at the moment it's created. Simply keeping up with the data flow and providing adequate storage for everything would be prohibitively expensive. And there's no real reason to store the data unless something exceptional occurs—such as a plane crash or other incident. But even this type of information would not be useful to most searchers.

Note: The Flight Tracker service obtains data via the Federal Aviation Administration. Flight Tracker has been licensed to several other Web sites including USA Today and Yahoo!. However, at the time of writing, TheTrip.com's version provides the greatest utility. Flightarrivals.com (http://www.flightarrivals.com) also promotes itself as an independent source of information for commercial airline flights in the U.S. and Canada.

Case 4 – Locating an Out of Print Book

Toni Thompson, a volunteer for the Make a Wish Foundation, needs a book and needs it quickly. Toni has agreed to "grant a wish" to a young child with a terminal disease. The child has requested a copy of *The Magic Wagon* by Dr. Frances Horwich, which her deceased grandmother once read to her. The only problem is that it's out of print.

Toni's local bookstore said it could help but finding a copy could take several weeks. So Toni has turned to the Web for help. She discovered that amazon.com could also help her track down a copy of an out of print book, but with the same time problem as her local bookstore. A quick search with Yahoo!, HotBot, and AltaVista turned up lots of mentions of the book in reviews and on personal Web sites, but no clues as to where she might be able to purchase the book.

Growing ever more upset, Toni calls her friend Brian, a frequent and accomplished Web user. Brian tells Toni about the Advanced Book Exchange (http://www.abebooks.com). Within a few seconds after entering the title and author information and clicking the search button, Toni has a list of ten used book dealers who can ship her the book overnight. In 15 hours the book is in her hands.

In pre-Internet days, finding an out of print or rare book was often very time consuming and expensive, if not flat-out impossible. General-purpose search tools could, in theory, help someone like Toni locate a dealer who has a copy of an out of print book for sale. In reality, however, search engines prefer not to index the catalogs of online retailers. Why?

Because inventory, especially in stores dealing with rare or one-of-a-kind items, tends to fluctuate. If a crawler indexes a catalog page offering a book and the book is sold, it will nonetheless turn up in search results until the crawler revisits the page.

As a specialized Invisible Web resource, the Advanced Book Exchange also offers advanced searching functions, limiting searches to author, title, publisher, and other book-specific attributes that would be difficult to express even in a torturously sophisticated query with the advanced search function of a general-purpose search engine.

Note: In addition to the Advanced Book Exchange, several other networks of used book dealers exist on the Web. These include:

Alibris (http://www.alibris.com)

Bibliofind (http://www.bibliofind.com)

21 North Main (http://www.21northmain.com)

Case 5 – Telephone Numbers and Zip Codes

Aaron Abrahamson lives in Buffalo, New York. He's written a letter to a friend who recently moved to Vancouver, British Columbia. Aaron has his friend's address, but not his zip code. He has spent the last two hours trying to find the correct code via several Internet search tools like Lycos and Yahoo!. He's found plenty of sites that offer lookups for U.S. addresses, but nothing for Canada.

Aaron's problem is twofold. First, general-purpose search engines aren't an appropriate place to search for a zip code. Far better would be a database that allowed precise entry of a specific street name and house number. Second, Aaron is using the wrong search term. What we call zip codes in the U.S. are known as "postal codes" in Canada and other countries.

About ready to give up, Aaron realizes that if he can look up his friend's telephone number in Vancouver he could simply call him and get the postal code directly from him. Aaron returns to his favorite search engine, Lycos, and types in his friend's name. He finds several mentions of his friend on Web pages but nothing with his home telephone number.

Could the Invisible Web assist Aaron in locating both the friend's postal code and telephone number? Yes, and within seconds. Aaron just needs to know where to look.

Canada Post, the Canadian Postal service, has an easy to use interactive postal look-up tool at http://www.canadapost.ca/CPC2/addrm/pclookup/pclookup.shtml. Aaron simply types his friend's street address into the appropriate boxes. Within two seconds he learns the postal code is V6J 5K5.

Finding a telephone number is a bit more of a challenge. Why? Because if Aaron's friend has an unlisted number, it will not be available online. Also, many phone directories exist online and they often contain different sets of data. Like search engines, some are more up to date than others.

Aaron checks an Invisible Web directory and learns of Canada411 at http://canada411. sympatico.ca/eng/person.html.

He enters his friend's name and then uses the pull-down menu to select British Columbia. In fact, the telephone directory also contains his friend's address and postal code.

Interestingly, the postal code Aaron found via the Canada411 directory is not the same as the one he located via Canada Post. He decides to use the one he found via the Canada Post database because this is the leading authority for that type of information. This is a good example of an Invisible Web resource maintained by a government agency that can be trusted as *the* authoritative source for information vs. what might be located using a general-purpose search engine.

Note: Infospace also offers a Canadian telephone directory at http://www.infospace.com/_1_43343463__info/canada.htm. In addition to Invisible Web resources to find telephone directories, the Web resource at http://www.teldir.com/eng/ is a terrific tool to have at the ready. If Aaron had been unsuccessful locating his friend's postal code with his first search, this directory of telephone directories would have served as a great alternative choice. As you're building your own collection of Invisible Web tools, it's important to remember that you can't always rely on a single source to provide all of your information needs.

Case 6 – Finding Online Images

Nathan Newman is trying to help his daughter, Nancy, with a school project. Nancy needs some information about paintings that can be found in the National Gallery of Art in Washington, D.C. A typical teenager, Nancy has waited to the last minute to begin her homework. Nathan and Nancy start work at 7pm on Sunday night for an assignment due Monday. No chance to visit the local public library or even call the museum.

What to do?

Nathan had read a review in a popular computer magazine about some U.S. government agencies and institutions that featured impressive Web sites. He knew nothing about the National Gallery's site, but thought it was worth a try. Visiting the National Gallery's homepage, Nathan and Nancy discover not only information about the National Gallery's collection but in many cases copies of many of the impressive paintings, sculptures, and other works of art found in the collection. The Gallery's site is entirely database-driven, which makes sense given the wide array of options it provides to its online patrons.

Nancy and her dad are lucky. Trying to find and access this treasure chest of authoritative information via a general-purpose search tool would have been impossible. All of this material is inaccessible to search engine spiders, making it a huge Invisible Web resource. Even if each one of these pages from the National Gallery was accessible via a general search tool, they could not be as easily searched without the options offered by the National Gallery's site itself, including subject, medium, and year.

They also learn two important lessons. It is very important to check a Web site thoroughly for Invisible Web resources. Access to materials in databases may not be immediately apparent from a cursory glance at a home page. Also, don't rely solely on Web site reviews as they are often superficial, overlooking or omitting Invisible Web resources.

Case 7 – Investment Research

Rebecca Reed is a diligent and prudent investor who prefers do her own research and analysis for her current and potential investments rather than relying on reports from her broker. The Web has been a boon for Rebecca, offering scores of sites with all manner of information.

Rebecca is growing tired, not of investing, but of having to go from one source to the next on the Web and having to reenter the company name or ticker symbol each time. One site provides her with exceptional fundamental information on the security. Another provides excellent charts of price and momentum activity. A third offers detailed "technical analysis" with a wide array of numeric data series that Rebecca can use in her own custom-designed stock screening programs. But no single site seems to give her everything she needs.

Recently an article in her local newspaper has alerted Rebecca to a resource that will save her time and provide her with even more useful information than she has ever been able to access.

The site is the inadequately named justquotes.com (http://www.justquotes.com).

The concept is simple and divine. Justquotes.com allows the user to enter the ticker symbol or company name once, then returns a results page with links pre-configured with the company's stock symbol for several hundred investing resources, including Rebecca's favorites mentioned above. Nearly all of these pre-configured links are indirect URLs with scripting commands that will extract specific information about the stock from an Invisible Web database.

Justquotes.com is a great example of a site that serves both as a useful pathfinder to specific (namely investing) Invisible Web resources, but that saves the time of the researcher by pre-configuring what amounts to custom searches with the stock symbol of interest to the searcher. To paraphrase the popular television commercial, "No search engine gonna do all that."

Case 8 – The Invisible Web Fails to Deliver!

Donald Davis feels very familiar and comfortable with the visible and Invisible Web. He has read numerous articles on the subject and knows his way around many of the better Invisible Web pathfinders. In fact, he recently accessed some key economic statistics via the Invisible Web.

Donald is trying to track down several newspaper articles for a business proposal he is writing and feels confident that his knowledge of the Invisible Web will come in very handy. Donald wants to frame some of his business plan with a few quotes from material published in the *Washington Post*, the *Houston Chronicle*, and *Dallas Morning News*.

Donald begins his search with the Web sites of each newspaper. From prior experience, he realizes he'll have to pay a small fee to access the articles from the newspapers' online archives. However, to his surprise, he discovers that the articles he's looking for simply aren't available from the newspapers' archives. Why? Because the archives are incomplete, with only relatively recent articles available.

For example, one article Donald needs is from the *Washington Post*, published in 1975. However, the *Post*'s Web archive only goes back to 1977. The article from the *Dallas Morning News* was published in 1980. The Morning News archive contains the full-text of articles only from 1985 forward.

Donald contacted his local public library for guidance. They checked the holdings of the Dow Jones Interactive proprietary information service for him. Unfortunately, the Dow Jones Interactive database contains only the full-text of newspaper articles from 1984 forward. It turns out the articles are not available anywhere (Web, value-added Web, or proprietary database) in electronic format.

What's left to do? Donald will likely need to hire an information broker, or call each newspaper or magazine and obtain the material directly from each source. The bottom line? The Invisible Web is not the solution to every information need.

Web researchers often forget that attempting to find older material in electronic format is often difficult, if not impossible. With so much attention being paid to both the visible and Invisible Web these days it is important to remember that a *massive* amount of material is not accessible on the Web, via the Web, or in any electronic format. It only exists in its original format or some other offline archive format like microfilm or microfiche.

Will everything in print ultimately be digitized and made available online? Not likely. The expense of converting materials from printed text to machine-readable format is often prohibitive. Much of what we have on the Web we owe to the generosity of venture capitalists willing to back experimental ventures in delivering online content. High-quality offline content will continue to migrate to the Web, but likely at a much slower pace than we've seen in the past.

CHAPTER 8

The Future:
Revealing the Invisible Web

The future Invisible Web will be both larger and smaller than today's Invisible Web. This seeming paradox can be explained by looking at the new technologies and methods being developed by information scientists bent on revealing the Invisible Web and making more online data accessible and useful. Many of the technical solutions are both elegant and relatively straightforward to implement. Simultaneously, existing techniques will be less arbitrarily constrained as the costs of computing power drops and network bandwidth increases.

But there will always be the perpetual tensions between speed and comprehensiveness, ease of use and power, costs and payoffs. Technology can go a long way toward opening up the realms of the Invisible Web, but in and of itself it's not sufficient. So while searchers using next-generation tools will likely be able to access much more of the Invisible Web via general-purpose search engines than they can today, the rate of growth of the Invisible Web is likely to outpace the enhanced capability of the tools.

In this chapter, we take a brief look at some of the most promising new approaches to making the Invisible Web visible. Some of these technologies may be in place by the time this book sees print. Others may never make it out of research labs—and we're certain there are still other projects operating in stealth mode, waiting for the ideal time to launch a competitive assault against the major search services.

Smarter Crawlers

At the most basic level, search engines will get much better at compiling truly comprehensive indexes of the Web. In part, they'll do this by enhancing their crawler programs to be smarter about how they operate. First generation crawlers use a non-selective approach to retrieving Web pages. This means they simply gather links from a Web page, put them in a queue, and then crawl them in the order they were added to the queue. In theory, since the Web is highly connected, crawlers will eventually find and download for indexing nearly all of the pages on the Web. In practice, because most search engines limit the depth of crawl on a Web site, most sites are only partially indexed.

As computing power, data storage, and bandwidth becomes less expensive, search engines will loosen or even eliminate their depth of crawl restrictions, striving to index all pages on a site. Nonetheless, since the Web continues to grow at a relentless rate, a crawler will still be limited to visiting a site on some sort of schedule, meaning that the pages in the index may not always reflect the freshest content on a site.

Smarter crawlers will attempt to learn more about a site and automatically adapt their schedule to return more frequently to popular or "important" sites to assure the freshest possible content. Pages that change frequently will be crawled more frequently, while crawlers will largely ignore slowly changing or static pages. Smart crawlers may also be programmed to make judgments about the relevance of a document and the quality of the links it contains. Poor quality or inappropriate documents will not be crawled, and therefore will not clutter up the index, ultimately meaning that search results will be "purer."

There will also be advances made in targeted crawlers. Cohen, McCallum, and Quass, in "Learning to Understand the Web" (2000), foresee a wide range of specialized "data-centric" search engines emerging. "It is likely that many such search engines will be developed, each specializing in a different topic. Topic-specific engines are also likely to vary in their depth of coverage, with some systems electing to impose a rich schema on a smaller subset of the Web, and others imposing a weak schema on a large subset of the Web. Ultimately the vast majority of queries that focus on common topics will be answered by one of a few dozen general-purpose databases; and of the remaining, special-purpose queries, most will be answered by one of a few thousand more specialized databases" (pp. 17-24).

The Promise and Pitfalls of Metadata

Metadata, or data about data, has long been held out as the Holy Grail for dramatically improving search engine performance. Essentially, metadata provides standardized information about a document, including things like the name of the document's author, a summary, and descriptive keywords. A primitive form of metadata ("keywords" and "description" meta tags) has been recognized since 1996, but it has been so widely abused by spammers that most search engines either ignore it or use it only peripherally in calculating relevance for a document.

Proposals for metadata standards abound. The standard that seems most likely to achieve something close to universal adoption is RDF (Resource Description Framework), which uses the syntax of XML (Extensible Markup Language). The goal of all metadata standards proposals is to go beyond machine-*readable* data and create machine-*understandable* data on the Web. Among other things, they provide the capability to introduce controlled vocabulary (often organized in thesaurus form) into the search equation. A controlled vocabulary can bring different terms, jargon, and concepts together. Though the standard will provide a structure for describing, classifying, and managing Web documents, it has its own set of vulnerabilities, and not everyone is sanguine about its prospects.

RDF will provide the most benefit to sites that can maintain control over the quality and integrity of the metadata authoring process. Specialized search services will be able to impose rules on Web authors that will require a greater level of internal consistency and validity in documents than exists today. For general search services, the benefits of metadata are more problematic, since a rich metadata language like XML offers a virtually infinite number of possibilities for spammers.

Some search engines, such as Northern Light, add their own metadata to pages as they index them. However, this value-added process is expensive, and unlikely to be adopted by other search engines. Metadata could realize its potential if a widely accepted certification authority gains popularity. To be certified, Web authors would be required to adhere to specific guidelines, similar to the privacy policy guidelines administered by TRUSTe.

Beyond Text

A large portion of the Invisible Web consists of non-text objects—images, sounds, streaming video, and other file formats that present problems for crawlers designed to capture text. Research into multimedia information retrieval is creating new tools that have the capability of extracting the unique features of multimedia data objects and allowing queries based on comparisons of these attributes.

For example:

- Find all images that have the same color distribution as this picture of Mt. Blanc.

- Locate X-ray images that show features similar to a fractured tibia.

- Locate all audio recordings of speeches by Federal Reserve Chairman Greenspan on the 1987 stock market crash.

In each query, the search engine is essentially performing pattern matching on specified attributes. These attributes may have been associated with individual images as metadata, or they might be inferred by software that has been trained to recognize them, using machine learning techniques.

As multimedia search becomes more sophisticated, it's likely that text-based queries will form only one part of the search interface. Interfaces on search engines will evolve to employ visual controls similar to those in graphics editing software, making it easier to refine or limit searches. For example, sliders could be used to specify a range of values. Color palettes could be combined with a "more like this" feature, and so on. All of these new interfaces will likely provide a very fine level of granularity of results for media types other than text.

Delving into Databases

As we discussed in Chapter 4, dynamic content stored in databases makes up a very large portion of the Invisible Web. Technically, there is no reason that current generation crawlers cannot access this information. Search engines do not index dynamic content because the scripting language used to assemble Web pages from a database can also be used to set "spider traps" for crawlers, ensnaring them in endless loops or worse, feeding them thousands or millions of pages of spam. To avoid spider traps, search engines avoid all dynamic content sites—an unfortunate situation, as the vast majority of dynamic sites provide useful information.

This situation could be remedied if search engines could establish a code of ethics for dynamic sites that would allow spidering of dynamic content while severely punishing abusers. One way this could occur is for search engines to charge Webmasters to crawl and index pages. Inktomi has begun an experiment with paid submission, and as part of the test they are allowing dynamic content, assuming that no one would be foolish enough to pay to submit a spider-trapped URL that would ultimately be banished from the index anyway.

Another approach would be to establish individual agreements between Web sites and search engines, specifying which pages should be included in the search engine's database. Alternately, entire trusted top-level domains could be opened up to crawlers—content in .gov or .edu domains, for example. The U.S. government's FirstGov search engine is an example of how this could work. FirstGov crawls pages in all .gov domains and includes many dynamic pages in its database.

Technology can help as well. Information can be extracted from databases using *wrapper induction* techniques, where software probes a database and examines the results to determine what kind of action to take. Agents that "understand" how to interact with database query forms can also be used to enter required parameters into forms and generate result pages that can be crawled and included in a search engine's database.

These are just a few of the techniques that might transcend the barriers databases present to current generation search engine technology. As promising as these methods are, it's important to bear in mind that if general-purpose search engines begin to crawl material in databases, they can't possibly offer the robust interfaces offered by the databases themselves. General-purpose search engines strive to have something for everybody, taking an "any answer is better than no answer" approach. Conversely, databases strive to provide very limited (but precise) information for a small number of users, taking the approach that "no answer at all is better than one that's incomplete or inaccurate." These radically differing approaches mean that if you're looking for precise, specific information, a database specializing in your target subject area will almost always give you better results than what you'll get from a general-purpose search engine.

Hypertext Query Languages

If the Web itself is considered as a large, unstructured database, it follows that query languages can be created that allow sophisticated query processing of Web content. The first generation of these languages includes W3QL and WebSQL. The next generation goes much further in scope and power, with languages such as STRUQL, FLORID, and WebOQL. These hypertext query languages seek to unify the Web, allowing sophisticated searching that's very similar to the kind available with Invisible Web databases today. But rather than being limited to one or just a few databases at a time, hypertext query languages may evolve that treat the entire Web as a single database.

Real-Time Crawling

In the best of all possible worlds, Web search would be a real-time process. You would enter a query and every page on the Web would be analyzed and assigned a relevance ranking. In reality, of course, this is impossible. But IBM's Fetuccino project brings real-time crawling a step closer by taking the results from any search engine and verifying, filtering, and augmenting those results by dynamically crawling in directions where relevant information is found (http://www.ibm.com/java/fetuccino/fetuccino-abstract.html).

Individual searchers could also undertake real-time crawling if the proper tools were made available. If you had your own personal crawler, for example, you could seed it with a set of URLs that you know contain useful information on a particular subject. When you turn the crawler loose, it would fetch these pages, then extract the links from each page and crawl the new set of pages. The crawler could continue this process until some sort of predefined goal was reached. The end result would be your own personal universe of documents that were relevant in some way to the initial set you seeded the crawler with.

Long Live the Invisible Web

Even if all of the future developments we have described come to fruition, the Invisible Web will still make up a vast portion of cyberspace. The rate of growth of information is simply so great that no general-purpose search tool will ever be able to effectively search *all* information sources on the Web without some sort of tradeoff. Even if crawlers get smarter, they will inevitably miss many resources, whether because of cost, data format, or timeliness issues. Even if Invisible Web databases become accessible via a general-purpose search engine, the native query tools offered by each individual database will always be the most efficient way to extract accurate information quickly from the database.

The bottom line is that the Invisible Web is here to stay. By taking the time to learn what it has to offer and mastering some of the incredible resources it has to offer, you'll become far more adept at satisfying your information needs than if you simply rely on general-purpose search engines and Web directories.

CHAPTER 9

The Best of the Invisible Web

Now that you know what the Invisible Web has to offer, you're probably eager to delve into its rich resources, but you face a similar challenge to the one confronted by early explorers of Terra Incognito. Without the benefit of a search engine to guide you, exactly *where* do you begin your search for information on the Invisible Web?

In this chapter, we discuss several Invisible Web pathfinders that make excellent starting points for the exploration of virtually any topic. We also introduce our directory of more than 1,000 hand-selected Invisible Web sites that make up the remaining chapters of this book. This introduction takes the form of the familiar "Frequently Asked Questions" (FAQ) section you see on many Web sites. We talk about the structure of the directory, how we selected our resources, and how to get the most out of the directory for doing your own searching.

Finally, we'll leave you with a handy "pocket reference" that you can refer to on your explorations—the top ten concepts to understand about the Invisible Web.

Invisible Web Pathfinders

Invisible Web pathfinders are, for the most part, Yahoo!-like directories with lists of links to Invisible Web resources. Most of these pathfinders, however, also include links to searchable resources that aren't strictly invisible. Nonetheless, they are useful starting points for finding and building your own collection of Invisible Web resources.

direct search

http://gwis2.circ.gwu.edu/~gprice/direct.htm
direct search is a growing compilation of links to the search interfaces of resources that contain data not easily or entirely searchable/accessible from general search tools like AltaVista, Google, and HotBot. The goal of direct search is to get as close as possible to the search form offered by a Web resource (rather than having to click through one or two pages to get there); hence the name "direct search."

InvisibleWeb.com

http://www.invisibleweb.com/
The InvisibleWeb Catalog contains over 10,000 databases and searchable sources that have been frequently overlooked by traditional searching. Each source is analyzed and described by editors to ensure that every user of the InvisibleWeb Catalog will find reliable information on hundreds of topics, from Air Fares to Yellow Pages. All of this material can be accessed easily by Quick or Advanced Search features or a browsable index of the InvisibleWeb Catalog. Unlike other search engines, this takes you directly to the searchable source within a Web site, even generating a search form for you to perform your query.

Librarians' Index to the Internet

http://www.lii.org/
The Librarians' Index to the Internet is a searchable, annotated subject directory of more than 7,000 Internet resources selected and evaluated by librarians for their usefulness to users of public libraries. LII only includes links to the very best Net content. While not a "pure" Invisible Web pathfinder, LII categorizes each resource as Best Of, Directories, Databases, and Specific Resources. Databases, of course, are Invisible Web resources. By using LII's advanced search feature, you can limit your search to return only databases in the results list. Advanced search also lets you restrict your results to specific fields of the directory (author name, description, title, URL, etc.). In effect, the Librarians' Index to the Internet is a laser-sharp searching tool for finding Invisible Web databases.

WebData
http://www.Webdata.com/Webdata.htm
General portal Web sites like Yahoo!, Excite, Infoseek, Lycos, and Goto.com, etc. are page-oriented search engine sites (words on pages are indexed), where WebData.com's searches are content-oriented searches (forms and databases on Web sites are indexed). WebData.com and the traditional search engines are often confused with each other when composed side by side because they look alike. However, results from searches on WebData.com return databases where the others return Web pages that may or may not be what a user is looking for.

AlphaSearch
http://www.calvin.edu/library/searreso/internet/as/
The primary purpose of AlphaSearch is to access the finest Internet "gateway" sites. The authors of these gateway sites have spent significant time gathering into one place all relevant sites related to a discipline, subject, or idea. You have instant access to hundreds of sites by entering just one gateway site.

ProFusion
http://www.profusion.com
ProFusion is a meta search engine from Intelliseek, the same company that runs InvisibleWeb.com. In addition to providing a sophisticated simultaneous search capability for the major general-purpose search engines, ProFusion provides direct access to the Invisible Web with the ability to search over 1,000 targeted sources of information, including sites like TerraServer, Adobe PDF Search, Britannica.com, *The New York Times*, and the U.S. Patent database.

An Invisible Web Directory

The remaining chapters in this book make up a directory of some of the best resources the Invisible Web has to offer. The directory includes resources that are informative, of high quality, and contain worthy information from reliable information providers that are not visible to general-purpose search engines. We give precedence to resources that are freely available to anyone with Web access. However, we do include a few select resources that are either free to search but have resulting fee-based content (such as Newslibrary.com), or charge a small fee to search and a fee to access full records. Some sites may be free to search and access full records, but require the user to register at no charge before granting access.

In general, we like the idea of comparing the resources available on the Invisible Web to a good collection of reference works. The challenge is to be familiar with some key resources prior to needing them. Information professionals have always done this with canonical reference books, and often with traditional, proprietary databases like Dialog and LexisNexis. We encourage you to approach the Invisible Web in the same way—consider each specialized search tool as you would an individual reference resource.

Frequently Asked Questions about the Directory

Why did you create the directory of Invisible Web resources?

To provide practical examples of what we discuss in the book and to highlight the variety of high quality information that can be found on the Invisible Web. We hope that our book appeals to a wide variety of Web users and researchers—that this directory has something for everyone. This is one of the reasons why the directory is so broad in scope. The Invisible Web resources we've selected range from a searchable bibliography about African Elephants to a road construction database for U.S. highways. From a database of Canadian statistics to an interactive calendar of events at the world's leading art museums. It's an eclectic collection, but we feel that every resource included represents one of the best sources of information available for its particular subject area.

Does this directory list every Invisible Web resource on the Internet?

No. While we have over 1,000 resources listed in the directory, this is just a relatively small portion of what's available. Because the Invisible Web is so huge and constantly changing, creating a totally comprehensive directory is virtually impossible. Our goal was to go for quality over quantity—though we continue to add new resources as we find them to the companion Web site at http://www.invisible-web.net.

Does every resource in the book contain 100% invisible data?

Not necessarily. Some Web sites have both visible and invisible portions—we cited the U.S. Library of Congress as just one example. If a site's invisible portion met our criteria for quality and usefulness, we included it even if there was substantial visible material as well. We have also chosen to include a few specialized, focused, and targeted search resources that are largely visible—they are still crucial in making the Web a useful and effective research tool. Remember that no single general-purpose search engine contains everything, and they are often out of date, due to crawler time lag in revisiting sites.

Does Invisible Web material ever become visible?

Absolutely! What was invisible when we wrote this book may be visible by the time you are reading this. Search spiders will often begin crawling new formats and types of pages with little or no notice. In fact, during the interval between when we finished the book and when it went to press, Google began to crawl and index PDF format files, which had previously been invisible to all general-purpose search engines. We fully expect this trend to continue as search engines strive to provide more comprehensive coverage of the Web.

Why do you list two URLs (Web addresses) for each resource?

We're all familiar with the frustrating "Page Not Found" message—URLs change and change often. To help avoid potential frustration, we've often included two URLs for each site in the directory. The first URL listed is generally the home page or primary entry for a site, and is a location that we deemed stable. These primary URLs are very useful for locating background about the resource and for finding further information about the subject of your search.

The second URL, the Search Form URL, will take you directly to the search interface provided by the resource—or no more than two clicks away from it. Search form URLs have a notorious reputation for changing, so be ready to go exploring if the URL doesn't work, by either using the primary URL for the site, or by playing with the outdated URL to explore for the new search form URL.

Some sites have a country name or the letter "B" next to them. What does that mean?

We marked most sites originating outside the U.S. with the country of origin. Of course, most of these resources will be of use to people around the globe, regardless of the country of origin.

The "B" next to an entry denotes that this database contains primarily bibliographic material. In most cases, the full text of the documents, books, or other materials referenced in the bibliography are not available via that database. However, they may be accessible elsewhere online, at your library, or via interlibrary loan.

Where do the descriptions for each directory entry come from?

In most cases they come from the resources themselves.

What are related entries?

Creating related entries for many resources was an effective way to share more URLs with you that have some relationship (primarily by subject) to a resource. As we move forward with the companion Web site, many of the related resources will be expanded to include their own full descriptions.

Can a resource be located in more than one chapter?

For the most part, each resource is listed just once, in the chapter where we think it best belongs. However, we fully recognize the fact that many of these resources could go in more than one chapter, and in a few cases we've duplicated listings. Trying to decide which category a resource was most appropriate for was a major challenge in creating the directory. The interdisciplinary nature of the Web is one of the things we find most exciting about it.

Since the directory does not list every Invisible Web site, how can a searcher most effectively use it?

We hope that you use the printed directory as a starting point to build your own collection of Invisible Web resources, maximized for your work and interests. Consider it a "virtual acquisition shelf" of material to get you started. Explore and allow the power of browsing and serendipity to work for you.

How much does it cost to search these Invisible Web databases?

An overwhelming majority of the material listed is free to search and access. In some cases you will need to register for access, but the registration process is generally quick and free.

Did you have a particular mindset when building the directory?

Yes. We kept in mind many of the concepts that a librarian would use when building a collection at his or her library. The bottom line is the quality of material and the authority of who is providing it. Here are a few of the other factors we considered when building the directory:

- **Content/Uniqueness**. Does the resource illustrate the wide variety of information available on the Invisible Web?

- **Truly Invisible?** Does the resource contain information that is not available via general-purpose search engines? In other words, is content generated dynamically; is the content in a format that engines don't handle; does the site specifically block search crawlers?

- **Utility**. Can the resource save the searcher's time when compared to a general-purpose search engine?

- **Authority**. Who is providing the data? Do they have a trustworthy reputation?

- **Cost**. Preferably free or low cost.

- **Timeliness**. Does the resource appear to be kept up-to-date?

- **Web Reputation**. What other reputable Web sites link to the resource? Where did we find out about it?

We also include some resources that are technically visible, but provide better results from searching the native interface of the resource rather than trying to find its content via a general-purpose search engine. For these sites, we asked:

- Does the specialized interface that the site provides allow for advanced search capabilities, such as Boolean queries, limiting, filtering, and so on?

- Does the site's search tool provide greater depth on a topic or subject, deeper than what's provided by a general search engine?

- Does the site's search tool allow results to be displayed in various orders and forms?

Our final question was always: Does it make it easier and more efficient to pull the needle from the haystack?

Is the directory available on the Web?

It is, at http://www.invisible-web.net. In fact, we plan to add all of the new Invisible Web resources we find to the Web-based version of the directory, so it's already substantially larger than what you'll find in the book. As an added bonus, the online version of the directory is keyword searchable. We encourage you to bookmark the directory and use it frequently for your own explorations of the Invisible Web.

In Summary: The Top 10 Concepts to Understand about the Invisible Web

As you begin your exploration and charting of the Invisible Web, here's a list of the top ten concepts that you should understand about the Invisible Web.

1. In most cases, the data found in an Invisible Web database or opaque Web database cannot be accessed entirely or easily via a general-purpose search engine.

2. The Invisible Web is not the sole solution to all of one's information needs. For optimal results, Invisible Web resources should be used in conjunction with other information resources, including general-purpose Web search engines and directories.

3. Because many Invisible Web databases (as well as opaque databases) search a limited universe of material, the opportunity for a more precise and relevant search is greater than when using a general search tool.

4. Often, Invisible Web and Opaque Web databases will have the most current information available online, since they are updated more frequently than most general-purpose search engines.

5. In many cases, Invisible Web resources clearly identify who is providing the information, making it easy to judge the authority of the content and its provider.

6. Material accessible "on the Invisible Web" is not the same as what is found in proprietary databases, such as Dialog or Factiva. In many cases, material on the Invisible Web is free or available for a small fee. In some cases material is available in multiple formats.

7. Targeted crawlers, which commonly focus on Opaque Web resources, often offer more comprehensive coverage of their subject, since they crawl more pages of each site that they index and crawl them more often than a general-purpose search engine.

8. To use the Invisible Web effectively, you must make some effort to have an idea of what is available prior to searching. Consider each resource as if it were a traditional reference book. Ask yourself, "What questions can this resource answer?" Think less of an entire site and more of the tools that can answer specific types of questions.

9. Invisible Web databases can make non-textual material searchable and accessible.

10. Invisible Web databases offer specialized interfaces that enhance the utility of the information they access. Even if a general-purpose search engine could somehow access Invisible Web data, the shotgun nature of its search interface simply is no match for the rifle-shot approach offered by most Invisible Web tools.

Chapter 10

Art and Architecture

Art and architecture resources have been abundant on the Web since the advent of the first graphical Web browsers in the early '90s. It's easy for an art lover to pay a virtual visit to the National Galleries of the U.S. or U.K., New York's famous Metropolitan Museum of Art, or countless other online exhibitions of fine arts. But, as with so many other wonderful resources available on the Invisible Web, good luck finding the artwork available for viewing at many online museums with a general-purpose search engine.

Images pose a special challenge for search engines. Since they contain no text, there's literally nothing for a general-purpose search crawler to index. Nonetheless, there's a lot of valuable information that can be associated with images, such as the title of the image, artist's name, the style of the image, time period, medium, and so on. For this reason, most online museums have built their collections using database technology, providing sophisticated browsing and search capabilities for their users. This, naturally, makes most online image collections part of the Invisible Web.

Even if the general-purpose search engines *could* somehow find these resources, as we've said elsewhere they can't possibly offer the power that's available to a searcher through the sophisticated interfaces offered by a database-driven information resource. This means that no matter how sophisticated general-purpose search engines become at finding art and architecture resources in the future, you'll almost always be better served by going directly to the source to access the visual treasures available via the Web.

There's more for the art lover or student than just pretty pictures. Notable resources in this chapter include the following:

- **Architecture Resources**, such as the Cities and Buildings Database, providing images of buildings and cities drawn from across time and throughout the world

- **Artist Information**, including Who's Who in American Art, an authoritative source for biographical information about America's notable artists

- **Gateways to Art and Architecture Resources**, such as ADAM (Art, Design, Architecture & Media Information Gateway), a comprehensive catalog of a wide array of art resources available on the Web

- **Reference Resources**, such as the Art and Architecture Thesaurus Browser, a comprehensive listing of the structured vocabulary used by art professionals to describe all aspects of art

See the Art and Architecture category on the companion Web site for additional Invisible Web resources on this topic at http://www.invisible-web.net.

Architecture

archINFORM (International Architecture Database)
http://www.archinform.net/
"This architectural database, originally emerging from records of interesting building projects from architecture students, has meanwhile become the largest online database for international architecture. This database includes over 9,500 built and unrealized projects from various architects and planners. The architecture of the 20th century is the main theme of this database. It's possible to look for a special project via an architect, town, or keyword with the indices or by using a query form."
Search Form URL: See Main Page

Cities and Buildings Database

http://content.lib.washington.edu/cities/

"The Cities/Buildings Database is a collection of digitized images of buildings and cities drawn from across time and throughout the world, available to students, researchers, and educators on the Web."

Search Form URL: See Main Page

Council on Tall Buildings Database

http://hrbd.ce.lehigh.edu

Limited access for nonmembers of the organization. "The High Rise Buildings Database, contains data on thousands of tall buildings: the latest facts and statistics, visual images and video, and listings of professional firms linked to specific buildings and specialty categories."

Search Form URL: http://hrbd.ce.lehigh.edu/hrbd_enter.html

Frank Lloyd Wright Building Locator

http://www.pbs.org/flw/l

Locate Frank Lloyd Wright buildings by ZIP code, state, building type, and building name.

Search Form URL: http://www.pbs.org/flw/locator/index.html

S*P*I*R*O (Architecture Slide Library)

http://arch.ced.berkeley.edu/resources/archslides.htm

"... visual online public access catalog to the Architecture Slide Library's (ASL) collection of over 200,000 35mm slides at the University of California at Berkeley."

Search Form URL: http://www.mip.Berkeley.EDU/spiro/

Artists

Artcyclopedia

http://www.artcyclopedia.com/index.html

Use Artcyclopedia to find museum-quality fine art on the Internet. The database contains links to more than 80,000 works by over 7,000 artists.

Search Form URL: See Main Page

The Union List of Artists Names Browser (ULAN)

http://www.getty.edu/gri/vocabularies/index.htm

"The ULAN is a structured vocabulary containing around 220,000 names and biographical information about artists and architects, including a wealth of variant names, pseudonyms, and language variants."

Search Form URL: http://shiva.pub.getty.edu/ulan_browser/

Who's Who in American Art

http://www.artstar.com

"Marquis Publication's 22nd Edition of Who's Who in American Art. This volume profiles 11,724 contributors to the States, Canada, and Mexico."

Search Form URL: http://www.artstar.com/bin/open_page? doc=330

Related Resources:

Artists in Canada Canada

http://www.chin.gc.ca/Resources/Research_Ref/Reference_Info/AICH/e_hp_aich.html

Galleries on the Web

American Political Prints in the Library of Congress

http://loc.harpweek.com/default.asp

"... access to one of the most important collections of American political prints. The Library of Congress collection has been catalogued and extensively annotated by Bernard F. Reilly, Jr. This catalog, which HarpWeek has the privilege of bringing to the public in electronic format, is an unmatched source of information on American political prints."

Search Form URL: http://loc.harpweek.com/default.asp

Axis U.K.

http://www.axisartists.org.uk/axishome/default.htm

"Axis is a national contemporary visual arts service providing information about artists and makers living/working in Britain to a national and international audience. It is the largest interactive database of contemporary British art on the Internet."

Search Form URL: http://www.axisartists.org.uk/database/gallery/imageview.asp

Collage (Corporation of London Library & Art Gallery Electronic) U.K.

http://collage.nhil.com/collagedev/index.html
"An image database containing 20,000 works from the Guildhall Library and Guildhall Art Gallery London."
Search Form URL: See Main Page

ExCALENDAR

http://www.excalendar.net/
"The official exhibition calendar of the world's leading art museums."
Search the exCALENDAR database for exhibitions by artist's name, exhibition title, city, keyword or museum name.
Search Form URL: See Main Page

Kyoto National Museum Online Database Japan

http://www.kyohaku.go.jp/
"This On-Line Catalogue currently includes about 2,000 of over 5,000 works owned by the Kyoto National Museum."
Search Form URL: http://www.kyohaku.go.jp/olc/menu00e.htm
Related Resources:
vanGogh Museum Amsterdam Collection
http://www.vangoghmuseum.nl/collection/catalog/alphaMart.asp?LANGID=0&SEL=1

Metropolitan Museum of Art Online Collection

http://www.metmuseum.org
"The Metropolitan Museum's online collection currently includes the entire Department of European Paintings and fifty highlights from each of the Museum's seventeen other curatorial departments, as well as fifty each from the Museum's libraries and from the database of the Antonio Ratti Textile Center. (As digitization of images proceeds, more objects will be made available online.)"
Search Form URL: http://www.metmuseum.org/collections/search.asp

National Gallery of Art (London) U.K.

http://www.nationalgallery.org.uk/
"The Collection spans the period from about 1260 to 1900 and consists of Western European paintings. The national collection of 20th-century art is held at Tate Modern and the national collection of

British Art is held at Tate Britain." Search by artist name, work number, or gallery number.

Search Form URL: http://www.nationalgallery.org.uk/collection/index.html

Related Resources:

National Portrait Gallery Collection and Research Records Search U.K.

http://www.npg.org.uk/live/collect.asp

Victoria and Albert Museum Images Online U.K.

http://www.vam.ac.uk/Explorer/Virtual/images/

National Gallery of Art (Washington D.C.)

http://www.nga.gov

Search the entire collection by artist name or title of work. Images are available for many items.

Search Form URL: http://www.nga.gov/search/search.htm

National Museum of American Art Digitized Collection

http://nmaa-ryder.si.edu

Search and view the holdings of this Smithsonian museum. Images are available for many items.

Search Form URL: http://nmaa-ryder.si.edu/helios/search.html

Rolling Stone Cover Art Archive

http://www.rollingstone.com

Browse all of the covers of this music magazine since its inception in 1967.

Search Form URL: http://www.rollingstone.com/sections/gallery/text/gallerycovers.asp?afl=

The Great Canadian Guide Canada

http://www.chin.gc.ca/

"Your premier Internet connection to Canadian museums, galleries and other attractions!"

Search Form URL: http://daryl.chin.gc.ca/Museums/English/index.html

Related Resources:

Directory of Canadian Museums Canada

http://www.chin.gc.ca/Museums/Cma/e_cma.html

The State Hermitage Museum Digital Collection Russia

http://www.hermitagemuseum.org

"...virtual gallery of high-resolution artwork images from the State Hermitage Museum." This site has IBM's Query by Image Content (QBIC) search technolgy available.
Search Form URL: http://www.hermitagemuseum.org/ fcgi-bin/db2www/browse.mac/category?selLang=English

The Thinker ImageBase

http://www.thinker.org/fam/thinker.html
"The ImageBase is a searchable image and text database of objects from the collections of the Fine Arts Museums of San Francisco (the de Young Museum and the Legion of Honor)."
Search Form URL: http://www.thinker.org/fam/advancedsearch.html

Gateways to Art and Architecture Resources

ADAM (Art, Design, Architecture & Media Information Gateway) U.K.

http://adam.ac.uk/
"ADAM, the Art, Design, Architecture & Media Information Gateway, is a searchable catalogue of 2,546 Internet resources that have been carefully selected and catalogued by professional librarians for the benefit of the UK Higher Education community."
Search Form URL: See Main Page

American Art Directory

http://www.artstar.com
"The American Art Directory, first published in 1898 as the American Art Annual, is now in its 57th year. Here you'll find up-to-date contact information, addresses, and activities for over 7,500 museums, libraries, organizations, and schools from around the world."
Search Form URL: http://www.artstar.com/bin/open_page?doc=331

Art Library Directory (IFLA)

http://iberia.vassar.edu/ifla-idal/
"This Directory is provided as a means to access nearly 3,000 libraries and library departments with specialized holdings in art, architecture,

and archaeology throughout the world. Data recorded for each institution includes address, telephone and tele-facsimile numbers, hours of operation, annual closings, and listings of professional personnel. It also includes electronic mail addresses of individual librarians and direct Web links to institutional home pages." Provided by the IFLA (International Federation of Library Associations and Institutions) Section of Art Libraries.
Search Form URL: See Main Page

Artcyclopedia
http://www.artcyclopedia.com/
"... a comprehensive index of every artist represented at hundreds of museum sites, image archives, and other online resources."
Search Form URL: See Main Page

Reference

The Art and Architecture Thesaurus Browser (AAT)
http://www.getty.edu/gri/vocabularies/index.htm
"The AAT is a structured vocabulary of around 125,000 terms, scope notes, and other information for describing fine art, architecture, decorative arts, archival materials, and material culture."
Search Form URL: http://shiva.pub.getty.edu/aat_browser/

CHAPTER 11

Bibliographies and Library Catalogs

Historians of information science consider the first "search engine" to be the card catalog system developed in the early 1900s by Paul Otlet and his colleagues at the Collective Library of Learned Societies in Brussels. Otlet's system was essentially an extensively cross-indexed bibliographic "database" that made use of early 20th-century high-tech features such as standardized 3x5 cards and categorized filing drawers—revolutionary breakthroughs for the time that led to the standardized cataloging systems we use today.

It's ironic, then, that today's Internet-accessible card catalogs and bibliographies are largely invisible to search engines—all the more so, since many of these resources are excellent finding aids for online information in and of themselves.

The resources in this chapter are primarily links to large library catalogs and authoritative bibliographic databases. These types of key resources are included:

- **Archive Catalogs**, such as the ARCHON British history archives and the *Directory of Digitized Collections*, which aims to be nothing less than the "memory of the world"

- **Key Web Resource Collections**, such as the *Librarians' Index to the Internet*, which offers links to many Invisible Web databases

- **Databases from Document Delivery Services**, (companies that sell individual articles) such as *UnCover's* descriptive briefs for more than 8.8 million articles that appeared in over 18,000 multi-disciplinary journals

See the Bibliographies and Library Catalogs category on the companion Web site for additional Invisible Web resources on this topic at http://www.invisible-web.net.

Bibliographies

21 North Main B
http://www.21northmain.com/
One of the many large databases containing used books for sale via various book dealers.
Search Form URL: See Main Page
Related Resources:
Bibliofind
http://www.bibliofind.com/
abebooks.com
http://www.abebooks.com/

Archisplus (Database of the Historical Archives of the European Commission) B
http://europa.eu.int/comm/secretariat_general/sg1/archives/home-en.htm
"... contains details of the references of files and organisational structure of the following European institutions: the European Coal and Steel Community (ECSC), the European Economic Community (EEC), the European Atomic Energy Community (EAEC or Euratom), and the current European Community from their inception to the present day."
Search Form URL: http://europa.eu.int/comm/secretariat_general/archisplus/cgi/archisdb?DisplayLang=en&Domain=Recherche

Archon (Historic Manuscripts) B, U.K.
http://www.hmc.gov.uk/archon/archon.htm
"ARCHON is the principal information gateway for U.K. archivists and

users of manuscript sources for British history. It is hosted and maintained by the Historical Manuscripts Commission."
Search Form URL: See Main Page

BOPCRIS (British Official Publications Collaborative Reader Information Service) B, U.K.

http://www.bopcris.ac.uk/
"... aims to save researchers wasting valuable research time and effort finding relevant British Official Publications over the period 1688-1995 by providing a Web-based bibliographic database which enables them ..."
Search Form URL: See Main Page

British Library Public Catalogue B, U.K.

http://blpc.bl.uk
"... information about the contents of a number of the Library's major collections."
Search Form URL: See Main Page
Related Resources:
British Library Newspaper Library Catalogue
http://www.bl.uk/collections/newspaper/newscat.html
British Library Manuscript Catalogue
http://molcat.bl.uk/
National Sound Archive Catalogue
http://cadensa.bl.uk/

COPAC (Consortium of University Research Libraries) B, U.K.

http://copac.ac.uk/
"COPAC provides FREE access to the merged online catalogues of 19 of the largest university research libraries in the U.K. and Ireland."
Search Form URL: http://copac.ac.uk/copac/wzgw?db=copact

Directory of Digitized Collections B, U.K.

http://thoth.bl.uk/
"This site aims to offer a listing of major digitized heritage collections and on-going digitization programmes worldwide. It is hoped that this will provide a single focal point of information on digitized collections. This site will act as the 'Memory of the World' virtual library, offering direct access to those collections where permission to link has been granted."
Search Form URL: See Main Page

Related Resources:
Digital Library Federation Public Access Collections
http://www.hti.umich.edu/cgi/d/dlfcoll/dlfcoll-idx

Folger Shakespeare Library Online Catalog (HAMNET) B
http://www.folger.edu
"The Folger Shakespeare Library® is an independent research library.
... A major center for scholarly research, the Folger houses the world's
largest collection of Shakespeare's printed works, in addition to a
magnificent collection of other rare Renaissance books and manuscripts on all disciplines—history and politics, theology and exploration, law and the arts. The collection, astonishing in its range and
variety, consists of approximately 280,000 books and manuscripts;
27,000 paintings, drawings, engravings, and prints; and musical
instruments, costumes, and films."
Search Form URL: http://shakespeare.folger.edu/

Library of Congress Online Catalog B
http://www.loc.gov/catalog/
"The Library of Congress Online Catalog (http://catalog.loc.gov/) is a
database of approximately 12 million records representing books, serials, computer files, manuscripts, cartographic materials, music, sound
recordings, and visual materials in the Library's collections. The
Online Catalog also provides references, notes, circulation status, and
information about materials still in the acquisitions stage."
Search Form URL: http://catalog.loc.gov/
Related Resources:
Library of Congress Archival Finding Aids
http://lcweb2.loc.gov/faid/faidquery.html

Linda Hall Library Online Catalog (LEONARDO) B
http://www.lhl.lib.mo.us/
"The LEONARDO online catalog contains the monograph and serial
records for the Linda Hall Library and for the Spencer Art Reference
Library of the Nelson-Atkins Museum of Art. Records for the collection
of the Engineering Societies Library are being added to the database.
Other collections to be added in the future include serials acquired
after 1989, technical reports, government documents, maps, and engineering standards and specifications." The Linda Hall Library is
located in Kansas City, Missouri.
Search Form URL: http://www.lhl.lib.mo.us/tas/leonard.htm

Minnesota Magazine Index B
http://www.mpls.lib.mn.us
"MNMag is an index of articles on local and statewide politics, news, current events, history and the arts that appear in nine Minnesota magazines. Produced since 1991 by the staff in the History Department at the Minneapolis Public Library, MNMag now includes over 12,000 citations."
Search Form URL: http://www.mpls.lib.mn.us/dbtw-wpd/magsrc.htm

NAIL (National Archival Information Locator) B
http://www.nara.gov/nara/nail.html
"NAIL contains information about a wide variety of NARA's [National Archives and Records Administration] holdings across the country. Although NAIL contains more than 3,000 microfilm publications descriptions, 607,000 archival holdings descriptions, and 124,000 digital copies, it represents only a limited portion of NARA's vast holdings."
Search Form URL: http://www.nara.gov/nara/searchnail.html

National Archives of Canada (ArchiviaNet) B, Canada
http://www.archives.ca
"ArchiviaNet is an automated research tool that allows you to access a vast amount of information from various databases and automated systems created by the National Archives of Canada."
Search Form URL: http://www.archives.ca/exec/naweb.dll?fs&0201&e&top&0

National Geographic Society Publications Database B
http//www.nationalgeographic.com
"The NGS Publications Index includes broad subject indexing to magazines, books, films and videos, educational products, map products, interactive features, and newsletters produced by the Society."
Search Form URL: http://www.nationalgeographic.com/publications/index.html

National Library of Canada Catalogue (resAnet) B, Canada
http://www.nlc-bnc.ca
"The National Library Catalogue is the largest collection of Canadiana in the world. It contains 2 million records with the holdings of the National Library of Canada."
Search Form URL: http://www.nlc-bnc.ca/amicus/nlccat-e.htm

Related Resources:
National Library of Canada Union Catalogue
http://www.nlc-bnc.ca/unioncat/eunion.htm

New York Public Library Finding Aids B

http://digilib.nypl.org/
"Finding aids are guides to archival and manuscript collections. Each finding aid will generally include background information on the creator of the collection, a general description of the content and organization of the collection as a whole, and a container list [that] provides box-by-box breakdown of the collection's contents."
Search Form URL: http://digilib.nypl.org/dynaweb/ead/nypl/

Newberry Library Online Catalog B

http://www.newberry.org
"The Newberry Library is an independent research library concentrating in the humanities with an active educational and cultural presence in Chicago. Privately funded, but free and open to the public, it houses an extensive non-circulating collection of rare books, maps, and manuscripts."
Search Form URL: http://www.newberry.org/nl/collections/collectionshome.html

NTIS (National Technical Information Service) Electronic Catalog B

http://www.ntis.gov
"Use this page to locate and order government publications and other products issued by NTIS since 1990. Searching capability is limited to titles and topics. Most records do NOT include product summaries (Abstracts)." This database has over 450,000 records. To search the complete NTIS database (over 2,000,000 million records) visit the Gov.Research_Center (fee-based).
Search Form URL: http://www.ntis.gov/search.htm
Related Resources:
Gov.Research_Center
http://grc.ntis.gov/

Online Archive of California B

http://www.oac.cdlib.org/
"... the Online Archive of California (OAC) is a digital information resource that facilitates and provides access to materials such as

manuscripts, photographs, and works of art held in libraries, museums, archives, and other institutions across California. The OAC is available to a broad spectrum of users—students, teachers, and researchers of all levels. Through the OAC, all have access to information previously available only to scholars who traveled to collection sites."
Search Form URL: http://www.oac.cdlib.org/dynaweb/ead/
Related Resources:
Integrated Digital Archive of Los Angeles (IDA-LA)
http://www.usc.edu/isd/locations/cst/idala/isla_collections.html

Online Books Page (The) B
http://digital.library.upenn.edu/books
The Online Books Page was founded in 1993 by John Mark Ockerbloom at Carnegie Mellon University. The index of individual titles includes books and definitive collections and major serial archives that meet rigorous criteria specified on the site. More than 12,000+ listings, updated frequently.
Search Form URL: http://digital.library.upenn.edu/books/search.html
Related Resources:
Internet Public Library Online Text Collection
http://www.ipl.org/reading/books/
National Academy Press
http://www.nap.edu/

Public Records Office/National Archives Online Catalogue B, U.K.
http://www.pro.gov.uk/default.htm
"The catalogue is a list of all the records (documents) deposited at the Public Record Office (PRO), by the government departments who originally used them." Several databases and interfaces are available.
Search Form URL: http://www.pro.gov.uk/finding/default.htm

RecordSearch: National Archives of Australia B, Australia
http://www.naa.gov.au
RecordSearch is the National Archives collection database. It contains descriptions of 80,000 collections (called series) and over 2,500,000 record items as well as details of about 9,000 creators and depositors.
Search Form URL: http://www.naa.gov.au/The_Collection/recordsearch.html

Related Resources:
RAAM-Register of Australian Archives and Manuscripts
http://www.nla.gov.au/raam/

UnCover Web B
http://uncweb.carl.org
UnCover is a document delivery company. This is not a full-text database. "UnCover is a database of current article information taken from
well over 18,000 multidisciplinary journals. UnCover contains brief
descriptive information for over 8,800,000 articles [that] have
appeared since Fall 1988. UnCover offers you the opportunity to order
fax copies of the articles from this database. UnCover is easy to use,
with keyword access to article titles and summaries."
Search Form URL: See Main Page
Related Resources:
INFOTRIEVE
http://www.infotrieve.com/
British Library Current Serials File U.K.
http://www.bl.uk/serials/

Library Catalogs

Compass (British Museum Materials) U.K.
http://www.thebritishmuseum.ac.uk
"COMPASS is an online display featuring objects chosen by the cura-
tors to reflect the extraordinary range of the British Museum's
collections."
Search Form URL: http://www.thebritishmuseum.ac.uk/
compass/ index.html

Directory of National Union Catalogs (IFLA)
http://www.ifla.org
"This Directory is a complete listing of all known current national union
catalogues in the world, including monograph, serial, and general
union catalogues. In order for catalogues to be included, they must be
both national (or international) and current. Closed catalogues and
regional or local catalogues are not listed. Specific subject catalogues
are included where known, as well as those with a general subject

coverage. Catalogues are listed even where there is no public access, although contact details are always provided." Provided by IFLA, the International Federation of Library Associations and Instituions.
Search Form URL: http://www.ifla.org/VI/2/duc/index.htm

LibDex

http://www.libdex.com
Library catalogs are some of the most popular types of resources found on the Invisible Web. Although we have listed several in this chapter, we have not even scratched the surface of the thousands that are available. To find more, we recommend visiting this comprehensive directory compiled by Peter Scott.
Search Form URL: See Main Page

Librarians' Index to the Internet

http://www.lii.org
"The Librarians' Index to the Internet is a searchable, annotated subject directory of more than 7,200 Internet resources selected and evaluated by librarians for their usefulness to users of public libraries. It's meant to be used by both librarians and non-librarians as a reliable and efficient guide to described and evaluated Internet resources."
Search Form URL: See Main Page

New Zealand Digital Library (The) New Zealand

http://www.nzdl.org/cgi-bin/library
Numerous databases about a wide variety of subjects. "The New Zealand Digital Library project is a research programme at The University of Waikato whose aim is to develop the underlying technology for digital libraries and make it available publicly so that others can use it to create their own collections."
Search Form URL: See Main Page of each collection.
Related Resources:
New Zealand Digital Library Example—Women's History: Primary Source Documents
http://www.nzdl.org/fast-cgi-bin/library?a=p&p=about&c=whist
New Zealand Digital Library Example—Virtual Disaster Library
http://www.nzdl.org/fast-cgi-bin/library?a=p&p=about&c=paho
New Zealand Digital Library Example—Digital Music Library
http://nzdl2.cs.waikato.ac.nz/cgi-bin/gwmm?c=meldex&a=page&p=coltitle

Scout Report Archives (The)

http://scout.cs.wisc.edu

"Surf smarter, not longer. Let the Internet Scout Project show you the way to the best resources on the Internet—then you can choose what's best for you. ... The Scout Report Archives is a searchable and browseable database to over five years' worth of the Scout Report and subject-specific Scout Reports. It contains [over 10,000] critical annotations of carefully selected Internet sites and mailing lists."

Search Form URL: See Main Page

Smithsonian Institution Online Collections

http://www.si.edu

"Over the past few years the Smithsonian has been digitizing its catalogues and has been appending images to these records. The Online Collections site is the portal through which these collections will ultimately be accessed. You will be able to use the portal site to search for topics or collections across the museums, allowing the user to locate and browse the Smithsonian's treasures."

Search Form URL: http://160.111.100.43/digilib/main.asp

Related Resources:

Smithsonian Institution Research Information System (SIRIS)

http://www.siris.si.edu/

Smithsonian Image Database

http://web2.si.edu/cgi-bin/image_archive.pl

CHAPTER 12

Business and Investing

Until a few years ago, online access to timely, high quality business and investing information was both expensive and difficult to obtain. Proprietary services like Dialog, LexisNexis, and Dow Jones operated as virtual oligopolies for authoritative business information. The Web, of course, changed all of that, with literally thousands of business-oriented Web sites appearing virtually overnight—many offering free content.

Much of this content is visible and accessible to search engines. But by the time a search engine's crawler has discovered information on a visible Web site, it may be out of date and worthless to a searcher who may need literally up-to-the-moment information to make a business or investment decision.

Fortunately, there are exceptional Invisible Web resources that can satisfy the need for fresh, authoritative business information. In this chapter, we provide a small sample of the many excellent business and investment resources available, and also touch on economics and finance sites, job listings (including often-difficult-to-find salary data), resources for competitive intelligence research and analysis, and much more.

These key resources are included:

- **Company Information Resources**, such as the *10Kwizard*, which offers access to the full text of documents filed with the U.S. Securities and Exchange Commission, in real time

- **U.S. and World Economic Information**, including *Economic Data* (via the Government Information Sharing Project), which provides interactive access to numerous U.S. Government databases in economics, education, and demographics

- **Investment Resources and Tools**, such as *Justquotes.com*, a simple, yet remarkably powerful tool that makes it easy to access investment information about a specific company from hundreds of online resources simply by entering the company's ticker symbol

- **Industry Specific Resources**, covering a wide array of industries

- **General Business Resources**, with links to Invisible Web sites covering topics such as consumer information, financial institutions, government contracts, jobs and careers, marketing, pensions, personal finances, research and development, real estate, tariffs and trade, and trade shows

See the Business and Investing category on the companion Web site for additional Invisible Web resources on this topic at http://www.invisible-web.net.

Company Information and Research

10Kwizard.Com (Public Company Filings)

http://www.10kwizard.com

One of many interfaces to this SEC EDGAR material. "10K Wizard provides free real-time online access and full-text search of the EDGAR system, thus providing the public a real-time link to the SEC's filings. 10K Wizard's market leading, proprietary search technology gives users the ability to not only view the latest SEC filings of more than 68,000 companies, but search historical filings, from the start date of each company's existence, by keywords, phrases and names." Additional resources are available after completing a free registration process.

Search Form URL: See Main Page

Related Resources:

FreeEDGAR

http://www.freeedgar.com
Securites and Exchange Commission Edgar
http://www.sec.gov/edgarhp.htm

Australian Business Register Australia

http://abr.business.gov.au/
"The Australian Business Register (ABR) Online is a publicly available, online database that contains some of the information that is provided by businesses when they register for an Australian Business Number (ABN)."
Search Form URL: See Main Page

Better Business Bureau Company Reports

http://www.bbb.com
A centralized database for Better Bureau Company Reports does not exist on the Web. However, this page provides links to the many offices in the U.S. and Canada that do make reports available online.
Search Form URL: http://www.bbb.org/reports/bizreports.asp

Business Credit USA

http://www.businesscreditusa.com/
Basic directory and credit information for 12 million U.S. companies. Additional information available for a fee.
Search Form URL: See Main Page
Related Resources:
Lycos Company Online
http://www.companiesonline.com/

CompanySleuth

http://www.companysleuth.com
"... information specialist providing free, legal, inside information on publicly traded companies. Company Sleuth scours the Internet for hard-to-find business information on your investments, competitors, partners, and clients."
Search Form URL: See Main Page

Disqualified Directors Register U.K.

http://www.companies-house.gov.uk
"The information available here is an extract from the Register of Companies and Register of Disqualified Directors, which are updated regularly."

Search Form URL: http://ws3.companieshouse.gov.uk/free/
Related Resources:
Basic Company Name and Address Index (Limited Free Data) U.K.
http://ws1.companieshouse.gov.uk/free/

dot com directory

http://www.dotcomdirectory.com
Utilizes the Network Solutions Domain Name Registration Database
to provide basic company information. This should be used in conjunction with other directory tools.
Search Form URL: http://www.dotcomdirectory.com/nsi/
advanced.htm

Ecomp Executive Compensation Database

http://www.ecomponline.com
Compensation data for executives at U.S. public companies.
Search Form URL: See Main Page

European High-Tech Industry Database

http://www.tornado-insider.com/radar/
"... research startups, investors, and advisors to high-tech Europe. You
can search through press releases of these companies and read their
profiles in the Radar database."
Search Form URL: http://www.tornado-insider.com/radar/
comp AdvSearchForm.asp

Federally Incorporated Companies Canada

http://strategis.ic.gc.ca
This database produced by the Canadian Government allows searching by corporation name, location, status, and more. It also allows
results sets to be sorted by corporate name or corporate number.
Search Form URL: http://strategis.ic.gc.ca/cgi-bin/sc_mrksv/
corpdir/dataOnline/corpns_se
Related Resources:
(Nova Scotia) Registry of Joint Stock Companies Database Search
http://www.gov.ns.ca/snsmr/rjsc/search.stm

Fortune 500

http://www.fortune.com
The well-known business list identifies the largest U.S. publicly traded companies.
Search Form URL: http://www.fortune.com/fortune/fortune500/
Related Resources:
Forbes Private 500 (Largest U.S. Privately Held Companies)
http://www.forbes.com/private500/
Forbes International 800
http://www.forbes.com/international800/
Inc. 500 Database (1982-2000)
http://www.inc.com/500/search/1,3762,,00.html

Herringtown

http://www.redherring.com
The Red Herring, a respected publication providing coverage of the information technology business, provides this database of startup companies. Content is provided by the companies themselves.
Search Form URL: http://www.redherring.com/herringtown/home/home.jsp
Related Resources:
The Industry Standard "Net Deals" Database
http://www.thestandard.com/deals

Kompass

http://www.kompass.com
"Every company worldwide [that] participates in business-to-business commerce may be listed in the Kompass Database." The free online version has limited data. Additional data available on the Web by subscription.
Search Form URL: See Main Page

Price Waterhouse Coopers Money Tree Survey

http://www0.mercurycenter.com/svtech/
"A searchable database of U.S. firms that received venture capital financing. This version is made available via the San Jose Mercury News."
Search Form URL: http://www.mercurycenter.com/svtech/companies/moneytree/
Related Resources:
Price Waterhouse Coopers Money Tree Survey

http://www.pwcmoneytree.com/
Venture Capital Firm Database
http://www.vfinance.com/home.asp?Toolpage=vencaentire.asp
Venture Capital Deal Monitor
http://www.vfinance.com/home.asp?ToolPage=vcim_search.asp

Red Herring Company and Person Search

http://www.redherring.com
Locate brief company overviews and executive biographies. Red
Herring covers the technology industry. The search interface is located
on the far-right of the page.
Search Form URL: http://www.redherring.com/companies/

SEDAR (Public Company Filings) Canada

http://www.sedar.com
"SEDAR is the System for Electronic Document Analysis and Retrieval,
the electronic filing system for the disclosure documents of public
companies and mutual funds across Canada."
Search Form URL: http://www.sedar.com/search/search_form_
pc.htm
Related Resources:
British Columbia Securities Commission Database
http://www.bcsc.bc.ca/bcscdb/default.asp

Silicon Valley Companies Database

http://www0.mercurycenter.com/svtech/
"A database of the 150 largest publicly traded Silicon Valley companies
for financial and company background."
Search Form URL: http://www.mercurycenter.com/svtech/
companies/db/

Thomas Register of American Manufacturers

http://www.thomasregister.com/
A reference room classic! Search 158,000 companies, 63,669 product &
service classification headings, and 135,415 brand names located in
both the U.S. and Canada. A free registration process is needed to
access data.
Search Form URL: See Main Page
Related Resources:
Thomas Register of European Manufacturers
http://www.tipcoeurope.com/

American Export Register
http://www.aernet.com/
Thomas Food Industry Register (U.S. and Canada)
http://www.tfir.com/

World Brands Database (Advertising Age)
http://adage.com/international/world_brands/index.html
"Search the database of 400 advertisers, and the agencies and 22 agency networks that handle the accounts."
Search Form URL: See Main Page

Consumer Resources

Consumer Product Safety Commission Product Recalls
http://www.cpsc.gov/
Search for recalls ordered by the CPSC since 1977.
Search Form URL: http://www.cpsc.gov/cgi-bin/recalldb/prod.asp
Related Resources:
Search for CPSC Recalls (by company) since 1977
http://www.cpsc.gov/cgi-bin/recalldb/firm.asp
(Australia) Product Recalls Australia
http://www.recalls.gov.au/

Strong Numbers
http://www.strongnumbers
"... calculate values for a wide variety of items based on prices from over 5 million online auctions each week."
Search Form URL: See Main Page

Economics – United States

Beige Book Archive
http://minneapolisfed.org
"The Beige Book is released two weeks prior to each FOMC meeting eight times per year. Each Federal Reserve bank gathers anecdotal

information on current economic conditions in its district through
reports from bank and branch directors and interviews with key busi-
nessmen, economists, market experts, and other sources."
Search Form URL: http://minneapolisfed.org/bb/

Business Loan Data (Small Business Administation)
http://www.sba.gov
Statistics about recently approved loans made to small businessess in
the U.S. Updated monthly.
Search Form URL: http://www.sba.gov/loans/business/

Economic Data (via Geospatial and
Statistical Data Center)
http://fisher.lib.Virginia.EDU/active_data/index.html
The Geospatial and Statistical Data Center at the University of Virginia
provides access to several economic resources. For a complete list see
the Center's homepage. Registration is required. A few examples
follow.
Search Form URL: See Main Page
Related Resources:
County Business Patterns
http://fisher.lib.virginia.edu/cbp/
Regional Economic Forecasts
http://fisher.lib.virginia.edu/projection/
State Personal Income (1969-1998)
http://fisher.lib.virginia.edu/spi/

Economic Data (via Government Information
Sharing Project)
http://govinfo.kerr.orst.edu/
The Government Information Sharing Project located at Oregon St.
University provides interactive access to numerous U.S. Government
databases in economics, education, and demographics. For a com-
plete list see the homepage of the GISP. A few examples follow.
Search Form URL: See Main Page
Related Resources:
Regional Economic Information System (1969-1997)
http://govinfo.kerr.orst.edu/reis-stateis.html
U.S. Imports/Exports History: 1994-1998
http://govinfo.kerr.orst.edu/impexp.html

Federal Reserve in Print B

http://www.frbsf.org

"An index to Federal Reserve research."

Search Form URL: http://www.frbsf.org/system/fedinprint/

Related Resources:

Federal Reserve Publications Catalog

http://app.ny.frb.org/cfpicnic/frame1.cfm

Free Lunch

http://www.economy.com

"Free access to over 1,000,000 economic and financial data series."

Free registration provides extra charting and graphing options.

Search Form URL: http://www.economy.com/freelunch/default.asp

Related Resources:

Economagic

http://www.economagic.com

National Agriculture Statistics Service Published Estimates Database United States Department of Agriculture (USDA)

http://www.usda.gov/nass/

"... U.S., state, and county level agricultural statistics for many commodities and data series."

Search Form URL: http://www.nass.usda.gov:81/ipedb/

Related Resources:

Census of Agriculture: 1987, 1992, 1997

http://govinfo.kerr.orst.edu/ag-stateis.html

USDA Economics and Statistics System

http://usda.mannlib.cornell.edu/reports/nassr/livestock/

php-bb/1998/hogs_and_pigs_03.27.98_REVISED_04.02.98

National Income and Product Accounts (NIPA) Tables

http://www.bea.doc.gov

Interactive access to these frequently used tables containing U.S. economic data.

Search Form URL: http://www.bea.doc.gov/bea/dn/nipaweb/

Related Resources:

Gross State Product Data

http://www.bea.doc.gov/bea/regional/gsp/

National Marine Fisheries Service Fishing Statistics

http://www.st.nmfs.gov/st1/commercial/

"The Fisheries Statistics & Economics Division of the National Marine Fisheries Service (NMFS) has automated data summary programs that anyone can use to rapidly and easily summarize U.S. commercial fisheries landings."
Search Form URL: See Main Page
Related Resources:
Marine Recrational Fisheries Statistics Survey Database
http://www.st.nmfs.gov/st1/recreational/database/index.html

Payment Systems Research Database B

http://www.chicagofed.org/paymentsystems/index.cfm
"The PSRC (Payment Systems Resource Center) includes a searchable database of payment systems research, links to related Web sites, and other information."
Search Form URL: http://www.chicagofed.org/payment
systems/search1.cfm

RECON (U.S. Regional Economic Data)

http://www.fdic.gov
From the FDIC (Federal Deposit Insurance Corporation). "Regional Economic Conditions (RECON) was originally designed to assist the FDIC in the examination process by providing economic information at the state, MSA (Metropolitan Statistical Area), and county levels. It is helpful in the analysis of risks facing financial institutions."
Search Form URL: http://www2.fdic.gov/recon/

U.S. Regional Economic Data

http://www.dismalscientist.com
"... view data on all 50 states and Washington D.C.; rank the different states using nearly 130 different criteria, in either ascending or descending order, for as few as ten or as many as 50 states and Washington D.C. ... You can also view data on nearly and 257 different metro areas; rank the different metro areas using nearly 60 different criteria, in either ascending or descending order, for as few as ten or as many as 257 different metro areas; or find a particular metro area by entering in a ZIP Code."
Search Form URL: http://www.dismal.com/regions/regions.stm

Economics – World

Asian Development Bank Developing Member Country Data
http://www.adb.org
Basic economic and trade statistics can be obtained in either Adobe Acrobat or Microsoft Excel formats.
Search Form URL: http://www.adb.org/Statistics/country.asp
Related Resources:
Asian Development Bank Regional Data
http://www.adb.org/Statistics/regdata.asp

Econbase B
http://www.elsevier.nl
Econbase provides access to abstracts from 64 scholarly economics journals (20,000 abstracts) published by Elsevier North-Holland Pergamon. This service allows users to search and read the full abstracts of all journals and access limited full-text content from selected publications.
Search Form URL: http://www.elsevier.nl/homepage/sae/econbase/menu.sht

Foreign Labor Statistics
http://www.bls.gov/flshome.htm
Basic labor statistics for many nations are made accessible by the U.S. Bureau of Labor Statistics.
Search Form URL: http://146.142.4.24/cgi-bin/surveymost?in
Related Resources:
Foreign Labor Statistics Java Interface
http://146.142.4.24/labjava/outside.jsp?survey=in

Inflation Calculator Canada
http://www.bankofcanada.ca/
"The Inflation Calculator uses monthly consumer price index (CPI) data from 1914 to the present to show changes in the cost of a fixed 'basket' of consumer purchases."
Search Form URL: http://www.bankofcanada.ca/en/inflation_calc.htm
Related Resources:

(U.S.) Consumer Price Index Calculator 1913- U.S.
http://woodrow.mpls.frb.fed.us/economy/calc/cpihome.html
How Much Is That?
http://www.eh.net/hmit/
Additional Inflation Calculators
http://www.dismalscientist.com/toolbox/calc_inflation.stm

Inter-American Development Bank Economic and Social Database

http://www.iadb.org
"The Economic and Social Data Base (ESDB) is the Inter-American
Development Bank's on-line data base for economic and social statis-
tics on its member countries." Countries are located in Latin America
and the Caribbean.
Search Form URL: http://database.iadb.org/esdbweb/scripts/
esdbweb.exe
Related Resources:
INTAL (Institute for the Integration of Latin America and the
Caribbean) External Trade Database

Laborsta (Labor Statistics)

http://www.ilo.org
"This dynamic application on Internet allows you to access data from
the International Labour Organization Bureau of Statistics. The data
available here are an extract of LABORSTA, the Bureau's principal
database. It consists mainly of annual time-series, which serve to publish the ILO Yearbook of Labour Statistics. The application presents
data covering 7 subjects in 23 tables."
Search Form URL: http://laborsta.ilo.org

National Labour Market Information System Canada

http://lmi-imt.hrdc-drhc.gc.ca
The Labour Market Information service provides general and detailed
information on local labour markets across Canada. This information
can help people to search for work, and to make general employment,
training, and career decisions. Produced by Human Resources
Canada.
Search Form URL: http://lmi-imt.hrdc-drhc.gc.ca/owa_lmi/owa/
sp_show_lmi?l=e&i=1
Related Resources:

Industry Profiles-Economic Analysis of Human Resources in Canadian Industries
http://www.hrdc-drhc.gc.ca/hrib/hrp-prh/ssd-des/english/industryprofiles/prsearch.shtml

Penn World Tables
http://datacentre.chass.utoronto.ca:5680/pwt/
Detailed economic statistics. The Penn World Tables currently comprise data for 152 countries and 29 subjects.
Search Form URL: See Main Page

Financial Institutions

Federal Reserve National Information Center Databases
http://www.ffiec.gov/nic/
Several resources providing detailed statistical data of U.S. banks.
Search Form URL: See Main Page
Related Resources:
Additional Financial Institution Related Databases
http://www.ffiec.gov/info_services.htm

Financial Institution and Branch Office Data, Federal Deposit Insurance Corporation (FDIC)
http://www.fdic.gov
"Searchable databases allow users to find institutions and their branches in order to determine their status as insured depository institutions, their financial condition and their condition relative to other institutions. The databases may also contain other financial and non-financial information about individual financial institutions as well as certain aggregate financial statistics for comparative use."
Search Form URL: http://www.fdic.gov/bank/individual/ index.html
Related Resources:
Is My Bank Insured?
http://www2.fdic.gov/structur/search/findoneinst.cfm
FDIC Summary of Deposit Data (Several Resources)
http://www2.fdic.gov/sod/

Find a Credit Union
http://www.ncua.gov
From the National Credit Union Administration.
Search Form URL: http://www.ncua.gov/data/CuDataExpanded.html
Related Resources:
Custom Credit Union Reports (NCUA)
http://www.ncua.gov/data/custmqry.html
Credit Union Search U.K.
http://www.abcul.org/members.cfm

Monetary Financial Institions in the European Union
http://www.ecb.int/mfi/mfi01.htm
"... Monetary Financial Institutions (MFIs) in the European Union and institutions subject to the Eurosystem's minimum reserve system."
The European Central Bank provides access to this data.
Search Form URL: https://mfi-assets.ecb.int/query_MFI.htm
Related Resources:
Assets Eligible for the Eurosystem's Monetary Policy
https://mfi-assets.ecb.int/query_EA.htm

General Business Resources

American Community Network
http://www.acn.net/
This resource offers several searchable databases with information on most American cities and towns. The site is designed for those in the site-selection and economic development professions. Free registration is required.
Search Form URL: See Main Page

Fire Loss Profiles (National Fire Incident Reporting System)
http://www.usfa.fema.gov/nfdc/statistics.htm
"... generate national and state fire loss reports based on NFIRS data."
Search Form URL: http://www.usfa.fema.gov/nfirs/
Related Resources:
Firefighter Fatality Database
http://www.usfa.fema.gov/nfdc/tally_report.cfm

List of Defaulted Borrowers (Health Education Loan Program)

http://defaulteddocs.dhhs.gov/

"The Health Resources and Services Administration (HRSA) has published this list of Health Education Assistance Loan (HEAL) borrowers who are in default, as required by section 709(c)(1) of the Public Health Service Act (the Act)."

Search Form URL: See Main Page

World Chambers of Commerce Directory

http://www.worldchambers.com

"This electronic directory contains information on over 10,000 chambers around the world, with hyperlinks to their Web sites."

Search Form URL: http://www.worldchambers.com/CF/index.htm

Related Resources:

U.S. Chamber of Commerce Directory

http://www.uschamber.com/Chambers/Chamber+Directory/default.htm

Government Contracts

CBD Net (*Commerce Business Daily*)

http://cbdnet.access.gpo.gov/index.html

"The Commerce Business Daily (CBD) lists notices of proposed government procurement actions, contract awards, sales of government property, and other procurement information. A new edition of the CBD is issued every business day. Each edition contains approximately 500-1,000 notices. Each notice appears in the CBD only once. The CBD databases online via GPO Access contain notices from December 2, 1996 forward."

Search Form URL: http://cbdnet.access.gpo.gov/search1.html

Related Resources:

PRO-NET (SBA Procurement Info)

https://pro-net.sba.gov/pro-net/search.html

Contracts Canada Canada

http://csi.contractscanada.gc.ca/csi/prod/xx/home.cfm

"This site contains information on contracts awarded by PWGSC on behalf of other federal government departments and agencies since April 1, 1997."

Search Form URL: http://csi.contractscanada.gc.ca/csi/prod/en/applctrl.cfm?cmd=start

U.S. Department of Defense Central Contractor Register

http://www.ccr2000.com

A database of vendors who are registered to do business with the United States Department of Defense.

Search Form URL: https://www.ccr.dlsc.dla.mil/ccrinq/scripts/oleisapi2.DLL/CCRinq.Isapidb.Normal?TARGET=SEARCH.TXT

Related Resources:

U.S. Department of Defense Business Opportunities
http://www.dodbusopps.com/

Industry-Specific Resources

A.M. Best Insurance Ratings

http://www.ambest.com

"Find A.M. Best financial strength rating, from A++ to F, for over 6,000 life/health, property/casualty, and international insurance companies." Registration is required. Basic information is free.
Comprehensive reports are available for a fee.

Search Form URL: http://www3.ambest.com/ratings/info.asp

AAAAgency Search (Advertising)

http://www.aaaagencysearch.com/

Web site of the American Association of Advertising Agencies. "Clients and consultants conducting agency searches will find in-depth profiles of the best ad agencies in the world, and can conduct user-friendly, comprehensive searches based on multiple criteria. All agencies listed are AAAA members."

Search Form URL: See Main Page

Related Resources:

Agency ComPile
http://www.agencycompile.com/

Automated Reporting Management Information System (ARMIS) (FCC)

http://www.fcc.gov/ccb/armis/

"... portal to a database containing financial and operational data of the nation's largest local exchange carriers that file this data in compliance with Part 43 of the Commission's Rules."

Search Form URL: http://www.fcc.gov/ccb/armis/db/

Biotech Alliance Database

http://www.recap.com

"ReCap's Biotech Alliance Database contains high-level summaries of more than 7,900 alliances in the life sciences [that] have been formed since 1978."

Search Form URL: http://www.recap.com/mainweb.nsf/HTML/alliance+frame?OpenDocument

Related Resources:

Biotech Clinical Trials Database

http://www.recap.com/mainweb.nsf/HTML/clinical+frame?OpenDocument

Biotech Agreement Database

http://www.recap.com/mainweb.nsf/employ+frame

Bluebook.Com (The)

http://www.thebluebook.com

"The Blue Book of Building and Construction is the Industry's leading source of regional, categorized construction information. The Blue Book features over 800,000 company listings with over 46,000 display ads and company profiles."

Search Form URL: See Main Page

eCirc

http://www.accessabc.com/

From the Audit Bureau Circulation. A "quick, concise online source for the latest top-line circulation information. eCirc lets you sort and search summarized circulation data by publisher title, U.S. SRDS number, or Canadian CARD classifications."

Search Form URL: http://abcas1.accessabc.com/ecirc/

Related Resources:

(U.K.) Audit Bureau of Circulations

http://www.abc.org.uk/

European Case Clearing House B
http://www.ecch.cranfield.ac.uk
"Established nearly 25 years, the European Case Clearing House (ECCH) is a unique source of case study materials for management education and training. ECCH is a nonprofit organisation and a registered charity. Over 16,000 titles are available for purchase."
Search Form URL: See Main Page
Related Resources:
Harvard Business School Cases and Teaching Material
http://www.hbsp.harvard.edu/products/cases/collections.html

Hotel and Properties Database (EventSource)
http://www.eventsource.com
"Comprehensive information about worldwide meeting sites including detailed descriptions, photos, and in-depth reviews …"
Search Form URL: http://www.eventsource.com/Main/Resource CenterMain.jsp?COMMAND=HOTELPROPERTY
Related Resources:
Venue Center (Trade Show Central)
http://ww0.tscentral.com/VenueCenter/

Institute for Operations Research and the Management Sciences (INFORMS) Annual Comprehensive Index Bibliographic Database B
http://www.informs.org
"… approximately 33,198 bibliographic entries. The entries for the period 1976 to 1987 come from INFORMS journals, while for the period 1988 to 1999 they come from a total of approximately 614 different INFORMS as well as non-INFORMS journals."
Search Form URL: http://www.informs.org/Biblio/ACI.html
Related Resources:
INFORMS Meeting Database
http://www.informs.org/Biblio/Meetings.html

Insurance Company Complaint Finder
http://www.insure.com
"… view insurance complaint rankings that are compiled by state insurance departments. (Not all states collect complaint statistics, so you may not see your own state here.)"
Search Form URL: http://www.insure.com/complaints/

Profile (Architectural Firms Database)

http://www.cmdg.com/profile/index.html

"ProFile on the Web is a search engine for locating architecture firms and businesses in the United States."

Search Form URL: http://www.cmdg.com/profile/search.html

Railroads and States

http://www.aar.org

Railroads and States highlights the freight railroad industry's contributions to the commerce, employment, and finances of the nation by providing state-by-state statistics of the U.S. freight railroad industry.

Search Form URL: http://www.aar.org/rrstates1998.nsf

Recent Advances in Manufacturing B

http://www.eevl.ac.uk/ram/aboutram.html

"Recent Advances in Manufacturing (RAM) is a database of bibliographic information for manufacturing and related areas. It covers items in well over 500 niche and mainstream journals and magazines, and also details of books, videos, and conference proceedings."

Search Form URL: http://www.eevl.ac.uk/ram/index.html

Registered Identification Number Database

http://www.ftc.gov/bcp/rn/

"A registered identification number or RN is a number issued by the Federal Trade Commission, upon request, to a business residing in the U.S. that is engaged in the manufacture, importing, distribution, or sale of textile, wool, or fur products. Such businesses are not required to have RNs. They may, however, use the RN in place of a name on the label or tag that is required to be affixed to these products."

Search Form URL: https://rn.ftc.gov/TextileRN/wrnquery$.startup

Related Resources:

CA Number Database Canada

http://strategis.ic.gc.ca/SSG/cp01120e.html

Standard Industrial Classification Search

http://www.osha.gov

"This page allows the user to search the 1987 version SIC manual by keyword, to access descriptive information for a specified 4-digit SIC."

Search Form URL: http://www.osha.gov/oshstats/sicser.html

Related Resources:

1997 NAICS (North American Industry Classification System) and 1987
SIC Correspondence Tables
http://www.census.gov/epcd/www/naicstab.htm

TV Database (Federal Communications Commission)

http://www.fcc.gov/
Locate basic directory and technical data for U.S. licensed television
stations.
Search Form URL: http://www.fcc.gov/mmb/vsd/tvq.html
Related Resources:
AM Radio Database
http://www.fcc.gov/mmb/asd/amq.html
FM Radio Database
http://www.fcc.gov/mmb/asd/fmq.html
FCC General Menu Reports (GenMen)
http://gullfoss2.fcc.gov/cgi-bin/ws.exe/genmen/index.hts

Investment Resources

Canadian Stock Charts Canada

http://www.globeinvestor.com
Obtain stock charts for Canadian and U.S. exchanges. Chart data
available for a five-year period.
Search Form URL: http://www.globeinvestor.com/static/hubs/
charts.html

Dow Jones Average Search

http://averages.dowjones.com
Obtain the High, Low, and Closing Averages for the Dow Jones
Industrial, Transportation, and Utility Indices for any date beginning
May 26, 1896.
Search Form URL: http://averages.dowjones.com/screen1.htm
Related Resources:
Other Dow Jones Averages Databases
http://208.198.167.32/

Financial Times Company Financials Database

http://www.globalarchive.ft.com

Obtain basic public company data for companies from numerous countries.
Search Form URL: http://www.globalarchive.ft.com/cb/cb_search.htm
Related Resources:
Wright Investor Services Company Profiles
http://profiles.wisi.com/profiles/Comsrch.htm
hemscott.NET U.K.
http://www.hemscott.net/

Historical Stock Quotes

http://www.bigcharts.com
One of many sites on the Web providing access to historical stock data. U.S. stocks only. In some cases this database provides access to material back to 1985.
Search Form URL: http://www.bigcharts.com/historical
Related Resources:
Financial Web Historical Quotes (10-12 years of Data)
http://www.stocktools.com/mkthistory.asp

Hoover's StockScreener

http://www.stockscreener.com
This tool allows you to identify U.S. public companies using various financial criteria.
Search Form URL: See Main Page
Related Resources:
Quicken Company Comparison Tool
http://quicken.excite.com/investments/comparison/
Morningstar Fund Selector (Mutual Funds)
http://screen.morningstar.com/FundSelector.html

InsiderScores.Com

http://www.insiderscores.com
"... tracks the trading skill and market timing of over 150,000 individual corporate insiders throughout the past 14 years. Users are given access to the very latest insider trades filed with the Securities and Exchange Commission in over 10,000 public companies. Users can view the complete personal transaction histories of individual executives and ranking/performance results dating back to 1986."
Search Form URL: See Main Page

IPO Super Search

http://www.edgar-express.com

Search for information of recent Initial Public Offerings using over 20 search criteria.

Search Form URL: http://www.edgar-online.com/ipoexpress/supersearch.asp

Related Resources:

IPO Underwriter Database

http://www.ipo.com/ipoinfo/unddir.asp

JustQuotes.Com

http://www.justquotes.com

A real timesaver for those doing public company research! This tool permits you to preconfigure a company name or ticker symbol into a database that provides one-click access to a massive list of research resources.

Search Form URL: See Main Page

Related Resources:

Investorama

http://www.investorama.com

NASDAQ Monthly Market Activity

http://www.nasdaqtrader.com

"View a monthly activity report for the Nasdaq Stock Market® or for an individual Nasdaq® market participant by entering an MPID. Information is available from January 1997."

Search Form URL:

http://www.nasdaqtrader.com/asp/tdMarkSpec.asp

Related Resources:

NASDAQ Monthly Share Volume Reports

http://www.nasdaqtrader.com/static/tdhome.stm

NASDAQ Monthly Short Interest Report

http://www.nasdaqtrader.com/asp/short_interest.asp

NASDAQ Day One (IPO) Report

http://www.nasdaqtrader.com/static/DayOneHome.stm

National Association of Securities Dealers Public Disclosure Database

http://www.nasdr.com/2000.htm

"The NASD Regulation℠ Public Disclosure Program is intended to help investors in their selection of an individual broker or securities firm. More specifically, the Public Disclosure Program provides an

effective mechanism for investors to obtain information about NASD member firms and their associated persons."
Search Form URL: http://pdpi.nasdr.com/pdpi/disclaimer_frame.htm

Nelson's World's Best Money Managers Rankings
http://www.nelnet.com
"Every quarter, The Nelson Investment Manager Database collects performance data from over 1,500 investment managers on over 4,500 portfolios. The World's Best Money Managers is a published service [that] screens, categorizes and ranks this performance data in a series of 200 ranking reports." Free registration is required.
Search Form URL: http://www.nelnet.com/wbmm/intro.htm

Stock Market Valuation Calculator
http://www.dismalscientist.com
Calculate the "fair value" of stocks by using this tool.
Search Form URL: http://www.dismalscientist.com/cgi/stocks.asp

Tokyo Stock Exchange Listed Company Directory
http://www.tse.or.jp/english/
Search for members using several criteria including industrial classification, first letter, or company name.
Search Form URL: http://www.tse.or.jp/ec/listed/eindex.html
Related Resources:
London Stock Exchange Listed Company Company Directory
http://www.londonstockexchange.com/companies/default.asp
Toronto Stock Exchange Listed Company Directory
http://www.tse.com/listed/comp_set.html

Jobs and Career Information

America's Job Bank
http://www.ajb.org/
"America's Job Bank is the biggest and busiest job market in cyberspace. Job seekers can post their resume where thousands of employers search every day, search for job openings automatically, and find their dream job fast. Employers can post job listings in the nation's largest online labor exchange, create customized job orders, and search resumes automatically to find the right people fast."

Search Form URL: See Main Page
Related Resources:
Employment Service Vacancies Search U.K.
http://www.employmentservice.gov.uk/vacancies/Search.htm
Job Bank Canada
http://jb-ge.hrdc-drhc.gc.ca/owa_job/owa/provRes?cLang=E

Flipdog

http://www.flipdog.com
The resources listed here are representative of the thousands of job
search sites found on the Internet. Most of the information in these
databases resides on the Invisible Web. Many of these tools offer
added benefits after registration.
Search Form URL: http://www.flipdog.com/js/loc.html
Related Resources:
Monster.Com
http://jobsearch.monster.com/
Careerbuilder.Com
http://www.careerbuilder.com/mjs/megasearch.html
Workopolis.Com Canada
http://jobs.workopolis.com/jobshome/db/work.search_cri

Immigration/Wage Salary Trends

http://www.erieri.com
"Review projected Occupational Employment Statistics compensation
based on 1998-2000" U.S. and Canadian data.
Search Form URL: http://www.erieri.com/doltrends/
Related Resources:
All Earners Beginning Expected Salary (U.S. Only)
http://www.salariesreview.com/surveys/freedata.cfm

International Salary Calculator

http://www.homefair.com
Compare the cost of living in cities throughout the world.
Search Form URL: http://www2.homefair.com/calc/intsalcalc. html?
NETSCAPE_LIVEWIRE.src=homefair

O*Net

http://www.onetcenter.org/
"The O*NET database includes information on skills, abilities, knowl-
edges, work activities, and interests associated with occupations. This

information can be used to facilitate career exploration, vocational counseling, and a variety of human resources functions, such as developing job orders and position descriptions and aligning training with current workplace needs."
Search Form URL: http://online.onetcenter.org/

Salary.Com Salary Wizard

http://www.salary.com
"The Salary Wizard accesses Salary.com's proprietary compensation database, which contains salary information on thousands of job titles. The Salary Wizard calculates salaries based on job title and geographic location."
Search Form URL: http://swz.salary.com/salarywizard/layoutscripts/swzl_newsearch.asp
Related Resources:
Dept. of Labor Wage Query System (National Compensation Survey)
http://146.142.4.24/cgi-bin/dsrv?nc
Dept. of Labor Wage Query System (National Compensation Survey) Java Interface
http://146.142.4.24/labjava/outside.jsp?survey=nc

Lookup Services

192.Com U.K.

http://www.192.com
A treasure chest of United Kingdom directory information. "192.com provides its users with free, fast access to the largest database of telephone and address information on the Internet. The content is continually updated and is enhanced with extensive cross-referencing." All this, makes 192.COM the focal point for information on the Internet. Free registration is required for limited free data.
Search Form URL: See Main Page

Anywho.Com (Telephone Directory)

http://www.anywho.com
One of many phone directory databases on the Internet. Anywho.com provides both residential and business listings. Listed here are just a few of the databases available.

Search Form URL: See Main Page
Related Resources:
Canada Yellow Pages Canada
http://www.Canadayellowpages.com/search/main.cgi?lang=
BT PhoneNet UK U.K.
http://www.bt.com/phonenetuk/
Online Telephone Book Directory
http://www.teldir.com/eng/

Reverse Telephone Directory

http://www.anywho.com
Search for telephone directory information by phone number.
Search Form URL: http://www.anywho.com/telq.html
Related Resources:
Reverse Telephone and Address Lookup
http://in-115.infospace.com/_1_43343463__info/reverse.htm
Reverse Telephone & Address Lookup Canada
http://www.infospace.com/info/reverse_ca.htm

Marketing Resources

New York Green Book

http://www.greenbook.org
The New York Chapter of the American Marketing Association provides free access to this searchable directory. It includes "the full range
of marketing research companies and services worldwide. It can help
you select the best research services for your needs."
Search Form URL: http://www.greenbook.org/greenbook/ search.cfm
Related Resources:
Focus Group Directory
http://www.greenbook.org/focus/focussearch.cfm
Quirk's Researcher SourceBook
http://www.quirks.com/source/index.htm
Selectline (Market Research Firm Database) U.K.
http://www.bmra.org.uk/selectline/index.html

ZIP Code Business Patterns (U.S. Census)

http://tier2.census.gov/zbp/index.html?

"ZIP Code Business Patterns provides data on total number of establishments and number of establishments by employment-size classes by detailed industry."
Search Form URL: See Main Page

Pension Resources

Employee Benefits INFOSOURCE B
http://www.ifebp.org
"... find information on U.S., Canadian, and international employee benefits and compensation topics. This comprehensive resource of industry-related information contains more than 60,000 summaries of more than 350 English-language journal and newsletter articles, research reports, and books." Registration is required.
Search Form URL: http://www.ifebp.org/infosource/default.asp

freeErisa.com
http://www.freerisa.com
Free registration is necessary to access data. "Welcome to freeERISA.com, your primary source for the latest available pension and benefit information for U.S. employers. Using freeERISA.com, you can locate, view, and download facsimiles of employers' most recent form 5500, as filed with the United States Department of Labor." Data about Public Pension Funds (state, county, and municipal government plans) is also available.
Search Form URL: See Main Page
Related Resources:
Employee Identification Number Search (EIN)
http://www.freeerisa.com/extras/SearchEIN.asp

Pension Benefit Guaranty Corporation Pension (PBGC) Search
http://www.pbgc.gov/
"The Pension Search Directory helps PBGC find people who are owed pensions they earned from private defined benefit pension plans that have been closed. These are traditional pensions that promise a specified monthly benefit at retirement."
Search Form URL: http://search.pbgc.gov/

Personal Finances

401K Calculator

http://www.dismalscientist.com

Calculate your savings with a 401K investment.

Search Form URL: http://www.dismalscientist.com/cgi/401K.asp

Related Resources:

Installment Loan Calculator

http://www.dismalscientist.com/toolbox/loan_calc.stm

RRSP Calculator Canada

http://www.quicken.ca/eng/taxes/calculators/rrsp/

ISA Growth Calculator U.K.

http://www.FTyourmoney.com/guides/isa/isas_1.jsp

College Student Consumables Cost of Living Calculator from ERI

http://www.erieri.com

"Information accessed illustrates a student's COL for consumables in any of over 6,700 U.S., Canadian, and international locations."

Search Form URL: http://www.erieri.com/cgi-bin/cdat.cgi

RateNet

http://www.rate.net

"... monitors and ranks interest rates and financial performance for over 11,000 financial institutions nationwide."

Search Form URL: See Main Page

Related Resources:

Bankrate.Com

http://www.bankrate.com

Philanthropy and Non-Profit Resources

Foundation Finder

http://fdcenter.org

"Use the Foundation Finder to search by name for basic information about foundations within the universe of more than 59,000 private and community foundations in the U.S."
Search Form URL: http://lnp.fdncenter.org/finder.html

Guidestar.Org
http://www.guidestar.org
Information on more than 640,000 nonprofit organizations in the U.S. GuideStar obtains information from a variety of sources, including the IRS Business Master File, digitization of Forms 990 data, and from individual organizations.
Search Form URL: http://www.guidestar.org/search/
Related Resources:
GrantSmart
http://www.grantsmart.org
Internal Revenue Service Database of Tax Exempt Organizations
http://www.irs.ustreas.gov/prod/bus_info/eo/eosearch.html
National Center for Charitable Statistics Form 990 Search
http://nccs.urban.org/990/

Heritage Assets Exemption Database U.K.
http://www.inlandrevenue.gov.uk/home.htm
"... database of tax-exempt heritage assets. The database gives details of assets exempted from capital taxes and how the public can see them."
Search Form URL: http://www.cto.eds.co.uk/

Idealist
http://www.idealist.org/
A searchable database of 20,000 nonprofit organizations in 150 countries.
Search Form URL: http://www.idealist.org/is/org_search.html

Philanthropic Studies Index B
http://www.ulib.iupui.edu/
"The Philanthropic Studies Index (PSI) is a reference tool to literature on voluntarism, nonprofit organizations, fundraising, and charitable giving. It began in a print format in 1991, and has evolved to an online version. PSI indexes material concerning topics and issues relevant to the nonprofit sector and philanthropy, which are published in both popular and scholarly journals."

Search Form URL: http://cheever.ulib.iupui.edu/psipublicsearch/
Related Resources:
Literature of the Non-Profit Sector B
http://lnps.fdncenter.org/

U.S. Tax Exempt Organizations

http://www.irs.gov
From the Internal Revenue Service. "... find out if your organization is exempt from federal taxation and how much of your contributions to them are tax deductible. This is an electronic version of the Publication 78 'Cumulative List of Organizations.'"
Search Form URL: http://www.irs.ustreas.gov/prod/bus_info/eo/eosearch.html

United Kingdom Register of Charities U.K.

http://www.charity-commission.gov.uk
"The Register of Charities contains details of registered charities in England and Wales. This means that such charities: have most of their assets held in England and/or Wales; have all or a majority of their trustees normally resident in England and/or Wales; or if the charity is set up as a company, is incorporated in England or Wales."
Search Form URL: http://www.charity-commission.gov.uk/cinprs/first.asp

Research and Development

CORDIS (Community Research & Development Information System)

http://www.cordis.lu
"The Community Research and Development Information Service provides information about Research and Development sponsored and supported by the European Union."
Search Form URL: http://dbs.cordis.lu/EN_GLOBALsearch.html

TECH-Net (U.S. Small Business Administration)

http://tech-net.sba.gov/
"Tech-Net is an electronic gateway of technology information and resources for and about small high-tech businesses. It is a search

engine for researchers, scientists, state, federal, and local government officials, a marketing tool for small firms, and a potential "link" to investment opportunities for investors and other sources of capital."
Search Form URL: http://tech-net.sba.gov/tech-net/search.html

TechTracS/TechFinder (NASA)
http://technology.larc.nasa.gov/default.html
"NASATechTracS—an up-to-date database of all NASA programs, technologies, and success stories [that] may have commercial potential and benefits."
Search Form URL: http://technology.larc.nasa.gov/techfinder/
Related Resources:
Federal Laboratory Profiles
http://flc2.federallabs.org/servlet/LinkAreaFramesetServlet?
LnArID=2000-07-07-16-59-11-531-eportney&LnArRegion= National

Real Estate

Directory of Major Malls
http://www.icsc.org/
"The Directory of Major Malls (DMM) is a directory of shopping centers concentrating on the primary centers in the industry with a Gross Leasable Area of 250,000 square feet and above. Through an agreement with DMM, the ICSC [International Council of Shopping Centers] is able to present a limited edition of the Directory through ICSCNET."
Search Form URL: http://www.icsc.org/dmm/dmm.html

Real Estate Retrieval System (FDIC)
http://www.fdic.gov
Properties for sale by the Federal Deposit Insurance Corporation.
Search Form URL: http://www2.fdic.gov/drrore/index.cfm
Related Resources:
Fannie Mae Owned Property Search
http://www.fanniemae.com/homes/index.html
HUD Homes for Sale
http://www.hud.gov/local/sams/ctznhome.html

Realtor.Com

http://www.realtor.com

A database of over 1.4 million properties for sale in the U.S. and
Canada. Searchable by State/Province, ZIP/Postal Code, or MLS number.
Search Form URL: http://www.realtor.com/FindHome/ default.asp
Related Resources:
Find a Neighborhood Database
http://www.realtor.com/FindNeig/default.asp

Recent Home Sale Purchase Prices

http://www.iown.com/

"... get a list of homes recently sold there, with the sale price and date.
Also get an overview of all sales activity in the area." Search by
address, city, or ZIP Code.
Search Form URL: http://rhs.iown.com/selling/rh_selling_
index.htm?MSPARTNER=stihpsh
Related Resources:
Home Price Check
http://dowjones.homepricecheck.com/
Land Registry Residential Price Report U.K.
http://www.landreg.gov.uk/ppr/interactive/

REIT (Real Estate Investment Trusts) Directory

http://www.nareit.com

Information provided by the National Association of Real Estate
Investment Trusts.
Search Form URL: http://secure.podi.com/cfdocs/nareitdir.cfm

Tariffs and Trade

Canadian Importers Database Canada

http://strategis.ic.gc.ca

"[The] Canadian Importers Database provides lists of companies
importing goods into Canada, by product and by city."
Search Form URL: http://strategis.ic.gc.ca/sc_mrkti/cid/engdoc/
index.html
Related Resources:
Canadian Company Capabilities
http://strategis.ic.gc.ca/sc_coinf/ccc/engdoc/homepage.html

Canadian Trade Data Online Canada

http://strategis.ic.gc.ca

"Trade Data Online provides the ability to generate customized reports on Canada's and U.S. trade with over 200 countries."

Search Form URL: http://strategis.ic.gc.ca/sc_mrkti/tdst/engdoc/ tr_homep.html

Foreign Agricultural Service Import/Export Data (United States Department of Agriculture (USDA)

http://ffas.usda.gov

"U.S. export/import data is available from FAS databases in two different forms: Bulk, Intermediate, and Consumer-Oriented (BICO) agricultural trade reports are available in both a calendar or fiscal year format. U.S. Trade Reports provides a more comprehensive commodity-by-commodity breakdown of exports and imports over a two- or five-year period."

Search Form URL: http://ffas.usda.gov/country.html

Related Resources:

Bulk, Intermediate, and Consumer-Oriented (BICO) Database

http://www.fas.usda.gov/scriptsw/bico/bico_frm.idc

U.S. Trade Reports

http://www.fas.usda.gov/scriptsw/ust2&5/ust_frm.idc

Tariff Wizard Canada

http://207.61.56.166/

"The Tariff Wizard has been created as a convenient reference only and has no official sanction. It has been designed to help you determine the proper classification of the goods you import."

Search Form URL: http://207.61.56.166/services/twiz98/twiz98e.cfm

Related Resources:

APEC (Asia Pacific Economic Cooperation) Tariff Database

http://www.apectariff.org/

U.S. International Trade Commission Interactive Tariff and Trade DataWeb

http://dataweb.usitc.gov/

Several interactive databases are available from this site including several with tariff and statistical data. For a complete list see the homepage of the USITC. A few examples follow.

Search Form URL: See Main Page

Related Resources:

USITC Tariff Database-2001
http://205.197.120.17/scripts/tariff.asp
U.S. Trade Summary (by region)
http://dataweb.usitc.gov/scripts/Regions.asp
U.S. Trade Balance (by partner country)
http://dataweb.usitc.gov/scripts/cy_m3_run.asp

U.S. State Exports Database (U.S. Department of Commerce)
http://www.ita.doc.gov/td/industry/otea/
Two interactive mapping databases. One can map exports from each
State to the world while the other maps exports from each State to a
selected country.
Search Form URL: http://ita.mapinfo.com/SCRIPTS/hsrun.hse/
single/ITA/MapXtreme.htx;start=HS_Intro

U.S. Trade Compliance Center Trade Agreements Database
http://www.mac.doc.gov/
"... centralized database for the fully searchable texts of more than 250
trade agreements. Herein are most of the trade agreements to which
the United States is a party and related documents [that] are important to business."
Search Form URL: http://www.mac.doc.gov/tcc/data/index.html
Related Resources:
U.S. Country Commerical Guides
http://www.usatrade.gov/Website/ccg.nsf

Trade Shows and Conventions

Convention Center and Visitors Bureau Directory
http://www.asaenet.org
Locate convention and visitor organizations throughout the world.
Provided by the American Society of Association Executives.
Search Form URL: http://info.asaenet.org/convctrs/cvbdir_SQL.cfm/
Related Resources:
ConventionBureaus.Com
http://www.conventionbureaus.com/

ExhibitorNet.Com: Directory of Trade Shows

http://www.tscentral.com/

Searchable directory of trade shows throughout the world. Numerous limiting tools.

Search Form URL: http://www.tscentral.com/EventCenter/

Related Resources:

TechCalendar (Info Tech Events)

http://www.techweb.com/calendar/advancedSearch

TradePort Trade Events Calendar

http://www.tradeport.org/cgi-bin/tradeport/events/
tradebase-form.pl

Las Vegas Show and Event Calendar

http://www.vegasfreedom.com/play-1.asp

Chapter 13

Computers and Internet

When Tim Berners-Lee conceived the Web, his vision included a wide range of information resources and even network-connected devices of virtually any kind. As the Web matures, we predict that Berners-Lee's vision will be realized, with many of the resources currently located on the Invisible Web becoming accessible to general-purpose search engines.

Meanwhile, computing and Internet resources are some of the most useful and fascinating parts of the Invisible Web. Ranging from simple utilities that help novices establish and maintain a personal Web site, to vast repositories of computer-related research, the sites we've chosen for this chapter represent a wide variety of sources (at many user levels) related to computers and the Internet.

These key resources are included:

- **Computer Science Resources**, such as *ResearchIndex*, a combination meta search engine and citation index that's actually capable of locating computer science research papers on the Invisible Web by creating a custom search database for you *in real time*

- **Internet Tools and Resources**, such as the *Allwhois Database*, an essential tool that allows you to find out who owns and operates any site on the Web

- **Personal Computing Resources**, such as the *MacAfee World Virus Map*, offering a real-time, bird's-eye view of where the latest viruses are infecting computers worldwide

See the Computers and Internet category on the companion Web site for additional Invisible Web resources on this topic at http://www.invisible-web.net.

Computers and Computing

Association of Computing Machinery (ACM) Digital Library B
http://www.acm.org
"As a service to the computing community, the Digital Library will continue to offer its search and bibliographic database resources to all visitors, for free." Registration is required. Full text can be purchased online at the time of the search.
Search Form URL: http://www.acm.org/dl

bitpipe
http://www.bitpipe.com
"Bitpipe collects, catalogs, and distributes corporate literature to other Web sites. For vendors, Bitpipe is like a wire service for professional literature such as white papers and case studies."
Search Form URL: See Main Page

CORA: Computer Science Research Paper Search Engine
http://cora.whizbang.com/
"Cora is a special-purpose search engine covering computer science research papers. It allows keyword searches over the partial text of Postscript-formatted papers it has found by spidering the Web. Cora provides access to over 50,000 research papers on all computer science subjects."
Search Form URL: See Main Page
Related Resources:
ResearchIndex
http://www.researchindex.com

CRA Forsythe List (Computer Researching Association)

http://www.cra.org
"A searchable database of Ph.D.-granting departments in disciplines related to computing in the United States and Canada."
Search Form URL: http://www.cra.org/reports/forsythe.html

DriverGuide.Com

http://www.driverguide.com
"With the help of thousands of our members, we have compiled a massive database of drivers and resources that is by far the most comprehensive on the Web." Free registration is required.
Search Form URL: See Main Page

McAfee World Virus Map

http://www.mcafee.com
"Get a real-time, bird's-eye view of where the latest viruses are infecting computers worldwide."
Search Form URL: http://mast.mcafee.com/mast/mass_ map.asp?
Related Resources:
MacAfee Virus Calendar
http://www.mcafee.com/anti-virus/calendar/default.asp
MacAfee Virus Information Library
http://vil.mcafee.com/default.asp

Microsoft Knowledge Base

http://www.microsoft.com
"Search the Microsoft Knowledge Base of technical support information and self-help tools for Microsoft products."
Search Form URL: http://search.support.microsoft.com/kb/c.asp
Related Resources:
Lotus Knowledge Base
http://www.support.lotus.com/lshome.nsf

Network World Fusion

http://www.nwfusion.com
An archive of material from the magazine and elsewhere beginning in 1994.
Search Form URL: http://search.nwfusion.com/
Related Resources:
CIO Archive
http://www.cio.com/archive/indexfront.html

Information WeekArchive
http://www.informationweek.com/maindocs/archive.htm

Networked Computer Science Technical Reference Library B

http://cs-tr.cs.cornell.edu

"NCSTRL (pronounced "ancestral") is an international collection of computer science research reports and papers made available for non-commercial use from a number of participating institutions and archives. Some of the documents in NCSTRL are part of the technical report collections of participating institutions."

Search Form URL: See Main Page

Related Resources:

Microsoft Research Publications Search

http://research.microsoft.com/scripts/pubs/query.asp

IBM Technical Paper Search

http://www.research.ibm.com/resources/paper_search.html

AT&T Labs External Publications Search

http://www.research.att.com/resources/extsearch/

ResearchIndex

http://www.researchindex.com

An amazing resource. "ResearchIndex is a scientific literature digital library that aims to improve the dissemination and feedback of scientific literature, and to provide improvements in functionality, usability, availability, cost, comprehensiveness, efficiency, and timeliness."

Search Form URL: See Main Page

SecuritySearch.net

http://www.securitysearch.net/

"SecuritySearch.net features searchable security, industry, and product news; an extensive and up-to-date directory and search engine of IT security Web sites; downloadable tools; white papers; and more."

Search Form URL: See Main Page

The Collection of Computer Science Bibliographies B

http://liinwww.ira.uka.de/bibliography/index.html

"This is a collection of bibliographies of scientific literature in computer science from various sources, covering most aspects of computer science. The about 1,400 bibliographies are updated monthly from their original locations such that you'll always find the most recent versions here."

Search Form URL: See Main Page

Internet Resources

Allwhois.com
http://www.allwhois.com/
"Check any domain name in the world. This search will find the "whois" database for the particular domain name and display the output below. If a "whois" database does not exist for a particular domain name, a Root Name Server query will check the domain's availability."
Search Form URL: See Main Page
Related Resources:
WHOIS (.GOV Domain)
http://www.nic.gov/cgi-bin/whois
AllWhois.Com (Domain ownership worldwide)
http://www.allwhois.com/

Cybercafe Search Engine
http://www.cybercaptive.com/
The Cybercafe Search Engine database contains listings for more than 6,000 verified cybercafes, public internet access points, and kiosks in 168 countries.
Search Form URL: See Main Page

Internet Traffic Report
http://www.internettrafficreport.com/
"The Internet Traffic Report monitors the flow of data around the world. It then displays a value between zero and 100. Higher values indicate faster and more reliable connections."
Search Form URL: See Main Page

ISPs.com
http://www.isps.com/
Find an Internet Service Provider, searching by area code, name, price, national, or toll-free providers with this database of over 5,000 ISPs.
Search Form URL: See Main Page

Marks Online Domain Name Search
http://www.marksonline.com
"... an enhanced domain name search [that] enables easy-to-use wild-card queries." Available only for the .com, .org, and .net, domains.
Search Form URL: http://www.marksonline.com/app/nicsearch

Meta-List

http://www.meta-list.net/query?acc=110en
Meta-List allows you to search for information in more than 170,000 public Internet-based newsletters and email discussion lists.
Search Form URL: See Main Page

NetLingo

http://www.netlingo.com
"NetLingo is a popular dictionary about the Internet language. It is a Web site with thousands of "cyberterms" that people use when communicating online or surfing the Web or conducting e-commerce transactions. It is a digital reference book that helps millions of people around the world learn about the most commonly used words, smileys, acronyms, and so on that keep sprouting up on the Internet."
Search Form URL: See Main Page
Related Resources:
Techweb Technology Encyclopedia
http://www.techweb.com/encyclopedia/
Webopedia
http://www.pcwebopaedia.com/
Free On-Line Dictionary of Computing
http://www.foldoc.org/

Network Solutions USA Internet Facts

http://www.dotcom.com
Several maps and graphs that illustrate domain name registrations by city, state, and metropolitan area.
Search Form URL: http://www.dotcom.com/facts/usmap.html#
Related Resources:
Network Solutions International Market Internet Facts
http://www.dotcom.com/facts/intmarket.html

Nua Internet Surveys

http://www.nua.ie/surveys
"Nua Internet Surveys is the authoritative source online for information on Internet demographics and trends."
Search Form URL: See Main Page

Search Engine Guide

http://www.searchengineguide.com/
Find topical search engines, portals, and directories on a huge variety
of topics, with this directory of more than 3,500 resources.
Search Form URL: http://www.searchengineguide.com/
searchengines.html

Chapter 14

Education

Educational resources abound on the Web. In addition to countless homework help sites, students can now access such high quality resources as the *Merriam-Webster Dictionary* or *National Geographic's MapMachine*—both, incidentally, largely Invisible Web sites.

The Invisible Web has far more education resources to offer than basic homework helpers. Whether you're a student looking for information on schools, an instructor looking for course materials, or an administrator looking for fund-raising resources, the Invisible Web has something for you.

These key resources are included:

> **Classroom and Teacher Support**, including the *Gateway to Educational Materials*, a consortium effort to provide educators with quick and easy access to the substantial, but uncataloged, collections of educational materials found on the Web

> • **Directories and Locators**, such as *Peterson's Graduate School Databases*, designed to help students narrow their search for the ideal school by focusing on key personal requirements.

> • **General Education Resources**, including *ERIC*, the Educational Resources Information Center. ERIC's database is the world's largest source of education information

- **Statistics Resources**, such as WebCASPAR, a database system designed to provide quick and convenient access to a wide range of statistical data focusing on U.S. universities and colleges

See the Education category on the companion Web site for additional Invisible Web resources on this topic at http://www.invisible-web.net.

Classroom and Teacher Support

Culturally and Linguistically Appropriate Services Database

http://clas.uiuc.edu/
"This Web site presents a dynamic and evolving database of materials describing culturally and linguistically appropriate practices for early childhood/early intervention services."
Search Form URL: http://clas.uiuc.edu/search.html

Gateway to Education Materials

http://www.thegateway.org/
"The Gateway to Educational Materials (GEM) project is a consortium effort to provide educators with quick and easy access to the substantial, but uncataloged, collections of educational materials found on various federal, state, university, nonprofit, and commercial Internet sites."
Search Form URL: http://www.enc.org/resources/search/

Mathline (Searchable Video Database)

http://www.pbs.org/teachersource/math.htm
"... professional development resource helps teachers quickly and easily find standards-based Mathline video clips and lesson plans on different mathematical topics and teaching techniques for grades K-12."
Search Form URL: http://www.pbs.org/teachersource/mathline/lessonplans/aboutvid.shtm

National Child Care Information Center Database

http://nccic.org/
"This database provides information on child care in U.S. states, the District of Columbia, and Puerto Rico."
Search Form URL: http://nautilus.outreach.uiuc.edu/eric/search.asp

Reading Pathfinder Database
http://readingpath.org/
"... goal is to make easily accessible the best available information on how to help children become competent readers by about third grade."
Search Form URL: http://ericps.crc.uiuc.edu/cgi-bin/readpath/searchrp.cgi

Directories and Locators

Canadian Colleges and Universities (CanLearn) Canada
http://www.canlearn.ca/
"... a complete listing of Canadian colleges and universities, including program and contact information."
Search Form URL: http://www.canlearn.ca/English/find/college&university/college.cfm
Related Resources:
Student Planner Occupations Databank Canada
http://216.208.47.164/canlearn/ci_prof.nsf/frmOccsIntro?OpenForm
Student Planner Learning Opportunities Databank Canada
http://216.208.47.164/canlearn/ci_prog.nsf/frmProgsIntro?OpenForm

College Opportunities Online (National Center for Education Statistics)
http://nces.ed.gov/ipeds/cool/
"IPEDS College Opportunities Online is your direct link to over 9,000 colleges and universities in the United States. If you are thinking about a large university, a small liberal arts college, a specialized college, a community college, a career or technical college, or a trade school, you can find them all here."
Search Form URL: http://nces.ed.gov/ipeds/cool/Search.asp
Related Resources:
Integrated Postsecondary Education Data System Peer Analysis System
http://nces.ed.gov/ipedspas/

Directory of Resources for Foreign Language Programs

http://www.cal.org/ericcll

"This Web-based directory of resources for improving elementary foreign language programs provides information about and links to national associations, professional organizations, state foreign language offices, funders, publishers of language learning materials, centers, clearinghouses, instructional materials Web sites, online publications, databases, regional conferences, and listservs."

Search Form URL: http://www.cal.org/ericcll/ncbe/fldirectory/

Related Resources:

Directory of Partial Immersion Language Programs in U.S. Schools, 1999

http://www2.cal.org/immersion/

Education Resource Organizations Directory

http://www.ed.gov/Programs/EROD/

"The Directory is intended to help you identify and contact organizations that provide information and assistance on a broad range of education-related topics."

Search Form URL: See Main Page

Related Resources:

Directory of Higher Education Organizations

http://www.educause.edu/ir/dheo.html

ERIC/AE Test Locator

http://ericae.net

Three separate databases are available to assist in locating tests and test reviews.

Search Form URL: http://ericae.net/testcol.htm

Related Resources:

ERIC/AE Full Text Internet Library

http://ericae.net/ftlib.htm

Foreign Language Test Database

http://www.cal.org/nclrc/fltestdb/

Guide to the Evaluation of Educational Experiences in the Armed Services

http://www.militaryguides.acenet.edu/

"For more than a half century the Guide to the Evaluation of Education Experiences in the Armed Services has been the standard reference work for recognizing learning acquired in military life. Since

1942, the American Council on Education has worked cooperatively with the U.S. Department of Defense, the armed services, and the U.S. Coast Guard in helping hundreds of individuals earn academic credit for learning acheived while serving their country."
Search Form URL: See Main Page

Higher Education Databases, (*U.S. News and World Report*)

http://www.usnews.com/usnews/misc/tools.htm
Several searchable databases with college information. Also note the school comparison option. The related resources for this entry are only a few of the resources available.
Search Form URL: See Main Page
Related Resources:
Community College Finder
http://www.usnews.com/usnews/edu/college/communit/commsrch.htm
College Search (The College Board)
http://www2.collegeboard.com/search/index.jsp

IIE (Institute of International Education) Passport

http://www.iiepassport.org/
Search a well known database of U.S. education experiences abroad. Registration is mandatory.
Search Form URL: See Main Page

National Public School/District Locator

http://nces.ed.gov/ccdweb/school/
"This School/District Locator will enable you to find the correct name, address, telephone number, NCES ID number, urbanicity (rural, large city, etc.), and other student and teacher information for public schools or school districts for school year 1998-99 as reported to NCES [National Center for Education Statistics] by state education officials in each state."
Search Form URL: http://nces.ed.gov/ccdweb/school/school.asp
Related Resources:
U.S. Private School Locator
http://nces.ed.gov/surveys/pss/locator/locator.html

Online Distance Education Catalog (Globewide Network Academy)

http://www.gnacademy.org/

"GNA's course and program catalog is a comprehensive directory of distance learning opportunities throughout the world." Over 23,000 courses are listed.

Search Form URL: http://www.gnacademy.org/mason/catalog/front.html

Related Resources:

Peterson's Lifelong Learning Resources

http://www.lifelonglearning.com/

Peterson's Graduate School Databases

http://iiswinprd01.petersons.com/gradchannel/

Locate graduate school programs in the U.S. and Canada.

Search Form URL: http://iiswinprd01.petersons.com/GradChannel/Search.asp

Related Resources:

Peterson's MBA Concentration Search

http://iiswinprd01.petersons.com/mba/search.asp

Peterson's Law School Search (via Dow Jones)

http://www.petersons.com/fcgi-bin/college-wsj-law.pl

Shaw Guides

http://www.shawguides.com

"More than 4,300 Learning Vacation & Creative Career Programs worldwide. Programs include Cultural Travel, Cooking School, Language Vacations, and Writers Conferences & Workshops."

Search Form URL: See Main Page

Financial Information and Scholarships

Finding Federal Dollars (After-School Programs)

http://www.afterschool.gov

"This database gives you one stop for information about more than 100 sources of federal funding for after-school and youth development programming."

Search Form URL: http://www.afterschool.gov/feddollar.html

Grants Awarded Database (*Chronicle of Higher Education*)
http://www.chronicle.com
"... search listings of foundation and corporate grants of $75,000 or more awarded to colleges and universities since 1995."
Search Form URL: http://www.chronicle.com/free/grants/

Public School District Finance Peer Search
http://nces.ed.gov/edfin/
"This search will allow you to compare the finances of a school district with its peers (those districts [that] share similar characteristics to the one you choose)."
Search Form URL: http://nces.ed.gov/edfin/search/search_ intro.asp

Scholarship Search U.K. U.K.
http://www.scholarship-search.org.uk/index.html
"Scholarship Search U.K. provides a freely searchable database of undergraduate scholarships offered by academic institutions, commercial organisations, and charitable trusts."
Search Form URL: See Main Page

U.S. News "Find a Scholarship"
http://www.usnews.com/usnews/edu/college/cohome.htm
Locate scholarship award information. Search by scholarship name and various other criteria.
Search Form URL: http://www.usnews.com/usnews/edu/dollars/ scholar/search.htm
Related Resources:
Fastweb Scholarship Database
http://www.fastweb.com
U.S. Federal School Code Search
http://www.ed.gov/offices/OSFAP/Students/apply/search.html

General Education Resources

Current Awareness—Education B
http://landmark-project.com/ca/index.php3
"Current Awareness is a monthly bibliography of the most recent educational literature from an extensive collection of journals. Produced by the

Division of Instructional Technology, North Carolina Department of Public Instruction in partnership with The Landmark Project."
Search Form URL: See Main Page
Related Resources:
Education WeekArchives
http://www.edweek.com/edsearch.cfm
Edupage Archive (E-Mail Newsletter)
http://www.educause.edu/pub/edupage/edupage.html

ERIC B
http://searcheric.org/
"The Educational Resources Information Center (ERIC) database is the world's largest source of education information. The database contains more than 1,000,000 abstractsof documents and journal articles on education research and practice. The documents in the database can be ordered from the ERIC Document Reproduction Service. Over 50,000 documents are now available online, on-demand. Journal articles can be ordered through various journal reprint services. ERIC is a federally funded project of the U.S. Department of Education, Office of Educational Research and Improvement."
Search Form URL: See Main Page
Related Resources:
ERIC Database (Second Interface)
http://www.askeric.org/Eric/
ERIC Document Reproduction Service (A source to purchase the full text of ERIC documents.)
http://www.edrs.com/
ERIC Digests (Full-Text)
http://www.ed.gov/databases/ERIC_Digests/index/

ERIC Calendar of Education Related Conferences
http://www.accesseric.org/
"The ERIC Calendar includes more than 700 international, national, regional, and state conferences scheduled for this year and next year. To provide contact information for sponsors who posted conferences in the past, the Calendar also includes last year's conference information. The Calendar database is updated throughout the year as new information becomes available."
Search Form URL: http://webprod.aspensys.com/education/ericconf/ericcal/introduction.asp

Music Education Search System B

http://www.music.miami.edu:591/mess/
The Music Education Search System comprises three databases. Music
Journals, Poland-Cady Abstract Collection, and the Boletin De
Investigacio Educativo Musical.
Search Form URL: See Main Page

National Center for Bilingual Education (NCBE) Bibliographic Database B

http://www.ncbe.gwu.edu/databases/index.htm
"… access to over 20,000 bibliographic citations and abstracts of materials from a variety of sources dealing with all aspects of the education of
linguistically and culturally diverse (LCD) students in U.S. schools."
Search Form URL: http://www.ncbe.gwu.edu/bibliographic/

National Teacher Recruitment Clearinghouse Search

http://www.recruitingteachers.org
"The National Teacher Recruitment Clearinghouse offers a gateway to
teacher recruitment job banks and job postings nationwide to help
teachers find jobs and school districts find teachers. Access to this job
bank portal and to the Clearinghouse resources is free."
Search Form URL: http://www.recruitingteachers.org/perl/
survey/ search.pl

Technologies for Learning Database

http://node.on.ca
"… a clearinghouse of information on the technologies used to
develop and deliver online education and training."
Search Form URL: http://node.on.ca/tfl/

Statistics

Eurybase: Education Systems in Europe

http://www.eurydice.org
Basic facts and statistics about education throughout Europe. The
EURYDICE European Unit of the European Commission (DG
Education and Culture) developed the database.
Search Form URL: http://www.eurydice.org/Eurybase/
Application/eurybase.htm

Related Resources:
The Doctorate in the European Region Database
http://doct.cepes.ro/cgi-bin/doctoratT.plx
Access to Higher Education [in Europe]
http://access.cepes.ro/cgi-bin/dbOleg.plx

Fast Facts (National Center for Education Statistics)

http://nces.ed.gov
This handy database is a one-stop shop for facts derived from the many
reports that the National Center for Education Statistics publishes.
Search Form URL: http://nces.ed.gov/fastfacts/index.asp

National Center for Education Statistics Quick Tables and Figures

http://www.nces.ed.gov
This search tool allows you to locate all tables/figures published in the
inventory of NCES' "Education Statistics Quarterly."
Search Form URL: http://nces.ed.gov/quicktables/index.asp

SESTAT

http://srsstats.sbe.nsf.gov/
"A comprehensive and integrated system of information about the
employment, educational and demographic characteristics of scientists and engineers in the United States."
Search Form URL: http://srsstats.sbe.nsf.gov/dataaccess_ java.html

WebCASPAR

http://caspar.nsf.gov/
" ... a National Science Foundation database system designed to provide quick and convenient access to a wide range of statistical data
focusing on U.S. universities and colleges and their science and engineering resources." Free registration is required.
Search Form URL: See Main Page

Chapter 15

Entertainment

Throughout this book, we've repeatedly made the point that many Invisible Web resources offer high-quality, authoritative information that's often not available on the visible Web. This doesn't mean that the Invisible Web is all work and no play. Rather, there are some excellent resources focusing on entertainment that are just as useful and comprehensive as their more "serious" kin.

In this chapter, we've assembled a varied sample of entertainment resources, covering amusements, movies, music, live performances, and other activities people do mostly for fun and pleasure. While these resources provide a lot of enjoyment for leisure-time activities, many are also of value to serious researchers as well.

Thes key resources are included:

- **Amusements**, such as the *All Game Guide*, with information on more than 25,000 games

- **Movies and Cinema**, including *Current Films in the Works* and the *Movie Review Query Engine*, in addition to the well-known *Internet Movie Database*

- **Music Resources**, ranging from the *All Music Guide*, which focuses primarily on contemporary music and musicians, to *OperaBase*

• **Performances**, including *Festivals.com's* database of more than 37,000 worldwide events

See the Entertainment category on the companion Web site for additional Invisible Web resources on this topic at http://www.invisible-web.net.

Amusements

All Game Guide
http://allgame.com/
"With coverage ranging from Pong to the newest next-generation products, the All Game Guide features an ever-growing inventory of over 25,000 games for more than 85 platforms."
Search Form URL: See main page

Internet Anagram Server
http://www.wordsmith.org/anagram/
Enter any word or phrase to generate a list of its anagrams (words or phrases formed by reordering the letters)
Search Form URL: See main page

The Roller Coaster Database
http://www.rcdb.com/
"The Roller Coaster Database is a comprehensive, searchable database with information and statistics on over 1,000 roller coasters in North America and Europe."
Search Form URL: See Main Page

General Entertainment Resources

Searchable Television Listings
http://www.clicktv.com
An example of an interactive and keyword-searchable television guide.
Search Form URL: http://www.clicktv.com/search.asp
Related Resources:
Searchable Television Listings Canada

http://www.clicktv.com/index.asp?cid=tvdc
Searchable Television Listings U.K.
http://www.radiotimes.beeb.com/servlet/controller?action=tvHome

Movies and Cinema

CineFiles (Pacific Film Archive)
http://www.bampfa.berkeley.edu/pfa/
"A database of reviews, press kits, festival and showcase program
notes, newspaper articles, and other documents from the Pacific Film
Archive Library's clippings files. The files contain documents from a
broad range of sources covering world cinema, past and present."
Search Form URL: http://www.mip.berkeley.edu/cinefiles/
Related Resources:
Pacific Film Archive Film Notes Database
http://www.bampfa.berkeley.edu/search/filmnotes.html

Cinema FreeNet
http://www.cinfn.com/
"This program allows you to search for relationships between movies,
actors, directors, and producers."
Search Form URL: See Main Page

Current Films in the Works
http://www.boxoffice.com
Boxoffice, a film industry trade publication, provides access to a list of
upcoming motion pictures. Each listing includes a short plot synopsis
and list of actors set to take part in the production.
Search Form URL: http://www.boxoffice.com/scripts/fiw.dll?DoSearch

Directory of International Film and Video Festivals (The)
http://www.britfilms.com/
The directory lists over 500 international film, television, and video
festivals, giving details on how and when to enter these events.
Compiled and published by the British Film Council.
Search Form URL: http://www.britfilms.com/fv/home.lasso
Related Resources:
The Film Festivals Directory
http://filmfestivals.com/ffs/search2.htm

Internet Movie Database

http://www.imdb.com

Nirvana for any move fan. The IMDB began as a small project in the United Kingdom and is now a service that is part of the Amazon.com family. Note the many additional search options on the search page.

Search Form URL: http://us.imdb.com/Search/

Related Resources:

Motion Picture Association of America Ratings Database

http://www.mpaa.org/movieratings/search/index.htm

British Board of Film Classification Database U.K.

http://www.bbfc.co.uk/website/Classified.nsf/$$Search

All Movie Guide

http://allmovie.com/

Inter-Play B

http://www.portals.org/interplay/

"Inter-Play provides easy access to the locations of printed plays in collections, anthologies, and periodicals. Most of the plays cited are not indexed in the standard printed play indexes such as Ottemiller's Index to Plays in Collections or H. W. Wilson's Play Index. For plays by the most familiar authors (e.g., Shakespeare), you should also consult your local library's catalog. Approximately 18,000 locations are currently cited to plays in many languages. Separately published plays are not included, as these may also be located through local library catalogs. Inter-Play is updated frequently in order to include recent publications."

Search Form URL: http://www.portals.org/interplay/play.html

Movie Review Query Engine

http://www.mrqe.com

This database contains movie reviews for 21,000 films. Reviews come from both newspaper and Internet-only sources.

Search Form URL: See Main Page

MovieFone

http://www.moviefone.com

A free directory of movies, showtimes, and theater locations throughout the U.S.

Search Form URL: See Main Page

Video Distributors Database

http://www.videolibrarian.com
Basic directory information for video distribution companies.
Search Form URL: http://www.videolibrarian.com/producers. html

Music

All Music Guide

http://allmusic.com/
This resource (search interface near the top of page) contains a treasure trove of information on musicians, albums, and songs.
Search Form URL: See Main Page
Related Resources:
All Music Guide (Classical)
http://allclassical.com/

ASCAP Music License Database

http://www.ascap.com/
"ACE is a database of song titles licensed by ASCAP (American Society of Composers, Artists, and Publishers) in the United States. For each title, you can find the names of the songwriters and the names, contact persons, addresses, and, in most cases, phone numbers of publishers to contact if you want to use the work. For most of the titles, you'll find some of the artists who have made a commercial recording."
Search Form URL: http://www.ascap.com/ace/search.cfm?
mode=search
Related Resources:
BMI (Broadcast Music Inc.) Repertoire Song Title Database
http://repertoire.bmi.com/
Carlin America (Music Publisher Database)
http://www.carlinamerica.com

Beethoven Bibliography Database B

http://www.sjsu.edu/depts/beethoven/database/database.html
"The Beethoven Bibliography Database is an exciting project that unites the continuing interest in the life and works of Ludwig van Beethoven with the advantages of computer technology and the Internet." Contains over 10,000 entries.
Search Form URL: http://sjsulib.sjsu.edu:83/

Related Resources:
Bach Bibliography
http://www.npj.com/bach/

Billboard Spotlight Reviews

http://www.billboard.com
Contains more than 30,000 original Billboard album reviews from
1970 through today.
Search Form URL: http://www.billboard.com/reviews/finder.asp
Related Resources:
Rolling Stone Album Review Search
http://www.rollingstone.com/sections/recordings/text/search.
asp?afl=

Canadian Music Periodical Index B, Canada

http://www.nlc-bnc.ca/cmpi/about_e.htm
"This database includes more than 25,000 entries indexed from 475
Canadian music journals, newsletters, and magazines from the late
nineteenth century to the present day. It focuses on articles and news
items covering all aspects of musical activity in Canada. Over 200 titles
are currently being indexed ..."
Search Form URL: http://www.nlc-bnc.ca/cmpi-bin/search/l=0

Hoagy Carmichael Collection (The)

http://www.dlib.indiana.edu/collections/hoagy/index.html
"... a complete catalog of the entire Carmichael Collection, access to
selected digital objects, and supplemental research information, such
as genealogy. The Hoagy Carmichael Collection contains sound
recordings of Hoagy's music, letters, photographs of him and his family, print and handwritten musical compositions, and more."
Search Form URL: http://www.dlib.indiana.edu/collections/
hoagy/search/index.html

Mudcat Café Digital Tradition Folksong Database (The)

http://www.mudcat.org/
Search or browse this resource containg the lyrics to over 8,000 folk
songs.
Search Form URL: http://www.mudcat.org/threads.cfm

Musica: The International Database of Choral Repertoire

http://www.musicanet.org/

"MUSICA is currently a choral documentary search tool as well as a pedagogic tool for conductors, musicologists, schools of music, musical federations, music stores, etc. ... but it is also for amateurs and people eager to know about the choral music repertoire."
Search Form URL: http://www.musicanet.org/en/cherchgb.htm
Related Resources:
http://www.musicanet.org/en/cherchgb.htm

Mutopia (Public Domain Sheet Music)

http://www.mutopia.org
"Seventy years after a composer dies, the copyright on his work expires and anyone can copy it. Music publishers, however, own the copyright on their typeset editions and therefore the only way to legally copy this music is to write it out or typeset it yourself and allow other people to make copies. This is the essence of Mutopia—a growing number of musical scores all typeset using GNU Lilypond by volunteers."
Search Form URL: http://www.mutopiaproject.org/browse.cgi

OperaBase

http://www.operabase.com/en/
This highly praised database offers numerous searching options for locating data about Opera. Note the special arrangement with the Grove Dictionary of Opera that provides full-text material in the database.
Search Form URL: See Main Page

Pollstar Concert Database

http://www.pollstar.com
Search for concert dates via several criteria including city and venue.
Search Form URL: See Main Page
Related Resources:
FestivalFinder (Music Festivals)
http://www.festivalfinder.com/search/index.cfm

RIAA Gold and Platinum Database

http://www.riaa.com
Information on recordings certified gold or platinum by the Recording Industry Association of America.
Search Form URL: http://www.riaa.com/Gold-Intro-2.cfm

ThemeFinder

http://www.themefinder.com

"The Themefinder database contains the initial portions of melodies for about 20,000 themes from Classical and Folksong repertoires. When searching for recordings and scores of particular works, we usually rely on title information. When title information is not available but melodies can be recalled, they can be searched using Themefinder."
Search Form URL: See Main Page

UBL Ultimate Band List
http://ubl.artistdirect.com/
A one-stop shop for information and resources for over 100,000 artists.
Search Form URL: See Main Page

Performances and Events

CultureFinder
http://www.culturefinder.com
Locate events and tickets for performances and events in major U.S. cities.
Search Form URL: See Main Page
Related Resources:
Playbill Theatre Database
http://www.playbill.com/cgi-bin/plb/theatre?cmd=search

Festivals.com
http://www.festivals.com/
"Festivals are the universal form of community celebration. Whether we call them fairs, festivals, feasts or fiestas, they bring people together in a public space for mutual expression. Search from more than 37,000 events around the world."
Search Form URL: See Main Page

London Theatre Guide U.K.
http://www.officiallondontheatre.co.uk/index.cfm
Find out what's playing with this official guide to the 50 major commercial and grant-aided theatres in central London.
Search Form URL: See Main Page

Playbill Theatre Listings

http://www.playbill.com

This well known theatre publication provides a searchable directory with show listings in North America and London.

Search Form URL: http://www.playbill.com/cgi-bin/plb/theatre?cmd=search

CHAPTER 16

Government Information and Data

Governments are prolific Web publishers—in fact, the U.S. government is the single largest producer of content for the Web, and other countries are putting more and more material on the Web every day. Several trends are accelerating the pace of government Web publishing, including cost-cutting efforts and mandates to reduce paperwork.

While there are numerous portals to government information on the Web, including FirstGov.gov, Hieros Gamos, UK Online, and others, most of these cover primarily visible Web materials. Unfortunately for the searcher who relies solely on general-purpose search engines, many government documents are published in PDF or other non-crawlable formats. Other sources of government information, especially statistics or other numeric data, reside in databases that are impenetrable to crawlers.

In this chapter, we highlight a selection of outstanding government Invisible Web resources. The sites we have selected primarily offer "general" types of information, directly from government entities themselves. And, since politicians and politics play such a crucial role in governmental activities, we've selected several political resources as well.

These key resources are included:

- **Directories and Locators**, such as the *Canadian Electoral District Locator*, which helps you locate information about each of Canada's 301 Electoral Districts

- **Government Documents**, including gateways like *GPO ACCESS*, a service of the U.S. Government Printing Office that provides free electronic access to a wealth of important information products produced by the Federal Government, and *RAPID (European Union News)*, a database giving a daily view of the activities of the European Union as presented by the Institutions in their press releases

- **Government Officials**, such as the *Mayors at a Glance* database of U.S. city leaders

- **Statistics**, including *InfoNation*, a database that allows you to view and compare the most up-to-date statistical data for the Member States of the United Nations

See the Government Information and Data category on the companion Web site for additional Invisible Web resources on this topic at http://www.invisible-web.net.

Directories and Locators

411 for Government: Carroll Publishing Government Directories U.S.

http://www.carrollpub.com
Search or browse Federal, State, and Municipal Government directories. Over 500,000 records. Additional Carroll Publishing resources are available for a fee.
Search Form URL: http://www.carrollpub.com/CitCenter/citcenter.asp
Related Resources:
Carroll's Who's New/Pending/Out and Vacancies in Government Databases
See Main Page
Carroll's GovSearch
http://www.carrollpub.com/govsearch/

About Counties (National Association of Counties)

http://www.naco.org
This resource contains numerous options to find U.S. county information. Included is a county official lookup.
Search Form URL: http://www.naco.org/counties/queries/index.cfm

Canadian Electoral District Locator Canada
http://www.elections.ca
Locate information about each of Canada's 301 Electoral Districts.
Search Form URL: http://www.elections.ca/intro.asp?section=
cir&document=index&lang=e
Related Resources:
Reistered Political Parties in Canada
http://www.elections.ca/content.asp?section=pol&document=
index&dir=par&lang=e&textonly=false

Directory of Federal Property Canada
http://www.tbs-sct.gc.ca/dfrp-rbif/
"The Directory of Federal Real Property is the central record and only
complete listing of real property holdings of the Government of
Canada. It is administered by the Real Property Management Division
of the Treasury Board Secretariat."
Search Form URL: http://www.tbs-sct.gc.ca/dfrp-rbif/home-
accueil.asp?Language=EN

Foreign Representatives in Canada Canada
http://198.103.104.118/Protocol/main.asp?sScreen=Basic
Several databases with directory-type data.
Search Form URL: See Main Page

GOLD (Government Online Directory) Australia
http://gold.directory.gov.au/tmpl/s.html
"GOLD is the official guide to the Australian Government's organisational structure, key personnel, and agencies. GOLD is a free Internet
service provided by AusInfo (a unit within the Department of Finance
and Administration)."
Search Form URL: See Main Page

Government Locator Information Service (GILS) U.S.
http://www.access.gpo.gov/su_docs/index.html
"The Government Information Locator Service (GILS) is an effort to
identify, locate, and describe publicly available Federal information
resources, including electronic information resources. GILS records
identify public information resources within the Federal Government,
describe the information available in these resources, and assist in
obtaining the information."

Search Form URL: http://www.access.gpo.gov/su_docs/gils/
index.html

Inforoute U.K.
http://www.hmso.gov.uk/inforoute/index.htm
"Inforoute is the new gateway to information held by UK Government
departments. It provides direct access to the Government's
Information Asset Register (IAR)."
Search Form URL: See Main Page
Related Resources:
U.K. Online Citizen Portal
http://www.ukonline.gov.uk/

Japan Government Locator System Japan
http://www.clearing.somucho.go.jp
Search for resources available from many Japanese Government
organizations.
Search Form URL: http://www.clearing.somucho.go.jp/cgi-bin/
HpSchSearch.cgi?LANG=1

Parline Database
http://www.ipu.org
"The PARLINE database (a derivative of Parliaments online) has been
developed by the Inter-Parliamentary Union and is regularly updated
on the basis of official information provided by national Parliaments."
Search Form URL: http://www.ipu.org/parline-e/parlinesearch.asp

General Government Resources

Good Practice Database (Cabinet Office) U.K.
http://www.bestpractices.org.uk
"The database holds information from a wide range of public service
providers on ideas they have introduced to improve the service they provide. It is designed to help you find out what others are doing so that you
can consider whether something similar might improve your service."
Search Form URL: http://www.bestpractices.org.uk/app/search.asp

Native American Consultation Database U.S.
http://www.cr.nps.gov/nagpra/nacd/

"The Native American Consultation Database is an easy way to identify a current contact for each Indian tribe, Alaska Native corporation,
and Native Hawaiian organization."
Search Form URL: http://www.cast.uark.edu/other/nps/nacd/

Government Documents

10 Downing Street News Search U.K.
http://www.number-10.gov.uk
Search for press releases from the Prime Minister of the United
Kingdom.
Search Form URL: http://www.number-10.gov.uk/search2.asp
Related Resources:
Prime Minister of Canada Site Search Canada
http://pm.gc.ca/Search.asp

1040.com
http://www.1040.com/
"Find, download, and print any tax form you need, visit links to the
IRS Web site, find the answers to your tax questions, and get the latest
news and information, all in one location."
Search Form URL: See Main Page

AGIP (Australian Government Index of Publications)
B, Australia
http://www.dofa.gov.au/agip/
"AGIP contains bibliographic entries of Commonwealth publications
for publications sold by the Government Info Shops [and] publications distributed through the Commonwealth Library Deposit and
Free Issue Schemes."
Search Form URL: http://203.2.143.24/webpac-bin/wgbroker? new+-
access+top

Catalog of U.S. Government Publications U.S.
http://www.access.gpo.gov
"The Catalog is a search-and-retrieval service that provides bibliographic records of U.S. Government information products. Use it to link
to Federal agency online resources or identify materials distributed to

Federal Depository Libraries. Coverage begins with January 1994 and new records are added daily."
Search Form URL: http://www.access.gpo.gov/su_docs/locators/cgp/index.html
Related Resources:
U.S. Government Online Bookstore Sales Product Catalog
http://bookstore.gpo.gov/
Federal Depository Library Finder U.S.
http://www.access.gpo.gov/su_docs/locators/findlibs/index.html
New Electronic Titles
http://www.access.gpo.gov/su_docs/locators/net/index.html

European Foreign Policy Bulletin EU

http://www.iue.it/EFPB/Welcome.html
"This full-text database brings together the documents issued by the European Union in the area of foreign policy since 1985."
Search Form URL: http://wwwarc1.iue.it/iue/fillf?form.html=form2efpb.html

GPO Access U.S.

http://www.access.gpo.gov
GPO Access is a service of the U.S. Government Printing Office that provides free electronic access to a wealth of important information products produced by the Federal Government. The information provided on this site is the official, published version and the information retrieved from GPO Access can be used without restriction, unless specifically noted. "GPO Access provides free online use of over 1,500 databases of Federal information in over 80 applications." Many of these resources contain Invisible Web data.
Search Form URL: See Main Page
Related Resources:
GPO Access Database Example—The Congressional Record
http://www.access.gpo.gov/su_docs/aces/aces150.html
GPO Access Database Example—The U.S. Government Manual
http://www.access.gpo.gov/nara/nara001.html
List of Additional GPO Access Databases
http://www.access.gpo.gov/su_docs/db2.html

Public Diplomacy Query (United States) U.S.

http://www.state.gov

"Public Diplomacy Query (PDQ), the open electronic archive of the International Information Programs (IIP), Department of State. The PDQ database comprises a wide array of official texts, statements, publications, reports, and other documents on U.S. foreign policy, international issues, and IIP overseas programs."
Search Form URL: http://usinfo.state.gov/products/pdq/pdq.htm

RAPID (European Union News) EU

http://europa.eu.int/rapid/start/welcome.htm
"RAPID is a database giving a daily view of the activities of the European Union as presented by the Institutions in their press releases."
Search Form URL: http://europa.eu.int/rapid/start/welcome.htm
Related Resources:
IDEA (Electronic Directory of the European Institutions)
http://europa.eu.int/idea/en/index.htm

THOMAS: Legislative Information on the Internet

http://thomas.loc.gov
A service of the Library of Congress, THOMAS provides access to U.S. Government legislation information.
Search Form URL: See Main Page

United Nations Daily Press Briefing Search UN

http://www.un.org/News/
Access the full text of U.N. press briefings beginning March 8, 1996.
Search Form URL: http://www.un.org/News/briefings/
Related Resources:
United Nations Press Release Search (full-text)
http://www.un.org/News/Press/

United Nations Voting Records UN

http://unbisnet.un.org/
"The voting records for all resolutions which were adopted—either without a vote or by roll-call or recorded vote—by the General Assembly beginning with its 38th session (1983-) and the Security Council beginning with its 1st year (1946-)."
Search Form URL: http://unbisnet.un.org/webpac-bin/
wgbroker?new+-access+top.vote
Related Resources:
United Nations Index to Speeches B

http://unbisnet.un.org/webpac-bin/wgbroker?new+-access+
top.speech

Weekly Checklist Catalogue [Canadian Government] Publications B, Canada

http://dsp-psd.pwgsc.gc.ca/dsp-psd/AboutDSP/DepoNew/table-
e.html

"The Weekly Checklist Catalogue is the Depository Services Program's
searchable catalogue of information about Canadian government
publications. The majority of publications described in this catalogue
are kept in the collections of more than 790 libraries in Canada and
another 147 institutions around the world."
Search Form URL: http://dsp-psd.pwgsc.gc.ca/search_form-e.html
Related Resources:
Depository Library Finder Canada
http://dsp-psd.pwgsc.gc.ca/depo_search-e.html

Government Officials

C-SPAN Congressional Vote Databases

http://www.c-span.org
Browse through key votes or search by member name, subject, month,
or ZIP Code. Data begins in 1994.
Search Form URL: http://congress.nw.dc.us/cgi-bin/issue.pl? dir=c-
span&command=votelib
Related Resources:
Roll Call U.S. Congress Directory
http://legislators.com/rollcall/congdir.html
U.S. Congress Foreign Travel Reports and Expenditures
http://clerkweb.house.gov/cgi-bin/jay2.pl

Mayors at a Glance Database

http://www.usmayors.org
From the U.S. Conference of Mayors. Short biographical information
on mayors for many U.S. cities.
Search Form URL: http://www.usmayors.org/USCM/cgi-bin/
database_search4.asp
Related Resources:
U.S. Council of Mayors Mayoral Election Results Database
http://www.usmayors.org/uscm/elections/99elections.asp

MP Lookup Canada
http://www.parl.gc.ca/information/about/people/
Locate members of the Canadian Parliament by Postal Code.
Search Form URL: http://www.parl.gc.ca/information/about/
people/house/PostalCode.asp?Source=SM
Related Resources:
Postal Codes by Constituency
http://www.parl.gc.ca/information/about/process/House/asp/
ConstPostalCode.asp

MPnetwork U.K.
http://194.128.65.140/home.asp?search=
Search for members of the British Parliament by postcode, surname,
constituency and party.
Search Form URL: See Main Page

Government Programs

Catalog of Federal Domestic Assistance
http://www.cfda.gov/
This imporant Federal Government publication contains information
on assistance programs administered by 57 Federal Agencies. "As a
potential applicant, always contact the agency information sources in
the program descriptions for the latest information concerning assistance programs."
Search Form URL: http://www.cfda.gov/public/faprs.htm
Related Resources:
Fedix (Federal Information Exchange)
http://content.sciencewise.com/fedix/index.htm
Minority Online Information Service (Molis)
http://content.sciencewise.com/molis/
Small Business Funding
http://services.sciencewise.com/content/search/results_
content.cfm

Federal Procurement Data System
http://fpds.gsa.gov
"The Official Statistical Data Base on Procurement Contract Transactions
of the U.S. Government (Executive Branch)" Procurement contract

transactions reported by approximately 65 U.S. Government, Executive Branch, departments, bureaus, agencies, and commissions. The largest exception to the requirement to report is the U.S. Postal Service.
Search Form URL: http://fpds.gsa.gov/Fpds/cust_reports.htm

National Lottery Award Search U.K.
http://www.culture.gov.uk/lottery/index.html
"Information about National Lottery Awards. You can search for: awards granted in your area; recent awards or those granted for a specific date; awards granted for a particular project; whether a specific award has been granted."
Search Form URL: http://www.culture.gov.uk/lottery_search/

Social Security Administration Frequently Asked Questions
http://www.ssa.gov
"More than 500 questions asked and answered." Questions can be searched or broswed.
Search Form URL: http://ssa-custhelp.ssa.gov/cgi-bin/ssa/

Politics, Policy, and International Relations

Country Indicators for Foreign Policy
http://www.carleton.ca/cifp/
"… an ongoing effort to identify and assemble statistical information conveying the key features of the economic, political, social, and cultural environments of countries around the world." Free registration is required.
Search Form URL: See Main Page

Database KOSIMO (Political Conflicts)
http://www.hiik.de/en/kosimo/kosimo.htm
"KOSIMO is the name of a database containing (at this time) 693 political conflicts from 1945 to 1999. Each conflict is coded with 28 variables." The online version allows users to search 6 variables. You can also choose to download the entire database.

Search Form URL: http://www.hiik.de/en/kosimo/kosimo_ querry.htm

FIRST (Facts on International Relations and Security Trends)

http://www.sipiri.se

"Facts on International Relations and Security Trends (FIRST) is a free-of-charge service for politicians, journalists, researchers, and the interested public. FIRST is a joint project of the International Relations and Security Network (ISN) and the Stockholm International Peace Research Institute (SIPRI)."

Search Form URL: http://first.sipri.se

Related Resources:

Comparing National Export Control Systems

http://projects.sipri.se/expcon/db1.htm

International Boundary News Database

http://www-ibru.dur.ac.uk

"The database contains over 10,000 boundary-related reports from a wide range of news sources around the world dating from 1991 to approximately six months before the current date." Provided by the International Boundary Research Unit at University of Durham.

Search Form URL: http://www-ibru.dur.ac.uk/database/data.html

Political Database of the Americas

http://www.georgetown.edu/pdba/english.html

"The Georgetown University Center for Latin American Studies' Political Database of the Americas was founded to fill a void in the electronic informational resources available to students, academics, policy analysts, and government officials on Latin American politics."

Search Form URL: See Main Page

Recent Lobbyist Registrations with the United States Congress

http://www.tray.com

This resource provides registration data for individuals who recently filed with the U.S. Secretary of the Senate's Public Records Office wanting to lobby the United States Congress.

Search Form URL: http://www.tray.com/bna/bna.exe

Related Resources:

Lobbyist Search Canada

http://strategis.ic.gc.ca/cgi-bin/sc_mrksv/lobbyist/bin/lrs.e/
view_search.phtml

Women in Politics Bibliographic Database B

http://www.ipu.org

The database is regularly updated to take account of new books and articles produced throughout the world on the subject of women in politics.
So far, it covers some 650 titles representing international, regional,
country-by-country, as well as thematic perspectives of the subject.
Search Form URL: http://www.ipu.org/bdf-e/BDfsearch.asp

Statistics

FedScope

http://www.fedscope.opm.gov

A completely interactive guide to locate statistics and other data about
U.S. Federal Government employment.
Search Form URL: See Main Page

Fedstats (United States Statistics)

http://www.fedstats.gov

"FedStats is the new window on the full range of official statistical
information available to the public from the Federal Government. Use
the Internet's powerful linking and searching capabilities to track economic and population trends, health care costs, aviation safety, foreign trade, energy use, farm production, and more. Access official
statistics collected and published by more than 70 Federal agencies
without having to know in advance which agency produces them."
Search Form URL: See Main Page

Infonation UN

http://www.un.org/Pubs/CyberSchoolBus/

"InfoNation is an easy-to-use, two-step database that allows you to
view and compare the most up-to-date statistical data for the Member
States of the United Nations."
Search Form URL: http://www.un.org/Pubs/CyberSchoolBus/
infonation/e_infonation.htm

State and County Quick Facts

http://www.census.gov

"State and County QuickFacts provides frequently requested Census Bureau information at the national, state, and county level."
Search Form URL: http://quickfacts.census.gov/qfd/index.html

Statistical Profiles of Canadian Communities Canada

http://www.statcan.ca
"This site contains information from the 1996 Census of Population conducted by Statistics Canada on May 14, 1996. A statistical profile is presented for all Canadian communities (cities, towns, villages, Indian Reserves and Settlements, etc.) highlighting information on education, income and work, families and dwellings, as well as general population information."
Search Form URL: http://ww2.statcan.ca/english/profil/
Related Resources:
First Nation Community Profiles Canada
http://esd.inac.gc.ca/fnprofiles/

CHAPTER 17

Health and Medical Information

According to a study from the Pew Internet and American Life Project, 47 percent of people who sought health information online said the information influenced their decisions about health and care. While it's good news that many people feel empowered to take a more active role in their own medical choices, many healthcare professionals are concerned about the quality of some of the health and medical information available online. Since anyone can publish on the Web, many quacks and outright charlatans have used the opportunity to create "medical information" Web sites that are at best misleading and at worst downright dangerous to users who accept what they offer without questioning the source.

Fortunately, there's a vast amount of authoritative information available on the Invisible Web, offered by healthcare organizations with unimpeachable reputations. Whether you're looking for information on diseases, medical procedures, pharmaceutical drugs, nutrition, clinical trials, or other healthcare related issues, the chances are good you'll find exceptionally high quality information using the resources we've gathered for this category.

These key resources are included:

- **Diseases and Conditions**, including the *HIV/Aids Treatment Directory (AmfAR's)*, a resource with data on current issues, clinical studies, treatments, and more

- **Healthcare and Medical Information**, including *Combined Health Information Database (CHID)*, a bibliographic database produced by health-related agencies of the Federal Government

- **Healthcare Professional Resources**, such as the *Internet Grateful Med*, which provides access to 13 medical databases

- **Locators**, such as *Nursing Home Compare*, which provides detailed information about the performance of every Medicare- and Medicaid-certified nursing home in the country

- **Research Resources**, such as *ClinicalTrials.gov*, which provides information to the public about current clinical research studies

See the Health and Medical Information category on the companion Web site for additional Invisible Web resources on this topic at http://www.invisible-web.net.

Diseases and Conditions

AIDS Economics Bibliographic Search B
http://www.worldbank.org/aids-econ
"AIDS Economics maintains a searchable database of new and important publications relevant to the economics of HIV/AIDS."
Search Form URL: http://www.worldbank.org/aids-econ/biblio.htm

Alcohol and Alcohol Problems Science Database (ETOH)— National Institute on Alcohol Abuse and Alcoholism (NIAAA) B
http://etoh.niaaa.nih.gov/
"The Alcohol and Alcohol Problems Science Database, commonly referred to as ETOH, is the most comprehensive online resource covering all aspects of alcohol abuse and alcoholism. Produced by the National Institute on Alcohol Abuse and Alcoholism (NIAAA), ETOH contains over 110,000 records and is accessed by both researchers and clinicians worldwide. Included in ETOH are abstracts and bibliographic references to journal articles, books, dissertation abstracts, conference papers and proceedings, reports and studies, and chapters in edited works. Updated monthly, ETOH contains research findings

from the late 1960s to the present, as well as historical research literature."
Search Form URL: http://etoh.niaaa.nih.gov/basic.htm
Related Resources:
Alcohol Studies Database
http://scc01.rutgers.edu/alcohol_studies/
Alcohol Industry & Policy Database (Marin Institute for the Prevention of Alcohol and Other Drug Problems)
http://marin.andornot.com/

BiblioSleep B
http://www.sleephomepages.org/
"BiblioSleep currently consists of all sleep and sleep-related papers from 1990 to the present. We are continuing to add yearly compendiums in order to accomplish our goal of making BiblioSleep a complete repository of sleep literature."
Search Form URL: http://www.websciences.org/bibliosleep/

Disease Surveillance Online Canada
http://www.hc-sc.gc.ca/hpb/lcdc/
Three searchable databases with statistical data on Cancer, Cardiovascular Diseases, and Notifiable Diseases.
Search Form URL: http://www.hc-sc.gc.ca/hpb/lcdc/webmap/index.html

Economics of Tobacco Control Database
http://www.worldbank.com
"Various tobacco/smoking related statistics (tobacco production, health expenditures, smoking prevalence) for numerous countries."
Search Form URL: http://www1.worldbank.org/tobacco/database.asp

European Database on AIDS and HIV Infection B
http://www.edoa.org/
"A bibliographic database focused on grey literature and educational material produced by a group of European documentation centers specialized in AIDS and HIV infection."
Search Form URL: See Main Page

HIV/Aids Treatment Directory (AmfAR's)
http://199.105.91.6/treatment/mainframe.asp

Several browsable and searchable resources with data on current issues, clinical studies, treatments, and more.
Search Form URL: See Main Page

PDQ (Physician Data Query) Comprehensive Cancer Database

http://cancernet.nci.nih.gov

"PDQ, NCI's (National Cancer Institute) comprehensive cancer database, contains peer-reviewed summaries on cancer treatment, screening, prevention, genetics, and supportive care; a registry of approximately 1,800 open and 10,300 closed cancer clinical trials from around the world; and directories of physicians, professionals who provide genetics services, and organizations that provide cancer care."
Search Form URL: http://cancernet.nci.nih.gov/pdq.html
Related Resources:
Cancerlit B
http://cancernet.nci.nih.gov/cancerlit.html
cancerTrials
http://cancernet.nci.nih.gov/trialsrch.shtml

PIE Database (Mental Health Policy)

http://www.mimh.edu/mimhweb/pie/

"PIE [Policy Information Exchange] maintains a comprehensive database of mental health policy related reports." Produced by the Missouri Institute of Mental Health.
Search Form URL: http://www.mimh.edu/mimhweb/pie/database/database.htm
Related Resources:
PIE Conference Database (Mental Health Conferences)
http://www.mimh.edu/mimhweb/pie/confrnc/confrnc.htm
Mental Health Services Research Database
http://cdmgroup.com/Ken-cf/MHRes.cfm

Rare Disease Database (National Organization for Rare Disorders)

http://www.rarediseases.org/

This database provides access to information on over 1,100 diseases. Abstracts are free to read online but access to full text is fee based. Also accessible are an Orphan Drug database, and a database of organizations.

Search Form URL: http://www.stepstn.com/nord/db/dbsearch/
search.htm

Tobacco Industry Documents

http://www.cdc.gov/tobacco/

"On July 17, 1998, the President of the United States issued an
Executive Memorandum highlighting the importance of tobacco
industry documents released as a result of recent tobacco litigation
and congressional subpoenas. ... The Tobacco Industry Documents
Web site has been designed to implement the President's Executive
Memorandum by increasing access to these tobacco industry docu-
ments and by making the documents more easily available via the
Internet. The Web site contains several components."

Search Form URL: http://www.cdc.gov/tobacco/industrydocs/
index.htm

Related Resources:

Tobacco Control Archives

http://galen.library.ucsf.edu/tobacco/

U.S. Department of Defense GulfLINK

http://www.gulflink.osd.mil/

"GulfLINK, the collection of recently declassified military and intelligence documents concerning Gulf War Illnesses, was created primarily as a database to be searched by users to retrieve desired
information."

Search Form URL: http://www.gulflink.osd.mil/cgi-bin/texis/
search/browse/

World Health Organization (WHO) Cancer Mortality Databank

http://www-dep.iarc.fr/

Cancer mortality data for many nations.

Search Form URL: http://www-dep.iarc.fr/dataava/globocan/
who.htm

Related Resources:

GloboCan (Java required)

http://www-dep.iarc.fr/dataava/globocan/globoJava.html

Atlas of Cancer Mortality in the United States 1950-1994

http://www.nci.nih.gov/atlas/

Your Cancer Risk

http://www.yourcancerrisk.harvard.edu/

Developed at the Harvard Center for Cancer Prevention. "Your Cancer Risk estimates your risk of cancer and provides personalized tips for prevention. It doesn't tell you if you'll get cancer or not. Anyone can use Your Cancer Risk, but it's most accurate for people age 40 and over who have never had any type of cancer."

Search Form URL: See Main Page

Images

Images from the History of Medicine

http://www.nlm.nih.edu

"This system provides access to the nearly 60,000 images in the prints and photograph collection of the History of Medicine Division (HMD) of the U.S. National Library of Medicine (NLM). The collection includes portraits, pictures of institutions, caricatures, genre scenes, and graphic art in a variety of media, illustrating the social and historical aspects of medicine."

Search Form URL: http://wwwihm.nlm.nih.gov/

Photoshare

http://www.jhuccp.org/mmc/

"The Media/Materials Clearinghouse (M/MC) photo library contains thousands of photographs related to population, public health, and related issues in developing countries. Photoshare is intended for use by communication specialists, editors, graphic designers, and publishers for nonprofit educational purposes. You may browse more than 3,600 photos through Photoshare online. The database is easy to search and grows monthly."

Search Form URL: http://db.jhuccp.org/mmc/photoshare/search.stm

Public Health Image Library

http://phil.cdc.gov/Phil/default.asp

Created by a Working Group at the Centers for Disease Control and Prevention (CDC), PHIL™ offers an organized, universal electronic gateway to CDC's pictures.

Search Form URL: http://phil.cdc.gov/Phil/search_page.asp

Healthcare and Medical Information

CDC Wonder (Centers for Disease Control)
http://wonder.cdc.gov/
"CDC WONDER is an easy-to-use system that provides a single point of access to a wide variety of CDC reports, guidelines, and numeric public health data."
Search Form URL: See Main Page

Combined Health Information Database (CHID)
http://chid.nih.gov/
"The CHID is a bibliographic database produced by health-related agencies of the Federal Government. This database provides titles, abstracts, and availability information for health information and health education resources."
Search Form URL: http://chid.nih.gov/detail/detail.html

DNA Patent Database
http://208.201.146.119/
"The DPD, a joint project of the Georgetown University's Kennedy Institute of Ethics and the Foundation for Genetic Medicine, allows free public access to the full text and analysis of all DNA patents issued by the United States Patent and Trademark Office (PTO)."
Search Form URL: See Main Page

English National Board (ENB) for Nursing, Midwifery, and Health Visiting—Healthcare Database B, U.K.
http://www.enb.org.uk
A bibliographic database of healthcare literature.
Search Form URL: http://www.enb.org.uk/hcd.htm

HazDat (Hazardous Substance Release/Health Effects Database)
http://www.atsdr.cdc.gov/atsdrhome.html
"HazDat, the Agency for Toxic Substances and Disease Registry's Hazardous Substance Release/Health Effects Database, is the scientific and administrative database developed to provide access to information on the release of hazardous substances from Superfund sites or from emergency events and on the effects of hazardous substances on the health of human populations."

Search Form URL: http://www.atsdr.cdc.gov/hazdat.html
Related Resources:
GATHER (Health Issues Spatial Data)
http://gis.cdc.gov/atsdr/

HealthComm KEY Database B

http://www.cdc.gov/od/oc/hcomm/
"The database contains comprehensive summaries of more than 200 articles about health communication research and practice. Articles selected for the database were published between 1986 and 1996 and describe U.S.-based public health interventions that have communication as a major component."
Search Form URL: See Main Page

International Digest of Health Legislation

http://www.who.int
"The International Digest of Health Legislation contains a selection of national and international health legislation. Texts of legislation are summarized in English or mentioned by their title. Where possible, links are provided to other Web sites that contain full texts of the legislation in question."
Search Form URL: http://www-nt.who.int/idhl/en/ConsultIDHL.cfm

Literature, Arts, and Medicine Database

http://endeavor.med.nyu.edu/lit-med/lit-med-db/
"The Literature, Arts, & Medicine Database is an annotated bibliography of prose, poetry, film, video, and art [that] is being developed as a dynamic, accessible, comprehensive resource in MEDICAL HUMANITIES, for use in health/pre-health and liberal arts settings." Each entry includes an annotation.
Search Form URL: See Main Page

NHS (National Health Service) Economic Evaluation Database U.K.

http://agatha.york.ac.uk/nhsdhp.htm
"Full economic evaluations in the scope of the NHS Economic Evaluation Database are regarded as cost-benefit analyses, cost-utility analyses, and cost-effectiveness analyses. Cost-minimisation analyses and cost-consequence analyses are also included."
Search Form URL: http://144.32.228.3/scripts/WEBC.EXE/NHSCRD/start

Related Resources:
National Health Service Pharmacy Database
http://www.nhs.uk/pharmacies/search_pharmacy.asp
NHS Local Health Services
http://www.nhs.uk/organisations/

Healthcare Professional Resources

Community Health Indicators
http://www.communityhealth.hrsa.gov/
Health assessment information at the county level for the United States.
Search Form URL: http://www.communityhealth.hrsa.gov/
searchCounty.asp

DIRLINE (Health and Biomedicine Resources)
http://www.nlm.nih.gov/hinfo.html
"DIRLINE (Directory of Information Resources Online) is the National
Library of Medicine's online database containing location and
descriptive information about a wide variety of information resources
including organizations, research resources, projects, and databases
concerned with health and biomedicine. This information may not be
readily available in bibliographic databases. Each record may contain
information on the publications, holdings, and services provided."
Search Form URL: http://dirline.nlm.nih.gov/

Doctors Guide: Congress (Conference and Meetings) Guide
http://www.docguide.com
"A Physician's Guide for Global Congress & Travel Planning. The
Congress Resource Centre (CRC) is a one-stop site of organised links
and information designed to facilitate planning and scheduling for a
featured congress."
Search Form URL: http://www.docguide.com/crc.nsf/
web-bySpec? OpenForm

HCUPnet (U.S. Hospital Statistics)
http://www.ahcpr.gov/data/hcup/hcupnet.htm
"A tool for identifying, tracking, analyzing, and comparing statistics on
hospitals at the national, regional, and state level."
Search Form URL: See Main Page

HSTAT (Healthcare Decision Making)

http://www.nlm.nih.gov
"HSTAT is a free, electronic resource that provides access to the full text of documents useful in healthcare decision making."
Search Form URL: http://text.nlm.nih.gov/

International Classification of Functioning, Disability, and Health

http://www.who.int/icidh/
"This volume contains the International Classification of Functioning, Disability and Health, known as ICIDH-2. The overall aim of the ICIDH-2 classification is to provide a unified and standard language and framework for the description of health and health-related states."
Search Form URL: See Main Page

Internet Grateful Med B

http://igm.nlm.nih.gov/
Internet Grateful Med provides access to 13 medical databases including: HealthSTAR; Bioethicsline, and AIDSLINE.
Search Form URL: See Main Page
Related Resources:
Jade (Medline Update Service)
http://www.biodigital.org/jade/
PubCrawler (Medline Update Service)
http://www.pubcrawler.ie/

National Guidelines Clearinghouse

http://www.guidelines.gov/
"The National Guidelines Clearinghouse (NGC) is an Internet Web site intended to make evidence-based clinical practice guidelines and related abstract, summary, and comparison materials widely available to healthcare professionals. NGC is operated by the U.S. Dept. of Health and Human Services, Agency for Healthcare Research and Quality (AHRQ) (formerly the Agency for Health Care Policy and Research [AHCPR]) in partnership with the American Medical Association (AMA), and the American Association of Health Plans (AAHP)."
Search Form URL: http://www.guidelines.gov/body_home_nf.asp?view=home

PubMed/Medline B

http://www.ncbi.nlm.nih.gov/

Medline is one of the world's preeminent medical literature databases. "PubMed is the National Library of Medicine's search service that provides access to over 11 million citations in MEDLINE, PreMEDLINE, and other related databases, with links to participating online journals." Medline is also available via numerous additional providers.
Search Form URL: http://www.ncbi.nlm.nih.gov/entrez/query.fcgi
Related Resources:
PubMed Central (Limited Full-Text Journal Access)
http://www.pubmedcentral.nih.gov/
The NCCAM Complementary and Alternative Medicine (CAM) Citation Index (Subset of Medline database)
http://156.40.39.5/
Biomedical Journal Title Search
http://bones.med.ohio-state.edu/abrv/

TRIP Database

http://www.tripdatabase.com
"The TRIP Database is a meta-search engine that searches across 61 sites of high-quality medical information. By searching the TRIP Database you have direct, hyperlinked access to the largest collection of 'evidence-based' material on the web as well as articles from premier online journals such as the BMJ, JAMA, NEJM, etc."
Search Form URL: See Main Page

WISQARS (Web-based Injury Statistics Query and Reporting System)

http://www.cdc.gov/ncipc/default.htm
"WISQARS™ (Web-based Injury Statistics Query and Reporting System) is an interactive system that provides customized injury-related mortality data useful for research and for making informed public-health decisions."
Search Form URL: http://www.cdc.gov/ncipc/osp/data.htm

Locators

American Hospital Directory

http://www.ahd.com
"The American Hospital Directory provides online, comparative data for most hospitals. Our database is built from Medicare claims data,

cost reports, and other public use files obtained from the federal Health Care Financing Administration." Limited data available for free. Additional data is fee-based.
Search Form URL: http://www.ahd.com/freeservices.php3

Certified Mammography Centers

http://www.fda.gov/cdrh/mammography/
"... access a listing by State and ZIP Code of all mammography facilities certified by the Food and Drug Administration (FDA) as meeting baseline quality standards for equipment, personnel, and practices under the Mammography Quality Standards Act of 1992 (MQSA)."
Search Form URL: http://www.fda.gov/cdrh/mammography/certified.html

HomeCare/Hospice Agency Locator

http://www.nahc.org/tango/hclocator/locator.html
"The HomeCare/Hospice Agency locator searches the most comprehensive database of over 22,500 home-care and/or hospice providers." The data is provided by the National Association for Homecare.
Search Form URL: http://www.nahc.org/Tango/HCLocator/locator.qry?function=form
Related Resources:
National Hospice & Palliative Care Organization Database (select "Find a Hospice Program")
http://209.141.207.182/

Hospital Records Database U.K.

http://hospitalrecords.pro.gov.uk/
"This database provides information on the existence and location of the records of hospitals in the U.K. The database currently contains over 2,800 entries."
Search Form URL: http://hospitalrecords.pro.gov.uk/scripts/searchscreen.asp

Nursing Home Compare

http://www.medicare.gov
"The primary purpose of this tool is to provide detailed information about the performance of every Medicare- and Medicaid-certified nursing home in the country."
Search Form URL: http://www.medicare.gov/NHCompare/Home.asp
Related Resources:

ExtendedCare.Com Provider Search
http://www.extendedcare.com/asp/pubprovidersearchform.asp

Substance Abuse Treatment Facility Locator

http://findtreatment.samhsa.gov/
"The Locator includes more than 11,000 residential treatment centers, inpatient drug treatment and alcohol treatment programs, and outpatient treatment programs for drug abuse and addiction and alcoholism. Listings include treatment programs for marijuana, cocaine, and heroin addiction, as well as drug and alcohol treatment programs for teenagers, adolescents, and adults."
Search Form URL: See Main Page

Nutrition

International Bibliographic Information on Dietary Supplements (IBIDS) B

http://ods.od.nih.gov/
"The International Bibliographic Information on Dietary Supplements (IBIDS) is a database of published, international, scientific literature on dietary supplements, including vitamins, minerals, and botanicals."
Search Form URL: http://ods.od.nih.gov/databases/ibids.html

Nutrition Analysis Tool 2.0

http://www.nat.uiuc.edu/
"NAT is provided as a public service by the Food Science and Human Nutrition Department at the University of Illinois. The tool is intended to empower individuals to select a nutrient-dense diet. It is not intended to replace the advice of a physician or health professional."
Search Form URL: http://www.nat.uiuc.edu/mainnat.html
Related Resources:
Fast Food Facts
http://www.ag.state.mn.us/consumer/health/fff.asp

United States Department of Agriculture (USDA) Nutrient Database for Standard Reference

http://www.nal.usda.gov
"This page provides access to Release 13 of the USDA Nutrient Database for Standard Reference. You can either view the data here or

download the data files and documentation in several different formats for use later on your computer. A search tool is also provided so you can look up the nutrient content of over 6,200 different foods directly from this home page."

Search Form URL: http://www.nal.usda.gov/fnic/cgi-bin/nut_search.pl

Patient Information and Consumer Resources

Health and Safety Executive (HSE) Public Register of Prosecutions U.K.

http://www.hse-databases.co.uk/prosecutions/

"This site gives details of all prosecution cases taken by HSE, since 1 April 1999, which resulted in a conviction. HSE enforces health and safety legislation for some industry sectors in the U.K. We cover factories, building sites, mines, farms, fairgrounds, quarries, railways, chemical plant, offshore and nuclear installations, schools, hospitals, and other places where there is a work activity."

Search Form URL: See Main Page

Manufacturer and User Facility Device Experience Database (MAUDE)

http://www.fda.gov/cdrh/

"MAUDE data represents reports of adverse events involving medical devices. The data consists of all voluntary reports since June 1993, user facility reports since 1991, distributor reports since 1993, and manufacturer reports since August 1996."

Search Form URL: http://www.fda.gov/cdrh/maude.html

Mayo Clinic

http://www.mayo.com

The Mayo Clinic provides access to "condition centers" with information on eleven medical conditions including Alzheimer's, Cancer, and Mental Health. Much of the information on the Mayo Clinic site resides on the Invisible Web.

Search Form URL: http://www.mayoclinic.com/home?id=SP3.1
Related Resources:
Mayo Clinic First-Aid and Self-Care Guide
http://www.mayoclinic.com/home?id=SP5.6

Medicare Health Plan Compare

http://www.medicare.gov
"Medicare Health Plan Compare helps you obtain detailed informa-
tion on Medicare's health plan options. By "comparison shopping,"
you can find the plans that are best for you."
Search Form URL: http://www.medicare.gov/MPHcompare/
Home.asp

Sanitation Inspections of International Cruise Ships

http://www.cdc.gov/nceh/vsp/vsp.htm
"Every vessel that has a foreign itinerary and that carries 13 or more
passengers is subject to twice-yearly inspections and, when necessary,
to reinspection by the Centers for Disease Control and Prevention
(CDC). To ensure a clean and healthful environment, cruise ships
must meet the criteria established by CDC. The score a ship receives
after inspection is published every 2 weeks in the Summary of
Sanitation Inspections of International Cruise Ships, commonly
referred to as the Green Sheet. The ship's level of sanitation is acceptable to CDC if its score on the inspection is 86% or higher."
Search Form URL: http://www2.cdc.gov/nceh/vsp/vspmain.asp

State Medicaid Policy Search Application (Health Care Finance Administration)

http://www.hcfa.gov/medicaid/
"The Medicaid State Plan section of HCFA's Web site represents our
effort to make the Medicaid State Plan materials available to the public in a convenient, searchable format."
Search Form URL: http://www.hcfa.gov/medicaid/stateplan/Map.asp

Toll-Free Hotlines, Health Information

http://sis.nlm.nih.gov/hotlines/index.cfm
"The National Library of Medicine is pleased to offer this online database of health-related organizations operating toll-free telephone
services. The database also includes information on services and publications available in Spanish."
Search Form URL: See Main Page

Transplant Patient Datasource, United Network for Organ Sharing (UNOS)

http://www.patients.unos.org/tpd/

"This site contains the most up-to-date center-specific results possible and is designed to help you learn more about the field of transplantation."

Search Form URL: http://www.patients.unos.org/tpd/

U.S. Army Physical Fitness Test Score Calculator

http://www.armytimes.com

Are you fit enough for the U.S. Army? Beware, this resource is not provided by the Army. Results are unofficial.

Search Form URL: http://cgi.mconetwork.com/cgi-bin/ptcalculator.pl

Related Resources:

U.S. Marines Body Fat Calculator

http://cgi.mconetwork.com/cgi-bin/marinebodyfat.pl

Pharmaceutical Drugs

Canadian Drug Product Database Canada

http://www.hc-sc.gc.ca/

"... provides product and company information for drug products marketed in Canada."

Search Form URL: http://www.hc-sc.gc.ca/hpb-dgps/therapeut/htmleng/dpd.html

Drug Information Database

http://www.familydoctor.org

"Find information about the drugs you are taking, including proper use and possible side effects." Provided by the American Academy of Family Physicians.

Search Form URL: http://www.familydoctor.org/cgi-bin/drugsearch.pl

Related Resources:

Drug Reaction Database

http://www.familydoctor.org/druginfo/

A to Z Drug Facts

http://www.drugfacts.com/DrugFacts/MedFacts/MedFactsTop50Page.jhtml

Research

CIHR Funding Database (Canada Institute of Health Research) Canada

http://www.cihr.ca/

"In this database, you will find information on currently funded researchers, such as: type of research funded, name of researchers, the institution and the city where the research is conducted, in Canada and abroad, the funding value of the research per year, and the e-mail address of the researcher."

Search Form URL: http://207.236.233.199/ExpertsDatabase/cihr_search_options.asp?language=eng

ClinicalTrials.gov

http://clinicaltrials.gov

"The U.S. National Institutes of Health, through its National Library of Medicine, has developed ClinicalTrials.gov to provide patients, family members, and members of the public current information about clinical research studies."

Search Form URL: http://clinicaltrials.gov/ct/gui/c/b

Related Resources:

Centerwatch

http://www.CenterWatch.com/

Cancer Research in Australia

http://cornhill.ludwig.edu.au/cara2/netscape/index2.html

Current Controlled Trials U.K.

http://www.controlled-trials.com

CRISP (Computer Retrieval of Information on Scientific Projects)

https://www-commons.cit.nih.gov/

"CRISP (Computer Retrieval of Information on Scientific Projects) is a searchable database of federally funded biomedical research projects conducted at universities, hospitals, and other research institutions. The database, maintained by the Office of Extramural Research at the National Institutes of Health, includes projects funded by the National Institutes of Health (NIH), Substance Abuse and Mental Health Services (SAMHSA), Health Resources and Services Administration (HRSA), Food and Drug Administration (FDA), Centers for Disease

Control and Prevention (CDCP), Agency for Healthcare Research and Quality (AHRQ), and Office of Assistant Secretary of Health (OASH)."
Search Form URL: http://crisp.cit.nih.gov/

Euroethics B

http://www.spri.se/spriline/sokforie.htm
"European Database on Medical Ethics. Euroethics is a European database of bibliographical references concerned with ethical issues in health care and biomedical research. Participating countries are France, Germany, the Netherlands, and Sweden." Menu-driven search also available.
Search Form URL: http://www.spri.se/spriline/sokforie.htm

National Research Register U.K.

http://www.update-software.com/National/nrr-frame.html
The National Research Register (NRR) is a register of ongoing and recently completed research projects funded by, or of interest to, the United Kingdom's National Health Service.
Search Form URL: See Main Page

New Medicines in Development Database

http://www,pharma.org
Provided by the Pharmaceutical Research and Manufacturers of America (PhRMA). "This database contains information on pharmaceutical products in the research and testing phase. Information has been obtained through government and industry sources based upon the latest information but may not be comprehensive. For more information about a particular product, please contact the individual company directly."
Search Form URL: http://www.phrma.org/searchcures/newmeds/webdb/

U.S. Department of Defense Biomedical Research Database

http://www.scitechweb.com/acau/brd/
"The areas of research, testing, and training include, but are not limited to, the following: infectious diseases, biological hazards, toxicology, medical chemical defense, medical biological defense, clinical medicine, clinical surgery, physical protection, training, graduate medical education, and instruction."
Search Form URL: See Main Page

Workplace Health and Safety

Mining Safety and Health Research: Common Information Service System

http://outside.cdc.gov:8000/ciss/Welcome.html

"CISS is an information system provided as a public service by NIOSH (National Institute for Occupational Safety and Health) Mining Safety & Health Research (formerly the U.S. Bureau of Mines). Thousands of publications are stored in this searchable database in bibliographic form and include abstracts. More recent publications are stored in the database in their entirety in PDF format. Full-text searches can be performed on these publications. The publications can then be viewed online, printed, or saved for future reference."

Search Form URL: http://outside.cdc.gov:8000/BASIS/ciss/pubs/pubs/SF

Occupational Safety and Health Administration (OSHA) Accident Investigation Search

http://www.osha.gov/

Enables the user to search the OSHA Accident Investigation Summaries (OSHA-170 Form).

Search Form URL: http://www.osha.gov/cgi-bin/inv/inv1

Related Resources:

OSHA Establishment Search

http://www.osha.gov/cgi-bin/est/est1

CHAPTER 18

U.S. and World History

Historians are by nature born archivists, and have created some truly fabulous repositories of U.S. and World History materials on the Invisible Web. Resources range from original source papers of famous people to fact databases to locators for historic sites. Many of the resources we've selected contain images and other multimedia materials.

These key resources are included:

- **Significant Collections**, including *The American Memory Collection*, with over 80 collections of digitized historical material from the National Digital Library at the Library of Congress

- **Source Materials**, such as the *Abraham Lincoln Primary Source Material Database*, a large multimedia database of primary source materials illustrating life in antebellum Illinois

- **Multimedia Repositories**, including *Picture Australia*, a large directory of links to images of a wide array of Australiana

See the U.S. and World History category on the companion Web site for additional Invisible Web resources on this topic at http://www. invisible-web.net.

United States History

Abraham Lincoln Primary Source Material Database
http://lincoln.lib.niu.edu/
"... a large multimedia database of primary source materials illustrating life in antebellum Illinois."
Search Form URL: http://lincoln.lib.niu.edu/aboutinfo.html

African American Women Writers of the 19th Century
http://digital.nypl.org/
"African American Women Writers of the 19th Century is a digital collection of some 52 published works by 19th-century black women writers. A part of the Digital Schomburg, this collection provides access to the thought, perspectives and creative abilities of black women as captured in books and pamphlets published prior to 1920. A full text database of these 19th and early 20th- century titles, this digital library is key-word-searchable."
Search Form URL: http://digital.nypl.org/schomburg/writers_ aa19/

American Memory Collection (The)
http://lcweb2.loc.gov/ammem/
Over 80 collections of digitized historical material from the National Digital Library at the Library of Congress.
Search Form URL: http://memory.loc.gov/ammem/mdbquery. html
Related Resources:
Canada's Digital Collections
http://collections.ic.gc.ca/

American Verse Project
http://www.hti.umich.edu
"The American Verse Project is a collaborative project between the University of Michigan Humanities Text Initiative (HTI) and the University of Michigan Press. The project is assembling an electronic archive of volumes of American poetry prior to 1920. The full text of each volume of poetry is being converted into digital form and coded in Standard Generalized Mark-up Language (SGML) using the TEI Guidelines, with various forms of access provided through the WWW."
Search Form URL: http://www.hti.umich.edu/english/amverse/
Related Resources:

Australian Literary and Historical Texts
http://setis.library.usyd.edu.au/ozlit/

Avalon Project at Yale Law School (The)

http://www.yale.edu/lawweb/avalon/avalon.htm
"The Avalon Project will mount digital documents relevant to the
fields of Law, History, Economics, Politics, Diplomacy, and
Government. We do not intend to mount only static text but rather to
add value to the text by linking to supporting documents expressly
referred to in the body of the text."
Search Form URL: See Main Page

California Shipwreck Database

http://shipwrecks.slc.ca.gov/
Information includes ship name, cause, type, captain name, and year
built.
Search Form URL: http://shipwrecks.slc.ca.gov/Database/Default.asp
Related Resources:
Canadian Ship Information Database
http://daryl.chin.gc.ca:8000/basisbwdocs/sid/title1e.html
Australian National Shipwreck Database
http://www.aima.iinet.net.au/databases/aimadata.html

Congressional Biographical Directory, U.S.

http://bioguide.congress.gov/biosearch/biosearch.asp
Locate short bios for all members of the United States Congress from
1774 to date.
Search Form URL: See Main Page

Digital Schomburg: Images of African Americans from the 19th Century

http://digital.nypl.org
"The Schomburg Center for Research in Black Culture of The New York
Public Library is pleased to offer this selection of images of 19th-century
African Americans. They are presented in the hope that they will at one
and the same time address some of your viewing, research, education, and
study needs and introduce you to the various types of visual images on the
African-American experience that are contained in the Photographs and
Prints Division of the Schomburg Center as well as other selected units of
the Research Libraries of The New York Public Library."
Search Form URL: http://digital.nypl.org/schomburg/images_aa19/

Emergence of Advertising in America (EAA) 1850-1920 (The)

http://scriptorium.lib.duke.edu/

"The Emergence of Advertising in America: 1850-1920 (EAA) presents over 9,000 images, with database information, relating to the early history of advertising in the United States. The materials, drawn from the Rare Book, Manuscript, and Special Collections Library at Duke University, provide a significant and informative perspective on the early evolution of this most ubiquitous feature of modern American business and culture."

Search Form URL: http://scriptorium.lib.duke.edu/eaa/

Related Resources:

adflip.com

http://www.adflip.com/

History and Politics Out Loud

http://www.hpol.org/

"HPOL is a collection of invaluable audio materials—some available for the first time on this Web site—capturing significant political and historical events and personalities of the twentieth century. The materials range from formal addresses delivered in public settings to private telephone conversations conducted from the innermost recesses of the White House."

Search Form URL: See Main Page

Lewis and Clark Journals Database

http://www.pbs.org/lewisandclark/

"The following journal excerpts were compiled by Florentine Films in preparation for the making of "Lewis and Clark: The Journey of the Corps of Discovery." The excerpts—drawn from the separate, more extensive journals of Captains Meriwether Lewis and William Clark, Sergeants Charles Floyd, Patrick Gass, and John Ordway, and Private Joseph Whitehouse—were then put together in chronological order. Altogether, the entries of these seven Corps members span March 3, 1804, to September 26, 1806, totalling more than 140,000 words."

Search Form URL: http://www.pbs.org/lewisandclark/archive/idx_jou.html

Making of America Project

http://moa.umdl.umich.edu/

"Making of America (MOA) is a digital library of primary sources in American social history from the antebellum period through reconstruction. The collection is particularly strong in the subject areas of education, psychology, American history, sociology, religion, and science and technology. The collection currently contains approximately 2,900 books and 50,000 journal articles with 19th-century imprints."
Search Form URL: http://moa.umdl.umich.edu/moa_search.html

Model Editions Partnership (The)
http://adh.sc.edu:80/
"The purpose of the Model Editions Partnership is to explore ways of creating editions of historical documents [that] meet the standards scholars traditionally use in preparing printed editions." The related resources for this entry are examples of the 12 resources available.
Search Form URL: See Main Page
Related Resources:
The Frederick Douglass Papers
http://adh.sc.edu:80/fd/fd-table.html
Abraham Lincoln Legal Papers
http://adh.sc.edu:80/ll/ll-table.html
The Marcus Garvey and UNIA Papers
http://adh.sc.edu:80/mg/mg-table.html

National Historic Landmarks Database
http://www2.cr.nps.gov/nhl/index.htm
Locate landmarks deemed "historic" by the National Park Service. Each record includes the reasons why a landmark has been designated as historic.
Search Form URL: http://tps.cr.nps.gov/nhl/
Related Resources:
U.S. Historic Federal Buildings
http://hydra.gsa.gov/pbs/centers/arts/index.htm

National Register [of Historic Places] Information System
http://www.cr.nps.gov/nr/
"Established under the National Historic Preservation Act of 1966, the National Register has identified and documented, in partnership with state, federal, and tribal preservation programs, more than 71,000 districts, sites, buildings, structures, and objects that are significant in American history, architecture, archeology, engineering, and culture.

Over 1 million contributing resources are included in the boundaries of National Register listings."

Search Form URL: http://www.cr.nps.gov/nr/research/nris.htm

Papers of Thomas A. Edison

http://edison.rutgers.edu/

A selection of material from the papers of Thomas A. Edison. This collection is taken from a massive print and microfilm archival project. Material in this database is from 1847-1898.

Search Form URL: See Main Page

Philadelphia Historical Digital Image Library (PHDIL)

http://jeffline.tju.edu/archives/phdil/phdil.html

"Containing over 3,000 images, PHDIL [Philadelphia Historical Digital Image Library] consists of a variety of photographs, artwork, and portraits."

Search Form URL: http://jeffline.lib.tju.edu:8806/photo_archive/owas_photo/photo_archive_search_img2.input_data

Related Resources:

Seattle Municipal Archives Photograph Collection

http://clerk.ci.seattle.wa.us/~public/phot1.htm

Suffragists Oral History Project

http://library.berkeley.edu/

"Seven major figures in twentieth-century suffragist history are represented here with full-length oral histories." From the University of California, Berkeley.

Search Form URL: http://library.berkeley.edu/BANC/ROHO/ohonline/suffragists.html

United States Historical Census Data Browser

http://fisher.lib.virginia.edu/census/

Material presented in this database describes the people and the economy of the U.S. for each state and county from 1790 to 1970.

Search Form URL: See Main Page

Western History Photos (Denver Public Library)

http://gowest.coalliance.org/

"Our online collection contains a selection of historic photographs from the collections of the Denver Public Library Western History/Genealogy Department and the Colorado Historical Society.

These collections, which contain more than one million items, document the history of Colorado and the American West. Currently our online collection contains some 70,000 images and catalog records of Native Americans, pioneers, early railroads, mining, Denver, and Colorado towns."

Search Form URL: http://gowest.coalliance.org/presearch.html

World History

British Columbia Visual Records Database Canada

http://www.bcarchives.gov.bc.ca

The Visual Records Database contains over 110,000 textual descriptions. Over 60,000 images are available online. Provided by the British Columbia Archive.

Search Form URL: http://www.bcarchives.gov.bc.ca/visual/ visual.htm

Cambodian Genocide Bibliographic Database B

http://www.yale.edu/cgp/

"The Cambodian Genocide Program is attempting to create an indexed catalogue of all known primary and secondary documentary resources pertaining to gross violations of human rights during the Khmer Rouge regime. At present the CGP Bibliographic Database (CBIB) contains over 3,000 records."

Search Form URL: http://www.yale.edu/cgp/

Related Resources:

Cambodian Genocide Photographic Database
http://www.yale.edu/cgp/databases/img.htm
Cambodian Genocide Biographic Database
http://www.yale.edu/cgp/databases/bio.htm
Cambodian Genocide Geographic Database
http://www.yale.edu/cgp/databases/geo.htm

Canada Heritage Directory Canada

http://www.chin.gc.ca

"The Heritage Directory provides detailed information about organizations, government departments, and agencies, primarily in Canada, [that] are engaged in heritage activities."

Search Form URL: http://www.chin.gc.ca/Museums/CHER/e_ hp_cher.html

Canadian Women Inventors Database Canada

http://napoleon.ic.gc.ca/

Search or browse this database of women inventors from Canada.
Each entry includes a brief biography.

Search Form URL: http://napoleon.ic.gc.ca/cipo/cdn_inv.nsf/
Home+Page+View/EnglishHome

Early Canadiana Online (ECO) Canada

http://www.canadiana.org

"Early Canadiana Online (ECO) is a full-text online collection of more
than 3,000 books and pamphlets documenting Canadian history from
the first European contact to the late 19th century. The collection is
particularly strong in literature, women's history, native studies, travel
and exploration, and the history of French Canada."

Search Form URL: http://www.canadiana.org/eco/index.html

Historical Atlas of Canada Online Learning Project Canada

http://mercator.geog.utoronto.ca/

This online atlas geared for students is full of interactive maps and
graphs. Portions of this tool use Java-based resources. The site suggests the use of Internet Explorer for full functionality.

Search Form URL: See Main Page

Napolean Image Database

http://www.napolean.org

A searchable library of images relating to "civil and military achieve-
ments of the First and Second Empire." Provided by the Napolean
Foundation.

Search Form URL: http://www.napoleon.org/us/us_cd/media/
me-principal.asp

Online Calendar of Henry James's Letters and a
Biographical Register of Henry James's Correspondents

http://jamescalendar.unl.edu/

"This Web site provides access to a database of all known letters written by Henry James and brief biographical information on the recipients of these letters. In addition, lists of all publication sources of the
letters, the repositories where the letters are held, and statistics of collected letters are provided."

Search Form URL: http://jamescalendar.unl.edu/search.htm

Perseus Digital Library

http://www.perseus.tufts.edu/

"The Perseus Project is an evolving digital library of resources for the study of the ancient world and beyond. Collaborators initially formed the project to construct a large, heterogeneous collection of materials, textual and visual, on the Archaic and Classical Greek world."

Search Form URL: See Main Page

Picture Australia Australia

http://www.pictureaustralia.org

"Picture Australia consists of links to images of all forms of Australiana, except for digitised full text and contemporary items that are restricted by copyright from display. Renditions of three-dimensional objects are included."

Search Form URL: See Main Page

SHIPDES (Ship DEScription)

http://www.library.tudelft.nl/mic/

"SHIPDES (SHIP DEScription) is a database containing over 19,000 specific ship descriptions. Searching can be done by specific data such as ship's name, ship type, length, width, draught, tonnage, speed, number of containers, etc. (info)." Provided by the Maritime Information Center at the Delf University of Technolgy in the Netherlands.

Search Form URL: http://delfi.library.tudelft.nl:4505/ALEPH/-/start/SHIPDES

Related Resources:

MARNA (MARitime Nautical) Database B

http://130.161.182.20:4505/ALEPH/-/start/mic01

United States Holocaust Memorial Museum Archive and Collection Search

http://www.ushmm.org

"The U.S. Holocaust Memorial Museum Archives' online catalog provides a means for searching and retrieving information for collections in its current holdings." The photo archive records contain a copy of the image.

Search Form URL: http://www.ushmm.org/uia-cgi/uia_form/db_group/collections

Related Resources:

United States Holocaust Memorial Library Catalog B

http://library.ushmm.org
International Directory of Organizations in Holocaust Education,
Remembrance, and Research.
http://ntdata.ushmm.org/ad/

World War II Poster Collection

http://www.library.northwestern.edu/govpub/
"The Government Publications Department at Northwestern
University Library has a comprehensive collection of over 300 posters
issued by U.S. Federal agencies from the onset of war through 1945."
Search Form URL: http://www.library.northwestern.edu/govpub/
collections/wwii-posters/index.html
Related Resources:
League of Nations Digitization Project
http://www.library.northwestern.edu/govpub/collections/
league/index.html

CHAPTER 19

Legal and Criminal Resources

People who use the Web to conduct legal research demand a lot from their information tools. Material should be current, authoritative, and easy to access since time can often be an issue.

The Invisible Web delivers many resources that meet these as well as other important criteria. Quality material that was once difficult to access in a timely manner, especially for free, is now only a few keystrokes or clicks away, if you know where to find it.

This chapter provides a sample of some of the Invisible Web resources that the legal researcher will find useful.

These key resources are included:

- **General Legal Resources**, such as *Oran's Law Dictionary*, a glossary of more than 6,000 legal definitions for the non-lawyer

- **Intellectual Property Resources**, including the *U.S. Patent Databases (U.S. Patent and Trademark Office)*, featuring the full text of every patent issued since 1976 and images of every patent issued since 1790

- **Laws, Codes, and Treaties Resources**, such as the *British and Irish Legal Information Institute (BAILII)* with comprehensive access to the laws of the U.K.

We also include attorney and law firm locators, crime resources, legal documents, and other legal information.

See the Legal and Criminal Resources category on the companion Web site for additional Invisible Web resources on this topic at http://www.invisible-web.net.

Attorney and Law Firm Locators

Kime's International Law Directory (Internet Edition)
http://www.smlawpub.co.uk/kimes/
"This annual international directory provides reliable and up-to-date information on law firms and chambers throughout the world, covering nearly 250 countries."
Search Form URL: http://www.smlawpub.co.uk/kimes/search.cfm
Related Resources:
Solicitors Online U.K.
http://www.solicitors-online.com/

Patent Attorneys and Agents Registered to Practice before the PTO
http://www.uspto.gov
"This Index contains contact information for 25,022 attorneys and agents with licenses to practice before the U.S. Patent and Trademark Office."
Search Form URL: http://www.uspto.gov/web/offices/dcom/
olia/oed/roster/index.html
Related Resources:
European Patent Attorneys Database
http://www.european-patent-office.org/reps/search.html

West Legal Directory
http://www.lawoffice.com
"West Legal Directory provides profiles of more than 1,000,000 lawyers and law firms, in addition to profiles of international counsel, corporate counsel, and U.S. government attorneys."
Search Form URL: http://www.lawoffice.com/direct/direct.asp?
form=name
Related Resources:
Martindale-Hubble Lawyer Locator
http://lawyers.martindale.com/marhub

Martindale-Hubble Lawyer Locator Canada Canada
http://lawyers.martindale.com/canada

Crime and Criminals

Arson and Explosives National Repository
http://www.atf.treas.gov
"The National Repository was established by congressional mandate
in 1996 as a national collection center for information on arson and
explosives-related incidents throughout the United States. The
National Repository databases incorporate information from various
sources such as the Bureau of Alcohol, Tobacco and Firearms; the
Federal Bureau of Investigation; and the United States Fire
Administration."
Search Form URL: http://www.atf.treas.gov/aexis2/index.htm

Campus Security Statistics
http://ope.ed.gov
"... reported criminal offenses for over 6,000 colleges and universities
in the United States."
Search Form URL: http://ope.ed.gov/security/Search.asp

Interpol Most Wanted
http://www.interpol.int/Public/Wanted/
"These Interpol 'Red Notices' represent only a tiny fraction of the
number of red notices issued by Interpol. The persons concerned are
wanted by national jurisdictions (or the International Criminal
Tribunals for the Former Yugoslavia and Rwanda, where appropriate),
and Interpol's role is to assist the national police forces in identifying
or locating those persons with a view to their arrest and extradition."
Search Form URL: http://www.interpol.int/Public/Wanted/
Search/Form.asp

Decisions

United States Supreme Court Opinions
http://guide.lp.findlaw.com/casecode/supreme.html

This database of U.S. Supreme Court Decisions includes material back to 1893.

Search Form URL:

Related Resources:

Supreme Court of Canada Judgements
http://www.lexum.umontreal.ca/csc-scc/en/index.html

Documents and Records

Federal Justice Statistics Database

http://fjsrc.urban.org

"The FJSP database is constructed from data files provided by the Executive Office for U.S. Attorneys (EOUSA), the Administrative Office of the U.S. Courts (AOUSC), the U.S. Sentencing Commission (USSC), and the Federal Bureau of Prisons (BOP). The AOUSC provides criminal court data, as well as data collected by the Pretrial Services Administration (PSA), the U.S. courts of appeals (APPEALS), and the Federal Probation Supervision Information System (FPSIS)."

Search Form URL: http://fjsrc.urban.org/noframe/wqs/q_intro.htm

Records and Information Management System (RIMS) (Federal Energy Regulatory Council)

http://www.ferc.fed.us

"The RIMS On The Web (RIMSweb) application is the Web-enabled equivalent to the Federal Energy Regulatory Commission (FERC) Records and Information Management System (RIMS). RIMSweb gives Internet users electronic access to RIMS document index information for 'mixed' and public documents, and view access for mixed and public document pages, and the capability of locally printing public document pages."

Search Form URL: http://www.ferc.fed.us/online/rims.htm

General Legal Resources

Child Abuse and Neglect Clearinghouse Organizations Database

http://www.calib.com/nccanch/

"The Organizations Database describes 129 national organizations that focus on child abuse and neglect or child welfare issues, have a significant child abuse and neglect/child welfare component, or have a related primary focus but can provide some information to the field. It does not include federal agencies, regional or local organizations, survivor groups, treatment programs, foreign organizations, or religious organizations."
Search Form URL: http://www.calib.com/nccanch/scripts/SearchPg.cfm

Federal Rules of Evidence
http://lii.law.cornell.edu/
A searchable and browsable version of the Federal Rules of Evidence made available by the Legal Information Institute at Cornell University.
Search Form URL: http://www.law.cornell.edu/rules/fre/overview.html
Related Resources:
Federal Rules of Civil Procedure
http://www.law.cornell.edu/rules/frcp/overview.htm
Federal Rules of Bankruptcy Procedure
http://www2.law.cornell.edu/cgi-bin/foliocgi.exe/frb?

Filed Comments Search (Federal Communications Commission)
http://www.fcc.gov/searchtools.html
"This tool allows you to research any document in the Electronic Comment Filing System (ECFS) including non-electronic documents that have been scanned into the system. ECFS includes data and images from 1992 onward."
Search Form URL: http://www.fcc.gov/searchtools.html

HUDOC
http://hudoc.echr.coe.int/hudoc/
"Database of the case-law of the supervisory organs of the European Convention on Human Rights."
Search Form URL: http://hudoc.echr.coe.int/hudoc/default.asp?Language=en&Advanced=1

Judicial Sector Indicators (World Bank)
http://www1.worldbank.org/legal/legal.html

"This is a World Bank information system to design performance indicators for the judicial sector. This information can be used by the individual countries to assess their performance and assist in planning for the future. In addition, judiciaries may be encouraged to exchange information about their progress in judicial reform, share experiences, and transfer know-how from the most successful judiciaries to those implementing reforms."

Search Form URL: http://www1.worldbank.org/legal/legop_judicial/percountry.html

Oran's Law Dictionary

http://www.wld.com

"A complete glossary of more than 6,000 legal definitions written for the non-lawyer."

Search Form URL: http://www.wld.com/conbus/orans/ Welcome.asp
Related Resources:
Law.Com Law Dictionary
http://dictionary.law.com/

U.S. Federal County/District Court Lookups

http://pacer.psc.uscourts.gov/lookup.html

Search for all counties in a district, district by county name, or details by county code.

Search Form URL: See Main Page

Intellectual Property

Delphion Intellectual Property Network

http://www.delphion.com/

"The Delphion Intellectual Property Network (IPN) has evolved into a premier Web site for searching, viewing, and analyzing patent documents. The IPN provides you with free access to a wide variety of data collections and patent information including ... United States patents, European patents and patent applications, PCT application data from the World Intellectual Property Office, Patent Abstracts of Japan, INPADOC family and legal status data, and IBM Technical Disclosure Bulletins."

Search Form URL: See Main Page

esp@cenet (European Patent Office) Patent Database

http://ep.espacenet.com/

"esp@cenet is a free service on the Internet provided by the European Patent Organisation through the EPO and the national offices of its members states: Austria, Belgium, Cyprus, Denmark, Finland, France, Germany, Hellenic Republic, Ireland, Italy, Liechtenstein, Luxembourg, Monaco, Portugal, Spain, Sweden, Switzerland, United Kingdom."

Search Form URL: See Main Page

Related Resources:

European Patent Office Board of Appeals Decisions

http://www.european-patent-office.org/dg3/search_dg3.htm

Federal Land Patents Database

http://www.glorecords.blm.gov/logon/logon.asp

"From the Bureau of Land Management—General Land Office. The GLO Records Automation staff has automated two million eastern records, issued between 1820 and 1908. The original documents are now stored in acid-free boxes and protected in fireproof temperature-controlled vaults, ensuring the preservation of this vital component of American heritage."

Search Form URL: See Main Page

Related Resources:

Bureau of Land Management Land and Mineral Records

http://www.blm.gov/lr2000/

Alaska Land Information System

https://www.ak.blm.gov/

U.S. Patent Databases (U.S. Patent and Trademark Office)

http://www.uspto.gov

Numerous searching options including full-text and bibliograhic databases. "Full text of all U.S. patents issued since January 1, 1976, and full-page images of each page of every U.S. patent issued since 1790."

Search Form URL: See Main Page

Related Resources:

Australia Patent Databases

http://www.ipaustralia.gov.au/patents/P_srch.htm

Canada Patent Database

http://patents1.ic.gc.ca/intro-e.html

U.K. Patent Search
http://www.patent.gov.uk/patent/dbase/index.htm

United States Copyright Office Records

http://www.loc.gov/copyright/rb.html
The Copyright Office databases are not Web accessible but require a
Telnet connection to access the command line system. "Copyright
Office records, including registration information and recorded documents, are available through LOCIS (Library of Congress Information
System). Two files, COHM and COHS, contain records for materials
registered for copyright since January 1978. These materials include
books, films, music, maps, sound recordings, software, multimedia
kits, drawings, posters, sculpture, serials, etc. A third file, COHD, has
references to documents that describe copyright legal transactions,
such as name changes and transfers."
Search Form URL: http://www.loc.gov/copyright/rb.html

WIPO (World Intellectual Property Organization)
Digital Library

http://www.wipo.int
"The WIPO Intellectual Property Digital Library (IPDL) Project has
been developed to provide electronic intellectual property informa-
tion to government sectors and individual users." Material from the
PCT Database.
Search Form URL: http://ipdl.wipo.int/

Laws, Codes, and Treaties

Annual Review of Population Law

http://www.law.harvard.edu/programs/annual_review/
"This database contains summaries and excerpts of legislation, consti-
tutions, court decisions, and other official government documents from
every country in the world relating to population policies, reproductive
health, women's rights, and related topics. It is produced jointly by
Harvard Law School and the United Nations Population Fund."
Search Form URL: http://cyber.law.harvard.edu/population/arpl.htm

Australasian Legal Information Institute

http://austlii.law.uts.edu.au/

"AustLII publishes public legal information—that is, primary legal materials (legislation, treaties, and decisions of courts and tribunals); and secondary legal materials created by public bodies for purposes of public access (law reform and royal commission reports, for example)."

Search Form URL: See Main Page

Related Resources:

SCALEplus Australia

http://scaleplus.law.gov.au/

British and Irish Legal Information Institute

http://www.bailii.org/

"Comprehensive Access to Freely Available British and Irish Public Legal Information."

Search Form URL: See Main Page

Related Resources:

United Kingdom Court Service Judgments Database

http://www.courtservice.gov.uk/judgments/judg_home.htm

Canadian Legal Information Institute

http://www.canlii.org/

"CANLII is a prototype site in the field of public and free distribution of Canadian primary law material. It was developed for the Federation of Law Societies of Canada by the University of Montreal's LexUM team."

Please take note that some material in this database is not complete.

Search Form URL: See Main Page

Related Resources:

Compilation of Provincial Law and Regulation Databases

http://www2.lexum.umontreal.ca/bv/classification1.cfm?
categorie=4&classement=1&lan=En

Canado-american Treaties

http://www.lexum.umontreal.ca/index_en.html

"This Web site provide free access to the text of all bilateral treaties established between the United States of America and Canada from 1783 to 1997."

Search Form URL: http://www2.lexum.umontreal.ca/ca_us/
index_en.html

CIS (Commonwealth of Independent States) Migration Legislation Database

http://www.iom.int/defaultmigrationweb.asp

This IOM (International Organization for Immigration) database contains migration-related legislation of countries of the Commonwealth of Independent States.

Search Form URL: http://www.iom.int/migrationweb/documents/Legislation/default.htm

Global Banking Law Database

http://www.gbld.org/

"The Global Banking Law Database (GBLD) is a joint project of the World Bank and the International Monetary Fund. The GBLD consists of a collection of commercial banking, central bank, and deposit insurance laws of jurisdictions that are representative of the regions of the world as well as international financial centers. The laws are available in English in both MS Word and PDF (Adobe Acrobat) formats."

Search Form URL: See Main Page

Global Legal Information Network (GLIN)

http://lcweb.loc.gov

"The Global Legal Information Network (GLIN) maintains and provides a database of laws, regulations, and other complementary legal sources. The documents included in the database are contributed by the governments of the member nations from the original official texts, which are deposited, by agreement of the members, in a server initially at the Library of Congress of the United States of America."

Search Form URL: http://lcweb2.loc.gov/law/GLINv1/GLIN.html

Municipal Codes Online (Seattle Public Library)

http://www.spl.org/govpubs/

Many cities around the U.S. place their municipal codes in Invisible Web databases. Use this page as a diretory to many of them.

Search Form URL: http://www.spl.org/govpubs/municode.html

Related Resources:

Municipal Codes Online (Municipal Code Corporation)

http://www.municode.com/database.html

Municipal Codes (American Legal Publishers)

http://www.amlegal.com/online_library.htm

Muncipal Codes On the Internet

http://www.generalcode.com/webcode2.html

National Criminal Justice Reference Service Full-Text Search

http://www.ncjrs.org/search.html

"Federal sources for crime and justice information, research, statistics, and funding opportunities. Searches more than 1,500 full-text publications on this site plus publications and other Web pages from NCJRS partner agency Web sites: the U.S. Department of Justice, Office of Justice Programs, and the White House Office of National Drug Control Policy."

Search Form URL: http://excalib1.aspensys.com/rware/ login.htm

Related Resources:

National Criminal Justice Reference Service Abstracts Database B

http://excalib1.aspensys.com/rware/abstract.htm

U.S. Department of Justice Crime & Justice Electronic Data Abstracts

http://www.ojp.usdoj.gov/bjs/dtdata.htm

U.S. Uniform Crime Reports County Data

http://fisher.lib.virginia.edu/crime/

National Fair Housing Case Database

http://www.fairhousing.com

"The National Fair Housing Advocate Online has made this case database available free of charge for basic legal research of housing discrimination cases. The cases are opinions of state and federal courts and HUD administrative law judges."

Search Form URL: http://www.fairhousing.com/legal_research/ case_database.htm

NATLEX (Labor Law) B

http://ilis.ilo.org/ilis/natlex/ilintrna.html

"NATLEX is a bibliographic database that contains information on national laws on labour, social security, and related human rights. It is the only legislative database in the labour field that endeavours to cover as many legal systems as possible throughout the world. Legal texts from about 180 countries and in more than forty languages are reviewed by a team of legal professionals."

Search Form URL: http://ilis.ilo.org/ilis/natlex/ilsearna.html# SearchFormE

Refugee Caselaw Site

http://www.refugeecaselaw.org/
"The site currently collects, indexes, and publishes selected recent
court decisions that interpret the legal definition of a 'refugee.' It
presently contains cases from the highest national courts of Australia,
Austria, Canada, Germany, New Zealand, Switzerland, the United
Kingdom, and the United States."
Search Form URL: See Main Page

Women's Right to Maternity Protection Database

http://www.cdinet.com/womensrights/home.html
Identifies maternity protection law in many world countries.
Search Form URL: http://www.cdinet.com/womensrights/
database.html

Chapter 20

News and Current Events

News and current events pose one of the most vexing challenges for Web searchers. The problem is that, while there is an abundance of high-quality news available on the Web, it's not easy to find news stories with general-purpose search engines. Many online newspapers deliberately remove stories relatively soon after they are published, stashing them away in archives that are only available for those willing to pay. And the notoriously poky schedule most Web crawlers follow means that even if a news story is found and indexed by a general purpose search engine, it'll likely be weeks or months after it's no longer "news."

Nonetheless, it is possible to search for news, and most of the best resources for doing so are on the Invisible Web. In this chapter, we've highlighted searchable news sources from a variety of media, including newspapers, television, and also Web multimedia formats.

These key resources are included:

- **Audio Resources**, such as *Speechbot,* a demonstration project that creates a searchable database of radio programming using voice recognition technology

- **News Search Resources**, including archives from the *International Herald Tribune,* the *Financial Times Global Archive,* and *Bloomberg Television Transcripts*

• **Video Resources**, such as the *ABC News Video Search*, allowing you to view broadcast news on your Web browser

See the News and Current Events category on the companion Web site for additional Invisible Web resources on this topic at http://www.invisible-web.net.

Audio

National Public Radio (NPR) Archive Search

http://www.npr.org

National Public Radio provides archival access to streaming audio (RealAudio) of most major news programs (All Things Considered, Morning Edition, Talk of the Nation, etc.). The unsophisticated search interface will allow you to search text abstracts of each program's content and then listen to the entire program or program segment. This material can also be browsed via the "Archives" link located at the homepage for each program. The archiving of most programs began in 1996.

Search Form URL: http://www.npr.org/search/

SpeechBot

http://speechbot.research.compaq.com/

A demonstration project that creates a searchable database of radio programming using voice recognition technology.

Search Form URL: See Main Page

Directories

Editor and Publisher Online Media Directory

http://www.mediainfo.com

Locate online media sources from around the world. Numerous searching options.

Search Form URL: http://emedia1.mediainfo.com/emedia/

Related Resources:

Newspapers Online

http://www.newspapersonline.com

News Search Resources

BizJournals.Com
http://bizjournals.bcentral.com/
Search the online contents of over 40 city business newspapers. This archive does not make the complete text of each journal available.
Search Form URL: http://bizjournals.bcentral.com/search.html

Bloomberg Television Transcript Search
http://www.bloomberg.com
Bloomberg Television, an all business news service, provides access to text transcripts of programming. Search by keyword or company ticker symbol.
Search Form URL: http://www.bloomberg.tveyes.com/trans_search.asp

CNN News Search
http://www.cnn.com
Search the large library of news material from the CNN, CNNSI (sports), and CNNFn (Business) Web sites. This resource makes new stories searchable shortly after publication.
Search Form URL: http://207.25.71.29/SEARCH/
Related Resources:
BBC News Search
http://news6.thdo.bbc.co.uk/hi/english/static/advquery/query.htm
Canadian Broadcasting Company News Search
http://cbc.ca/search/

Cold North Wind Newspaper Archive Project
http://www.coldnorthwind.com
"Cold North Wind (CNW) is building the Paper of Record™ digital archive of newspapers from 1700 to the present day."
Search Form URL: http://www.coldnorthwind.com/products/por.htm

Financial Times Global Archive
http://www.globalarchive.ft.com
"The global archive is a unique free source containing over 10 million articles from 2,000 publications. The news database is updated on a 24/7 basis from selected international publishers and agencies. Search

the five-year archive of the *Financial Times* newspaper as well as archives of European, Asian, and American business sources."
Search Form URL: See main page

INFOQUICK B, Australia

http://www.slnsw.gov.au/
"INFOQUICK provides a comprehensive index to articles about Australia and Australians, published in the Sydney Morning Herald and associated publications: Sun Herald, Eastern Herald, Northern Herald, and Good Weekend from 1988 onwards."
Search Form URL: http://www.slnsw.gov.au/infoquick/

International Herald Tribune Search

http://www.iht.com
Search material from this respected newspaper. Archive contains material beginning in 1996.
Search Form URL: http://www.iht.com/advancedsearch.html

Legacy.Com Newspaper Obituary Search

http://www.legacy.com
"Find recent obituaries from more than 1,000 newspapers." U.S. and Canadian newspapers.
Search Form URL: http://www.legacy.com/LegacySubPage1.asp?
Page=ObitFinder

Moreover

http://www.moreover.com
Although much of the actual news content itself is on the Invisible Web, Moreover provides access to over 1,800 web-based news resources by either category browsing or keyword searching. Remember, tools like Moreover can be of added value because of the "time lag" involved in the general search engines' crawling material.
Search Form URL: http://www.moreover.com/news/index.html
Related Resources:
Search.Com News Search
http://www.search.com/search?channel=5
TotalNews
http://www.totalnews.com
Special Libraries Association News Division—Directory of News Archives on the Web
http://www.ibiblio.org/slanews/internet/archives.html

Newslibrary.Com

http://www.newslibrary.com

Search the Newslibrary.Com archives for content from numerous papers including the *Denver Post, Philadelphia Inquirer*, and *Miami Herald*. The archive is free to search but registration is required. You will be charged for the articles you choose to download. Many newspapers offer free full-text content for a limited period, often for the first 7 to 14 days after publication. Upon conclusion of the free period, many newspapers institute a free search, pay-per-article scheme. Others offer free content for longer periods. Remember, these tools are essential for news searching because of search spider time lag. A few examples follow.

Search Form URL: See Main Page

Related Resources:

Washington Post (First 14 days free)

http://washingtonpost.com/wp-srv/searches/mainsrch.htm

New York Daily News

http://www.mostnewyork.com/-/-/-/search.asp

Los Angeles Times (First 14 days free)

http://www.latimes.com/archives/

Northern Light News Search

http://www.northernlight.com

"A searchable 2-week archive of real-time news from 56 continuously updated newswires." After material is removed from this database, it is available in the fee-based Northern Light "Special Collection." Also be aware of Northern Light's free "Alert" service.

Search Form URL: http://www.northernlight.com/news.html

Related Resources:

NewsTracker (alert tool available)

http://nt.excite.com/

Net2One (alert tool available)

http://www.net2one.com/

Television News Archives: Evening News Abstracts

http://tvnews.vanderbilt.edu

"The Archive began taping the evening news broadcasts of the three major networks, ABC, CBS, and NBC, on August 5, 1968. This collection has been abstracted with story-level descriptions." A useful tool to assist in locating the dates of specific news events. The actual broadcasts have not been digitized. The related resources for this entry do not provide material online. They are searchable catalogs of fee-based material.

Search Form URL: http://tvnews.vanderbilt.edu/search.html

Related Resources:

Footage.Net (Archive Footage)

http://www.footage.net/search/

BBC Library Sales (Archive Footage)

http://www.bbcfootage.com/

Newsfilm Library (Fox Movietone Newsreels)

http://www.sc.edu/newsfilm/index.html

The Times Archive Search U.K.

http://www.thetimes.co.uk/

There are several options available to search *The Times* of London back to January 1, 1996.

Search Form URL: http://www.thetimes.co.uk/section/0,,103,00. html

Related Resources:

The Guardian U.K.

http://www.guardian.co.uk/Archive/0,4271,210474,00.html

The Electronic Telegraph U.K.

http://www.telegraph.co.uk/et?ac=004188635558125&rtmo=
rrrrrrrq&atmo=rrrrrrrq&pg=/search/callfx.html

Video

ABC News Video Search

http://www.abcnews.com

Use this search engine to access streaming video news clips from ABC News. The search box is located on the right side of the page and is labled "Virage Video Search."

Search Form URL: http://abcnews.go.com/sections/us/video_
index/video_index.html

Related Resources:

The NewsHour with Jim Lehrer Video Search

http://www.pbs.org/newshour/video/

FNCEO with Neil Cavuto

http://www.fnceo.com

Fox News Channel's Neil Cavuto conducts interviews with the CEOs of major companies and with business leaders. Database can be browsed or searched by the person's or company's name.

Search Form URL: See Main Page

Related Resources:

Fox News Channel Video Archives (Fee-Based)

http://fn.emediamillworks.com/

CNBC/Dow Jones Business Video (Fee-Based)

http://www.cnbcdowjones.com/

Scientific American Frontiers Video Archive

http://www.pbs.org

Search an expanding archive of material from this PBS program. View program segments or an entire program.

Search Form URL: http://www.pbs.org/saf/archive.htm

Related Resources:

CNET Video Search

http://www.cnet.com/cnettv/0-3614.html

C-SPAN Campaign 2000 Video Archives

http://www.c-span.org/campaign2000/search

Chapter 21

Searching for People

Most people would agree that the best place to look for a person's phone number is a telephone book, not an encyclopedia. Yet many of these same people turn to a general-purpose search engine, which is more akin to an encyclopedia than a phone book, to search for information about people.

A better choice is to use specialized people-finding tools and databases, many of which are found on the Invisible Web. These people finders can help you locate not only telephone numbers and addresses, but email addresses, genealogical background information, school and employment histories, and many other types of personal details. They can help you find experts or professionals, such as doctors or attorneys. And some provide richly detailed biographical information about contemporary famous people or historical figures. We've selected a wide range of people finders to illustrate the breadth of information about people available on the Web that's difficult, if not impossible, to locate using general-purpose search engines.

These key resources are included:

- **Famous and Historical People**, including the thousands of profiles available via the *Biography.com Database*

- **Group and Affiliation Directories**, with resources such as the *American Medical Association Physician Select* service and the *Certificated Pilots Database (U.S.)*

- **Online White Pages and Lookup Tools**, such as the *Meta Email Search Agent* and the *Reverse Telephone Directory*

- **Veterans and Military Resources**, including *The Virtual Wall (Vietnam Veterans Memorial Wall)*

See the Searching for People category on the companion Web site for additional Invisible Web resources on this topic at http://www. invisible-web.net.

Famous and Historical People

Biography.com Database
http://www.biography.com
A database of over 20,000 short bios on a wide variety of people.
Search Form URL: See Main Page

Canadian Who's Who 1997 Canada
http://www.utpress.utoronto.ca
"Search the biographies of more than 15,000 prominent Canadians by name, birthdate, city, or full text." Please note that this is not the most current edition available. A newer edition is available for purchase.
Search Form URL: http://www.utpress.utoronto.ca/cww/cw2w3.cgi

Catalog of Scientific Community in the 16th and 17th Centuries
http://es.rice.edu/ES/humsoc/Galileo/
"This catalog is a collection of 631 detailed biographies on members of the scientific community during the 16th and 17th centuries with vital facts about individuals and their contributions to science. The information here was compiled by the late Richard S. Westfall, Professor in the Department of History and Philosophy of Science at Indiana University. While the scope of Dr. Westfall's research is immense, the information is concise and very well organized. All individuals in the catalog are systematically described by ten categories using twenty searchable fields."

Search Form URL: http://es.rice.edu/ES/humsoc/Galileo/
Catalog/catalog.html

PeopleTracker

http://www.forbes.com/peopletracker/
"Track over 120,000 executives and members of the Forbes rich and
celebrity lists." Registration (free) required.
Search Form URL:
http://www.forbes.com/peopletracker/protected/exec_tracker.jhtml

World Biographical Index 7 (The)

http://www.biblio.tu-bs.de/acwww25u/wbi_en/wbi.html
"This database is based on the 7th CD-ROM edition of the World
Biographical Index containing 2.8 million short biographical entries
for eminent individuals who lived in North and South America,
Western and Central Europe, Africa, Australia, New Zealand, and
Oceania. This edition is also a compiled index to many biographical
archives."
Search Form URL: See Main Page

Genealogy Resources

Cyndi's List of Genealogy Sites on the Internet

http://www.cyndislist.com/
There are hundreds of thousands of genealogical resources, many of
them databases, on the Invisible Web. An excellent place to begin
genealogy research is at Cyndi's List. Although it's not Invisible itself,
this compilation has over 89,000 well cataloged genealogy resources
including many Invisible Web and Opaque Web resources.
Search Form URL: See Main Page

FamilySearch

http://www.familysearch.org
Over 660 million names in this searchable name database. "The
Church of Jesus Christ of Latter-day Saints has been gathering
genealogical records across the world for more than a century to help
its members and others in family history research."
Search Form URL: http://www.familysearch.org/Eng/Search/
frameset_search.asp

Social Security Death Index

http://ssdi.rootsweb.com/

"One of the largest and easiest to access databases used for genealogical research is the Social Security Death Index (SSDI).... Clues and facts from the SSDI often can be used to further genealogical research by enabling you to locate a death certificate, find an obituary, discover cemetery records and track down probate records."

Search Form URL: http://ssdi.rootsweb.com/cgi-bin/ssdi.cgi

Related Resources:

Detailed Orientation to the Social Security Death Index

http://www.rootsweb.com/~rwguide/lesson10.htm

Group and Affiliation Directories

American Board of Medical Specialties
"Who's Certified" Database

http://www.abms.org

Search for credentialed medical specialists. The ABMS and the American Medical Association recognizes 24 medical specialty boards.

Search Form URL: http://www.abms.org/newsearch.asp

American Institute of Architects (AIAA)
Architect Finder (The)

http://www.aiaaccess.com/

Locate architects in the U.S. using several criteria.

Search Form URL: See Main Page

American Medical Association Physician Select

http://www.ama-assn.org

"AMA Physician Select provides basic professional information on virtually every licensed physician in the United States and its possessions, including more than 690,000 doctors of medicine (MD) and doctors of osteopathy or osteopathic medicine (DO)."

Search Form URL: http://www.ama-assn.org/aps/amahg.htm

Related Resources:

American Board of Medical Specialties Certification Search

http://www.abms.org/newsearch.asp

American Dental Association Member Directory

http://www.ada.org/directory/dentistsearchform.html

Dentists Register and Rolls of Dental Auxiliaries U.K.
http://www.gdc-uk.org/search_ind.htm

Burwell World Directory of Information Brokers

http://www.burwellinc.com/bedirectory.html
"The searchable Internet version of The Burwell World Directory of Information Brokers, the world's most comprehensive international database of professional information. ... Nearly 1,000 entries representing 38 countries are currently identified in the database. The inclusion of foreign language and country expertise is a reflection of the international nature of today's business environment and our ever-increasing worldwide communications capability."
Search Form URL: http://www.andornot.com/ibdb/power.html
Related Resources:
AIIP (Association of Independent Information Professionals) Member Directory
http://www.aiip.org/memberdirectoryhome.asp

Certificated Pilots Database (U.S.)

http://www.landings.com
"This database contains around 600,000 pilots and you can specify searches using different options."
Search Form URL: http://www.landings.com/_landings/pages/search_amd.html
Related Resources:
A&P Mechanics Database
http://www.landings.com/_landings/pages/search_apm.html
Aviation Medical Examiners Database
http://www.landings.com/_landings/pages/search_ame.html

CPA Directory

http://www.cpadirectory.com
Searchable online directory of Certified Public Accountants and accounting firms in the United States.
Search Form URL: http://www.cpadirectory.com/search_advanced.cfm

DocFinder (U.S.)

http://www.docboard.org/

This compilation brings together the official licensing databases for many States. Compilation is provided by the "Administrators in Medicine's (AIM) member state medical and osteopathic boards." Search Form URL: See Main Page

Judges of the United States Courts

http://www.fjc.gov/
"The Federal Judges Biographical Database contains the service record and biographical information for all judges who have served on the U.S. District Courts, U.S. Circuit Courts, U.S. Courts of Appeals, and the Supreme Court since 1789."
Search Form URL: http://air.fjc.gov/history/judges_frm.html

National Press Club Directory of News Sources

http://npc.press.org
One of many searchable databases on the Web that provide the reporting community with experts on a variety of topics.
Search Form URL: http://npc.press.org/who/sources.htm
Related Resources:
(Canada) National Expertise Index
http://strategis.ic.gc.ca/sc_innov/cite/engdoc/search.html
(Canada) National Research Council Expertise Database
http://www.nrc.ca/expertise/

National Register of Health Service Providers in Psychology U.S.

http://www.nationalregister.com
"National Register of Health Service Providers in Psychology (National Register) is the largest credentialing organization for psychologists. As a credentialing body, it evaluates the education, training, and experience of licensed psychologists to determine if they meet the criteria for recognition as a credentialed health service provider in psychology." Registration (free) required.
Search Form URL: http://www.nationalregister.com/osd.html

Translation Services Directory (American Translators Association)

http://www.atanet.org
"Use this searchable database to find a translator or interpreter. This online directory features the profiles of more than 4,000 translators and interpreters."
Search Form URL: http://www.americantranslators.org/tsd_listings/

U.S. Amateur Radio Call Sign Lookup

http://www.ualr.edu/~hamradio/

Directory data on FCC licensed U.S. amateur radio opearators.

Search Form URL: http://callsign.ualr.edu/callsign.shtml

Online White Pages and Lookup Tools

192.Com U.K.

http://www.192.com

A treasure chest of United Kingdom directory information. "192.com provides its users with free, fast access to the largest database of telephone and address information on the Internet. The content is continually updated and is enhanced with extensive cross-referencing." All this, makes 192.com the focal point for information on the Internet. Free registration is required for limited free data.

Search Form URL: See Main Page

Anywho.Com (Telephone Directory)

http://www.anywho.com

One of many phone directory databases on the Internet, Anywho.com provides both residential and business listings. Listed here are just a few of the databases available.

Search Form URL: See Main Page

Related Resources:

Canada Yellow Pages Canada

http://www.Canadayellowpages.com/search/main.cgi?lang=

BT PhoneNet UK U.K.

http://www.bt.com/phonenetuk/

Online Telephone Book Directory

http://www.teldir.com/eng/

Canada 411 Canada

http://canada411.sympatico.ca/eng/person.html

Canadian white pages directory.

Search Form URL: See Main Page

InfoSpace

http://www.infospace.com

Look up addresses, telephone numbers, email addresses, and other information for people all over the world.
Search Form URL: See Main Page

MESA (MetaEmailSearchAgent)

http://mesa.rrzn.uni-hannover.de/
This database searches six email address databases simultaneously.
Search Form URL: See Main Page

National Adoption Directory (National Adoption Information Clearinghouse)

http://www.calib.com/naic/
"The National Adoption Directory database is updated daily, and includes state-by-state listings of public officials, as well as public and licensed private adoption agencies and support groups for adoptive parents and for people searching for birth relatives."
Search Form URL: http://www.calib.com/naic/database/nadd/naddsearch.cfm
Related Resources:
National Adoption Information Clearinghouse National Organizations Directory
http://www.calib.com/naic/database/nat/srchorgs.cfm
National Adoption Information Clearinghouse Searchable Documents Database B
http://www.calib.com/naic/database/index.htm

Reverse Telephone Directory

http://www.anywho.com
Search for telephone directory information by phone number.
Search Form URL: http://www.anywho.com/telq.html
Related Resources:
Reverse Telephone and Address Lookup
http://in-115.infospace.com/_1_43343463__info/reverse.htm
Reverse Telephone & Address Lookup Canada
http://www.infospace.com/info/reverse_ca.htm

WED—World Email Directory

http://www.worldemail.com/
"More than 18 million email addresses and phone addresses worldwide."
Search Form URL: See Main Page

Veterans and Currently Serving Military

Canadian Virtual War Memorial Canada

http://www.vac-acc.gc.ca/

"This site contains a registry of information about the graves and memorials of more than 116,000 Canadians and Newfoundlanders who served valiantly and gave their lives for their country. The site also contains digital images of photographs and personal memorabilia about individual Canadians."

Search Form URL: See Main Page

Civil War Soldiers and Sailors System

http://www.itd.nps.gov/cwss/index.html

"The Civil War Soldiers and Sailors System is a computerized database containing very basic facts about servicemen who served on both sides during the Civil War. The initial focus of the CWSS is the Names Index Project, a project to enter names and other basic information from 5.4 million soldier records in the National Archives."

Search Form URL: See Main Page

Related Resources:

Illinois Civil War Veterans Database

http://www.cyberdriveillinois.com/departments/archives/datcivil.html

Commonwealth War Graves Commission Debt of Honour Register U.K.

http://www.cwgc.org/

"This Register provides personal and service details and places of commemoration for the 1.7 million members of the Commonwealth forces who died in the First or Second World Wars. (A record some 60,000 civilian casualties of the Second World War is provided without details of burial location.)"

Search Form URL: http://yard.ccta.gov.uk/cwgc/register.nsf

Related Resources:

Australian War Memorial Databases

http://www.awm.gov.au/database/

POW/MIA Database

http://lcweb2.loc.gov/pow/

This database has been established to assist researchers interested in investigating the U.S. Government documents pertaining to U.S. military personnel listed as unaccounted for as of December 1991. The title of this collection is "Correlated and Uncorrelated Information Relating to Missing Americans in Southeast Asia."

Search Form URL: http://lcweb2.loc.gov/pow/powquery.html

The Virtual Wall (Vietnam Veterans Memorial Wall)

http://www.thevirtualwall.org/

Search and browse a virtual version of the Vietnam Veterans Memorial Wall.

Search Form URL: http://www.thevirtualwall.org/search/search_index.htm

United States Navy Directory (X.500)

http://www.navydirectory.smartlink.navy.mil/

"The current Navy X.500 directory supports NAVY personnel, civilian and military, working in Navy and Joint agencies." Personnel who are overseas or in sensitive or routinely deployable Units are not accessible from the Internet.

Search Form URL: See Main Page

Chapter 22

Public Records

Before the Web existed, accessing public records generally meant making a trip to the office or agency where the records were physically located, or paying an agent to visit the office on your behalf. These days, however, public records maintained by cities, states, and provinces and other governmental agencies are increasingly available via the Web.

Unfortunately, there is little standardization or cooperation among and between public agencies in terms of how records are made available. Sometimes new systems are designed to replace existing systems, with Web accessibility as a high priority. In other cases, existing legacy systems are simply adapted, not always elegantly, to the Web. But in almost all cases, public records are squarely in the realm of the Invisible Web, and require some extra sleuthing by the searcher to locate and access.

The range of public records is vast—licenses, land records, labor market data, campaign finance records—these are just a few of the types of records in the public domain. In this chapter, we offer a select sample of what's available—a comprehensive catalog of Web-based public records would constitute another book in itself. Our aim is to show you some of the possibilities to stimulate your own creative thinking on how to find public records via the Web.

These key resources are included:

- **General Public Records Resources**, such as the comprehensive directory of *Property Assessment Databases*

- **Location-Specific Public Records Resources**, including Pennsylvnia's *PALMDIS (Labor Market Data)* and New York's *Financial Disclosure Information System*

See the Public Records category on the companion Web site for additional Invisible Web resources on this topic at http://www.invisible-web.net.

General Public Records Resources

Federal Election Commission Financial Reports
http://www.fec.gov
The actual financial reports filed by campaigns and committees are available on the Web. Now you can view the reports as they were originally submitted, something that once required a trip to your state elections office or the FEC in Washington. The related references in this section do an outstanding job of "massaging" the FEC data to create several specialized search tools and reports.
Search Form URL: http://herndon1.sdrdc.com/fecimg/query.html
Related Resources:
FEC Info
http://www.fecinfo.com
Center for Responsive Politics
http://www.crp.org

Internal Revenue Service Section 527 Notice Search
http://www.irs.gov
"Most political organizations are required to notify the IRS both electronically and in writing that they are political organizations described in section 527 of the Internal Revenue Code. The required notice form is Form 8871, Political Organization Notice of Section 527 Status."
Search Form URL: http://www.irs.gov/bus_info/eo/8871.html

KnowX
http://www.knowx.com
This fee-based service is a one-stop shop to many publicly available public record databases.
Search Form URL: See Main Page
Related Resources:
QuickInfo.Net (Fee-Based)
http://www.quickinfo.net/

Property Assessment Databases
http://www.people.virginia.edu/~dev-pros/Realestate.html
Many government jurisdictions in the U.S. and Canada make property assessment data available on the Invisible Web. Instead of listing all of them, visit this resource for a comprehensive guide.
Search Form URL: See Main Page

Search Systems Public Records Databases
http://www.pac-info.com/
Over 2,300 Free Searchable Public Record Databases.
Search Form URL: See Main Page

UnclaimedPersons.Com
http://www.unclaimedpersons.com
"The purpose of this Web site is to provide information to the public regarding a deceased loved one for whom next of kin has never been located. Coroner's departments, Medical Examiner's offices and Sheriff's departments throughout the United States oftentimes conduct an investigation for which a deceased person's identity is known; however, due to various reasons, family member(s) could not be located."
Search Form URL: http://www.unclaimedpersons.com/search.asp

Location-Specific Public Records

Bill Tracking Database California
http://www.leginfo.ca.gov/
"The full text of bills, resolutions, and constitutional amendments and their status, history, votes, analyses, and veto messages are available."
Search Form URL: http://www.leginfo.ca.gov/bilinfo.html
Related Resources:

Bill Tracker Michigan
http://198.109.122.10/find.asp
Legislative Information System Virginia
http://leg1.state.va.us/

Business and License Complaints History Search Hawaii
http://www.ehawaiigov.org/
"This search is designed to help the public obtain basic information about complaints that have been filed against companies that conduct business in the State of Hawaii." The interface is at the bottom of the page.
Search Form URL: http://www.ehawaiigov.org/serv/rico

Charitable Organizations Database Arizona
http://www.sosaz.com/
"The Office of the Secretary of State, Charitable Organizations, is a filing office designed to provide the public with information regarding specific charities."
Search Form URL: http://www.sosaz.com/scripts/Charity_search_engine.cgi/
Related Resources:
Charities Database Oregon
http://www.state.or.us/cgi-bin/OrgQuery.pl/
Charitable Organizations Database Maryland
http://www.sos.state.md.us/sos/charity/html/search.html
Charities Search Minnesota
http://www.ag.state.mn.us/charities/Char_srch.asp

Community Profiles Database Missouri
http://www.ecodev.state.mo.us/medms/default.htm
Obtain basic demographic data for all Missouri communities.
Search Form URL: http://www.ecodev.state.mo.us/medms/comm.htm
Related Resources:
Community Database Alaska
http://www.dced.state.ak.us/mra/CF_COMDB.htm

Corporation Database Alabama
http://www.sos.state.al.us/business/corporations.cfm
"The Corporations Division operates as a depository for records of domestic corporate entities and foreign entities that have qualified to

transact business in Alabama. The types of entities we serve include For-Profit Corporations, Non-Profit Corporations, Limited Liability Companies, Limited Partnerships, and Registered Limited Liability Partnerships."
Search Form URL: http://www.sos.state.al.us/sosinfo/inquiry.cfm
Related Resources:
Corporation Database Arizona
http://159.87.17.11/cgi-bin/wspd_cgi.sh/WService=wsbroker1/main.html
Corporation Database Arkansas
http://www.sosweb.state.ar.us/corps/incorp/
Business Entity Search Utah
http://www.state.ut.us/serv/bes

Corrections Offender Information Network Florida
http://www.dc.state.fl.us/inmateinfo/inmateinfomenu.asp
Several searchable databases including Inmate Population Information Search and Inmate Escape Information Search.
Search Form URL: See Main Page
Related Resources:
Inmate Search Illinois
http://www.idoc.state.il.us/inmates/search.htm
Inmate Population Information Search New York
http://207.198.24.23:84/kinqw00
Inmate Information Center Los Angeles County
http://pajis.lasd.org/ajis_search.cfm

Crime Database Chicago
http://12.17.79.6/
"... search the Chicago Police Department's database of reported crime. You will be able to see maps, graphs, and tables of reported crime. The database contains 90 days of information [that] you can access in blocks of up to 14 days. Data is refreshed daily. However, the most recent information is back-dated 7 days from today's date."
Search Form URL: See Main Page
Related Resources:
Automated Regional Justice Information System Crime Maps/Reports San Diego County
http://www.arjis.org/

Election Return Archives Missouri
http://sosweb.sos.state.mo.us/

Search for official election results from the Missouri Secretary of State's office. Coverage begins in 1996.
Search Form URL: http://sosweb.sos.state.mo.us/enrweb/electionselect.asp

Elections Canada Financial Reports Databases Canada
http://www.elections.ca
Two databases are available. One database searches contributions and expenses of political parties. The other database focuses on the contributions and expenses of candidates. Note that the page where you choose which database to search is also invisible.
Search Form URL: http://www.elections.ca/content.asp?section=fin&document=finindex&lang=e&textonly=false

Financial Disclosure Information System New York
http://www.elections.state.ny.us
"The Election Law was recently amended to provide for mandatory electronic financial disclosure by political committees registered with the State Board of Elections. Availability of disclosure reports on the Internet was also mandated. In accordance with these new requirements, the State Board developed electronic filing software and an Electronic Filing Database, which the public may view or search on the Internet."
Search Form URL: http://www.elections.state.ny.us/finance/fdismenu.htm
Related Resources:
Historical Campaign Finance Data Vermont
http://www.sec.state.vt.us/seek/fin_seek.htm
Campaign Finance Information System Delaware
http://elba.state.de.us/servlet/DECFIS
Campaign Finance Data Kansas
http://www.sec.state.vt.us/seek/fin_seek.htm

Health Data Warehouse Ohio
http://www.odh.state.oh.us/Data/whare/WhseMain.htm
"The Department of Health collects data about more than 100 health topics."
Search Form URL: See Main Page
Related Resources:
Public Health Databases Georgia

http://www.ph.dhr.state.ga.us:8090/ehi/owa/user_menu.main
WITHIN Wisconsin
http://www.state.wi.us/agencies/oci/ohci/qcmain.htm

Health Facility Report Card Search Iowa
http://www.dia-hfd.state.ia.us
"There are over 800 licensed and/or certified healthcare facilities in
the State of Iowa. With the Report Card Health Facility Locator you can
create a list of facilities to view Report Card information."
Search Form URL: http://www.dia-hfd.state.ia.us/reportcards/
default.asp

In-Depth Analysis of Revenues Illinois
http://www.ioc.state.il.us/
Compose reports to analyze State of Illinois revenue data. Basic
reports available via the State Comptroller homepage.
Search Form URL: http://www.ioc.state.il.us/iw/Expert/Rev/
ERSummary.cfm

Land Records Alaska
http://www.dnr.state.ak.us/pic/index.htm
This site offers access to the DNR [Department of Natural Resources]
State Status Plats and the Historical Indices. It also offers access to the
DNR Land Administration System (LAS) to provide case file sum-
maries and case file abstracts.
Search Form URL: http://www.dnr.state.ak.us/cgi-bin/lris/
landrecords

Licensed Child Care Facilities Indiana
http://www.state.in.us/fssa/
Search for facilities licensed by the Indiana Family and Social Services
Administration.
Search Form URL: http://www.state.in.us/fssa/database/ homes.html

Lobbyist Activity Reports Texas
http://www.ethics.state.tx.us/index.html
Search by month/year or by lobbyist name. Database coverage begins
in 1992.
Search Form URL: http://www.ethics.state.tx.us/dfs/lar.html
Related Resources:
Lobbyist Spending on Georgia Lawmakers Georgia

http://www.accessatlanta.com/partners/ajc/reports/lobbyists/
search.html
Lobbyist Lists Florida
http://www.leg.state.fl.us/Lobbyist/index.cfm?RequestTimeout=500&
Mode=Lists&Submenu=2&Tab=lobbyist
Lobbyist Public Registry Ontario
http://lobbyist.oico.on.ca/Integrity/RegistrationPublic.nsf/
ApprovedByType?OpenView

Marriage and Divorce Verification Colorado

http://www.cdphe.state.co.us/
"Search on all marriages (from 1975 to November 2000) and divorces
(from 1968 to November 2000) in the state of Colorado."
Search Form URL: http://www.quickinfo.net/madi/comadi.html
Related Resources:
Marriage Inquiry System Clark County, NV/Las Vegas
http://www.co.clark.nv.us/recorder/mar_srch.htm

New York City Department of Health Restaurant Inspection Database New York

http://www.nyc.gov/html/doh/html/rii/index.html
Search for restaurant name or location to find out about the most
recent significant violations issued.
Search Form URL: http://207.127.96.244/scripts/webfood.pl
Related Resources:
Resturant Inspection Search Boston
http://www.ci.boston.ma.us/isd/disclaimer.asp
Restaurant Health Inspection Reporting System Denver
http://www.denvergov.org/eh/default.asp
Department of Health Services Restaurant Rating Los Angeles County
http://www2.dhs.co.la.ca.us/search.html

Occupational License Search Alaska

http://www.dced.state.ak.us/occ/
"This database contains over 30,000 occupational/professional
licenses issued by the Alaska Division of Occupational Licensing and
its licensing boards."
Search Form URL: http://www.dced.state.ak.us/occ/search3.htm

PALMIDS (Labor Market Data) Pennsylvania

http://www.lmi.state.pa.us/palmids/default.asp

"PALMIDS [Pennsylvania Labor Market Information Database System] contains data on a wide variety of employment, economic, career-related, and education topics. It is intended to serve the information needs of jobseekers, employers, students, educational curriculum planners, workforce and economic development agencies, and the general public."
Search Form URL: See Main Page
Related Resources:
VELMA Virgina
http://www.vec-velma.state.va.us/velma/
WILMA Washington
http://www.wilma.org/

Pesticide Database Oklahoma

http://www.kellysolutions.com/ok/
"This information is compiled solely from pesticide registration data submitted by companies who wish their products to be sold in the state of Oklahoma, combined with data from the EPA with regard to ingredients, pests, and sites."
Search Form URL: See Main Page

School Data (Dataquest) California

http://data1.cde.ca.gov/dataquest/
"DataQuest helps you find facts about California Schools and districts."
Search Form URL: See Main Page

Vital Statistics Query System California

http://www.dhs.ca.gov./hisp/chs/chsindex.htm
"The Vital Statistics Query System has been developed to provide an interactive Internet interface to obtain tabular summaries and statistical reports from California's birth and death vital statistics databases. The selection process is broken down into four levels."
Search Form URL: http://www.dhs.ca.gov./hisp/applications/vsq/vsq.cfm
Related Resources:
SPOT Tennessee
http://web.utk.edu/~chrg/hit/main/SPOT/frames/SPOT/nfindex.htm

Chapter 23

Real-Time Information

Real-time information is probably the "purest" type of Invisible Web data, and it's not likely that general-purpose search engines will ever make any effort to include it in their indices. Real-time information is almost always stored in databases that are constantly updated in real or near-real time. In some cases, such as stock quotes or airline flight arrival information, each update obliterates the previous data record. Even if a search engine *could* somehow crawl and index this information, it would be like isolating a single frame from a feature length movie.

In other cases, real-time data is preserved, but the key point is that it is archived data in raw form, which a searcher cannot easily manipulate. Examples include barometric or temperature observations, the readings from a seismograph, or imagery streamed from space probes. This data, while valuable to a few select technologists who can interpret it, is largely useless to searchers who are seeking *processed information*. Some people call these huge data reservoirs the "Deep Web," and while it's certainly true that this data is Web-accessible, including these huge databases as part of the Invisible Web dramatically overstates the size of information useful to most searchers. While the "Deep Web" may be as much as 500 times larger than the visible Web, our studies indicate that the truly useful Invisible Web is only two to 50 times larger.

In this chapter, we offer some of the more useful real-time information resources available on the Invisible Web.

These key resources are included:

- **Government Information**, including the current *U.S. House Floor Proceedings*, offering a minute-by-minute update of each legislative day

- **Space and Satellite Information**, such as *NASA Real-Time Data*, which monitors the progress of the International Space Station, the Space Shuttle, and other NASA projects

- **Transportation Information**, including the awesome *Graphical Flight Tracker* that shows you the position and flight details of any currently in-flight commercial aircraft using information taken directly from its cockpit

See the Real-Time Information category on the companion Web site for additional Invisible Web resources on this topic at http://www.invisible-web.net.

Environment

AirNow (Real-Time Air Pollution Data)
http://www.epa.gov/airnow/
Several resources are available that monitor air quality in the U.S. The "Where I Live" portion of the site provides access to real-time data.
Search Form URL: http://www.epa.gov/airnow/where/

Real-Time Stream Flow Water Data, USGS (United States Geological Survey)
http://water.usgs.gov/realtime.html
"The U.S. Geological Survey (USGS) stream-gauging program provides streamflow data for a variety of purposes that range from current needs, such as flood forecasting, to future or long-term needs, such as detection of changes in streamflow due to human activities or global warming."
Search Form URL: See Main Page
Related Resources:
National Water Information System (Historical Data)
http://waterdata.usgs.gov/nwis-w/US/

Recent Marine Data, National Buoy Data Center

http://seaboard.ndbc.noaa.gov/

Current (real-time) data from buoys located in U.S., Canadian, and U.K. waters.

Search Form URL: http://seaboard.ndbc.noaa.gov/Maps/rmd.shtml

Related Resources:

Costal Water Temperature Guide (NODC)

http://www.nodc.noaa.gov/dsdt/cwtg/

PORTS (Physical Oceanographic Real-Time System)

http://co-ops.nos.noaa.gov/d_ports.html

Tides Online

http://tidesonline.nos.noaa.gov/

"Offering near real-time tidal and storm surge water level observation data and plots."

Search Form URL: See Main Page

Government

House Floor Proceedings, Current U.S.

http://clerkweb.house.gov

The Office of the Clerk, United States House of Representitives provides this minute-by-minute ticker for the current legislative day.

Search Form URL: http://clerkweb.house.gov/floor/current.htm

Related Resources:

Today's House Proceedings

http://www.house.gov/daily/log.html

Real-Time 911 Dispatches, Seattle Fire Department

http://www.ci.seattle.wa.us/fire/

Real-Time access to 911 calls as they are dispatched by the Seattle Fire Department.

Search Form URL: http://www2.cityofseattle.net/fire/GetDate PubTab.asp

Miscellaneous Tracking

PackTrack (Package Tracking)
http://www.packtrack.com
Track packages for 38 carriers using this single search tool.
Search Form URL: See Main Page

PublicRadioFan.Com
http://www.publicradiofan.com/
"... database of program listings for hundreds of public radio stations around the world."
Search Form URL: See Main Page

Space and Satellite

Earth View
http://www.fourmilab.ch/cgi-bin/uncgi/Earth/action?opt=-p
This astonishing tool lets you play around with real-time views of Earth from the Sun or the Moon, view the night side of the planet, add topo lines or cloud cover, and then zoom in or out.
Search Form URL: See Main Page
Related Resources:
Solar System Live
http://www.fourmilab.ch/cgi-bin/uncgi/Solar/action?sys=-Sf

J-Track 3-D Satellite Locator
http://liftoff.msfc.nasa.gov/realtime/JTrack/Spacecraft.html
"The tracking system calculates an approximate location for a list of satellites (including spacecraft). Each satellite is assigned a color used for displaying the ground trace, captions, location, and countdown clock."
Search Form URL: See Main Page

NASA Real-Time Data
http://spaceflight.nasa.gov/realdata/index.html
Several databases including resources that provide real-time tracking information of the Space Shuttle and International Space Station.
Search Form URL: See Main Page
Related Resources:

J-Track 3-D Satellite Locator
http://liftoff.msfc.nasa.gov/realtime/JTrack/Spacecraft.html

PDS Planetary Image Atlas

http://www-pdsimage.wr.usgs.gov/ATLAS.html
"The PDS Planetary Image Atlas uses existing PDS image products and
software known as MapMaker to generate seamless, tailor-made image
maps of a variety of planetary bodies. You will be able to specify the latitude and longitude limits of your map, plus scale and map projection."
Search Form URL: See Main Page

Stock Quotes

Stock Quotes

http://markets.ft.com/markets/home/us/
Thousands of Web sites offer real-time or near real-time quotes along
with other tools such as interactive charts. This database from the
Financial Times is representative of many of them. Quotes from several U.S. and European exchanges are available. Obtain quote by
entering ticker symbol or company name in the "Get Quote" box.
Search Form URL: See Main Page

Transportation

Flight Tracker

http://www.thetrip.com
Find out the current status of any flights of many U.S. and
Internationl airlines while they are in the FAA computer system. Java
application will continuously graph movement of aircraft on map.
Search Form URL: http://www.trip.com/trs/trip/flighttracker/flight_
tracker_home.xsl
Related Resources:
Web Trax Flight Tracking
http://216.33.28.152/

Heathrow Airport Flight Arrivals Information U.K.

http://www.baa.co.uk/main/airports/heathrow

Constantly updated database with flight arrival information. Other airports have arrival and departure data.
Search Form URL: http://www.baa.co.uk/main/airports/heathrow/flight_arrivals_frame.html
Related Resources:
Schipol Airport Flight Information Netherlands
http://www.schiphol.nl/engine/indexfilm01groot.html?url=/home/flight_information/index.html&lang=en&tab=navigation
Narita Flight Information Japan
http://www.narita-airport.or.jp/airport/flight/index_e.html
Flight Arrivals U.S., Canada
http://www.flightarrivals.com

Real-Time Airport Status U.S.
http://www.faa.gov
Find the latest delay information for major U.S. airports.
Search Form URL: http://www.fly.faa.gov/
Related Resources:
Airport Advisories Database
http://www.fly.faa.gov/advisories/
Airport Arrival Demand Chart
http://www.fly.faa.gov/AADC/aadc.html
National Airspace System Status
http://www.fly.faa.gov/ois/

Traffic Incident Information, California Highway Patrol
http://cad.chp.ca.gov/
A real-time display of California Highway Patrol activity.
Search Form URL: See Main Page
Related Resources:
Houston Real-Time Traffic Map
http://traffic.tamu.edu/traffic.html
Chicagoland Expressway Congestion Map
http://www.ai.uic.edu/GCM/CongestionMap.html
Puget Sound Region Traffic Map
http://www.wsdot.wa.gov/PugetSoundTraffic/

Train Arrival Information, Amtrak
http://www.amtrak.com
Locate the arrival time at any station for any train in the Amtrak system.

Search Form URL: http://reservations.amtrak.com/novus/
process-form?home&arrival

Weather

International Weather Conditions

http://weather.noaa.gov
National Weather Service conditions for hundreds of U.S. locations.
Search Form URL: http://weather.noaa.gov/pd/usframes.html
Related Resources:
International Weather Conditions
http://weather.noaa.gov/weather/ccworld.html

Worldwide School WeatherNet

http://www.aws.com
Real-time weather observations from automated weather stations
located around the U.S. and Canada.
Search Form URL: http://aws.com/globalwx.html
Related Resources:
Current Weather Conditions International
http://weather.noaa.gov/weather/ccworld.html
Current Weather Conditions U.S.
http://weather.noaa.gov/pd/usframes.html

Chapter 24

Reference

As we noted in an earlier chapter, one of the most pernicious myths about the Internet is that you can find "anything" on the Web. While this is far from true, there are still countless high-quality, authoritative reference resources residing on the Invisible Web.

Many of the resources described in this chapter could have easily been placed in other chapters. Our key criterion for placing them in this chapter on reference resources is that they are all the types of tools and resources that a librarian would want close at hand. Another challenge we faced was that many of these resources could have been placed in multiple categories *within* this chapter. Whenever possible, we chose to categorize by subject matter rather than by functionality, which is why you'll find the *American Booksellers Association Member Directory* in the *Books* category rather than the *Associations* category, for example.

These key resources are included:

- **Associations**, including the extensive *Gateway to Associations* database

- **Consumer Resources**, such as the *U.S. Automobile Recall Database*

- **Dictionaries, Glossaries,and Translation Resources**, including the *Acronym Finder*, the whimsical yet powerful *Lexical FreeNet* (a combination thesaurus, rhyming dictionary, pun generator, and concept navigator), and *Verbix*, which conjugates verbs in over 50 languages

- **Journals and Periodicals**, including *Publist*, a database of information for more than 150,000 publications

- **Locators**, such as the *Public Library Locator* and the *U.S. Zip Code+4 Database*

These are just a few of the resources in this chapter. As with all resources selected for this book, these represent only a small sample of what's available on the Invisible Web. We continually add new resources to the companion Web site for this book. For additional reference resources, point your browser to http://www.invisible-web.net.

Associations

American Society of Home Inspectors (ASHI) Inspector Search

http://www.ashi.com

Search for members within a certain radius of a ZIP code. "ASHI is the largest and most respected professional association for home inspectors in North America, with nearly 5,500 Members and Candidates ..."
Search Form URL: http://www.ashi.com/fi.cfm

Gateway to Associations

http://www.asaenet.org/main/

From the American Society for Association Executives, this database has links to over 6,500 associations. Searchable by keyword and category.
Search Form URL: http://info.asaenet.org/gateway/Online
Assoc Slist.html
Related Resources:
AssociationCentral.com
http://www.associationcentral.com
AssociationsCanada
http://www.associationscanada.com/Profiles/

QueerAmerica

http://www.queeramerica.com

"QueerAmerica is a database published by OutProud, The National Coalition for Gay, Lesbian, Bisexual, and Transgender Youth. With over 4,000 entries, it's the largest collection of lesbigay resources in the nation, and includes information on community centers, support organizations, PFLAG (Parents, Families & Friends of Lesbians and Gays) chapters, lesbigay youth groups, and more. These can be great places to meet friends, get questions answered, or find support."
Search Form URL: See Main Page

The Scholarly Societies Project
http://www.scholarly-societies.org
Contains a searchable database and several directories. Information on over 1,600 societies from around the world.
Search Form URL: http://www.lib.uwaterloo.ca/cgi-bin/public/opentext/pat2db?specfile=/fsys2/opentext/ssp/full/ssp.p2w

Awards

Academy Awards (Oscars) Database
http://www.oscars.org
"The database contains information concerning the Academy Awards[®] from 1927 to the present." A separate database is available for scientific and technical awards.
Search Form URL: http://www.oscars.org/awards_db/index.html
Related Resources:
Tony Awards Database
http://www.tonys.org/archives/pastwinners/index.html
Emmy Awards Database
http://www.emmycast.org/awards/search.asp
Grammy Award Database
http://www.grammy.com/awards/search.php3

Database of Award Winning Children's Literature
http://www2.wcoil.com/~ellerbee/childlit.html
Create customized reading lists using winning entries for numerous children's book awards.
Search Form URL: http://www2.wcoil.com/~ellerbee/childlit.html

Olympic Winners Database

http://www.britannica.com

A database of Olympic medal winners from 1896 to the present.

Search Form URL: http://www.britannica.com/olympics/record/

Pulitzer Prize Database

http://www.pulitzer.org

"The Pulitzer Prize Web site includes a database of winners and nominated finalists for each prize category. In addition, for winners from 1995 to the present, there is a complete inventory of winning cartoons, photos, and texts of journalism articles."

Search Form URL: http://www.pulitzer.org/Archive/Search/search.html

Related Resources:

Nobel Prize Laureate Search

http://www.nobel.se/search/laureate.html

Books

American Booksellers Association Member Directory

http://www.bookweb.org/bookstores/

Information on over 4,500 independent bookstores in the United States.

Search Form URL: http://www.bookweb.org/bd-bin/search_bd

Book Browser Calendar of Author Signings and Events

http://www.bookbrowser.com

Locate author signings, television appearances, lectures, and more.

Search Form URL: http://www.bookbrowser.com/Storytellers/Calendar.html

Related Resources:

Authors on the Highway

http://www.publishersweekly.com/highway/

ISBN Publishers' Directory Canada

http://www.nlc-bnc.ca

"The Canadian ISBN (International Standard Book Number) Publishers' Directory contains name and contact information for most Canadian publishers, past and present, who use the ISBN system. It

currently lists some 20,000 publishers who use ISBNs for their Canadian publications."
Search Form URL: http://www.nlc-bnc.ca/isbndir-bin/search/l=0

New York Times Book Reviews
http://www.nytimes.com
Keyword search *The New York Times* Book Section from 1997. Access full-text book reviews from 1980. Free registration is necessary to read reviews.
Search Form URL: http://search.nytimes.com/books/search/
Related Resources:
New York Review of Books Archive
http://www.nybooks.com/nyrev/archives.html

Publishers Weekly Bestseller Lists
http://www.bookwire.com
"Search *Publishers Weekly* hardcover lists from 1991 to date."
Search Form URL: http://www.bookwire.com/bookinfo/searchform PW.html

Calculators

Martindale's Calculators Online Center
http://www-sci.lib.uci.edu/HSG/RefCalculators.html
The Invisible Web is home to many interactive calculators. Although this directory is not on the Invisible Web, the data that they make accessible is found on the IW. This comprehensive compilation has links to over 12,000 calculators.
Search Form URL: See main page

U.S. Dept. of Energy/EPA Automobile Fuel Economy
http://www.fueleconomy.gov/
Find the mpg (miles per gallon) for cars and trucks. Data available for 1985-2001.
Search Form URL: http://www.fueleconomy.gov/feg/findacar. htm
Related Resources:
U.S. Regional Gasoline Costs
http://www.eia.doe.gov/emeu/rtecs/gascosts/start.html
U.S. Vehicle Emissions Guide (EPA)
http://www.epa.gov/autoemissions/select.htm

Fuel Consumption Guide Canada
http://autosmart.nrcan.gc.ca/pubs/fcg2_e.cfm

Universal Currency Converter

http://www.xe.net/ucc/

The Universal Currency Converter allows you to perform interactive foreign exchange rate conversion on the Internet. "Over 180 currencies available."

Search Form URL: http://www.xe.net/ucc/full.shtml

Consumer Resources

NADAGuides.Com

http://www.nadaguides.com

Prices from the consumer edition of the well known vehicle pricing guides. Vehicle pricing for Boats, Truck Campers, Motor Homes, Park Model RVs, Travel and Camping Trailers, Motorcycles, ATVs, Snowmobiles, Personal Watercraft, Aircraft, New Car Pricing, and Classic, Collectible and Special Interest Cars and Trucks.

Search Form URL: See Main Page

Related Resources:

Kelly Blue Book

http://www.kbb.com

Edmunds Used Vehicle Appraiser

http://www.edmunds.com

U.S. Automobile Recall Database

http://www.nhtsa.dot.gov

Recall information from the National Highway Traffic Safety Administration.

Search Form URL: http://www.nhtsa.dot.gov/cars/problems/ recalls/recall_links.html

Related Resources:

Vehicle Recalls Online Database Canada

http://www.tc.gc.ca/securiteroutiere/Recalls/search_e.asp

Underwriters Laboratory Certification Database

http://www.ul.com

"... access the most current information on more than 110,000 UL Listings of products and 4,000 Registered firms by company name, product name, geography, file number, or guide information."
Search Form URL: http://www.ul.com/database/

Dictionaries, Glossaries, and Translation Resources

Acronym Finder
http://www.acronymfinder.com
"The Web's most comprehensive database of acronyms, abbreviations, and initialisms. 180,000+ definitions!"
Search Form URL: See Main Page
Related Resources:
BioABACUS (Abbrvieations and Arcronyms in Biotechnology)
http://www.nmsu.edu/~molbio/bioABACUShome.htm

American Sign Language Browser
http://commtechlab.msu.edu/
"... an online American Sign Language (ASL) browser where you can look up video of thousands of ASL signs and learn interesting things about them."
Search Form URL: http://commtechlab.msu.edu/sites/aslweb/index.html

Art and Architecture Thesaurus Browser (AAT)
http://www.getty.edu/gri/vocabularies/index.htm
"The AAT is a structured vocabulary of around 125,000 terms, scope notes, and other information for describing fine art, architecture, decorative arts, archival materials, and material culture."
Search Form URL: http://shiva.pub.getty.edu/aat_browser/

Cambridge Dictionaries Online
http://dictionary.cambridge.org/
Keyword search four Cambridge publications: *Cambridge International Dictionary of English, Cambridge Dictionary of American*

English, Cambridge International Dictionary of Idioms, Cambridge International Dictionary of Phrasal Verbs.
Search Form URL: See Main Page
Related Resources:
Merriam-Webster Dictionary and Thesaurus
http://www.m-w.com
Wordsmyth
http://www.wordsmyth.com

EuroDicAutom

http://eurodic.ip.lu
Eurodicautom is the multilingual terminological database of the European Commission's Translation Service. Initially developed to assist in-house translators, it is today consulted by an increasing number of other EU officials, as well as by language professionals throughout the world.
Search Form URL: See Main Page
Related Resources:
International Telecommunications Union Terminology Database
http://www.itu.int/search/wais/Termite/
FAO Term (Food and Agriculture Organization)
http://www.fao.org/FAOTERM/
International Labor Organization Term Database
http://ilis.ilo.org/ilis/ilisterm/ilintrte.html

Glossary of Communications Terms

http://www.getcommstuff.com
Produced by the Telecommunications Industry Association. Over 5,800 terms in the database.
Search Form URL: http://www.getcommstuff.com/glossary/
Related Resources:
Telecom Acronym Database
http://www.tiaonline.org/resources/acronym.cfm

Jane's Defence Glossary

http://www.janes.com
"... database contains over 20,000 defense-related acronyms and abbreviations."
Search Form URL: http://www.janes.com/defence/glossary/

Lexical FreeNet

http://www.lexfn.com/

"This program allows you to search for relationships between words, concepts, and people. It is a combination thesaurus, rhyming dictionary, pun generator, and concept navigator."
Search Form URL: See Main Page

Library and Information Science Dictionary and Glossary
http://eubd1.ugr.es/tony/risweb.isa
Several searchable databases including the IFLA (International Federation of Library Associations and Institutions) Glossary.
Search Form URL: See Main Page

OnTerm Canada
http://www.onterm.gov.on.ca/
The government of Ontario's bilingual terminology database. "Contains over 12,000 entries in two databases, OFFICIAL GOVERNMENT NAMES and GENERIC NAMES, which can be searched simultaneously."
Search Form URL: See Main Page

RhymeZone
http://rhyme.lycos.com
Enter a word and find ryhmes, homophones, similar sounding words, similar spelled words, and much more.
Search Form URL: See Main Page

Verbix
http://www.verbix.com/index.html
Conjugate verbs online in over 50 languages.
Search Form URL: http://www.verbix.com/languages/index.html

Voice of America Pronunciation Guide
http://www.voa.gov
Locate the correct pronunciation of names for people in the news. Many names contain an associated RealAudio file that allows you to hear the name pronounced.
Search Form URL: http://www.voa.gov/pronunciations/index.cfm

Food and Beverages

Language of the Food Industry: Glossary of Supermarket Terms
http://www.fmi.org

The Food Marketing Institute provides free searchable/browsable access to this reference tool that contains over 20,000 terms.
Search Form URL: http://www.fmi.org/facts_figs/glossary_ search.cfm

Local Harvest

http://www.localharvest.org
Database of farms and other services throughout America where you can purchase locally grown food.
Search Form URL: See Main Page

SOAR (Searchable Online Archive of Recipes)

http://soar.berkeley.edu/recipes/
A browsable and searchable database of over 67,000 recipes.
Search Form URL: See Main Page
Related Resources:
Epicurious Recipe Database
http://www.epicurious.com/e_eating/e02_recipes/recipes.html

Winefiles.Org

http://www.winefiles.org
"... authoritative information on wine, wine making and grape growing, including the business, technology, and history associated with wine ... coverage is worldwide with a special emphasis on California."
Search Form URL: See Main Page
Related Resources:
Oxford Companion to Wine
http://www.wine.com/oxford/index.shtml

Zagat Restaurant Surveys

http://www.zagats.com
"... access to restaurant ratings and reviews for 45 cities and regions ..."
Search Form URL: See Main Page
Related Resources:
Wine Spectator Restaurant Database
http://www.winespectator.com/Wine/Spectator/rest

General Reference Resources

AIDS Memorial Quilt Search

http://www.aidsquilt.org

"The names that fill this database are those of individuals memorialized on the AIDS Memorial Quilt. In all, there are more than 83,000 names."
Search Form URL: http://www.aidsquilt.org/Newsite/searchquilt. htm

American Kennel Club Events Calendar and Awards Search

http://www.akc.org/dic/events/
"... display the plans for future events and the awards/results of past events. You can search for an event using any combination of: event name, state(s), competition type, and time range. You can also display a calendar of events and unofficial weekly wins."
Search Form URL: http://www.akc.org/dic/events/search/index.cfm

Bluebook.com (The)

http://www.thebluebook.com
"The Blue Book of Building and Construction is the Industry's leading source of regional, categorized construction information. The Blue Book features over 800,000 company listings with over 46,000 display ads and company profiles."
Search Form URL: See Main Page

Canadian Encyclopedia (The)

http://www.thecanadianencyclopedia.com
The full-text of this well-known encyclopedia is searchable and accessible for free.
Search Form URL: See Main Page

Directory of Scholarly and Professional E-Conferences (The)

http://www.n2h2.com/KOVACS/
"The Directory of Scholarly and Professional E-conferences screens, evaluates, and organizes discussion lists, newsgroups, MUDS, MOO'S, Muck's, Mushes, mailing lists, interactive Web chat groups, etc. (e-conferences) on topics of interest to scholars and professionals for use in their scholarly, pedagological, and professional activities. "
Search Form URL: See Main Page
Related Resources:
Topica Newsletter and Internet List Directory
http://www.topica.com
Catalist
http://www.lsoft.com/catalist.html

Fugitive Fact File (Hennepin County Library)

http://www.hennepin.lib.mn.us

"The Fugitive Fact File was compiled by Hennepin County Library staff from information files maintained at individual libraries throughout the Hennepin County Library System. The purpose of this database, which brings information from those many files together into one online resource, is to assist patrons in locating hard-to-find and elusive information. All of the data and resources collected here have been used by library staff to answer reference questions."

Search Form URL: http://www.hennepin.lib.mn.us/pub/search/ fff_public.html

Microsoft Design Gallery Live

http://cgl.microsoft.com

Searchable database of clip art, sounds, and animation provided by Microsoft. Make sure to pay close attention to the licensing agreement.

Search Form URL: See Main Page

Standard Industrial Classification Search

http://www.osha.gov

"This page allows the user to search the 1987 version SIC manual by keyword, to access descriptive information for a specified 4-digit SIC."

Search Form URL: http://www.osha.gov/oshstats/sicser.html

Related Resources:

1997 NAICS (North American Industry Classification System) and 1987 SIC Correspondence Tables

http://www.census.gov/epcd/www/naicstab.htm

United Nations System: Days, Decades, Years Database

http://www.unesco.org

"Included are the International Days, Decades, and Years proclaimed and observed (when in force) by the United Nations and its Specialized Agencies."

Search Form URL: http://www.unesco.org/general/eng/infoserv/db/international-events-form.shtml

Universal Postal Union Statistics

http://www.upu.int

"The International Bureau of the Universal Postal Union (UPU) has published postal statistics regularly since its foundation. Since the first

edition in 1875, these statistics have been amended and improved in order to meet as closely as possible the postal world's expectations and need for information."
Search Form URL: http://www.upu.int/ap/ssp_browse.menu0?p_language=AN

Writer's Digest Guidelines Database

http://www.writersdigest.com
"... browse more than 1,500 guidelines, prepared by book and magazine editors themselves."
Search Form URL: http://www.writersdigest.com/guidelines/index.htm

xrefer

http://www.xrefer.com
"xrefer contains encyclopedias, dictionaries, thesauri, and books of quotations from the world's leading publishers. All cross-referenced, all in one place—providing you with a single source for reliable factual information."
Search Form URL: See Main Page
Related Resources:
Bartleby.com
http://www.bartleby.com

Journals and Periodicals

Jake

http://jake.med.yale.edu
"Jake (Jointly Administered Knowledge Environment) is a reference source [that] makes finding, managing, and linking online journals and journal articles easier for students, researchers, and librarians. Jake does this by managing online resource metadata with a database union list, title authority control, linking tools, and a local holdings layer."
Search Form URL:
Related Resources:
JAKE (Experimental Interface)
http://mercury.lib.sfu.ca/~tholbroo/sfujake/search.cgi

Publist

http://www.publist.com

This database provides publication information for over 150,000 magazines, journals, newsletters, and other periodicals.

Search Form URL: http://www.publist.com/search.html

Library/Online Searching

Canadian Subject Headings Canada

http://www.nlc-bnc.ca/csh/csh-e.htm

"CSH is a list of standard subject headings (in English) on Canadian topics, which complements Library of Congress Subject Headings (LCSH) and is compatible with LCSH in its underlying principles."

Search Form URL: http://www.nlc-bnc.ca/cshweb/index-e.htm

DIALOG/DataStar Full-Text Database

http://library.dialog.com

"... tool for retrieving targeted information about the more than 30,000 LEXISNEXIS sources."

Search Form URL: See Main Page

Related Resources:

OCLC Participating Institution Search

http://www.oclc.org/oclc/forms/pisearch.htm

LexisNexis Source Locator

http://www.lexisnexis.com/lncc/sources/

Source Available in Dow Jones Interactive

http://askdj.dowjones.com/content/PubDir/index.asp

Gale Group Reference Review Archive

http://www.galegroup.com/reference/reference.htm

"The Reference Reviews Archive includes the reviews of James Rettig, Peter Jacso, Blanche Woolls, David Loertscher, and John Lawrence." Reviews date back to 1997. New reviews are accessible via the top-level page.

Search Form URL: http://www.galegroup.com/servlet/Reference ReviewSearchPageServlet

Librarian's Yellow Pages

http://www.librariansyellowpages.com

"... constantly updated database has products and services from 2,000+ library vendors ... with full-text, keyword searchable listings."
Search Form URL: See Main Page

NoodleBib (Bibliography Creator)

http://www.noodletools.com
"NoodleBib is a Web application that allows you to create and edit your MLA-style bibliographies online."
Search Form URL: http://www.noodletools.com/noodlebib/index.html
Related Resources:
Noodlequest (Search Tool Selection Aid)
http://www.noodletools.com/noodlequest/main.php3

Locators

Alternative Fuel Stations (Alternative Fuels Data Center)

http://www.afdc.doe.gov/
"The Alternative Fuels Data Center lists refueling site locations (stations) for compressed natural gas (CNG), 85% methanol and 15% gasoline (M85), 85% ethanol and 15% gasoline (E85), liquefied petroleum gas (LPG), liquefied natural gas (LNG), as well as electric charging stations located throughout the United States. We gather this information from retailers, trade organizations, and general literature."
Search Form URL: http://afdcmap.nrel.gov/nrel/

Federal Depository Library Directory

http://www.access.gpo.gov
"The Federal Depository Library Directory is the official GPO directory that includes information on all Federal depository libraries, such as names, addresses, telephone numbers, etc." The libraries permit access to large collections of government documents. Any person can visit Federal depository libraries and use the collections. The information available covers all topics.
Search Form URL: http://www.access.gpo.gov/su_docs/fdlp/tools/ldirect.html

Fone Finder

http://www.primeris.com/fonefind/

"Fone Finder is a free, public search engine that finds the geographic location of any phone number in the world."
Search Form URL: See Main Page

Guide to Military Installations Worldwide U.S.
http://www.militarycity.com
Army Times Publishing provides the directory of U.S. Military installations located in the U.S. and overseas.
Search Form URL: http://www.militarycity.com/moves/baseguide.html

Mailbox and Packing Store Database
http://www.bnl.com/mb/
"These stores offer services such as copying, faxing, mailbox rental, packaging and shipping through various shippers, mail forwarding, voice mail, and many, many more services."
Search Form URL: See Main Page

Museum Locator (Museum Research Board)
http://seeing2020.com/museums/index.html
"Find contact information for nearly 7,500 museums throughout the United States."
Search Form URL: http://seeing2020.com/museums/lookup.htm
Related Resources:
Museum Finder U.K.
http://www.24hourmuseum.org.uk/find_fr.htm

Public Library Locator
http://nces.ed.gov/surveys/libraries/
"The Public Library Locator is a tool to help you locate information about a public library or a public library service outlet when you know some, but not all of the information about it. The information in this locator has been drawn from the NCES Public Libraries Survey."
Search Form URL: http://nces.ed.gov/surveys/libraries/liblocator/default.asp
Related Resources:
Public Library Comparison Tool
http://nces.ed.gov/surveys/libraries/publicpeer/

Red Cross Chapter Locator
http://www.redcross.org
Locate your local chapter of the American Red Cross. Search by ZIP code.
Search Form URL: http://www.redcross.org/where/where.html

U.S. Post Office Locator

http://www.framed.usps.com/ncsc/

Find the address of the post office that delivers the mail to your address. The addresses of other local post offices will also be displayed.

Search Form URL: http://www.framed.usps.com/ncsc/locators/find-po.html

Related Resources:

U.S. Postal Inspection Service Office Locator

http://www.framed.usps.com/ncsc/locators/find-is.html

U.S. Post Office Business Center Locator

http://www.framed.usps.com/ncsc/locators/find-pbc.html

U.S. ZIP Code+4 Database

http://www.usps.gov

Find the ZIP code for any U.S. address.

Search Form URL: http://www.usps.gov/ncsc/lookups/lookup_zip+4.html

Related Resources:

Canadian Postal Code Lookup

http://www.canadapost.ca/CPC2/addrm/pclookup/pclookup.shtml

U.K. Postcode Finder

http://www.royalmail.co.uk/paf/

Australia Postcode Search

http://www.auspost.com.au/postcodes/

Visa/Plus ATM Locator

http://www.visa.com

Locate machine locations in many countries.

Search Form URL: http://www.visa.com/pd/atm/main.html

Related Resources:

The Mastercard/Maestro/Cirrus ATM Locator

http://www.mastercard.com/atm/

Maps and Geography

Canadian Geographic Names (Name Query) Canada

http://geonames.nrcan.gc.ca/

"Toponyms, or geographical names, are used by us all every day to describe our surroundings and to tell others where we have been or where we plan to go. When we use maps we expect the names to help

us identify features of the landscape, and perhaps even to throw light on the local history of an area."
Search Form URL: http://geonames.nrcan.gc.ca/english/ cgndb.html
Related Resources:
Canadian Geographic Names (Coordinate Query)
http://geonames.nrcan.gc.ca/english/cgndb_coord.html
Northwest Territories Geographic Names Database
http://www.pwnhc.learnnet.nt.ca/programs/geodb.htm
Prince Edward Island Places Database
http://www.gov.pe.ca/where.php3

GEONet Names Server

http://164.214.2.59/gns/html/index.html
"The GEOnet Names Server (GNS) provides access to the National Imagery and Mapping Agency's (NIMA) database of foreign geographic feature names. Approximately 20,000 of the database's 3.5 million features are updated monthly with names information approved by the U.S. Board on Geographic Names (US BGN)." Geographic Area of Coverage is worldwide excluding the United States and Antarctica.
Search Form URL: See Main Page
Related Resources:
Geographic Names Information System (U.S. and Antarctica)
http://mapping.usgs.gov/www/gnis/
U.S. Gazetteer
http://www.census.gov/cgi-bin/gazetteer

Getty Thesaurus of Geographic Names

http://www.getty.edu/gri/
"The TGN is a structured vocabulary containing around 1,000,000 names and other information about places. The TGN includes all continents and nations of the modern political world, as well as historical places. It includes physical features and administrative entities, such as cities and nations. The emphasis in TGN is on places important for art and architecture."
Search Form URL: http://shiva.pub.getty.edu/tgn_browser/
Related Resources:
Gazetteer of Australia
http://kaos.erin.gov.au/database/MAN200R.html
Get-a-Map U.K.
http://getamap.ordnancesurvey.co.uk/getamap.asp

How Far Is It?

http://www.indo.com/distance/

"This service uses data from the U.S. Census and a supplementary list of cities around the world to find the latitude and longitude of two places, and then calculates the distance between them (as the crow flies)."

Search Form URL: See Main Page

Related Resources:

Flight Route Calculator (Distance between two airports)

www.landings.com/_landings/pages/search_dist_apt.html

MapBlast

http://www.mapblast.com

Interactive maps and driving directions. Maps for many countries. Take note of the many advanced search options.

Search Form URL: See Main Page

Related Resources:

Maporama

http://www.maporama.com

Streetmap.co.uk U.K.

http://www.streetmap.co.uk/

Whereis Street Atlas Australia

http://www.whereis.com.au/

Maptech Map Server

http://www.maptech.com

"The largest online mapping resource for topographic maps and charts for land, sea, and air. Browse, view, print, and email the maps for free."

Search Form URL: http://navigator2.maptech.com/homepage/ index.cfm

Related Resources:

Topozone

http://www.topozone.com/

Toporama Canada

http://toporama.ctis.nrcan.gc.ca/

National Atlas of the United States

http://www.nationalatlas.gov

From the U.S. Geological Survey. "This Atlas updates a large bound collection of paper maps that was published in 1970. Like its predecessor, this largely digital National Atlas promotes greater national geographic awareness. It delivers easy to use, map-like views of America's natural and sociocultural landscapes."

Search Form URL: http://nationalatlas.gov/natlas/natlasstart.asp
Related Resources:
Tiger Mapping Service
http://tiger.census.gov/
National Atlas of Canada
http://atlas.gc.ca/
The Atlas of South Australia
http://www.atlas.sa.gov.au/

National Geographic Society Map Machine

http://www.nationalgeographic.com/maps/
An interactive collection of atlas maps, dynamic maps, and basic country facts.
Search Form URL: See Main Page
Related Resources:
Rand McNally Downloadable (.pdf) U.S. State and Thematic Maps
http://www.randmcnally.com/rmc/explore_maps/exmDownLoad.jsp

RandMcNally U.S. Road Construction Database

http://www.randmcnally.com
"Avoid possible delays. Find out about road construction projects in the U.S. and Canada that may affect your trip." The database is updated twice a month.
Search Form URL: http://www.randmcnally.com/rmc/tools/road ConstructionSearch.jsp

U.K. Ordnance Survey Get-A-Map U.K.

http://www.ordsvy.gov.uk
Search for and view a selection of Ordnance Survey maps online.
Search for locations by placename, Postal Code, or grid reference.
Search Form URL: http://getamap.ordnancesurvey.co.uk/getamap.asp

Sports

International Tennis Federation Player's Database

http://www.itftennis.com
"Extending back to 1977, the ITF database covers over 20 years of records for all male and female players who have competed in a major event during that time."
Search Form URL: http://onlinesql.itftennis.com/select.htm

Major Leaugue Baseball Player Search

http://www.totalbaseball.com

Find basic biographical and statistical information for most current
and former Major League players.

Search Form URL: http://www.totalbaseball.com/stats/mlbstat. html

NCAA Statistics

http://www.ncaa.org

Up-to-date statistics for college sports in the United States. The statistics for a few sports (Basketball, Baseball) are in Invisible Web databases. However, due to the timely nature of this information general
search tools may miss regular updates.

Search Form URL: http://www.ncaa.org/stats/

Travel

Airline Coding Directory

http://www.iata.org

Obtain official airline codes for over 9,000 locations around the world.

Search Form URL: http://www.iata.org/codes/index.asp

Airline Flight and Fare Database from ITA Software

http://www.itasoftware.com

Hundreds of searching options exist to find airfares on the Internet. ITA
Software is developing new airfare search technology and is licensing the
technology to airlines and Internet travel services. The software was
developed at the Artificial Intelligence Laboratory at MIT.

Search Form URL: http://beta.itasoftware.com/servlet/
cvgdispatch/

Related Resources:

FareChase

http://www.farechase.com

Qixo

http://www.qixo.com

Amtrak Timetable

http://www.amtrak.com

"Browse schedules and fares, purchase tickets, or review a previous
reservation."

Search Form URL: http://reservations.amtrak.com/
Related Resources:
European Rail Timetable Database
http://bahn.hafas.de/bin/detect.exe/bin/query.exe/e
VIA Rail Canada Timetable
http://www.viarail.ca/en.fram.hora.tari.html

Hotelguide.Com

http://www.hotelguide.com
"Find accommodations anywhere using Hotelguide.com—the largest
hotel directory on the Internet."
Search Form URL: http://www.hotelguide.com/search.cfm

Hotel-Motel Master List

http://www.usfa.fema.gov
"The Hotel-Motel National Master List provides you with the ability to
search for specific hotels and motels that meet fire and life safety
requirements of the Hotel-Motel Act of 1990."
Search Form URL: http://www.usfa.fema.gov/hotel/search.cfm

Journeys Made Simple

http://www.transportforlondon.gov.uk
Plan your itinerary on the London Transport System.
Search Form URL: http://www.transportforlondon.gov.uk/jp_
index.html
Related Resources:
Subway Navigator (Many Cities)
http://www.subwaynavigator.com/

Trail Finder

http://www.gorp.com
An interactive directory to locate trails (running, biking, snowmobil-
ing, etc.) in the U.S. and British Columbia.
Search Form URL: http://gorptools.gorp.com/GORPApps/trails/
search_form.asp

Travel Offices Worldwide Directory

http://www.towd.com
"The TOWD is your guide to official tourist information sources. The
Directory lists only official government tourism offices, convention
and visitors bureaus, chambers of commerce, and similar agencies

[that] provide free, accurate, and unbiased travel information to the public."
Search Form URL: See Main Page

Visit Your Parks (U.S. National Parks)

http://www.nps.gov
This National Park Service guide allows you to choose from a large list of criteria and have a list of National Parks that meet those criteria returned to you.
Search Form URL: http://www.nps.gov/parks/search.htm
Related Resources:
Recreational Opportunities on Federal Lands
http://www.recreation.gov/
Park Search (Worldwide Info)
http://www.llbean.com/parksearch/

WhatsGoingOn.com

http://www.whatsgoingon.com/
"... the tools to travel to the most interesting and outrageous places and rituals on the planet."
Search Form URL: See Main Page

Weather

Weatherbase

http://www.weatherbase.com/
"Weatherbase℠ is your one authoritative source for finding monthly weather records and averages for more than 10,200 cities worldwide."
Search Form URL: See Main Page

Weatherplanner

http://www.weatherplanner.com
A tool that predicts the weather in the U.S. up to one year in advance.
Search Form URL: See Main Page

CHAPTER 25

Science

The very heart of science revolves around research and the collection of data—so what better way to store and manipulate it than with a database? The Invisible Web is rife with scientific databases that allow amateur and professional scientists alike to access and analyze information across a broad spectrum of disciplines. Some scientific resources on the Invisible Web have been enhanced to allow extensive interactivity, in effect allowing users to conduct their own experiments with the data. And, as with many other subject areas, there are also extensive scientific bibliographic and document collections available to the searcher.

In this chapter, we attempt to offer a sample of what's available for a wide array of scientific fields. While much of this information is highly specialized and only useful to researchers in particular niches, it uniformly demonstrates the high quality of information available to searchers willing to explore the regions of the Invisible Web.

These key resources are included:

- **Agriculture, Biology, and Botany**, including the *FAOSTAT Statistical Database Collection (Food and Agriculture Organization of the United Nations)*, *GeneCards*, a database of human genes, their products, and involvement in disease, and the *Plants Database* from the U.S. Dept. of Agriculture

- **Chemistry, Earth Sciences, and Energy**, with resources like *Chemfinder.com*, the *Worldwide Volcano Database*, and the *Nuclear Explosions Database*

- **Environmental Resources**, including the *ENTRI (Environmental Treaties Database)*, *Envirofacts* from the Environmental Protection Agency, and *NatureServe*, authoritative conservation information on more than 50,000 plants, animals, and ecological communities

- **General Science Resources**, such as the *PrePRINT Network*, a gateway to preprint servers; *sciBase*, with access to more than 12 million scientific articles; and many, many other resources

See the Science category on the companion Web site for additional Invisible Web resources on this topic at http://www.invisible-web.net.

Agriculture

AGRICOLA B
http://www.nal.usda.gov
"AGRICOLA (AGRICultural OnLine Access) is a bibliographic database of citations to the agricultural literature created by the National Agricultural Library and its cooperators. Production of these records in electronic form began in 1970, but the database covers materials in all formats, including printed works from the 15th century."
Search Form URL: http://www.nal.usda.gov/ag98/ag98.html
Related Resources:
U.S. Agricultural Research Service Database Compilation
http://www.ars.usda.gov/arsdb.html
U.S. Agricultural Research Service Expert Database
http://www.nps.ars.usda.gov/fte/

Anro (Australian Agriculture) Australia
http://www.infoscan.com.au/contents/index.html
A collection of six Australian databases focusing on Agriculture and Natural Resources.
Search Form URL: See Main Page

FAOSTAT Statistical Database Collection (Food and Agriculture Organization of the United Nations)

http://apps.fao.org

"FAOSTAT is an online and multilingual database currently containing over 1 million time-series records covering international statistics in the following areas: Production, Trade, Food Balance Sheets, Fertilizer and Pesticides, Land Use and Irrigation, Forest Products, Fishery Products, Population Agricultural Machinery, and Food Aid Shipments."

Search Form URL: http://apps.fao.org/page/collections

Related Resources:

FAO Media Archive (Photographs)

http://www1.fao.org/media_user/_home.html

Biology

African Elephant Database B

http://www.chebucto.ns.ca/~drigby/eli3.htm

"The bibliography has been developed to facilitate the work of African elephant ecology researchers, field staff, and resource managers." Over 3,500 annotated references.

Search Form URL: http://dev.chebucto.ns.ca:8080/

Canadian Bird Trends Database Canada

http://www.cws-scf.ec.gc.ca

"The Canadian Bird Trends Database is a retrieval system that provides the user with information on Canadian bird species including: population trends, range distribution, and national conservation designations."

Search Form URL: http://www.cws-scf.ec.gc.ca/Trends

Related Resources:

http://www.cws-scf.ec.gc.ca/Trends/

E-Nature Field Guides

http://www.enature.com

"The complete guide to over 4,800 North American plants and animals." Excellent advanced search features.

Search Form URL: http://www.enature.com/guides/select_ group.asp

FishBase

http://www.fishbase.org

"... a global information system with all you ever wanted to know about fishes. FishBase is a relational database with fish information to cater to different professionals such as research scientists, fisheries managers, zoologists, and many more. FishBase on the Web contains practically all fish species known to science."

Search Form URL: http://www.fishbase.org/search.cfm

GeneCards

http://bioinformatics.weizmann.ac.il

"GeneCards is a database of human genes, their products, and their involvement in diseases. It offers concise information about the functions of all human genes that have an approved symbol, as well as selected others [gene listing]."

Search Form URL: http://bioinformatics.weizmann.ac.il/cards/

Integrated Taxonomic Information System (Biological Names)

http://www.itis.usda.gov/plantproj/itis/index.html

"The Integrated Taxonomic Information System (ITIS) is a partnership of U.S., Canadian, and Mexican agencies, other organizations, and taxonomic specialists cooperating on the development of an online, scientifically credible, list of biological names focusing on the biota of North America."

Search Form URL: http://www.itis.usda.gov/plantproj/itis/itis_query.html

Related Resources:

The International Plant Names Index

http://tc.huh.harvard.edu/

ISIS (International Species Information System)

http://www.worldzoo.org/

"ISIS is an international nonprofit membership organization (U.S. 501c3) [that] serves nearly 550 zoological institutional members, from 54 countries, worldwide." The abstracts listed here contain the holdings of member zoos.

Search Form URL: http://www.worldzoo.org/abstract/ abstract.htm

Man and the Biosphere Species Databases

http://ice.ucdavis.edu/mab/

"The Information Center for the Environment, in association with the Man and the Biosphere (MAB) Programs of UNESCO and the United States, is developing databases of vascular plant and vertebrate animal occurrences on the world's biosphere reserves and other protected areas. Currently, the MABFlora (for vascular plants) and MABFauna (for vertebrate animals) databases contain records from over 740 protected areas in 103 countries. The MABFlora and MABFauna databases are continually updated as additional data are received."
Search Form URL: See Main Page

Redlist (Threatened Species Database)
http://www.redlist.org
"The IUCN (International Union for Conservation of Nature and Natural Resources) Red List of Threatened Species provides taxonomic, conservation status, and distribution information on taxa that have been evaluated using the IUCN Red List Categories."
Search Form URL: http://www.redlist.org/search.asp
Related Resources:
Species at Risk Canada
http://www.speciesatrisk.gc.ca/Species/English/

Zoo and Aquarium Directory (American Zoo and and Aquarium Association)
http://www.aza.org/
Search for members by name or state. Most entries contain a brief overview of zoo/aquarium along with a link to the Web site.
Search Form URL: http://www.aza.org/members/zoo/

Botany

Canadian Poisonous Plants Information System Canada
http://sis.agr.ca/brd/poisonpl/
"The Canadian Poisonous Plants Information System presents data on plants that cause poisoning in livestock, pets, and humans. The plants include native, introduced, and cultivated outdoor plants as well as indoor plants that are found in Canada. Some food and herbal plants are also included that may cause potential poisoning problems."
Search Form URL: http://sis.agr.ca/brd/poisonpl/poison.html

Peanut Literature Database B

http://nespal.cpes.peachnet.edu

"A searchable collection of references to peanut research articles and information."

Search Form URL: http://nespal.cpes.peachnet.edu/home/ pnutdb/

Related Resources:

Rice Bibliography B

http://ricelib.irri.cgiar.org:81/screens/opacmenu.html

Plants Database

http://plants.usda.gov

Developed by the U.S. Department of Agriculture, this is an excellent one-stop source about plants. Topics covered include plant character-istics and cultural significance.

Search Form URL: See Main Page

Related Resources:

Species and Parks: Flora and Fauna in U.S. National Parks

http://endeavor.des.ucdavis.edu/NPS/

The Postcode Plants Database U.K.

http://www.nhm.ac.uk/science/projects/fff/

REFORGEN (Forestry)

http://www.fao.org/forestry/

"The FAO Global Information System on forest genetic resources. Information in the system can be divided into two major groups: (i) data by species on status and activities in the field of forest genetic resources in a given country, (ii) data on institutions active in the field of forest genetic resources in a given country."

Search Form URL: http://www.fao.org/montes/for/form/ FOGENRES/reforgen/

Related Resources:

Distribution of Forests (Country Profiles)

http://www.fao.org/forestry/fo/country/nav_world.jsp

Chemistry

Beilstein Abstracts

http://www.chemweb.com

"Users are able to access titles, abstracts, and citations from the top journals in organic and related chemistry, published from 1980 to the present. There are currently approximately 600,000 articles in the Beilstein Abstracts Database." Free registration for the Chemweb site is required.

Search Form URL: http://www.chemweb.com/databases/beilstein

Related Resources:

Chemistry Preprint Server

http://preprint.chemweb.com/

ChemGuide (Foused Crawler)

http://www.chemweb.com/databases/chemguide/chemguide.html

ChemIDplus

http://www.nlm.nih.gov/pubs/factsheets/chemidplusfs.html

Chemfinder.Com

http://www.chemfinder.com

Locate the properties of many chemicals.

Search Form URL: See Main Page

Related Resources:

Chemical Acronyms Database

http://129.79.137.107/cfdocs/libchem/searchu.html

National Institute of Science and Technology (NIST) WebBook

http://www.nist.gov

"This database contains thermochemical data for over 5,000 organic and small inorganic compounds, reaction thermochemistry data for over 8,000 reactions, IR spectra for over 7,500 compounds, mass spectra for over 10,000 compounds, UV/Vis spectra for over 400 compounds, electronic/vibrational spectra for over 3,000 compounds, constants of diatomic molecules (spectroscopic data) for over 600 compounds, ion energetics data for over 14,000 compounds, and thermophysical property data for 16 fluids. There are many avenues for searching the database."

Search Form URL: http://webbook.nist.gov/

Related Resources:

Elemental Data Index

http://physics.nist.gov/PhysRefData/Elements/cover.html

Additional NIST "Standard Reference" Databases

http://www.nist.gov/srd/online.htm

Solvents Database (SOLV-DB)

http://solvdb.ncms.org/index.html

"The National Center for Manufacturing Sciences presents SOLV-DB, your one-stop source for solvents data."

Search Form URL: http://solvdb.ncms.org/solvdb.htm

THERMODEX (Thermochemical Data) B

http://thermodex.lib.utexas.edu/

"ThermoDex contains records for printed and Web-based compilations of thermochemical and thermophysical data for chemical compounds and other substances. You can select one or more compound types and link them to one or more property terms, and ThermoDex will return a list of handbooks that might contain this data."

Search Form URL: See Main Page

Earth Sciences

Abandoned Mines Land Inventory System

http://www.osmre.gov/osmaml.htm

"The Abandoned Mine Land Inventory System is a computer system used to store, manage, and report on the Office of Surface Mining's Inventory of Abandoned Mines Land Problems. This includes both problems in need of reclamation and those that have been reclaimed." A small download and a telnet connection are needed to access this database.

Search Form URL: http://www.osmre.gov/aml/inven/zamlis.htm

ASTIS (Arctic Science and Technology Information System)
Canada, B

http://www.aina.ucalgary.ca/astis/

"The Arctic Science and Technology Information System (ASTIS) database contains over 47,000 records describing publications and research projects about northern Canada. ASTIS is maintained by the Arctic Institute of North America at the University of Calgary, and is made available for free with support from the Canadian Polar Commission."

Search Form URL: http://www.aina.ucalgary.ca/scripts/minisa. dll?HOME

Related Resources:

Nunavut Environmental Database (NED)
http://136.159.147.171/ned/

Atlas of Antarctic Research

http://usarc.usgs.gov/
"... designed to promote greater geographic awareness of the continent and the digital geospatial data that describe it. It provides a common base for displaying research results and data collected, as well as descriptions of ongoing and past projects, when they become available for display."
Search Form URL: http://usarc.usgs.gov/antarctic_atlas/
Related Resources:
Composite Gazetteer of Antarctica
http://www.pnra.it/SCAR_GAZE
Geographic Names Information System-Antarctica
http://mapping.usgs.gov/www/gnis/antform.html
SPIRLIB Antarctica B
http://www.spri.cam.ac.uk/lib/spriant.htm

Earthquake Engineering Abstracts B

http://www.eerc.berkeley.edu
EEA covers the world literature in earthquake engineering since 1971. Contents include selected technical reports, conference papers, monographs, and journal articles.
Search Form URL: http://www.eerc.berkeley.edu/cgi-bin/ texhtml? form=eea
Related Resources:
Earthquake Image Information System (EQIIS)
http://www.eerc.berkeley.edu/eqiis.html
Quakeline B
http://mceer.buffalo.edu/utilities/quakeline.html

Earthquake Search

http://www.neic.cr.usgs.gov/neis/
From the National Earthquake Information Center. Access earthquake information throughout history by using this database.
Search Form URL: http://wwwneic.cr.usgs.gov/neis/epic/ epic.html
Related Resources:
National Eathquake Database Canada
http://www.seismo.nrcan.gc.ca/nedb/eq_db_e.html

GEOLEX

http://ngmsvr.wr.usgs.gov/

"GEOLEX is a search tool for lithologic and geochronologic unit names. ... The Geolex database contains 16,005 entries. 75% of the unit names from the USGS Geologic Names Committee (GNC) card catalog have been entered in the database. Several thousand unit names remain to be checked and entered."

Search Form URL: http://ngmsvr.wr.usgs.gov/Geolex/geolex_home.html

Mineral Resources Online Spatial Data

http://mrdata.usgs.gov/

"... digital databases of geologic, lithologic, geochemical, geophysical, and mineral deposit information." This database is made available by the United States Geological Survey.

Search Form URL: See Main Page

Related Resources:

U.S. Coal Resource Database

http://energy.er.usgs.gov/products/databases/USCoal/index.htm

U.S. Coal Quality Database

http://ngmsvr.wr.usgs.gov/Other_Resources/rdb_coalqual.html

Publications of the United States Geological Survey B

http://usgs-georef.cos.com/

"The [biblopgraphic] database provides access to the publications of the USGS and includes references to U.S. Geological Survey reports and maps published from 1880 to date, references to non-USGS publications with USGS authors published from 1983 to date, and 225 references to reports produced by the Hayden, King, Powell, and Wheeler surveys." A subset of the GeoRef Database.

Search Form URL: http://usgs-georef.cos.com/cgi-bin/search

Remote Sensing Glossary (Canadian Center for Remote Sensing)

http://www.ccrs.nrcan.gc.ca

"... glossary database contains comprehensive listings for radar, optical, and airborne remote-sensing terms and their related acronyms."

Search Form URL: See Main Page

TerraServer

http://www.terraserver.com

A source for overhead imagery of the Earth. Material from over 60 countries. "The TerraServer started as a joint research project between Aerial Images, Inc., Microsoft, the USGS, and Compaq."
Search Form URL: http://www.terraserver.com/advfind.asp
Related Resources:
GlobeXplorer
http://www.globexplorer.com/applet.htm

Worldwide Volcano Database
http://www.ngdc.noaa.gov/seg/hazard/volcano.shtml
"Worldwide Volcano Database contains more than 4,300 listings of volcanic eruptions from [the year] 79 [A.D.] to 1997."
Search Form URL: http://www.ngdc.noaa.gov/seg/hazard/vol_srch.shtml
Related Resources:
Interactive Volcano Map
http://idl.ngdc.noaa.gov/cgi-bin/seg/haz/volc_world.pl

Energy

Atlas for the Solar Radiation Data Manual for Flat-Plate and Concentrating Collectors
http://rredc.nrel.gov/solar/
"These maps show the general trends in the amount of solar radiation received in the United States and its territories. They are spatial interpolations of solar radiation values derived from the 1961-1990 National Solar Radiation Data Base (NSRDB) and published in the Solar Radiation Data Manual for Flat-Plate and Concentrating Collectors."
Search Form URL: http://rredc.nrel.gov/solar/old_data/nsrdb/redbook/atlas/
Related Resources:
Atlas for the Solar Radiation Data Manual for Buildings
http://rredc.nrel.gov/solar/old_data/nsrdb/bluebook/atlas/

Department of Energy Information Bridge
http://www.osti.gov/bridge/
DOE Information Bridge provides free and convenient access to full-text and bibliographic records of Department of Energy (DOE)

research and development reports in physics, chemistry, materials, biology, environmental sciences, energy technologies, engineering, computer and information science, renewable energy, and other topics.
Search Form URL: See Main Page

Energy Database (Energy Technology Data Exchange) B

http://www.etde.org
"ETDE's Energy Database is available to anyone in an ETDE member country. ... ETDE, through its member countries, provides an extensive bibliographic database announcing published energy research and technology information." Registration is required.
Search Form URL: See Main Page

Monthly Energy Review Database

http://www.eia.doe.gov/mer/
Interactive query of energy statistics beginning in 1973.
Search Form URL: http://tonto.eia.doe.gov/mer/

Nuclear Explosions Database

http://www.ausseis.gov.au/databases/
"AGSO (Australian Geological Survey Organisation) maintains a database of nuclear explosions with the location, time, and size of explosions around the world since 1945."
Search Form URL: http://www.ausseis.gov.au/information/
structure/isd/database/nukexp_query.html

Nuclear Power Plant Databases

http://www.insc.anl.gov/
"... retrieve an up-to-date list of world's power plants along with the basic information and operational status ..."
Search Form URL: http://www.insc.anl.gov/plants/index.html

Power Reactor Information System

http://www.iaea.org/programmes/a2/
"Since 1970, the IAEA [International Atomic Energy Agency] has been collecting and publishing data about the world's nuclear power plants. In order to facilitate the analysis of power plant performance and to produce relevant publications, the data were computerized in 1980, and the Power Reactor Information System (PRIS) was implemented. Since then, PRIS has been continuously updated and improved, and it now constitutes the most complete data bank on nuclear power reactors in

the world. It has been widely used and today constitutes an essential source of information on nuclear power."
Search Form URL: See Main Page
Related Resources:
Additional Nuclear Power Related Databases
http://www.iaea.org/databases/dbdir/fulllist.htm

Engineering

American Society of Civil Engineers (ASCE) Civil Engineering Database B
http://www.asce.org
"The Civil Engineering Database (CEDB) is designed to provide easy bibliographic access to all ASCE publications. The database covers ASCE documents published since 1973. It provides access to all the journals, conference proceedings, books, standards, manuals, magazines, and newsletters." Over 80,000 entries.
Search Form URL: http://www.pubs.asce.org/cedbsrch.html

Edinburgh Engineering Virtual Library
http://www.eevl.ac.uk/
"EEVL (the Edinburgh Engineering Virtual Library) is a U.K.-based guide to engineering information on the Internet. It is a free service, created and run by a team of information specialists from Heriot-Watt University, with input from a number of other universities in the U.K. The site features a catalogue of quality engineering resources (selected by subject consultants), targeted engineering search engines, bibliographic and events databases, including the Recent Advances in Manufacturing bibliographic database, a directory of science and technology librarians, an Engineering on the Internet bibliography, and Hot Links to useful sites."
Search Form URL: See Main Page

Material Safety Datasheets
http://msds.pdc.cornell.edu/
A searchable collection of approximately 250,000 sheets collected from various sources including the U.S. Department of Defense MSDS Database.
Search Form URL: http://msds.pdc.cornell.edu/msdssrch.asp

Related Resources:
Hazardous Chemicals Database
http://ull.chemistry.uakron.edu/erd/

U.S. Army Corp of Engineers Digital Visual Library
http://images.usace.army.mil/main.html
"The photographic and graphic images located on this Web site are
provided to visually communicate programs, projects, and events of
the U.S. Army Corps of Engineers and are made available through the
combined efforts of team members throughout the Corps. The searchable library consists of photographs, illustrations, artwork, clipart,
logos, maps, and posters of a majority of the Corps of Engineers civil
and military projects from around the world."
Search Form URL: See Main Page

World Register of Large Dams (Abriged Version)
http://genepi.louis-jean.com/cigb/index.html
This resource is an abridged version of the World Register of World
Dams produced by International Council of Large Dams (ICOLD).
Search Form URL: http://genepi.louis-jean.com/cgi-bin/
cigb-registre.pl?language=en

Environment

ENTRI (Environmental Treaties Database)
http://sedac.ciesin.org/entri/
"A comprehensive online search service for finding information about
environmental treaties and national resource indicators. The ENTRI
system is unique in allowing you to construct queries that integrate
these different types of data."
Search Form URL: See Main Page

Envirofacts (EPA)
http://www.epa.gov/enviro/index_java.html
"... a single point of access to select U.S. EPA environmental data. This
Web site provides access to several EPA databases that provide you
with information about environmental activities that may affect air,
water, and land anywhere in the United States."
Search Form URL: See Main Page

Related Resources:
Enviromapper
http://www.epa.gov/enviro/html/em/index.html
Housing and Urban Development Environmental Maps (E-Maps)
http://www.hud.gov/emaps/
Scorecard
http://www.scorecard.org

Enviroment Databases (The Right-To-Know Network)

http://www.rtknet.org
"The Right-to-Know Network provides free access to numerous databases, text files, and conferences on the environment, housing, and sustainable development. With the information available on RTK NET, you can identify specific factories and their environmental effects; analyze reinvestment by banks in their communities; and assess people and communities affected."
Search Form URL: http://www.rtknet.org/rtkdata.html

GeoMAC (Wildland Fire Support)

http://wildfire.usgs.gov/wildfire/
"GeoMAC is an Internet-based mapping application, originally designed for firefighting coordination centers and incident command teams to access online maps of current fire locations and perimeters using standard Web browsers ..."
Search Form URL: See Main Page
Related Resources:
http://wildfire.usgs.gov/website/fireinfo/viewer.htm?Title=
Wildfire%20Information

Great Barrier Reef Online Image Catalogue (The) Australia

http://www.gbrmpa.gov.au/corp_site/info_services/library/
index.html
"The Great Barrier Reef Image Collection is a vast pictorial resource, available to the staff of the Great Barrier Reef Marine Park Authority, as well as outside agencies. The collection comprises over 50,000 original colour 35 mm transparencies, together with several thousand black and white and colour images."
Search Form URL: http://www.gbrmpa.gov.au/corp_site/info_
services/library/resources/image_collection/index.html
Related Resources:
ReefBase (Global Information System on Coral Reefs)
http://www.reefbase.org/database/default.asp

Green House Gas State Action List (EPA)

http://yosemite.epa.gov/globalwarming

"EPA compiled this database on states actions affecting GHG [Green House Gas] emissions to enable state decision makers to obtain information on the types of policies that are under consideration or being implemented by their colleagues. Although the database focuses primarily on actions motivated by state governments, it also includes local (i.e., county and municipal level) activities that are often conducted in partnership with the state or through a state grant."

Search Form URL: http://yosemite.epa.gov/globalwarming/ghg.nsf/StatePolicyOptionsSearch?OpenForm

Historical Incident Reports (Oil Spills/Chemical Accidents)

http://www.incidentnews.gov

"This database contains reports and images from about 1,000 incidents such as oil spills and chemical accidents that happened from 1977 to 1999. Generally, it includes reports on incidents to which NOAA responded, as well as some significant incidents in which NOAA was not involved. The database includes mainly U.S. incidents, but also significant incidents that occurred elsewhere." Current reports can be accessed via the main URL.

Search Form URL: http://www.incidentnews.gov/incidents/history.htm

Related Resources:

Properties of Crude Oils and Oil Products

http://www.etcentre.org/cgi-win/oil_prop_cgi.exe?Path=\Website\river\

INFOTERRA

http://www.nies.go.jp/db/index-e.html

"INFOTERRA, the Global Environmental Information Exchange Network has been designed by the United Nations Environmental Programme (UNEP) to stimulate and support the exchange of environmental information between partners. The system is operated at the national level by national focal points. As of March 2000, 178 countries participated in INFOTERRA and information sources registered in INFOTERRA numbered about 8,000."

Search Form URL: http://www.nies.go.jp/db/infoterra/index-e.html

Municipal Water Use Database Canada

http://www3.ec.gc.ca/MUD/eng/Default.cfm

"... information on water usage, wastewater treatment, and water pricing methods in Canadian municipalities."

Search Form URL: http://www3.ec.gc.ca/MUD/eng/Search Request.cfm

National Environmental Directory

http://environmentaldirectory.eelink.net/

"... a directory of more than 13,000 organizations in the United States concerned with environmental issues and environmental education."

Search Form URL: See Main Page

National Pollutant Release Inventory Canada

http://www.ec.gc.ca/pdb/npri/index.html

"NPRI data provide a publicly available annual record of releases and transfers of listed pollutants from facilities operating in Canada."

Search Form URL: http://www.npri-inrp.com/queryform.cfm

NatureServe

http://www.natureserve.org

"A source for authoritative conservation information on more than 50,000 plants, animals, and ecological communities of the United States and Canada."

Search Form URL: See Main Page

Pesticide Database (Pesticide Action Network)

http://www.pesticideinfo.org/

"... one-stop location for current toxicity and regulatory information for pesticides."

Search Form URL: See Main Page

Sector Facility Indexing Project

http://es.epa.gov/oeca/sfi/

The SFIP brings together environmental and other information from a number of data systems to produce facility-level profiles for five industry sectors (petroleum refining, iron and steel production, primary nonferrous metal refining and smelting, pulp manufacturing, and automobile assembly). SFIP information relates to compliance and inspection history, chemical releases and spills, demographics of the surrounding population, and production.

Search Form URL: http://es.epa.gov/oeca/sfi/access.htm

Supplemental Environmental Project (SEP) National Database

http://es.epa.gov/oeca/

"A Supplemental Environmental Project (SEP) is an environmental project that a violator voluntarily agrees to perform as part of the settlement of an enforcement action. Although the violator is not legally required to perform a SEP, his cash penalty may be lower if he chooses to perform an acceptable SEP. An acceptable SEP must improve, protect, or reduce risks to public health or the environment."

Search Form URL: http://es.epa.gov/oeca/sep/searchsep.html

Tree Conservation Database

http://www.wcmc.org.uk/trees/

"The Tree Conservation Database holds information on threatened species and others of conservation concern. This database is used to generate The World List of Threatened Trees, and the information is available here in interactive format."

Search Form URL: http://www.wcmc.org.uk/cgi-bin/SaCGI.cgi/trees.exe?FNC=database__Aindex_html

USEPA/OPP Pesticide Products Database

http://www.cdpr.ca.gov/

"The California Department of Pesticide Regulation is working closely with the USEPA Office of Pesticide Programs to develop Internet access to data sets that are of significant value to both organizations. In addition, the general public and chemical and agricultural industries will also find these data to be of use. Brief registration information on approximately 89,000 products is currently online. The data include: product number and name, company number and name, registration date, cancellation date and reason (if cancelled), and product manager name and phone number."

Search Form URL: http://www.cdpr.ca.gov/docs/epa/m2.htm

World Lakes Database

http://www.ilec.or.jp/

"... data for more than 500 lakes from 73 countries."

Search Form URL: http://www.ilec.or.jp/database/database.html

General Science Resources

GrayLIT Network

http://www.osti.gov/graylit/

"A science portal of technical reports ... The GrayLIT Network makes the gray literature of U.S. Federal Agencies easily accessible over the Internet. It taps into the search engines of distributed gray literature collections, enabling the user to find information without first having to know the sponsoring agency."

Search Form URL: See Main Page

PrePRINT Network B

http://www.osti.gov/preprint/

"The Department of Energy's PrePRINT Network is a searchable gateway to preprint servers that deal with scientific and technical disciplines of concern to DOE. Such disciplines include the great bulk of physics, materials, and chemistry, as well as portions of biology, environmental sciences, and nuclear medicine."

Search Form URL: http://www.osti.gov/preprint/ppnsearch.html

PubSCIENCE B

http://pubsci.osti.gov/

"PubSCIENCE provides users the capability to search across a large compendium of peer-reviewed journal literature with a focus on the physical sciences and other disciplines of concern to the Department of Energy (DOE)."

Search Form URL: http://pubsci.osti.gov/srchfrm.html

sciBASE B

http://www.thescientificworld.com

"sciBASE gives you free access to the world's premier database of scientific, technical, and medical research literature. sciBASE currently includes approximately 12 million articles published since 1993 in more than 20,000 journals. sciBASE is updated daily with approximately 7,000 new articles."

Search Form URL: http://www.thescientificworld.com/scibase/search.asp

WISDOM (Science Policy Data) U.K.

http://wisdom.wellcome.ac.uk/wisdom/spinhome.html

"This database contains summaries of articles related to science policy from over 150 journals and newspapers. Topics include U.K. and international research policy, research funding and management, research ethics, and public understanding of science published since March 1992."
Search Form URL: See Main Page

Mathematics and Physics

arXiv.org e-Print archive
http://xxx.lanl.gov/
Since August 1991, arXiv.org (formerly xxx.lanl.gov) is a fully automated electronic archive and distribution server for research papers. Covered areas include physics and related disciplines, mathematics, nonlinear sciences, computational linguistics, and neuroscience.
Search Form URL: http://xxx.lanl.gov/form
Related Resources:
High Energy Physics Conference Database
http://www.slac.stanford.edu/spires/conferences/

Sloane's Online Encyclopedia of Integer Sequences
http://www.research.att.com/~njas/sequences/index.html
Search for integer sequences.
Search Form URL: See Main Page

Oceanography

Bathing Water Quality in the European Union: Tourist Atlas
http://europa.eu.int/water/water-bathing/tourist.html
"The Tourist Atlas provides an easy way to find out what the bathing water quality is in your country or your holiday destination."
Search Form URL: http://europa.eu.int/water/cgi-bin/bw.pl

REEF Database (Marine Species Data)
http://www.reef.org/
"From the database you can generate a variety of reports on marine fish species distribution and abundance patterns."
Search Form URL: http://www.reef.org/data/database.htm

Tide and Current Predictor

http://cirp.wes.army.mil:8080/

After selection of a region, this database predicts local tide times for locations worldwide. Chart and graph tools are also available.

Search Form URL: See Main Page

Tsunami Database (Events)

http://www.ngdc.noaa.gov/seg/hazard/tsu.shtml

"This database provides information on tsunami events from 49 B.C. to the present in the Mediterranean and Caribbean Seas, and the Atlantic, Indian, and Pacific Oceans."

Search Form URL: See Main Page

Related Resources:

Tsunami Database (Runups)

http://www.ngdc.noaa.gov/seg/hazard/tsrnsrch.html

Research and Development

Community of Science Workbench Databases

http://www.cos.com

The Community of Science offers for free (registration required) several exemplary resources as part of the COS Workbench. Resources include an Experts database containing over 460,000 scholars and researchers worldwide, the Funded Research Database, the Funding Opportunities Database (over 25,000 grants and awards, alert tool available), and a meetings and conference database. COS also makes several fee-based databases available to members.

Search Form URL: http://www.cos.com/services/workbench.shtml

Related Resources:

National Science Foundation Awards Search

https://www.fastlane.nsf.gov/a6/A6AwardSearch.htm

NSERC Awards Search Engine Canada

http://www.ost.qc.ca/CRSNG/Projsearch.htm

Defence Research Reports B, Canada

http://pubs.crad.dnd.ca/pcow1e.html

"... a database of scientific and technical research produced by and for Defence Research and Development Canada (DRDC) over the past 50 years."

Search Form URL: http://pubs.crad.dnd.ca/pcow1e.html

Federal R&D Project Summaries

http://www.osti.gov

"Federal R&D Project Summaries provides a portal to information about Federal research projects, complete with full-text single-query searching across databases residing at different agencies."

Search Form URL: http://fedrnd.osti.gov/

GrantsNet

http://www.grantsnet.org

"... one-stop resource to find funds for training in the biomedical sciences and undergraduate science education." Free registration is required.

Search Form URL: http://www.grantsnet.org/search/srch_ menu.cfm

International Directory of Testing Laboratories (ASTM)

http://www.astm.org/labs/NEW/index.html

"The ASTM [American Society for Testing and Materials] International Directory of Testing Laboratories is an online full-text search for services and locations of testing laboratories."

Search Form URL: See Main Page

NASA Technical Reports Server

http://www.nasa.gov

"The NASA Technical Report Server is an experimental service that allows users to search the many different abstract and technical report servers maintained by various NASA centers and programs."

Search Form URL: http://techreports.larc.nasa.gov/cgi-bin/NTRS

Research Ship Schedules

http://oceanic.cms.udel.edu/ships/

"The Ocean Information Center (OCEANIC) maintains a searchable database of international cruise schedules and ship information for deep-water research vessels that are 40 meters or longer. Other research vessels are considered on a case-by-case basis."

Search Form URL: http://oceanic.cms.udel.edu/ships/ship_ gen.asp

Related Resources:

Research Ships Specifications

http://oceanic.cms.udel.edu/ships/ship_info_query.asp

Scientific and Technical Information Network (STINET) (U.S. Department of Defense) B

http://stinet.dtic.mil/

"Public STINET is free of charge and only requires registration upon document ordering. It provides access to citations to unclassified unlimited documents that have been entered into DTIC's [Defense Technical Information Center] Technical Reports Collection from late December 1974 to present as well as some full-text reports for those citations."

Search Form URL: http://stinet.dtic.mil/str/index.html

Scientific Research in Yellowstone National Park

http://www.wsulibs.wsu.edu/yellowstone/

"... bibliographic database of nearly 10,000 citations to scientific journal articles, books, proceedings, abstracts, videos, dissertations and theses, raw data, reports, letters, and manuscripts dealing with Yellowstone National Park."

Search Form URL: http://www.wsulibs.wsu.edu/ris/risweb.isa

Software Centers Directory

http://www.esi.es

ESI Software Centres Directory is a directory of R&D and Technology Transfer Centres working in Software Engineering. These centres can be university departments, private centres, government initiatives, working groups, etc.

Search Form URL: http://www.esi.es/Information/SCentres/

Space and Astronomy

Complete Sun and Moon Data for One Day

http://www.usno.navy.mil

"You can obtain the times of sunrise, sunset, moonrise, moonset, transits of the Sun and Moon, and the beginning and end of civil twilight, along with information on the Moon's phase ..."

Search Form URL: http://aa.usno.navy.mil/aa/data/docs/RS_OneDay.html

Related Resources:

Moon Phases Calculator (North America Only)

http://www.co-ops.nos.noaa.gov/astronomical.shtml

Dictionary of Nomenclature of Celestial Objects

http://cdsweb.u-strasbg.fr/

"Designations of astronomical objects are often confusing. Astronomical designations (also called Object Identifiers) have been collected and published by Lortet and collaborators in Dictionaries of Nomenclature of Celestial Objects outside the solar system ... This Info service is the electronic look-up version of the Dictionary, which is updated on a regular basis; it provides full references and usages about 10,608 different acronyms."

Search Form URL: http://vizier.u-strasbg.fr/cgi-bin/Dic

Earth from Space

http://earth.jsc.nasa.gov/

"The NASA Space Shuttle Earth Observations Photography database of over 375,000 images ... Within this set of web pages, you will find several ways to search the database and view multiple resolutions of each image with captions."

Search Form URL: See Main Page

Related Resources:

Earthrise

http://earthrise.sdsc.edu/

NASA Image eXchange

http://nix.nasa.gov

Mission and Spacecraft Library (The)

http://msl.jpl.nasa.gov/

"The Mission and Spacecraft Library is a catalog of space mission information designed for use by the public. Although much of the information contained in the database is technical in nature, the purpose of the library is to provide top-level descriptions of various spacecraft missions without too much aerospace geek-speak."

Search Form URL: See Main Page

Multiyear Interactive Computer Almanac (MICA) Web Version

http://aa.usno.navy.mil/AA/

"... enables you to obtain many kinds of astronomical data, including celestial coordinates, sidereal time, lunar and planetary configurations and aspects, and rise/set times. Specify the type of calculation you want below, click on the 'Continue' button, and fill in the form that will appear. The computations are performed by MICA, the

Multiyear Interactive Computer Almanac. The basis of the calculations is the same as for the Astronomical Almanac."
Search Form URL: http://aa.usno.navy.mil/AA/data/docs/WebMICA_2.html

SIMBAD Astronomical Database B

http://simbad.u-strasbg.fr/Simbad
"The SIMBAD astronomical database provides basic data, cross-identifications and bibliography for astronomical objects outside the solar system."
Search Form URL: http://simbad.u-strasbg.fr/sim-fid.pl

Solar System Simulator

http://space.jpl.nasa.gov/
View the Planets of the Solar System as if viewed from a variety of locations and dates.
Search Form URL: See Main Page

United States Space Command Satellite/Space Catalog

http://www.spacecom.af.mil
"The Space Control Center tracks nearly 9,000 man-made objects, softball-size and larger, orbiting Earth. About seven percent of these objects are operational satellites, 15 percent are rocket bodies, and the remainder are fragmentation and inactive satellites. The 1st Command and Control Squadron compiles all the information on these objects and produces the 'Satellite Catalog.' This catalog is maintained for military use and is also provided to NASA who is the conduit for distribution to other U.S. and international agencies."
Search Form URL: http://www.spacecom.af.mil/usspace/satcat.htm
Related Resources:
Space Orbit 3-D Visualization Tool
http://neo.jpl.nasa.gov/orbits/

Weather and Meteorology

Historical Significant Events Imagery Database (HSEI)

http://www.ncdc.noaa.gov
"Hundreds of selected satellite images capturing some of the more important weather and environmental events over the last 30 years."
Search Form URL: http://www5.ncdc.noaa.gov/cgi-bin/hsei/ hsei.pl?directive=welcome

National Climatic Data Center Storm Events

http://www.ncdc.noaa.gov

Use the NCDC Storm Event database to find various types of storms recorded in your county or use other selection criteria as desired. All Weather Events from 1993 - presnt, as entered into Storm Data.
Search Form URL: http://www4.ncdc.noaa.gov/cgi-win/wwcgi.dll?wwEvent~Storms

UV Index

http://www.epa.gov/sunwise

"Developed by the National Weather Service (NWS) and EPA, the UV Index predicts the next day's ultraviolet radiation levels on a 0-10+ scale, helping people determine appropriate sun-protective behaviors." Search by ZIP code.
Search Form URL: http://www.epa.gov/sunwise/uvindex.html

CHAPTER 26

Social Sciences

From anthropology to demographics to military resources to religion, the social sciences category covers a broad range of human activity. While many of these resources are relatively pure databases of statistical information, such as census data or the status of development projects around the world, others focus on "softer," more subjective types of information, such as gender or religious studies.

These key resources are included:

- **Demographic Information**, such as the *U.S. Census Lookup*, with extensive interactive tools that allow you to create customized tables using myriad criteria

- **Development Resources**, including *Data Query: World Development Indicators*, the world's most extensive collection of data about development

- **Gender Studies**, such as *gender Inn: Women and Gender Studies Database*, providing access to more than 6,000 specialized resources in American and English literature

- **Military Resources**, including the *Air University Index to Military Periodicals*

- **Religion Resources**, such as the *American Religion Data Archive* and the *Directory of Religious Centers*

See the Social Sciences Information category on the companion Web site for additional Invisible Web resources on this topic at http://www. invisible-web.net.

Anthropology

Anthropology Review Database B
http://wings.buffalo.edu/ARD/
"The Anthropology Review Database is intended to improve the level of access of anthropologists to anthropological literature by making them more aware of what is being published and helping them to evaluate its relevance to their own interests."
Search Form URL: See Main Page
Related Resources:
Anthropological Index Online
http://lucy.ukc.ac.uk/cgi-bin/uncgi/Search_AI/search_bib_ai/anthind

Archaeology

National Archeological Database—Reports B
http://www.cast.uark.edu/other/nps/nadb/
"National Archeological Database, Reports module, is an expanded bibliographic inventory of approximately 240,000 reports on archeological investigation and planning, mostly of limited circulation. This "gray literature" represents a large portion of the primary information available on archeological sites in the U.S. NADB-Reports can be searched by state, county, work type, cultural affiliation, keyword, material, year of publication, title, and author."
Search Form URL: http://www.cast.uark.edu/other/nps/nadb/nadb.mul.html
Related Resources:
ArcHSearch (Area Data) U.K.
http://ads.ahds.ac.uk/catalogue/

Canadian Archaeological Radiocarbon Database Canada
http://www.canadianarchaeology.com/localc14/c14search.htm

Demographics

Demographic Data (via Government Information Sharing Project)

http://govinfo.kerr.orst.edu/
The Government Information Sharing Project located at Oregon St. University provides interactive access to numerous U.S. Government databases in economics, education, and demographics. For a complete list, see the home page of the GISP. A few examples follow.
Search Form URL: See Main Page
Related Resources:
U.S.A. Counties
http://govinfo.kerr.orst.edu/usaco-stateis.html
Population Estimates by Age, Sex, and Race: 1990-1997
http://govinfo.kerr.orst.edu/pe-stateis.html
Equal Employment Opportunity File
http://govinfo.kerr.orst.edu/eeo-stateis.html

EASI Quick Reports & Analysis (Demographic Data)

http://www.easidemographics.com/
Easy Analytic Software offers several free databases that contain basic U.S. demographic material. The free service listed here allows users to choose from 12 different demographic variables and create 11 different reports.
Search Form URL: http://www.easidemographics.com/reports/easi_free_reports.phtml

Population Index B

http://popindex.princeton.edu
"Population Index, published since 1935, is the primary reference tool to the world's population literature. It presents an annotated bibliography of recently published books, journal articles, working papers, and other materials on population topics."
Search Form URL: http://popindex.princeton.edu/search/ index.html
Related Resources:
POPLINE (via Grateful Med)

http://igm.nlm.nih.gov/
POPINFORM (Most Recent POPLINE Records)
http://db.jhuccp.org/popinform/index.stm

U.S. Census Bureau International Database

http://www.census.gov
Access country statistics for many nations. Material available in text or spreadsheet formats.
Search Form URL: http://www.census.gov/ipc/www/idbacc.html
Related Resources:
U.S. Census International Bureau Population Pyramids
http://www.census.gov/ipc/www/idbpyr.html

U.S. Census Lookup

http://www.census.gov
Create customized tables using myriad criteria with U.S. Census Data. This resource is one of the best examples of what the Invisible Web has to offer.
Search Form URL: http://venus.census.gov/cdrom/lookup
Related Resources:
U.S. Census Basic Table Generator
http://www.oseda.missouri.edu/mscdc/profiles/xtabs3.mainmenu.html
U.S. Census Tract Street Locator
http://tier2.census.gov/ctsl/ctsl.htm

United Kingdom National Statistics U.K.

http://www.statistics.gov.uk
Official Statistics of the United Kingdom. This site has numerous search options to both free and fee-based material. The link below is to StatStore, which provides free online access to over 1,900 statistical datasets.
Search Form URL: http://www.statistics.gov.uk/statbase/
datasets2.asp

World Data Sheet

http://www.prb.org
"This database contains data on 85 demographic variables for 221 countries in the world, for 28 world regions and sub-regions, for the world as a whole, for the United States as a whole, and for the 50 states and the District of Columbia."
Search Form URL: http://www.worldpop.org/prbdata.htm

Development Resources

Data Query: World Development Indicators

http://www.worldbank.org

"Data Query offers free access to a segment of the World Development Indicators (WDI) database, the world's most extensive collection of data about development. This segment includes 54 time-series indicators for 206 countries and 17 groups, spanning 5 years (1995 to 1999)."

Search Form URL: http://devdata.worldbank.org/data-query/

ELDIS (Development Data)

http://nt1.ids.ac.uk/eldis/eldis.htm

"ELDIS provides an ever-increasing number of descriptions and links to a variety of information sources, including online documents, organisation's WWW sites, databases, library catalogues, bibliographies, email discussion lists, research project information, map, and newspaper collections."

Search Form URL: http://nt1.ids.ac.uk/eldis/eldsea.htm

Related Resources:

INDEV (India Development Information Network) Databases

http://www.indev.nic.in/indevdb/default.htm

Photobank—UNESCO (United Nations Educational, Scientific, and Cultural Organization)

http://upo.unesco.org/photobank.asp

"The collection—covering a wide range of subjects related to the Organization's fields of competence: education, science, culture, and communication—was started in 1946 when UNESCO was founded, and currently contains over 10,000 digitalized images. More will become available as the rest of the collection is digitalized and further developed so as to ensure a more equitable balance of subjects and countries."

Search Form URL: See Main Page

USAID (U.S. Agency for International Development) Development Experience System

http://www.dec.org/

"The Development Experience System (DEXS) is a family of bibliographic databases that contains records for over 100,000 Agency

technical and program documents. The purpose of the DEXS is to strengthen USAID's development projects, activities, and programs by making these development experience documents available to USAID offices and mission staff, other donor agencies, LDC government agencies, LDC institutions, and the public worldwide."
Search Form URL: http://www.dec.org/partners/dexs_public/

General Resources

Association of Research Libraries (ARL) Statistics
http://fisher.lib.virginia.edu/
"For 1962-63 through 1998-99 data you can list data for any of the current 111 academic ARL members, or you can compute statistics for any ARL data categories. You can also download the data in ASCII (.txt) or .wk1 format."
Search Form URL: http://fisher.lib.virginia.edu/newarl/

DARE: Directory in Social Sciences—Institutions, Specialists, Periodicals
http://www.unesco.org/
"11,000 worldwide references to social science research and training institutions, specialists, documentation and information services, and social science periodicals; references to peace, human rights, and international law training and research institutions."
Search Form URL: http://www.unesco.org/general/eng/infoserv/db/dare.html

National Recreation Database B (Some full-text), Canada
http://www.lin.ca/htdocs/rcentre.cfm
Produced by the Leisure Information Network. Contains information on "practical resources from the front lines."
Search Form URL: http://www.lin.ca/htdocs/findrs.cfm
Related Resources:
Youth at Risk Success Stories Database Canada
http:// www.lin.ca/lincfm/yar/yarsearch.cfm

NISSO Sexology Database (Netherlands Institute for Social Sexological Research) B
http://www.nisso.nl/ndbe.htm

"The collection of about 55,000 documents contains monographs, reports, conference proceedings, periodicals, articles, papers, brochures, etc." Abstracts are included with most entries.
Search Form URL: http://www.nisso.nl/cgi-bin/nph-nisso_search.pl?language=us&db=nissomain

Pavnet (Patnership Against Violence) Research Database

http://www.nal.usda.gov/pavnet/
"The PAVNET Research Database is an online, searchable source of information about current Federally funded research on violence."
Search Form URL: http://www.nal.usda.gov/pavnet/ search2.html
Related Resources:
Center for the Study and Prevention of Violence Literature Database
http://www.colorado.edu/cspv/infohouse/violit/

Washington Post Poll Database

http://www.washingtonpost.com/wp-dyn/politics/
Results of *Washington Post* national polls on a variety of subjects. Material begins in January of 1998.
Search Form URL: http://www.washingtonpost.com/wp-srv/politics/polls/vault/vault.htm

Gender Studies and Data

gender Inn: Women and Gender Studies Database B

http://www.uni-koeln.de/phil-fak/englisch/datenbank/e_ index.htm
"gender Inn is a searchable database providing access to over 6,000 records pertaining to feminist theory, feminist literary criticism, and gender studies focusing on English and American literature."
Search Form URL: See Main Page

Genderstats

http://www.worldbank.com
From the World Bank. Statistics on topics used in the study of gender. Statistics from many countries are available.
Search Form URL: http://genderstats.worldbank.org/

Medieval Feminist Index B

http://www.haverford.edu/library/reference/mschaus/mfi/mfi.html

"The Medieval Feminist Index covers journal articles, book reviews, and essays in books about women, sexuality, and gender during the Middle Ages. Because of the explosion of research in Women's Studies during the past two decades, scholars and students interested in women during the Middle Ages find an ever-growing flood of publications. Identifying relevant works in this mass of material is further complicated by the interdisciplinary nature of much of the scholarship."
Search Form URL: See Main Page

Women, Work, and Gender Database B

http://www.wsu.edu/~mnofsing/womenwrk.htm
"Database of annotated citations to scholarly research materials."
Search Form URL: http://www.wsulibs.wsu.edu/ris/risweb.isa/

Latin America

Fidel Castro Speech Databases

http://lanic.utexas.edu
"0'Castro Speech' is a database containing the full text of English translations of speeches, interviews, and press conferences by Fidel Castro, based upon the records of the Foreign Broadcast Information Service (FBIS), a U.S. government agency responsible for monitoring broadcast and print media in countries throughout the world. These records are in the public domain."
Search Form URL: http://lanic.utexas.edu/info/search/castro.html

Handbook of Latin American Studies B

http://lcweb2.loc.gov/hlas/hlashome.html
"The Handbook is a bibliography on Latin America consisting of works selected and annotated by scholars. Edited by the Hispanic Division of the Library of Congress, the multidisciplinary Handbook alternates annually between the social sciences and the humanities. Each year, more than 130 academics from around the world choose over 5,000 works for inclusion in the Handbook. Continuously published since 1935, the Handbook offers Latin Americanists an essential guide to available resources."
Search Form URL: http://lcweb2.loc.gov/hlas/mdbquery.html

Military Resources

Air University Index to Military Periodicals B
http://www.dtic.mil/search97doc/aulimp/main.htm
"... a subject index to significant articles, news items, and editorials from English language military and aeronautical periodicals. ... This Index contains citations since 1990 and is updated quarterly in combination with the hard-copy version of Air University Library's Index to Military Periodicals."
Search Form URL: See Main Page

Military Images Photo Library
http://www.militarycity.com
MilitaryCity.com provides this database. Images of aircraft, missiles, ships, and much more.
Search Form URL: http://www.militarycity.com/newsroom/images.html

Psychology

Jourlit/Bookrev Database (American Psychoanalytic Association) B
http://apsa.org
"The Jourlit and Bookrev databases, originated by Drs. Stanley Goodman and Vann Spruiell, together constitute a huge bibliography of psychoanalytic journal articles, books, and book reviews. Including files supplied by others, the complete set of references consists of almost 30,000 entries."
Search Form URL: http://apsa.org/lit/

Links to Psychological Journals: The Journal Locator in Psychology and the Social Sciences B
http://www.wiso.uni-augsburg.de/sozio/hartmann/psycho/journals.html
"... an index of 1,600+ online psychology and social science journals. It links you to journal home pages and journal information on the Web."
Search Form URL: See Main Page

Research and Development

FundSource
http://www.decadeofbehavior.org/
"A search tool for research funding in the Behavioral and Social Sciences."
Search Form URL: http://www.decadeofbehavior.org/fundsource/index.html

Religion

American Religion Data Archive
http://www.arda.tm
"The American Religion Data Archive collects quantitative data sets for the study of American religion."
Search Form URL: See Main Page

Beliefnet Dictionary
http://www.beliefnet.com
Beliefnet.com provides a searchable and browsable version of the *HarperCollins Dictionary of Religion.*
Search Form URL: http://www.beliefnet.com/glossary/index.asp

Bible Browser (The)
http://www.stg.brown.edu
Search several versions of *The Bible.*
Search Form URL: http://www.stg.brown.edu/webs/bible_browser/pbeasy.shtml

Directory of Religious Centers
http://www.fas.harvard.edu/~pluralsm/html/database.html
"The Pluralism Project [at Harvard University] maintains an extensive directory of religious centers in the United States. At present, this directory exists in a sortable database, with listings of nearly 3,500 centers across the United States. It does not include information on Christian or Jewish centers, as these can be readily found in the local phone book; however, it does include listings for Buddhist, Hindu, Jain, and Zoroastrian Temples, as well as Baha'i and Pagan Centers,

Islamic Centers and Masajid, Sikh Gurdwaras, and Tao Centers and Temples."
Search Form URL: http://www.fas.harvard.edu/~pluralsm/directory/directory.cgi

English Religious Resources

http://etext.lib.virginia.edu/
Search and browse several *Bibles, The Book of Morman, The Koran,* and a concise encyclopedia of religion.
Search Form URL: http://etext.lib.virginia.edu/relig.browse.html

Islamic Countries, Statistics (SESRTCIC)

http://www.sesrtcic.org/
SESRTCIC (Statistical, Economic, and Social Research for Islamic Countries) provides access to over 180 statistical indicators for 56 countries.
Search Form URL: See Main Page

Quaran Browser

http://www.stg.brown.edu
Search and view passages or individual words from the *Quaran.* Several translations are available to search.
Search Form URL: http://www.stg.brown.edu/webs/quran_browser/pqeasy.shtml

RAMBI (The Index of Articles on Jewish Studies) B

http://sites.huji.ac.il/jnul/index.html
"RAMBI—The Index of Articles on Jewish Studies—is a selective bibliography of articles in the various fields of Jewish studies and in the study of Eretz Israel. Material listed in Rambi is compiled from thousands of periodicals and from collections of articles—in Hebrew, Yiddish, and European languages—mainly from the holdings of the Jewish National and University Library, a world center for research on the Jewish people and Eretz Israel. The main criterion for inclusion in the bibliography is that the article be based on scientific research, or contain important information for such research."
Search Form URL: http://sites.huji.ac.il/jnul/rambi/

CHAPTER 27

Transportation

Searchers in need of transportation information have access to some unique Invisible Web resources. In addition to traditional databases that make facts, statistics, and bibliographic information available, a number of services provide real-time information on various transportation resources.

Whether you're looking for comprehensive transportation safety records or something as simple as whether a particular flight is on schedule, the resources we've selected for this chapter will help you save time and locate the most accurate information for your needs.

These key resources are included:

- **Air Transportation Resources**, including the *U.S. Airline On-Time Database*, which tracks the performance of major North American airlines, and the *Aviation Accident Synopsis* from the National Transportation Safety Board

- **Automotive Resources**, such as *Safer*, providing U.S. Motor-Carrier Information

- **General Transportation Resources**, including *Canadian Transportation Resources* and the *Global Transport Analyzer*

- **Maritime and Railroad Resources**, such as the *Equasis* registry of merchant ships and the *Federal Railroad Administration Safety Databases*

See the Transportation category on the companion Web site for additional Invisible Web resources on this topic at http://www.invisible-web.net.

Air

Airline Certificate Information (Federal Aviation Administration)

http://av-info.faa.gov/default.asp

"Contains information pertaining to scheduled airline certification, operations, and aircraft counts by make and model."

Search Form URL: http://av-info.faa.gov/OpCert.asp

AirNav Airport Database

http://www.airnav.com

"AirNav provides free detailed aeronautical information on airports and navigational aids in the U.S. We offer some fast database searches, allowing the pilot to retrieve information [that] may assist in flight planning." Take note of the advanced search options.

Search Form URL: http://www.airnav.com/airports/

Related Resources:

Navaid Information

http://www.airnav.com/navaids/

Aviation Accident Synopsis (National Transportation Safety Board)

http://www.ntsb.gov/aviation/aviation.htm

"The database contains information from 1983 and later about civil aviation accidents within the United States, its territories and possessions, and in international waters. Incidents investigated by the Safety Board are also contained in the database in the same form as accidents."

Search Form URL: http://www.ntsb.gov/aviation/Accident.htm

Related Resources:

FAA Incident Data System

http://nasdac.faa.gov/asp/fw_fids.asp
Near Mid-Air Collision System
http://nasdac.faa.gov/asp/fw_nmacs.asp
NTSB Safety Recommendations to the FAA
http://nasdac.faa.gov/asp/fw_searchus.asp

Registered Aircraft Databases

http://www.landings.com
This site is a compilation of links to databases that provide airplane
registration data for many countries.
Search Form URL: http://www.landings.com/_landings/pages/
search.html
Related Resources:
Canadian Civil Aircraft Register
http://www.tc.gc.ca/aviation/activepages/ccarcs/default_e.asp
Canadian Civil Aircraft Register (Historical)
http://www.tc.gc.ca/aviation/activepages/ccarcs/history/
default_e.asp

U.S. Airline On-Time Database

http://www.bts.gov
"These data are collected to assist consumers of air transportation in
making decisions based on air carrier service quality. ... Currently, the
on-time performance database tracks Alaska, America West,
American, Continental, Delta, Northwest, Southwest, TWA, United,
and USAIR. These airlines account for more than 90% of domestic
operating revenues. Each of these airlines earns 1% or more of total
domestic scheduled passenger revenue; therefore Federal regulations
require that they report on-time performance data."
Search Form URL: http://www.bts.gov/cgi-bin/oai/ontime_js.pl
Related Resources:
FAA/APO Data System (Historic Air Traffic Data)
http://www.apo.data.faa.gov/

World Aircraft Accident Summary (WAAS) Fatal Airline Accident Subset

http://www.waasinfo.net/
"... contains a subset of the accident information maintained in the
World Aircraft Accident Summary (WAAS) database. The World
Aircraft Accident Summary (WAAS) produced on behalf of the British
Civil Aviation Authority, by Airclaims Limited, provides brief details of

all known major operational accidents to jet and turboprop aircraft and helicopters and the larger piston-engined types worldwide."
Search Form URL: See Main Page

Automobile

National Safety Council Defensive Driving Training Locator
http://www.nsc.org/training/
Locate defensive driving programs in the U.S. and other selected countries.
Search Form URL: http://www.nsc.org/training/selectagency.cfm

Safer (U.S. Motor-Carrier Information)
http://www.safersys.org/
"The Federal Motor Carrier Safety Administration (FMCSA) has provided carrier safety data to industry and the public for many years via telephone requests. The Safety and Fitness Electronic Records (SAFER) System now makes it possible to offer this information electronically. Limited SAFER functions are now provided free of charge over the Internet."
Search Form URL: See Main Page

Traffic Calming Library B
http://www.ite.org
"The Traffic Calming Library contains a searchable database of reports, articles, and other documents related to traffic calming. In some cases the full publication is available online and in others only a source listing or abstract is available."
Search Form URL: http://www.ite.org/traffic/

General Transportation Resources

Canadian Transportation Databases Canada
http://www.tc.gc.ca
From Transport Canada. A collection of several databases featuring statistics for numerous modes of transport. Data can also be downloaded into spreadsheet format.

Search Form URL: http://www.tc.gc.ca/pol/en/t-facts_e/ Statistical_ Data_Menu.htm

Directory of Forensic Experts in Transportation Engineering

http://www.ite.org

"The ITE (Institute of Transportation Engineers) Directory of Forensic Experts in Transportation Engineering is provided to ease the search for an expert witness in transportation. Searches for a consultant can be performed by: name, location, and specialty area."

Search Form URL: http://www.ite.org/expert.htm

Fatality Analysis Reporting System

http://www-fars.nhtsa.dot.gov/

"The Fatality Analysis Reporting System (FARS) contains data on all vehicle crashes in the United States that occur on a public roadway and involve a fatality in the crash. This Web site provides instant access to FARS data via the Query Engine, Wizard, and Reports Library."

Search Form URL: See Main Page

Global Transport Analyzer (Shipping Data)

http://www.joc.com

The Journal of Commerce provides access to several databases with shipping data.

Search Form URL: http://www.joc.com/gta/

Related Resources:

U.S. River Statistics—Lock Characteristics Query

http://155.75.103.129/ndc/lockchar_query.htm

U.S. River Statistics—Commodity Ton and Barges By Direction Query

http://www.wrsc.usace.army.mil/ndc/commodity_query.htm

Port Facilities Database

http://155.75.103.44/inetpub/PortFacility/find.asp

PATH Database (Intelligent Transport Systems) B

http://www4.nationalacademies.org/trb/tris.nsf/web/path

"The California PATH Database provides access to the largest and most comprehensive collection of bibliographic information on Intelligent Transportation Systems (ITS)."

Search Form URL: http://www.dcdata.com/path/path.htm

Transborder Surface Freight Data

http://www.bts.gov/ntda/tbscd

"Interactively query the Transborder Surface Freight Database online. You can select the particular U.S. state or border port, mode of transportation, time period, and commodities in which you are interested, and a table will automatically be generated for you."
Search Form URL: http://www.bts.gov/ntda/tbscd/search.html

TRIS (Transportation Research Information Service) B
http://ntl.bts.gov/
"TRIS contains more than 400,000 records of published transportation research. Bibliograpic information only."
Search Form URL: http://199.79.179.82/sundev/search.cfm

Maritime

Equasis (Merchant Ships)
http://www.equasis.org/
Equasis aims at collecting and disseminating quality and safety-related information on the world's merchant ships provided to it by holders of such information. Registration is mandatory.
Search Form URL: See Main Page

Port State Information eXchange
http://www.uscg.mil
"The Port State Information Exchange (PSIX) system contains vessel specific information derived from the United States Coast Guard's Marine Safety Information System (MSIS). The information contained in PSIX represents a snapshot of Freedom of Information Act (FOIA) data compiled within the MSIS database. Information on unclosed cases or cases pending further action is considered privileged information and is precluded from the PSIX system."
Search Form URL: http://psix.uscg.mil/Default.asp

U.S. Coast Guard Vessel Documentation
http://www.st.nmfs.gov/st1/index.html
"Our query program only retrieves data about vessels [that] usually are craft that are 5 net tons or larger and are documented by the USCG. Craft less than 5 net tons ('boats') are numbered by individual states."

Search Form URL: http://www.st.nmfs.gov/st1/commercial/
landings/cg_vessels.html
Related Resources:
U.S. Coast Guard Vessel Documentation (Name Search)
http://www.st.nmfs.gov/st1/commercial/landings/cg_vessel2.html

Vessel Query Registration System Canada

http://www.tc.gc.ca/ShipRegistry/
"In Canada registration is basically a title system for the ownership of
ships. It is similar in nature to title systems applicable to land registry.
Registration is mandatory for every ship that exceeds 15 gross tons. Ships
not required by law to register may do so on a voluntary basis.
Registration allows for name approval, mortgage registration, protection
of the Crown. There are approximately 46,500 ships on Register totaling
4.7 million gross tons. In addition Canadian shipowners own 100 vessels
of 2.2 million gross tons, which they operate under foreign flags."
Search Form URL: http://www.tc.gc.ca/ShipRegistry/menu.asp?
lang=e

Railroad

Federal Railroad Administration Safety Databases

http://www.fra.dot.gov
"... run detailed and summary reports on FRA's databases, which
encompass Railroad Accidents/Incidents, Railroad Inspections, and
Highway-Rail Crossing information. Users can enter specific query
criteria and produce output reports (including color maps) of the
results." Use the menu at the top of the page to select the "query"
page.
Search Form URL: http://safetydata.fra.dot.gov/officeofsafety/

Glossary

authority. Authority asks who is the provider of the information and what reputation or special knowledge they have to make it accessible. Put another way, authority looks at what makes a person or entity qualified to provide the information. In the print world, the authority of a book is often determined by the reputation of the author and publisher. This is a major issue in the Web world because there is little or no control over what can be placed on the Web.

Boolean. A system of logical operators (AND, OR, NOT) that allows true-false operations to be performed on search queries, potentially narrowing or expanding results when used in conjunction with keywords.

citation analysis. Used in the Web environment to determine the linkages (cites), who links to whom, from one Web page to another. How and by what means are Web documents connected? This concept is used in relevance ranking and as a resource discovery tool. Citation indexing and analysis was pioneered by Dr. Eugene Garfield and has been used in the academic world for some time.

client-based search tools. Small software programs that reside on the searcher's computer that often query multiple search engines simultaneously. Many programs offer additional features such as the removal of duplicate hits and advanced relevance ranking.

client-server computing. A form of computing where data resides on many decentralized computers (servers) and is accessed and manipulated by programs called clients residing on users' computers.

controlled vocabulary (thesaurus). A standardized set of terms used to describe similar items. Web-based information about soft drinks may be indexed under such terms as "soda," "soda-pop," "pop," "cola," "carbonated beverages," "soft drinks," and even brand names like "Coke." A controlled vocabulary links all these terms so that a keyword search on any one of them provides results for all.

crawler (Web crawler, spider). A software robot used by search engines to autonomously find and retrieve Web pages to be included in a search engine's index.

database aggregators. Services that compile searchable databases from individual publishers, allowing access to all information through a single common interface. Dialog from the Thomson Corporation is a well-known example.

dead link. A hyperlink that refers to a page that has been renamed or removed from a Web server. Clicking a dead link will result in a "not found" message. A certain percentage of links in all Web directories and search engine indexes are dead links because of the highly volatile nature of the Web.

deep Web (Invisible Web). Often confused with the Invisible Web, the deep Web refers to databases and other extensive repositories of information that may—or may not—be truly Invisible Web resources.

directory (Web directory). A hand-selected collection of links to Web sites, created manually by human beings (as opposed to the automated processes used by search engines). Typically organized in a hierarchical structure, making it easy to browse for information by category.

distributed search. A decentralized system that relies on more than one computer to provide search results. Napster and Gnutella are examples of distributed search systems.

dynamic Web pages. Pages assembled "on the fly" from content stored in databases based on user input, saved settings, or other variable information. Dynamic pages can be highly customized to fit user needs. Also, databases provide a robust environment for Web sites, so Web developers increasingly use them. Many dynamic Web pages are invisible to search engines.

false drop. In a search result set, an item (hit) that is returned, which is determined irrelevant (by the searcher) to the information need.

fee-based. Material that costs money to access and/or retrieve. Many proprietary databases, as well as content provided by **database aggregators**, are fee-based.

field searching. Restricting or **limiting** search results to portions of documents located in one or more specific **HTML** field, such as the document title, body, or images.

File Transfer Protocol (FTP). A protocol (set of rules) for sending and receiving files of all types between computers connected to the Internet.

focused crawling (targeted crawling). A technique used to limit the types of pages included in a search engine's database to a particular topic, category, or domain.

frames. A method used to simulate multiple windows in a single Web page. Information in a frame can change independently of other frames, allowing Web designers to "lock" content that will always remain in place even while the contents of other frames change.

Gnutella. A **peer-to-peer** distributed search system that allows a Gnutella user to search for files on the computers of other Gnutella users in real time.

hit. An item in a result set that is determined to be relevant to the searcher's information need, as specified by the search query.

hypertext. A system that allows computerized objects (text, images, sounds, etc.) to be *linked* together. A hypertext link points to a specific object; clicking the link opens the file associated with the object.

intelligent crawling (smart spidering). Techniques that go beyond the basic "find and fetch" techniques used by most Web crawlers. Often used by **focused crawlers** to limit crawling to specific domains.

interactive database. A resource that allows the user to interact with the data set, sorting by various criteria. Search engines are interactive databases.

Invisible Web. Text pages, files, or other often high-quality information available via the World Wide Web that general-purpose search engines cannot, due to technical limitations, or will not, due to deliberate choice, add to their indices of Web pages. Sometimes erroneously referred to as the "deep Web" or "dark matter."

keyword. A word or phrase entered in a query form that a search system attempts to match in text documents in its database.

limit (limiting). Using search engine structure to reduce the returned set of possible hits by specifying certain criteria such as Web page date, country of origin, or by using **field searching** to restrict the search to specific parts of Web pages.

metasearch engine. A search engine that simultaneously searches other search engines and aggregates the results into a single result list. Metasearch engines typically do not maintain their own indices of Web pages.

natural language. Entering a search query exactly as if the question were being written or spoken. Natural Language Processing (NLP) is a technique used by search engines to break up or "parse" the search into a query the engine can understand.

"on the fly." Dynamic Web pages that are assembled in real time, as opposed to static HTML pages. An example could be your MyYahoo.Com page that contains the information (news, sports, weather, etc.) that you select. When you call for the page, it is built "on the fly" and sent to your browser.

Opaque Web. Content that *could* be indexed by search engines, but is not, for several reasons.

pay for placement. Paying a search engine to include the description of a Web page near the top of a result list for a specific keyword.

peer-to-peer (P2P). Two or more computers interacting directly with one another without going through a central server or directory. Many **distributed search** systems such as Gnutella and Napster use a P2P model.

precision. A measure of **relevance**, calculated by dividing the number of relevant documents retrieved in response to a query by the total number of documents in a search engine index.

proprietary database. Information services that restrict access to registered or paying customers. Although Web-accessible, proprietary databases such as Dow Jones Interactive and LexisNexis often use specific and robust search syntax, are often fee-based, and contain material that is difficult to access elsewhere.

protocol. A set of rules that specify how computer hardware and software should behave.

proximity operators. Commands that allow the search engine to identify and present words or phrases within a certain distance of one another. An example is NEAR. In the case of AltaVista Advanced Search, limiting a search with the NEAR operator requires search terms to be found within ten words (in either direction) of one another.

query. Keywords or phrases entered into a search form that the search engine uses to attempt to find the most relevant matching documents for those keywords.

recall. A measure of **relevance**, calculated by dividing the number of relevant documents retrieved in response to a query by the total number of relevant documents in the search engine's entire index.

recrawl. Finding and fetching a page that already exists in a search engine's index.

relevance. The degree to which a retrieved Web document matches a user's query or information need. Relevance is often a complex calculation that weighs many factors, ultimately resulting in a score that's expressed as a percentage value.

Robots Exclusion Protocol. A set of rules that enable a Webmaster to specify which parts of a server are open to search engine crawlers, and which parts are off-limits. See http://info.webcrawler.com/mak/projects/robots/exclusion.html for details.

search engine. A Web service that automatically gathers and indexes Web pages using powerful software, helping searchers find relevant Web documents by simply entering a **query** into a search form.

shadow sites. Often referred to as a "mirror or mirrored site." A server that stores and presents to the user an exact copy of another server's content. This technique is often used to reduce traffic at one or more specific sites. It is also used to bring data closer to the location of the end-user, thereby saving load time.

spam. Bogus, illegitimate, or deceptive content, often presented to users in an intrusive or unwanted manner. Junk e-mail is commonly referred to as spam; junk Web pages are known as spam pages.

spamdex. Creating pages that achieve high relevance rankings for particular keywords, but have little or nothing to do with the keywords. Alternately, submitting thousands or millions of bogus pages to a search engine with the hope that some of the pages will be indexed.

spider. See **crawler**.

Telnet. A *terminal emulation* program that runs on your computer, allowing you to access a remote computer via a TCP/IP network and execute commands on that computer as if you were directly connected to it.

thesaurus. A printed or electronic resource that associates the vocabulary used by searchers with that used by professional indexers and catalogers. Approved terms are displayed and relationships amongst terms are illustrated.

utility. Along with **precision, recall,** and **relevance**, utility asks how *useful* a suggested resource in satisfying a user's information need.

Web robot. See **crawler**.

Z39.50. "Z39.50 is a national standard that defines a protocol for computer-to-computer information retrieval. Z39.50 allows a user in one system to search and retrieve information from other computer systems (that have also implemented Z39.50) without knowing the search syntax that is used by those other systems." From Library of Congress WWW/Z39.50 Gateway Web Page at: http://lcweb.loc.gov/z3950/gateway.html#about.

References

Berners-Lee, Tim. Subject Listing. 2 Oct. 2000
(http://www.w3.org/History/19921103-hypertext/hypertext/
DataSources/bySubject/Overview.html)

Bright Planet. "The Deep Web: Surfacing Hidden Value." 1 Aug. 2000
(http://128.121.227.57/download/deepwebwhitepaper.pdf)

Broder, Andrei, et al. "Graph Structure In The Web." Paper Presented at
Ninth International World Wide Web Conference. Amsterdam,
Netherlands. 15-19 May 2000. 6 Dec. 2000 (http://www.
almaden.ibm.com/cs/k53/www9.final/)

Bush, Vannevar. "As We May Think." Atlantic Monthly July 1945:
101-108. 16 Nov. 2000 (http://www.theatlantic.com/unbound/
flashbks/computer/bushf.htm)

Cerf, Vinton. A Brief History of the Internet and Related Networks. 3
Nov. 2000 (http://www.isoc.org/internet/history/cerf.html)

Cohen, William W., Andrew McCallum, and Dallan Quass. "Learning to
Understand the Web." IEEE Data Engineering Bulletin 23.3
(2000): 17-24.

Connolly, Dan. A Little History of the World Wide Web. 11 Oct. 2000
(http://www.w3.org/History.html)

Deutsch, Peter. "Archie—A Darwinian Development Process." IEEE Internet Computing 4.1 (2000). 16 Aug. 2000 (http://www.computer.org/internet/v4n1/deutsch.htm)

Economics of Tobacco Control Country Reports Database. The World Bank Group. 15 Dec. 2000   (http://www1.worldbank.org/tobacco/database.asp)

ERIC. Educational Resources Information Center. 4 Nov. 2000 (http://www.accesseric.org)

Fetuccino. IBM Research. 14 Nov. 2000 (http://www.ibm.com/java/fetuccino/fetuccino-abstract.html)

FlightTracker. 17 Nov. 2000 (http://www.trip.com/ft/home/0,2096,1-1,00.shtml)

Hafner, Katie, and Matthew Lyon. When Wizards Stay Up Late. New York: Touchstone, 1998:6.

Hoover's Online - The Business Network. 19 Oct. 2000 (http://www.hoovers.com/)

Inktomi Slurp. 30 Oct. 2000 (http://www.inktomi.com/slurp.html)

Kahn, Robert E, and Vinton G Cerf. What Is The Internet (And What Makes It Work). Internet Policy Institute. 15 Oct. 2000 (http://www.internetpolicy.org/briefing/12_99_story.html)

Koehler, Wallace. "Digital Libraries and World Wide Web Sites and Web Page Persistence." Information Research 4.4 (1999). 7 Oct. 2000 (http://www.shef.ac.uk/~is/publications/infres/paper60.html)

Koll, Matthew. "Major Trends and Issues in the Information Industry." ASIDIC Newsletter 1998. 16 Nov. 2000 (http://www.asidic.org/techsumf99.html)

Labour Market Information. Human Resources Development Canada. 20 Oct. 2000 (http://lmi-imt.hrdc-drhc.gc.ca/owa_lmi/owa/sp_show_lmi?l=e&i=1)

Lawrence, Steve, and Lee Giles. "Accessibility of Information on the Web." Nature 400 (1999): 107-109.

Leiner, Barry M, et al. A Brief History of the Internet. 10 Oct. 2000 (http://www.isoc.org/internet/history/brief.html)

Notess, Greg. <u>Search Engine Statistics: Database Overlap</u>. 29 Nov. 2000 (http://searchengineshowdown.com/stats/overlap.shtml)

<u>Project Xanadu</u>. 20 Nov. 2000 (http://www.xanadu.net)

ResearchIndex. NEC Research Institute. 20 Dec. 2000 (http://www.researchindex.com)

Speechbot. Compaq Corporate Research. 1 Dec. 2000 (http://www.speechbot.com)

<u>Understanding the Internet: Transcript</u>. PBS. 14 Oct. 2000 (http://www.pbs.org/uti/utitranscript.html)

<u>The Web Robots Page</u>. 18 Oct. 2000 (http://info.webcrawler.com/mak/projects/robots/robots.html)

About the Authors

Chris Sherman is President of Searchwise, a Boulder, Colorado-based Web consulting firm, and Associate Editor of SearchEngineWatch.com. He is a frequent contributor to *Information Today, Online* Magazine, *EContent,* and other information industry journals, and his previous books include *The McGraw-Hill CD ROM Handbook,* and *The Elements of Basic, The Elements of Cobol,* and *The Elements of Pascal* from John Wiley & Sons.

Chris has more than 20 years of experience in developing multimedia and Internet applications. Early in his career, he worked on prototypes of many products and concepts that are now commonplace, such as CD ROM and multimedia technologies and interactive cable television. Later, he was Vice President of Technology for a global management consulting firm based in Amsterdam.

Chris has written about search and search engines since 1994, when he developed online searching tutorials for several clients. From 1998 to 2001, he was the Web Search Guide for About.com. Other clients have included International Data Corporation, Andersen Consulting, Motorola, Levi-Strauss, Porsche, United Technologies, and the Scripps Clinic. Chris holds a Master's degree in Interactive Educational Technology from Stanford University and a Bachelor's degree in Visual Arts and Communications from the University of California, San Diego.

Gary Price is a library and information research consultant based in suburban Washington D.C.

A native of the Chicago area, Gary earned his Master's of Library and Information Science degree from Wayne State University in Detroit, Michigan. He also holds a Bachelor of Arts degree from the University of Kansas in Lawrence, Kansas.

From 1995 through April 2001, Gary worked as a Reference Librarian at the Virginia Campus of George Washington University in Ashburn, VA. Currently, he maintains a consulting relationship with the University.

Gary is the creator and compiler of several well-known Web research tools including Price's List of Lists and Direct Search, a compilation of Invisible Web databases. He is also the creator and editor of The Virtual Acquisition Shelf and News Desk. This weblog resource posts news and other resources of interest to the online researcher. His compilations have been mentioned in numerous publications including *The Washington Post*, *The New York Times*, and *The Chronicle of Higher Education*.

Gary is a frequent speaker at professional and trade conferences and is a regular contributor to *Searcher* magazine. He is a member of the Special Libraries Association.

In his life away from the computer he can often be found scanning and reading magazines, at the movie theater, or listening to all types of music.

Index

A

A to Z Drug Facts, 256
AAAAgency Search, 178
Abandoned Mines Land Inventory
    System, 350
ABC News Video Search, 288
abebooks.com, 154
About Counties, 228
About.com, 23
Abraham Lincoln Legal Papers, 265
Abraham Lincoln Primary Source
    Material Database, 262
abstracts, 15, 39
academic information resources
    program selection, 102
    scholarly journals, 104
    SearchEdu.Com, 42
    subject bibliographies, 100
Academy Awards Database, 321
Access to Higher Education (Europe),
    216
AccuWeather, 102
Acronym Finder, 325
acronyms, 325, 326, 349
activism, 107–108
ADAM (Arts, Design, Architecture &
    Media Information Gateway)
    (U.K.), 103, 151

Adflip.com, 264
adoption, 298
adult sites, tactics of, 25
Advanced Book Exchange, 120–121
Advertising Age (World Brands
    Database), 169
advertising information resources,
    178, 264
African-American Women Writers of
    19th Century, 262
African-Americans, 19th century, 262,
    263
African Elephant Database, 345
after-school programs, 212
Agency ComPile, 178
Agency for Healthcare Research and
    Quality (AHRQ), 250,
    257–258
AGIP (Australian Government Index
    Publications), 231
AGRICOLA, 344
Agricultural Research Service
    Database, U.S., 344
agriculture information resources,
    171, 195, 344–345
AIDS Economics Bibliographic
    Search, 242
AIDS Memorial Quilt Search, 328–329

AIIP (Association of Independent Information Professionals) Member Directory, 295
air transportation information resources, 382–384
Air University Index to Military Periodicals, 377
Airline Certificate Information, 382
Airline Coding Directory, 339
Airline Flight and Fare Database, 339
airline flight information, 60, 66–67, 119–120, 339
Airline On-Time Database, U.S., 383
AirNav Airport Database, 382
AirNow (Real-Time Air Pollution Data), 312
Airport Advisories Database, 316
Airport Arrival Demand Chart, 316
Alcohol and Alcohol Problems Science Database (ETOH), 242–243
Alcohol Industry & Policy Database, 243
Alcohol Studies Database, 243
alerts, 51, 97
Alibris, 98, 121
All Earners Beginning Expected Salary (U.S.), 186
All Game Guide, 218
All Music Guide, 221
Allwhois.com, 203
AlphaSearch, 137
AltaVista
    company links, 106
    crawling efficiency study, 29, 72
    debut, 16
    indexing of file formats, 74
    LawCrawler, 41
    LookSmart and, 23
    nontextile searching, 57–58
    translation tools, 101
Alternative Fuel Stations, 333
A.M. Best Insurance Ratings, 178
Amateur Radio Call Sign Lookup, U.S., 297
Amazon.com, 103
America Online (AOL), 47
American Art Directory, 151
American Association of Health Plans (AAHP), 250

American Board of Medical Specialties (ABMS) "Who's Certified" Database, 294
American Booksellers Association Member Directory, 322
American Community Network, 176
American Dental Association Members Directory, 294
American Export Register, 169
American FactFinder, 102
American Hospital Directory, 251–252
American Institute of Architects, 294
American Kennel Club Events Calendar and Awards Search, 329
American Marketing Association, 188–189
American Medical Association (AMA), 250, 294–295
American Memory Collection, The, 87–88, 99, 262
American political prints, LOC, 148
American Psychoanalytic Association, 377
American Psychological Association (APA), 42
American Religion Data Archive, 378
American Sign Language Browser, 325
American Society for Association Executives (ASAE), 196, 320
American Society of Civil Engineers (ASCE) Civil Engineering Database, 355
American Society of Composers, Artists and Publishers (ASCAP), 221
American Society of Home Inspectors (ASHI), 320
American Verse Project, 262
Americans and Aquarium Association, 347
America's Job Bank, 185–186
Amtrak, 316–317, 339–340
amusements, 218
anagrams, 218
analysis, browser agents, 50
annotations, 23, 24, 39
Annual Review of Population Law, 278

Anro (Australian Agriculture), 344

Antarctica, 56, 351

Anthropological Index Online, 370

Anthropology Review Database, 370

AnyWho.Com, 97, 187–188, 297

A&P Mechanics Database, 295

APEC tariff database, 195

archaeology information resources, 152, 370–371

Archie, 4–5, 6–7, 58

archINFORM (International Architecture Database), 146

Archisplus (Database of the Historical Archives of the European Commission), 154

Architect Finder, The, 294

architecture information resources, 145–147, 151–152, 181, 265

archive catalog goals, 153

ArchiviaNet (National Archives of Canada), 157

Archon (Historical Manuscripts), 154–155

ArcHSearch (U.K.), 370

armed services information resources. *See also* specific databases

    Army Physical Fitness Test Score Calculator, 256

    directories, 299

    educational experiences, 210–211

    images, 377

    military installations worldwide, 334

    military periodicals, 377

    navy personnel, 300

    SearchMil.Com to, 42

Army Corps of Engineers Digital Virtual Library, U.S., 356

Army Physical Fitness Test Score Calculator, U.S., 256

ARPANET, 2–3

Arson and Explosives National Repository, 273

Art and Architecture Thesaurus Browser (AAT), 325

Art, Design, Architecture & Media Information Gateway, 103

art information resources, 103, 122–123, 147–151

Art Library Directory (IFLA), 151–152

Artcyclopedia, 147, 152

artists, 147–148

Arts and Architecture Thesaurus Browser (AAT), 152

arXiv.org e-Print archive, 362

ASCAP Music License Database, 221

Asia-Pacific Economic Cooperation (APEC), 195

Asian Development Bank Developing Member Country Data, 173

Asian Development Bank Regional Data, 173

AskERIC, 83–84

Association of Computing Machinery (ACM), 200

Association of Research Libraries (ARL) Statistics, 374

Associationcentral, 320

associations, 320–321

AssociationsCanada, 320

asterisk(*) symbol, 89–90

ASTIS (Arctic Science and Technology Information System), 350

astronomy information resources, 365–367

Atkinson, Bill, 10

Atlas for the Solar Radiation Data Manual for Buildings, 353

Atlas for the Solar Radiation Data Manual for Flat-Plate and Concentrating Collectors, 353

Atlas of Antarctic Research, 351

Atlas of Cancer Mortality in United States, 245

Atlas of South Australia, 338

AT&T Labs External Publications Search, 202

auctions, online, 169

audio information resources. *See also* non-text content

    History and Politics Out Loud, 264

    National Sound Archive Catalogue, 155

    NPR, 284

    retrieval, 130

    SpeechBot, 65, 284

Audit Bureau Circulation, eCirc, 179

Australia
agriculture, 344
Atlas of South Australia, 338
cancer research, 257
gazetteer, 336
Government Online Directory, 229
Images, 269
INFOQUICK, 286
National Archives of, 159–160
Postcode Search, 335
Whereis Street Atlas, 337
Australian Business Register (ABR),
165
Australian Geological Survey
Organization (AGSO), 354
Australian Government Index of
Publications (AGIP), 231
Australian Legal Information
Institute, 278–279
Australian Literary and Historical
Texts, 263
Australian National Shipwreck
Database, 263
Australian Patents Databases, 277
Australian War Memorial Databases,
299
authority
content providers, 106–107
directory resources, 141
Invisible Web, 91–92, 95, 96
URL information, 108
Authors on the Highway, 322
Automated Regional Justice
Information System Crime
Maps/Reports (San Diego
County), 305
Automated Reporting Management
Information System (ARMIS)
(FCC), 179
Automated Weather Source, 102–103
Automobile Fuel Economy, 323
automobile information resources,
323, 384
Automobile Recall Database, U.S.,
324
autonomous agents, origins of, 14–16
Avalon Project at Yale Law School,
the, 263
Aviation Accident Synopsis (NTSB),
382–383

Aviation Medical Examiners
Database, 295
award information resources, 100,
321–322, 329, 363
Axis (U.K.), 142

B

Bach Bibliography, 222
Backflip, 111, 113
bait and switch tactics, 25, 68–69
bands, lists of, 224
Bank of Canada Inflation Calculator,
173–174
Bankrate.Com, 190
Bankruptcy Procedure, Federal Rules
of, 275
Bartleby.com, 331
baseball, 339
Basic Company Name and Address
Index (U.K.), 166
Bathing Water Quality in the
European Union: Tourist
Atlas, 362
BBC Library Sales, 288
BBC News Search, 285
Beethoven Bibliography Database,
221–222
Beige Book Archive, 169–170
Beilstein Abstracts, 343–349
Beliefnet Dictionary, 378
Berners-Lee, Tim
background, 1
communication goals, 17–19
Enquire Within Upon Everything,
8–10
first Web directory, 12–13
format negotiation, 68
World Wide Web prototype, 10–12
Better Business Bureau Company
Reports, 165
beverage information resources,
327–328
biases
corporate Web sites, 106
indexing of text, 35
subtlety of, 107
targeted directories and, 40
URL information, 108
Vortals, 43–44
Bible Browser, The, 378

Bibliofind, 98, 121, 154
bibliographic material
    code for, 140
    Invisible Web, 154–160
    searchable, 100
BiblioSleep, 243
BigCharts.com, 99, 116, 183
Bill Tracker (Michigan), 304
Bill Tracking Database (California),
    303–304
Billboard Spotlight Reviews, 222
BioABACUS, 325
Biographical Register of Henry James'
    Correspondents, 268
Biography.com Database, 292
biology resources, 345–350
Biomedical Journal Title Search, 251
Biotech Agreement Database, 179
Biotech Alliance Database, 179
biotechnology, abbreviations and
    acronyms, 325
birds, Canada, 345
bitpipe.com, 200
BizJournals.Com, 285
Bloomberg Television Transcript
    Search, 285
Bluebook.Com, The, 179, 329
body fat calculator, U.S. Marines, 256
Book Browser Calendar of Author
    Signings and Events, 322
book information resources, 98–99,
    120–121, 154, 322–323
bookmarks, 111–113
bookwire.com, 323
Boolean, definition, 6
BOPCRIS (British Official
    Publications Collaborative
    Reader Information Service),
    155
botany resources, 347–348
Bright Planet study, 82
British and Irish Legal Information
    Institute, 279
British Columbia Securities
    Commission Database, 168
British Columbia Visual Records
    Database, 267
British Library Current Serials File,
    160
British Library Manuscript

Catalogue, 155
British Library Newspaper Library
    Catalogue, 155
British Library Public Catalogue, 155
British Museum Materials
    (Compass), 160
broken links. *See* links, broken
browser agents, 43, 48–50
browsers, graphical, 11
browsing
    directories, 82–83
    point-and-click interfaces, 18
    searching and, 18–22
BT PhoneNet UK, 297
building and construction industry,
    179
Bulk, Intermediate and Consumer-
    Oriented (BICO) Database,
    195
bulletin boards, 7
BullsEye Pro, 51
Bureau of Labor Statistics, 173
Bureau of Land Management, 277
Burwell World Directory of
    Information Brokers, 295
Bush, Vannevar, 9
Business and License Complaints
    History Search (Hawaii), 304
Business Entities Search (Utah), 305
business information resources
    company directories, 100
    company facts, 106
    corporate Web sites, 106
    Delphion Intellectual Property
        Network, 84–85
    historical stock quotes, 99
    Hoover's Business Profiles, 64
    Hoover's Online, 85
    INTA Trademark Checklist, 84–85
    jobs, 100–101
    Northern Light Special Collection,
        47
    patents, 98
    public company filings, 96–97
    Thomas's Register of American
        Manufacturers, 85
Business Loan Data (SBA), 170
Business Resources, 163–197
business to business (B2B) sites,
    43–44

C

C-SPAN Campaign 2000 Video
    Archives, 289
C-SPAN Congressional Vote
    Databases, 234
calculators, 323–324
California Highway Patrol, traffic
    incidents, 316
California, Online Archive of, 159
California Shipwreck Database, 263
Calishain, Tara, 110
Cambodian Genocide Bibliographic
    Database, 267
Cambridge Dictionaries Online, 325
Cambridge International Dictionary
    of English, 99
Cambridge University, 39
Campaign Finance Data (Kansas),
    306
Campaign Finance Information
    System (Delaware), 306
campaigns, political
    2000, 289
    Financial Disclosure Information
        System (NY), 306
    Financial Report Databases
        (Canada), 306
    financing information, 102
    Historical Campaign Finance
        Data (Vermont), 306
Campus Security Statistics, 273
Canada
    ArchiviaNet, 157
    British Columbia Visual Records
        Database, 267
    CA Number Database, 181
    colleges and universities, 209
    Defense Research Reports, 363
    depository library finder, 234
    Disease Surveillance Online, 243
    Electoral District Locator, 229
    foreign representatives in, 229
    government contracts, 177–178
    importers database, 194
    inflation calculator, 173–174
    Job Bank, 186
    labour market, 174–175
    lobbyist search, 237–23/8
    MP Lookup, 235
    Municipal Water Use Database, 359
    museums and galleries, 150
    national atlas, 338
    postal codes, 121–122
    Prime Minister of Canada site
        search, 231
    resAnet, 157–158
    Reverse Telephone & Address
        Lookup, 188
    RRSP calculator Net, 190
    searchable TV listings, 218–219
    SEDAR, 168
    statistical profiles of communi-
        ties, 239
    stock charts, 182
    Supreme Court Judgments, 274
    tariff wizards, 195
    Toronto Stock Exchange, 185
    trade data online, 195
    VIA Rail Timetable, 340
    Weekly Checklist Catalogue of
        Publications, 234
    Workopolis, 186
    Yellow Pages, 188, 297
Canada 411, 122, 297
Canada Heritage Directory, 267
Canada Institute of Health Research
    (CIRH), 257
Canada Patents Database, 277
Canada Post, 122
Canada Yellow Pages, 188, 297
Canada-American Treaties, 279
Canada's Digital Collections, 262
Canadian Archaeological
    Radiocarbon Database, 371
Canadian Bird Trends Database, 345
Canadian Broadcasting Company
    News Search, 285
Canadian Broadcasting Corp., 89
Canadian Civil Aircraft Register, 383
Canadian Company Capability, 194
Canadian Drug Products Database,
    256
Canadian Encyclopedia, The, 329
Canadian Geographic Names,
    335–336
Canadian Importers Database, 194
Canadian Legal Information
    Institute, 279
Canadian Music Periodical Index,
    100, 222

Canadian Poisonous Plants Information System, 347
Canadian Postal Code Lookup, 335
Canadian Ship Information Database, 263
Canadian Subject Headings, 332
Canadian Trade Data Online, 195
Canadian Transportation Databases, 384–385
Canadian Virtual War Memorial, 299
Canadian Who's Who 1997, 292
Canadian Women Inventors Database, 268
cancer, 243, 244, 245, 246, 257
Cancer Mortality Data for Many Nations, 245
Cancer Research Australia, 257
Cancerlit, 244
cancerTrials, 244
CanLearn (Canada), 209
cardiovascular disease, 243
career resources, 185–187
CareerBuilder.Com, 101, 186
Caribbean, ESDB database, 174
Carmichael, Hoagy, 222
Carnegie Mellon University, 15, 159
Carroll Publishing Company Government Directories, U.S., 228
Carroll's GovSearch, 228
cartography, 40. See also maps
Castro, Fidel, 376
Catalist, 329
Catalog of Scientific Community in the 16th and 17th Centuries, 292
Catalog of U.S. Government Publications, 231–232
Cavuto, Neil, 289
CBD Net, 177
CDC Wonder, 247
Census Bureau International Database, U.S., 372
census data
    agriculture, 171
    historical, 266
    lookup, 372
    U.S., 102
Census International Bureau Population Pyramids, U.S., 372

Census Lookup, U.S., 372
Census of Agriculture, 171
Center for Responsive Politics, 302
Center for the Study and Prevention of Violence Literature, 375
Centers for Disease Control and Prevention (CDCP), 246, 247, 255, 257–258
CenterWatch, 97–98, 257
Cerf, Vint, 3
Certified Mammography Centers, 252
Certified Pilots Database (U.S.), 295
Certified Public Accountants (CPA) Directory, 295
cgi-bin, 80
Chambers of Commerce, 177
Charitable Organizations Database (Arizona), 304
Charitable Organizations Database (Maryland), 304
Charities Database (Oregon), 304
Charities Search (Minnesota), 304
ChemFinder.Com, 349
ChemGuide, 349
Chemical Accidents, Historical Incident Reports, 358
Chemical Acronyms Database, 349
ChemIDplus, 349
chemistry information resources, 348–350, 356
Chemistry Preprint Server, 349
Chemweb, 348–349
Chicagoland Expressway Congestion Map, 316
Child Abuse and Neglect Clearinghouse Organizations Database, 274–275
childcare, NCCIC database, 208
children's book awards, 321
Choral Repertoire, International Database of, 222–223
Chronicle of Higher Education, 213
Cindi's List of Genealogy Sites on the Internet, 293
CineFiles, 219
cinema, 219–221
Cinema FreeNet, 219
CIO Archive, 201

CIS (Commonwealth of Independent States) Migration Legislation Database, 280

citations
index of, 67
outbound links, 108
subject bibliographies, 100

Cities and Buildings Database, 147

Civil Engineering Database, ASCE, 355

Civil Procedure, Federal Rules of, 275

Civil War Soldiers and Sailors System, 299

classics, Web resources, 39

client-based Web search, 43, 50–51

clinical trials information resources, 97–98, 179, 244, 257

ClinicalTrials.gov, 97, 257

cloaking, 68–69

CNBC/Dow Jones Business Video, 289

CNET Video Search, 289

CNN, robots.txt file use, 89

CNN New Search, 285

coal, 352

Coal Quality Database, U.S., 352

Coal Resource Database, U.S., 352

Coast Guard Vessel Documentation, U.S., 386–387

Coastal Water Temperature Guide, 313

Cold North Wind Newspaper Archive Project, 285

Collage (Corporation of London Library & Art Gallery Electronic), 149

Collection of Computer Science Bibliographies, 202

College Board, The, 211

College Opportunities Online, 209

College Search, 211

College Students Consumables Cost of Living Calculator, 190

Colorado State University, 16

Combined Health Information Database (CHID), 247

commerce, Internet and, 12

Commerce Business Daily, 177

Committee Profiles Database (Missouri), 304

Common Information Services System (CISS), Mining Safety and Health Research, 259

common sense, 109

Commonwealth War Graves Commission Debt of Honour Register (U.K.), 299

Community College Finder, 211

Community Database (Alaska), 304

Community Health Indicators, 249

Community of Science Workbench Databases, 363

companies. *See* business information resources

Company Information, 164–169

CompanySleuth, 165

Compaq, 29, 65, 72, 284

Compass (British Museum Materials), 160

competitive intelligence resources, 39–40, 100

Compilation of Provincial Law and Regulations Database (Canada), 279

complaints, insurance companies, 180

Complete Sun and Moon Data for One Day, 365

Composite Gazetteer of Antarctica, 351

compressed file formats, 58, 74–75

CompuServe, 47

Computer Researching Association (CRA), 201

computing information resources, 199–202

concerts, Pollstar Database, 223

conferences
education, 214
mental health, 244
online, 329
physics, 362
planning, 180

Congress Resource Center (CRC), 249

Congress, U.S., 234, 237–238

Congressional Biographical Directory (U.S.), 263

Consumer Price Index Calculator (U.S.), 173–174

Consumer Product Safety
Commission (CPSC) Product
Recalls, 169
consumer resources, 169, 254–256,
324
content sites, 78–79
Contracts Canada, 177–178
Convention Center Directory, 196
convention resources, 196–197
ConventionBureaus.Com, 196
COPAC (Consortium of University
Research Libraries), 155
Copernic, 51
Copyright Office Records, U. S., 278
copyrighted content, 48, 105
copyrights, United States, 278
CORA, 200
coral reefs, 357
CORDIS (Community Research &
Development Information
System), 192
Corporation Database (Alabama),
304–305
Corporation Database (Arizona), 305
Corporation Database (Arkansas),
305
Corrections Offender Information
Network (Florida), 305
costs
depth of crawl, 70–71
directory resources, 141
frequency of crawl, 71–72
scholarly journals, 104
value-added search services,
46–48
costs of living, 187, 190
Council of Mayors Mayoral Election
Results Database, U.S., 234
Council on Tall Buildings Database,
147
counties, U.S., 170, 228, 236, 238–239
Country Commercial Guides, U.S.,
196
Country Indicators for Foreign Policy,
236
County Business Patterns, 170
county government, 228
coverage
metasearch engines and, 46
search indexes, 53–54

Web directories, 25
CPA Directory, 295
CRA (Computer Researching
Association), 201
crawlers
comprehensiveness, 53–54
databases and, 59–61
depth of crawlers, 70–71
efficiency, 29
focused, 38–43
functioning of, 27–29
future of, 128
lag time, 33
the opaque Web, 70–72
origins of, 14–16
passwords and, 63
real-time, 132
Robots Exclusion Protocol, 72–73
search engine use of, 26
spider traps, 65–66
crawling, cost of, 32–33
credibility, Invisible Web, 91–92
Credit Union Search (U.K.), 176
credit unions, 176
Crime Database (Chicago), 305
criminal resources, 271–282
CRISP (Computer Retrieval of
Information on Scientific
Projects), 257–258
Culturally and Linguistically
Appropriate Services
Database, 208
CultureFinder, 224
currency conversion, 324
current awareness resources,
109–111, 213–214
Current Controlled Trials (U.K.), 257
current events resources, 283–289
Current Weather Conditions
International, 317
Current Weather Conditions U.S., 317
customization
databases, 60–61
invisible Web, 93
local weather, 102.103
MetaCrawler, 45
research toolkits, 111, 113
Cybercafe Search Engine database,
203
cyberterms, 204

D

dams, register of, 356

DARE: Directory in Social Sciences — Institutions, Specialists, Periodicals, 374

dark matter, definition, 57

Data Query: World Development Indicators, 373

Database of Award-Winning Children's Literature, 321

databases. *See also* specific databases
  content storage, 78–79
  crawlers and, 67–68
  customization, 60–61
  document delivery services, 154
  dynamic content, 130–132
  keywords searchable, 14
  relational, 61, 75
  search engines and, 59–61
  specialized content focus, 93
  Web interface access, 7

dates, timeliness and, 108–109

deep Web, 57, 82–83

Defense Advanced Research Projects Agency (DARPA), U.S., 1, 3

Defense Research Reports (Canada), 363

Defensive Driving Training Locator (NSC), 384

Delphion Intellectual Property Network, 98, 276

Demographic Data (Government Information Sharing Project), 371

demographic information resources, 102, 216, 371–372

dentists, 294–295

Dentists Register and Rolls of Dental Auxiliaries (U.K.), 295

Denver Public Library, Western History Photos, 266–267

Department of Agriculture (USDA), 171
  Economics and Statistics System, 171
  Foreign Import/Export Data, 195
  nutrient database for standard reference, 253–254
  Plants Database, 348

Department Of Commerce (DOC), U.S., State Exports Database, 196

Department of Defense (DOD), U.S.
  Advanced Research Projects Agency (ARPA), U.S., 2
  Biomedical Research Database, 258
  Business Opportunities, 178
  Central Contractor Register, 178
  GulfLINK, 245
  STINET, 365

Department of Energy (DOE), U.S.
  Information Bridge, 353–354
  PrePRINT Network, 361

Department of Energy/EPA Automobile Fuel Economy, U.S., 323

Department of Health and Human Services, U.S., NGC, 250

Department of Health Services Restaurant Rating (Los Angeles County), 308

Department of Justice (DOJ), U.S.
  Crime & Justice Electronic Database Abstracts, 281

Department of Labor (DOL), U.S.
  pension information, 189
  Wage Query System, 187

Depository Library Finder (Canada), 234

Deutsch, Peter, 5

Development Experience System (DEXS), USAID, 373–374

development information resources, 192–193, 373–374

DIALOG/DataStar Full-Text Database, 332

dictionaries, 99, 204, 276, 325–327, 378. *See also* Specific dictionaries

Dictionary of Nomenclature of Celestial Objects, 366

dietary supplements, 253

Digital Library Federation Public Access Collections, 156

Digital Schomburg, 262, 263

Digitized Collections (U.K.), Directory of, 155

direct search, 136

directories. *See also* specific directories
 browsing, 82
 editorial policies, 24–25
 examples, 22–26, 294–297
 hierarchical, 20–21, 82–83
 issues with, 24–26
 open vs. closed models, 23
 origins of, 12–13
 search engines and, 36
 search tool functions, 19
 size of, 24
 structure, 20–21
 supplemental search results, 23–24
 targeted, 38–43
DIRLINE (Health and Biomedicine
  Resources), 249
disabilities, ICIDH-2, 250
"disallow" commands, 89–90
disclaimers, 68–69
discussion lists, 204
Disease Surveillance Online
  (Canada), 243
diseases, notifiable, 243
Disqualified Directors Register (U.K.),
  165–166
Distribution of Forests, 348
DNA Patent Database (DPD), 247
DocFinder (U.S.), 295–296
Doctorate in the European Region
  Database, 216
Doctors Guide, Congress Guide, 249
document delivery services, 154
documents, governmental, 231–234
Dogpile, 45
dogs, AKC, 329
domain names
 Allwhois.com, 203
 dot com directory, 166
 focused crawlers and, 42
 Mark's Online search, 203
 network solutions, 204
 registration, 12
dot com directory, 166
"dot-com" domain name registration,
  12
Dow Jones, 104
Dow Jones Average Search, 182
Dow Jones Interactive, 125
Dreilinger, Daniel, 16
Drug Information Database, 256

Drug Reaction Database, 256
duplicates, 28, 33
dynamic content databases, 130–131
dynamically generated content,
  60–61, 65–66, 80, 81

E

E-mail, 7, 204
E-mail directory, 298
E-Nature Field Guides, 345
Early Canadiana Online, 268
Earth from Space, 366
earth science information resources,
  350–353
Earth View, 314
Earthquake Engineering Abstracts,
  351
Earthquake Image Information
  System (EQIIS), 351
Earthquake Search, 351
Earthrise, 366
EASI QuickReport & Analysis, 371
eCirc, 179
Ecomp Executive Compensation
  Database, 166
Economagic, 171
Economic and Social Database
  (ESDB), 174
economics information resources,
  100
 financial institutions, 175–176
 general business, 176–177
 government contracts, 177–178
 industry-specific, 178–182
 Tobacco Control Country Data
   Report Database, 64
 United States, 169–173
 world, 173–175
Economics of Tobacco Control
  Database, 243
EDGAR Online, 48
Edinburgh Engineering Virtual
  Library, 355
Edison, Thomas A., papers of, 266
Editor and Publisher Online Media
  Directory, 284
editors, directories, 22–26
Edmonds Used Vehicle Appraiser, 324
education information resources,
  207–216

education information resources (*cont.*)
Access to Higher Education
(Europe), 216
AskERIC, 83–84
classroom support, 208–209
directories, 209–212
ERIC database, 79
financial information, 212–213
Gateway to Educational Materials
Project, 83–84
general, 213–215
Historical Atlas of Canada Online
Learning Project, 268
locators, 209–212
scholarship information, 212–213
SearchEdu.Com, 42
statistics, 215–216
teachers support, 208–209
Education Resource Information
Clearinghouse (ERIC), 79
Education Resources Organizations
Directory, 210
Education WeekArchives, 214
Edupage Archive, 214
EEVL (Edinburgh Engineering Virtual
Library), 39
ELDIS (Development Data), 373
Election Canada, Financial Report
Databases, 306
Election Return Archives (Missouri),
305–306
elections, 229, 305–306. *See also* polit-
ical information resources
Electric Library, 47–48
Electronic Telegraph, The (U.K.), 288
Elemental Data Index, 349
elephants, 345
Emergence of Advertising in America
(EAA) 1850-1929, 264
Emmy Awards Database, 321
Employee Benefits INFOSOURCE, 189
Employee Identification Number
(EIN) Search, 190
employment resources, 100–101,
185–187, 209, 215, 308–309
Employment Service Vacancies
Search (U.K.), 186
emulators, 17
Energy Database, 354
energy information resources,

353–355
Energy Technology Data Exchange,
354
engineering information resources,
39, 156, 216, 355–356, 385
Engineering Societies Library, 156
English National Board for Nursing,
Midwifery, and Health
Visiting — Healthcare
Database, 247
English Religious Resources, 379
Enquire Within Upon Everything,
8–10
entertainment resources, 217–225
amusements, 218
general, 218–219
movies and cinema, 219–221
music, 221–224
ENTRI (Environmental Treaties
Database), 356
Envirofacts, 99, 356–357
Enviromapper, 357
Environment Databases (the Right-
to-Know Network), 357
environmental information
resources, 99, 312–313,
356–360
Environmental Protection Agency
(EPA)
Automobile Fuel Economy, 323
Envirofacts, 356–357
Green House Gas State Action
List, 358
SEP National Database, 360
Environmental Treaties Database
(ENTRI), 356
Epicurious Recipe Database, 328
Equal Employment Opportunity File,
371
Equasis (Merchant Ships), 386
ERI, college students consumables
cost of living, 190
ERIC (Educational Resources
Information Center), 83–84,
214
ERIC/AE Full Text Internet Library,
210
ERIC/AE Test Locator, 210
esp@cenet (European Patent Office),
277

ETOH (Alcohol and Alcohol Problems Science Database), 242–243
EuroDicAutom, 101, 326
Euroethics, 258
European Case Clearing House (ECCH), 180
European Central Bank, 176
European commission
  education systems, 215–216
  historical archives, 154
European Convention on Human Rights
  HUDOC, 275
European Database on AIDS and HIV Infection, 243
European Foreign Policy Bulletin (EU), 232
European High-tech Industry Database, 166
European Organization for Nuclear Research (CERN), 1
European Patent Attorneys Database, 272
European Patent Office, 277
European Rail Timetable Database, 340
European Union
  bathing water quality, 362
  directory of institutions, 233
  Monetary Financial Institutions, 176
  RAPID, 233
Eurybase, 215–216
Evaluating the Quality of Information on the Internet (Tyburski), 109
EventSource, 180
Evidence, Federal Rules of, 275
ExCALENDAR, 149
Excite, 16, 60
executable formats, 58, 74–75
ExhibitorNet.Com, 197
experts, locators, 296. *See also* specific directory
ExtendedCare.Com, 253

F

familydoctor.org, 256
FamilySearch, 293
Fannie Mae Owned Property Search, 193

FAO (Food and Agriculture Organization, U.N.), 340, 345
FAOSTAT, 345
FareChase, 339
Fast Facts, education statistics, 216
Fastweb Scholarship Database, 213
Fatality Analysis Reporting System, 385
Fecinfo.Com, 102
Federal Aviation Administration (FAA), 120, 316, 382
Federal Communications Commission (FCC)
  Amateur Radio Call Sign Lookup, 297
  ARMIS, 179
  Filed Comments Search, 275
  General Menu Reports, 182
  radio databases, 182
  TV database, 182
Federal County/District Court Lookups, U.S., 276
Federal Deposit Insurance Corporation (FDIC), 100, 172, 175, 193
Federal Depository Library Directory, 333
Federal Depository Library Finder U.S., 232
Federal Domestic Assistance, Catalog of, 235
Federal Election Commission (FEC), 102, 302
Federal Energy Regulatory Council, RIMS, 274
Federal Justice Statistics Database, 274
Federal Laboratory Profiles, 193
Federal Lands Patents Database, 277
Federal Motor Carrier Safety Administration (FMCSA), 384
Federal Procurement Data System, 235–236
Federal Property (Canada), Directory of, 229
Federal Railroad Administration Safety Databases, 387
Federal R&D Project Summaries, 364
Federal Reserve in Print, 171

Federal Reserve National Information Center Databases, 175
Federal Reserve Publications Catalog, 171
Federal School Code Search, U.S., 213
Federal Trade Commission (FTC), 181
Federally Incorporated Companies (Canada), 166
Fedix (Federal Information Exchange), 235
FedLaw service, 41
FedScope, 238
Fedstats, 238
fee-based Web-accessible services, 52
FestivalFinder, 223
Festivals.com, 224
Fetuccino project, 132
Fidel Castro Speech Databases, 376
File Transfer Protocol (FTP), 3–4
Filed Comments Search (FCC), 275
files, early search tools, 3–8
Film Festivals Directory, The, 219
Filo, David, 15
Financial Deposit Insurance Corporation (FDIC), 175
Financial Disclosure Information System, 306
Financial Institution and Branch Office Data, 175
financial institutions, 175–176
Financial Times
    Company Financial Database, 182–183
    European Companies Premium Research, 100
    Global Archive, 285–286
Financial Web Historical Quotes, 183
Find a Neighborhood Database, 194
Finding Federal Dollars, 212
Fine Arts Museum of San Francisco, 151
fire information resources
    Fire Loss Profiles, 176
    Firefighter Fatality Database, 176
    Seattle 911 fire dept. dispatches, 313
    Wildland Fire Support, 357
Fire Loss Profiles, 176
Firefighter Fatality Database, 176
FIRST (Facts of International Relations and Security Trends), 237
First Nation Community Profiles Canada, 239
FirstGov.Gov, 42, 131
FishBase, 346
fishing, 171–172
Flash formats, 58, 74–75
Fletcher, Jonathon, 15
Flight Arrivals U.S., Canada, 316
Flight Route Calculator, 337
Flight Tracker, 119–120, 315
Flightarrivals.com, 120
Flipdog, 101, 186
FLORID, 132
Flyswat, 49
FNCEO with Neil Cavuto, 289
Focus Group Directory, 189
focused crawlers, 38–43
Folger Shakespeare Library Online Catalog (HAMNET), 156
Fone Finder, 333–334
Food and Agriculture Organization (FAO) U.N., 340, 345
Food and Drug Administration (FDA)
    CRISP database, 257–258
    mammography centers, 252
Food Marketing Institute, The, 327–328
food resources, 327–328
Footage.Net, 288
Forbes
    International 800, 167
    Private 500, 167
Forbes 500
    direct URLs, 79
Foreign Agricultural Service Import/Export Data, 195
Foreign Labor Statistics Java Interface, 173
foreign language programs, 210
Foreign Language Tests Database, 210
foreign policies, 236
Foreign Representatives in Canada, 229
Forensic Experts in Transportation Engineering, Directory of, 385
forestry, 348

format negotiation, 68
forms
    database Web interfaces, 67–68
    HTML, 64–65
Forsyth list (CRA), 201
Fortune 500, 167
forums, 7
Foundation Center, 101
Foundation Finder, 101, 190–191
411 For Government, 228
401K Calculator, 190
Fox Movietone Newsreels, 288
Fox News Channel Video Archives, 289
frames, crawler coverage and, 53
Frank Lloyd Wright Building Locator, 147
Frederick Douglass Papers, The, 265
Free Lunch, 171
Free On-line Dictionary of Computing, 204
Free Pint, 110–111
FreeEDGAR, 97, 164–165
freeErisa.com, 189
freight railroads, 181
Fuel Consumption Guide Canada, 324
Fugitive Fact File (Hennepin County Library), 330
Fuld & Company, 39–40
functional assessments, ICIDH-2, 250
FundSource, 378

G

"Galactic Network" (Licklider), 2
Gale Group Reference Review Archive, 332
galleries, art, 148–151
games, 218
gasoline, 323, 333
Gateway to Associations, 320
Gateway to Educational Materials (GEM) Project, 83–84, 208
GATHER (Health Issues Spatial Data), 248
Gazetteer, U.S., 336
Gazetteer of Australia, 336
gender Inn: Women and Gender Studies Database, 375
Genderstats, 375

genealogy resources, 293–294
GeneCards, 346
Geographic Names Information Systems (U.S. and Antarctica), 336, 351
geography resources, 335–336
GEOLEX, 352
Geological Survey, U.S., 312, 337–338
GeoMAC (Wildland Fire Support), 357
GEONet Names Server, 336
Georgetown University, 237, 247
Geospatial and Statistical Data Center, 170
Get-a-Map U.K., 336
Getty Thesaurus of Geographic Names, 336
Giles, Lee, 71
GILS (Government Locator Information Service), 229–230
Global Banking Law Database, 280
Global Legal Information Network (GLIN), 280
Global Transport Analyzer (Shipping Data), 385
global warming, 358
globalinvestor.com, 182
Globe Wide Network Academy, 212
GlobeXplorer, 353
GloboCan, 245
glossaries, 325–327
Glossary of Communications Terms, 326
GOLD (Government Online Directory) (Australia), 229
Good Practice Database (U.K.), 230
Google, 23, 67, 107
Gopher, origins of, 5–6
GoTo search engines, 15
government. *See also* Specific agencies
    information, U.S., 42
    paperwork reduction, 59
    restricted records, 104
government information resources, 227–239. *See also* political information resources; specific agencies
    directories, 228–230

government information resources
(*cont.*)
documents, 231–234
general, 230–231
international relations, 236–238
locators, 228–230
officials, 234–235
programs, 235–236
real-time, 313
statistics, 238–239
Government Information Sharing
Project, 170, 371
Government Locator Information
Service (GILS), 229–230
Government Online Bookstore Sales
Product Catalog, U.S.,
231–232
Government Printing Office, U.S.,
231–232
GPO Access (U.S.), 232
Grammy Awards Database, 321
grant information, 101, 191, 213, 364
Grants Awarded Database, 213
GrantSmart, 191
GrantsNet, 364
Grateful Med, 250
Gray, Mathew, 14
GrayLIT Network, 361
Great Barrier Reef Online Image
Catalog, The, 357
Great Canadian Guide, The, 150
Green House Gas State Action List, 358
Gross State Product Data, 171
Grove Dictionary of Opera, 223
Guardian, The (U.K.), 288
Guide to Military Installations
Worldwide, 334
Guide to the Evaluation of
Educational Experiences in
the Armed Services, 210–211
Guidestar.Org, 191
Gulf War illnesses, 245
GulfLINK, 245

H

Hall, Justin, 12
HAMNET (Folger Shakespeare
Library Online Catalog), 156
Handbook of Latin American Studies,
376

Hann, William, 110–111
Harvard Business School Cases and
Teaching Material, 180
Harvard Law School, 278
Hazardous Chemicals Database, 356
HazDat (Hazardous Substance
Release/Health Effects
Database), 247–248
HCUPnet, 249
Health and Safety Executive (HSE)
Public Register of
Prosecutions (U.K.), 254
Health Care Financing
Administration (HCFA), 255
Health care professional resources,
249–251
Health Data Warehouse (Ohio),
306–307
Health Education Assistance Loan
(HEAL) Program, 177
Health Facility Report Card Search
(Iowa), 307
health information resources,
241–259. *See also* medical
information resources
clinical trials, 97–98
diseases and conditions, 242–246
Health Data Warehouse (Ohio), 306
Health Facility Report Card Search
(Iowa), 307
healthcare professionals, 249–251
HSTAT (Health Care Decision
Making), 250
images, 246
locators, 251–253
National Health Information
Center, 86
nutrition, 253–254
patient information, 254–256
pharmaceutical drugs, 256
Public Health Databases
(Georgia), 306
research, 257–258
WebMD, 86
WITHIN (Wisconsin), 307
workplace health and safety, 259
Health Resources and Services
Administration (HRSA), 177,
257–258
HealthComm KEY Database, 248

Heathrow Airport Flight Arrivals Information, 315–316
hemscott.NET (U.K.), 183
Hennepin County Library, Fugitive Fact File, 330
Heriot-Watt University Library, 111
Heritage Assets Exemption Database (U.K.), 191
Herringtown, 167
hierarchical graph structure, 20–21
High-energy Physics Conference Database, 362
Higher Education Databases, 211
Higher Education Organizations, Directory of, 210
Historic Federal Buildings, U.S., 265
Historical Atlas of Canada Online Learning Project, 268
Historical Campaign Finance Data (Vermont), 306
Historical Census Data Browser, U.S., 266
Historical Incident Reports (Oil Spills/Chemical Accidents), 358
Historical Significant Events Imagery Database (HSEI), 367
History and Politics Out Loud (HPOL), 264
history resources. *See also* genealogy
    British manuscript sources, 154–155
    Cambridge University, 39
    documents, 99
    examples, 261–270
    images, 99
    medicine, 246
    Medieval Feminist Index, 375–376
    stock quotes, 99, 115–117
History Resources, World History, 267–270
HIV/AIDS, 243–244
Hoagy Carmichael Collection, The, 222
Holocaust Memorial Museum Archive and Collection Search (U.S.), 269–270
Home Price Check, 194
HomeCare/Hospice Agency Locator, 252

homosexuality, 320–321
Hoover's Business Profiles, 64
Hoover's Stock Screener, 183
hospice locator, 252
Hospital Records Database (U.K.), 252
Hospital Statistics (U.S.), 249
HotBot, 57–58, 112
hotel and properties database, 180
Hotel-Motel Master List, 340
hotelguide.Com, 340
Hotlinks, 113
House Floor Proceedings, Current, 313
Housing And Urban Development Environmental Maps (E-Maps), 357
Houston Real-Time Traffic Map, 316
How Far Is It?, 337
How Much Is That?, 174
HSTAT (Health Care Decisionmaking), 250
HTML (HyperText Markup Language)
    communications and, 18
    creation of, 11
    direct vs. indirect URLs, 79–81
    forms, 64–65
HTTP (HyperText Transfer Protocol), 11
HUD Homes for Sale, 193
HUDOC, 275
Human Resources Canada, 174–175
human resources, O*Net, 186–187
humanities, Cambridge University, 39
HyperCard, 10
hypertext
    definition, 2
    directory use of, 22
    search engines and, 62–63
    Xanadu and, 10
    Xerox implementation, 10
HyperText Markup Language (HTML), 11, 62
hypertext query languages, 132
HyperText Transfer Protocol (HTTP), 11

I

IBM, 29, 72, 132, 202
IDEA (Electronic Directory of European Institutions), 233

Idealab, 15
Idealist, 191
IFLA (Directory of National Union
    Catalogs), 160–161
IIE (Institute of International
    Education) passports, 211
images. *See also* non-text content
    ALT 10, 58
    Art Gallery holdings, 103
    graphical Web browsers, 11
    health information, 246
    historical, 99
    online, 122–123
    retrieval, 130
    Smithsonian Database, 162
Images from the History of Medicine,
    246
Images of African-Americans to 19th-
    century, 263
imports, Canada, 195
Imports/Exports History, U.S., 170
In-Depth Analysis of Revenues
    (Illinois), 307
Inc. 500 Database, 167
INDEV (India Development
    Information Network)
    Databases, 373
indexers
    citations, 67
    non-text formats, 58–59
    search engine, 26, 29–30
    timeliness of, 31
indexes, search engine, 13–16, 19, 21
indexing
    associative, 9–10
    early search engines, 13–16
India Development Information
    Network, 373
Industry Standard "Net Deals"
    Database, 167
Inflation Calculators, 173–174
Infonation (U.N.), 238
INFOQUICK (Australia), 286
information brokers, 125, 295
information services, 104
Information Week Archive, 202
INFORMS (Institute for Operations
    Research and the
    Management Sciences), 180
Inforoute (U.K.), 230

Infoseek, 16
InfoSpace, 97, 122, 297–298
INFOTERRA, 358
INFOTRIEVE, 160
Initial Public Offerings (IPOs), 184
injuries, mortality data, 251
Inktomi, 23, 66
Inmate Information Center (Los
    Angeles County), 305
Inmate Population Information
    Search (New York), 305
Inmate Search (Illinois), 305
InsiderScores.com, 183
Installment Loan Calculator, 190
Institute for Operations Research and
    the Management Sciences
    (INFORMS), 180
Insurance Company Complaints
    Finder, 180
insurance industry, A.M. Best ratings,
    178
INTAL (Institute for the integration of
    Latin America and the
    Caribbean) External Trade
    Database, 174
Integrated Digital Archive of Los
    Angeles (IDA-LA), 159
Integrated Economic Information
    System, 346
Integrated Postsecondary Education
    Data System Peer Analysis
    System, 209
Intellectual Property, 276–278
intellectual property resources,
    84–85, 276–278
Intelliseek, ProFusion, 45, 137
Inter-American Development Bank
    Economic and Social
    Database, 174
Inter-Play, 220
Interactive Volcano Map, 353
interest rates, 190
Internal Revenue Service (IRS)
    Business Master File, 191
    1040.com, 231
    Database of Tax-Exempt
        Organizations, 191, 192
    Section 527 Notice Search for, 302
International Atomic Energy Agency
    (IAEA), 354–355

International Bibliographic
    Information on Dietary
    Supplements (IBIDS), 253
International Boundary News
    Database, 237
International Classification of
    Functioning, Disability, and
    Health, 250
International Digest of Health
    Legislation, 248
International Directory of
    Organizations in Holocaust
    Education, Remembrance
    and Research, 270
International Directory of Testing
    Laboratories (ASTM), 364
International Federation of Library
    Associations and Institutions
    (IFLA), 160–161
International Film and Video
    Festivals, The Directory of,
    219
International Herald Tribune Search,
    286
International Labor Organization
    Bureau of Statistics, 174
International Labor Organization
    Term Database, 326
International Monetary Fund, Global
    Banking Law Database, 280
International Plant Names Index, 346
International Relations and Security
    Network (ISN), FIRST data-
    base, 237
International Salary Calculator, 186
International Telecommunications
    Union Terminology
    Database, 326
International Tennis Federation
    Players Database, 338
International Trade Commission
    Interactive Tariff and Trade
    DataWeb, U.S., 195–196
International Trademark Association
    (INTA), 84–85
International Weather Conditions,
    317
Internet
    Invisible Web, 56–61, 95–96,
        135–137, 138–142
    network protocol, 17
    origins, 2–3
    protocols, 7, 68–69
    public access points, 203
    research, 110
    service providers, 203
    visible Web and, 1–16
    Web and, 7
Internet Anagram Server, 218
Internet Archives Database at McGill
    University, 5
Internet Grateful Med, 250
Internet information resources,
    203–205
Internet Intelligence Index, 39–40
Internet Movie Database, (IMDB),
    220
Internet protocols, 7, 68–69
Internet Public Library Online Text
    Collection, 159
Internet Resources Newsletter, 111
Internet Service Providers (ISPs), 203
Internet Traffic Reports, 203
Interpol Most Wanted, 273
inverted index structures, 20–21
investment information resources,
    123–124, 182–185
Investment Resources, 163–197
invisibility
    types of, 70–75
    visibility and, 77–90
Invisible Web
    definition, 56–61
    directory FAQs, 138–142
    pathfinders, 135–137
    top 10 concepts, 142–143
    when to use, 95–96
Invisible-Web.net, 79, 142
InvisibleWeb.com, 136
IP delivery, 68–69
IPO SuperSearch, 184
IPO Underwriter Database, 184
Is My Bank Insured?, 175
ISA Growth Calculator (U.K.), 190
ISBN Publishers' Directory (Canada),
    322–323
ISIS (International Species
    Information Systems), 346
Islamic Countries, Statistics
    (SESRTCIC), 379

ISPs.com, 203
ITA Software, 339

J

J-Track 3-D Satellite Locator, 314
Jade (MEDLINE Update Service), 250
Jake (Jointly Administered
    Knowledge Environment),
    331
James, Henry, correspondence, 268
Jane's Defence Glossary, 326
Japan, 149, 185, 230
javascript in URLs, 80
Jerry's Guide to the Internet, 15
Jewish studies, 379
Job Bank Canada, 186
job information resources, 100–101,
    185–187
Jones, Joel, 12
Jones, Rhett "Jonzy," 7
Jourlit/Bookrev database, 377
Journal Locator in the Psychology
    and Social Sciences, The,
    377
journals, resources, 331–332, 377
Journeys Made Simple, 340
Judges of the United States Courts,
    296
Judicial Sector Indicators, World
    Bank, 275–276
Jughead, 6–7
JustQuotes.Com, 124, 184

K

Kahle, Brewster, 8
Kejin, 49
Kelly Blue Book, 324
keywords
    definition, 6
    metadata and, 129
    metasearch engines and, 46
    metatag source codes and, 68–69
    search engines and, 19
    searching with, 19
Kime's International Law Directory,
    272
KnowX, 104, 303
Koll, Matthew, 34
Kompass, 167
KOSIMO, 236–237

Kyoto National Museum Online
    Database (Japan), 149

L

labor law, NATLEX, 281
labor statistics, 173, 174
Laborsta, 174
lag time, crawlers, 33
lakes, 360
Land Records (Alaska), 307
Land Registry Residential Price
    Report (U.K.), 194
Landmark Project, The, 214
Language of the Food Industry:
    Glossary of Supermarket
    Terms, 327–328
Las Vegas Show and Event Calendar,
    197
Latin America, 174, 237, 376
Law.Com Law Dictionary, 276
LawCrawler, 41
Lawrence, Steve, 71
League of Nations Digitization
    Project, 270
Legacy.Com Newspaper Obituary
    Search, 286
legal information resources, 271–282
    codes, 278–282
    crime and criminals, 273
    decisions, 273–274
    directories, 272–273
    directory of judges, 296
    documents and records, 274
    general, 274–276
    health legislation, 248
    HSE register of prosecutions
        (U.K.), 254
    intellectual property, 276–278
    LawCrawler, 41
    laws, 278–282
    treaties, 278–282
legislative information resources, 233
Lehrer, Jim, 288
Leita, Carole, 110
LEONARDO (Linda Hall Library
    Online Catalog), 156
lesbigay resources, 320–321
Lewis and Clark Journals Database,
    264
Lexical FreeNet, 326–327

LexisNexis, 104
LexisNexis Source Locator, 332
LibDex, 161
Librarians' Index to the Internet (LII),
    110, 136
Librarians Yellow Pages, 332–333
libraries
    catalogs, 98–99
    SearchEdu.Com, 42
Library and Information Science
    Dictionary and Glossary, 327
Library Catalogs, 160–162
Library of Congress
    American Memory Collection, 262
    American Memory Project, 99
    American political prints, 148
    Copyright Office Records, 278
    Online Catalog, 156
    Web sites, 78, 86–89
library/online searching resources,
    332–333
Licensed Child Care Facilities
    (Indiana), 307
Licklider, J.C.R., 2
Lincoln, Abraham, 262, 265
Linda Hall Library Online Catalog
    (LEONARDO), 156
linguistic information resources, 39
links
    broken, 50, 54, 72
    browsing, 19
    hypertext, 2
    outbound, 108
    search engine coverage, 34
listing fees, 25–26
literary resources, 39, 248
Literature, Arts, and Medicine
    Database, 248
Literature of the Non-profit Sector,
    192
Lobbyist Activity Reports (Texas),
    307–308
lobbyist regulations, U.S. Congress,
    237–238
Lobbyist Search Canada, 237–238
Lobbyists Lists (Florida), 308
Lobbyists Public Registry (Ontario),
    308
Lobbyists Spending on Georgia
    Lawmakers, 307–308

Local Harvest, 328
logical operators, Boolean, 6
London Stock Exchange Listed
    Company Directory, 185
London Theatre Guide, 224
London Times, 89
London Transport System, 340
LookSmart, 22–26
lookup services, 187–188
Los Angeles Times, 89–90, 287
lotteries (U.K.), 236
Lotus Knowledge Base, 201
Lycos, 15, 112
Lycos Company Online, 165

M

Macintosh HyperCard, 10
magazines, full text, 105
Mailbox and Packing Store Database,
    334
mailing lists, 7
Major League Baseball Player Search,
    339
Major Malls (DMM), Directory of, 193
Making of America (MOA) Project,
    264–265
Makulowich, John, 12
malls, directory of, 193
mammography, certified centers, 252
Man and the Biosphere Species
    Database, 346–347
Manufacturer and User Facility
    Device Experience Database
    (MAUDE), 254
MapBlast, 97, 337
Maporama, 337
Mapquest, 97
maps, 40, 97, 316, 335–337, 357
Maptech Map Server, 337
Marcus Garvey and UNIA Papers, 265
Marin Institute for the Prevention of
    Alcohol and Other Drug
    Problems, 243
Marine Recreational Fisheries
    Statistics Survey Database,
    172
Marine Safety Information System
    (MSIS), U.S.C.G., 386
Marines Body Fat Calculator, U.S.,
    256

maritime information resources, 386–387

marketing information resources, 188–189

Mark's Online Domain Names Search, 203

MARNA (Maritime Nautical) Database, 269

Marriage and Divorce Verification (Colorado), 308

Marriage Inquiry System (Clark County, NV/Las Vegas), 308

Martindale-Hubbel Lawyer Locator, 272–273

Martindale's Calculators Online Center, 323

MasterCard/Maestro/Cirrus ATM Locator, 335

Material Safety Data Sheets (MSDS), 355–356

mathematics information resources, 208, 362. *See also* statistics

Mathline, 208

MAUDE (Manufacturer and User Facility Device Experience), 254

Mauldin, Michael, 15

Mayo Clinic, 254–255

Mayors at a Glance Database, 234

McAfee Virus Information Library, 201

McAfee World Virus Map, 201

McBryan, Oliver, 15

McCahill, Mark, 5–6

McGill University, 4–5

Media/Materials Clearinghouse (M/MC), 246

medical information resources, 241–259. *See also* health information resources

Medicare Health Plan Compare, 255

Medieval Feminist Index, 375–376

MEDLINE, update services, 250

meeting planning, 180

MEMEX, 9–10

mental health policy, PIE database, 244

Mental Health Services Research Database, 244

Merriam Webster's Collegiate Dictionary, 99

Merriam-Webster Dictionary and Thesaurus, 326

MESA (MetaE-mailSearchAgent), 298

Meta-List.net, 204

meta tags
cloaking, 68–69
no index, 63, 73, 90

MetaCrawler, 16, 44–45

metadata, 62, 129

metasearch engines, 16, 43, 44–46

meteorology information resources, 367–368

Metropolitan Museum Of Art Online Collection, 149

Microsoft, 10, 201, 202

Microsoft's Design Gallery Live, 330

military. *See* armed services

Military Images Photo Library, 377

Mineral Resources Online Spatial Data, 352

minimum alternative (ALT) text, 58

Mining Safety and Health Research, 259

Minnesota Magazine Index (MNMag), 157

Minority Online Information Service (Molis), 235

mirror sites, 78–79

Mission and Spacecraft Library, The, 366

MNMAG (Minnesota Magazine Index), 157

Model Editions Partnership, The, 265

money management, Nelsons rankings, 185

Monster.Com, 186

Monthly Energy Review Database, 354

Moon Phases Calculator, 365

Moreover, 286

Morningstar Fund Selector, 183

Mosaic, 11

motor carriers, 384

Movie Review Query Engine, 220

MovieFone, 220

movies, 219–221

MP Lookup (Canada), 235

MPnetwork (U.K.), 235

MSN fall-through search results, 23

Mud Café Digital Tradition Folk Song Database, The, 222

multimedia, 130. *See also* non-text content
Multiyear Interactive Computer Almanac (MICA) Web Version, 366–367
Municipal Code Online, 280
Municipal Water Use Database (Canada), 359
Museum Locator (Museum Research Board), 334
Music Education Search System, 214
music information resources, 221–225
Musica, 222–223
Mutopia, 223
mutual funds, 183

N

NADAGuides.com, 324
NAICS (North American Industry Classification System), 182
NAIL (National Archival Information Locator), 157
Napoleon Image Database, 6 8
Narita Flight Information, 316
NASA
    Earth from Space, 366
    Image eXchange, 366
    Real-Time Data, 314–315
    Technical Reports Server, 364
    TechTracS/TechFinder, 193
NASDAQ, 184
National Academy Press, 159
National Adoption Directory, 298
National Adoption Information Clearinghouse, 298
National Aeronautics and Space Administration. *See* NASA
National Agriculture Statistics Service Published Estimates Database, 171
National Airspace System Status, 316
National Archeological Database — Reports, 370–371
National Archival Information Locator (NAIL), 157
National Archives and Records Administration (NARA), 157
National Archives of Canada (ArchiviaNet), 157

National Association of Counties, 228
National Association of Securities Dealers (NSAD) Public Disclosure Database, 184–185
National Atlas of Canada, 338
National Atlas of the United States, 337–338
National Center for Bilingual Education (NCBE), 215
National Center for Charitable Statistics Form 990 Search, 191
National Center for Education Statistics, 209, 216
National Childcare Information Center (NCCIC) database, 208
National Climatic Data Center Storm Events, 368
National Compensation Survey, 187
National Credit Union Administration, 176
National Criminal Justice Reference Service, 281
National Earthquake Database Canada, 351
National Environmental Directory, 359
National Expertise Index (Canada), 296
National Fair Housing Case Database, 281
National Fire Incident Reporting System, 176
National Gallery of Art (London), 149–150
National Gallery of Art (Washington D.C.), 122–123, 150
National Geographic Publications Database, 157
National Geographic Society Map Machine, 338
National Guidelines Clearinghouse (NGC), 250
National Health Service (NHS)
    local health services, 249
    NRR, 258
    pharmacy database, 249
National Highway Traffic Safety Administration (NHTSA)
    recall information, 324

National Historic Landmarks Database, 265
National Hospice & Palliative Care Organization Database, 252
National Income and Product Accounts (NIPA) Tables, 171
National Institute for Occupational Safety and Health (NIOSH), Mining Safety and Health Research, 259
National Institute of Science and Technology (NIST) WebBook, 349
National Institute on Alcohol Abuse and Alcoholism (NIAAA), 242–243
National Institutes of Health (NIH), 257–258
National Labour Market Information System (Canada), 174–175
National Library of Canada
    Canadian Music Periodical Index, 100
    Catalogue (resAnet), 157–158
    Union Catalogue, 158
National Library of Medicine (NLM)
    ChemIDplus, 349
    ClinicalTrials.gov, 257
    DIRLINE, 249
    Grateful Med, 250
    MEDLINE, update services, 250
    POPLINE, 372
    toll-free hotlines, health information, 255
National Lottery Award Search (U.K.), 236
National Marine Fisheries Service (NMFS) Fishing Statistics, 171–172
National Museum Of Art Digitized Collection, 150
National Organization for Rare Disorders, 244–245
National Park Service, landmarks database, 265
National Park Service, U.S., 341
National Pollutant Release Inventory (Canada), 359
National Portrait Gallery and Research Records Search (U.K.), 150
National Press Club Directory of New Sources, 296
National Public Radio (NPR) Archive Search, 284
National Public School/District Locator, 211
National Recreation Database (Canada), 374
National Register Information System, 265–266
National Register of Health Service Providers in Psychology (U.S.), 296
National Research Council Expertise Database (Canada), 296
National Research Register (NRR) (U.K.), 258
National Safety Council Defensive Driving Training Locator, 384
National Science Foundation, WebCASPAR, 216
National Science Foundation (NSF), U.S., 12
National Science Foundation (NSF) Awards Search, 363
National Sound Archive Catalogue, 155
National Teacher Recruitment Clearinghouse Search, 215
National Technical Information Service Electronic Catalog, 158
National Transportation Safety Board (NTSB), aviation accidents, 382–383
National Union Catalogs (IFLA), Directory of, 160–161
National Water Information System, 312
Native American Consultation Database, 230–231
NATLEX, 281
NatureServe, 359
Navaid Information, 382
navigation
    the early Web, 12–13
    hubs, 82–83
    sites, 78–79
Navy personnel, 300

NBCi, 22
NCAA Statistics, 339
NCSTRL (Networked Computer Science Technical Reference Library), 202
Near Mid-Air Collision System, 383
NEC research Institute, 67
Nelson, Ted, 10
Nelson-Atkins Museum of Art, 156
Nelson's World's Best Money Managers Rankings, 185
NetLingo.com, 204
Net2One, 287
Network Solutions, 204
Network Solutions Domain Name Registration Database, 166
Network World Fusion, 201–202
Networked Computer Science Technical Reference Library (NCSTRL), 202
New Electronic Titles (GPO), 232
New Medicines in Development Database, 97, 258
New York City Department of Health Restaurant Inspection Database, 308
New York Daily News, 287
New York Green Book, 188
New York Public Library Finding Aids, 158
New York Review of Books Archive, 323
New York Times Book Reviews, 323
New Zealand Digital Library, The, 161
Newberry Library Online Catalog, 158
news resources, 283–289
Newsfilm Library, 288
newsgroups, 7
NewsHour with Jim Lehrer Video Search, 288
newsletters online, 204
Newslibrary.Com, 105, 287
newspapers, 105, 124–125, 155, 284, 286. *See also* specific newspapers
Newspapers Online, 284
NewsTracker, 287
NEXRAD Doppler radar images, 102
NHS (National Health Service) Economic Evaluation Database, 248–249
NISSO Sexology Database, 374–375
"no index" meta tags, 73, 90
Nobel e-museum, 100
Nobel Prize Laureate Search, 322
Nobel prizes, 100
non-profit resources, 191–192
non-text content, 58–59. *See also* audio; images; multimedia; video
  coverage, 53–54
  crawlers and, 66
  indexing, 35
  Invisible Web searches, 143
  search engines and, 57–58
NoodleBib (Bibliography Creator), 333
Noodlequest (Search Tool Selection Aid), 333
North American Industry Classification System (NAICS), 182
  SIC Correspondence Tables, 330
Northern Light
  maps, 97
  News Search, 287
  Special Collection, 47, 104
Northwest Territories Geographic Names Database, 336
NoteCards (Xerox), 10
Notess, Greg, 34
notifiable diseases, 243
Nova Scotia, Registry of Joint Stock Companies Database, 166
NSERC Awards Search Engine Canada, 363
NTIS (National Technical Information Service) Electronic Catalog, 158
Nua Internet Surveys, 204
Nuclear Explosions Database, 354
Nuclear Power Plant Databases, 354
Nunavut Environmental Database (NED), 351
Nursing Home Compare, 252–253
Nutrition Analysis Tool 2.0, 253
nutritional information resources, 253–254

O

obituaries, newspaper, 286
Occupational License Search
    (Alaska), 308
Occupational Safety and Health
    Administration (OSHA)
    Accident Investigation Search,
    259
    SIC search, 181–182, 330
Ocean Information Center, Research
    Ship Schedules, 364
oceanography information resources,
    362–364
Ockerbloom, John Mark, 159
OCLC Participating Institution
    Search, 332
Oddens, Roelof P., 40
Odden's Bookmarks, 40
Office of Assistant Secretary of Health
    (OASH), 257–258
*Official Netscape Guide to Internet
    Research* (Calishain), 110
oil, crude, 358
Oil Spills, Historical Incident Reports,
    358
Olympic Winners Database, 322
192.Com (U.K.), 187, 297
OneLook, 99
O*Net, 186–187
Online Archive of California (OAC),
    158–159
Online Books Page, The, 159
Online Calendar of Henry James'
    Letters, 268
Online Distance Education Catalog,
    212
Online Public Access Catalogs
    (OPACs), 98
Online Telephone Book Directory,
    188, 297
OnTerm (Canada), 327
opaque Web, 70–72
Open Directory Project (ODP), 22–26,
    25
OperaBase, 223
Oran's Law Dictionary, 276
O'Reilly & Associates, 12
Organization for Nuclear Research
    (CERN), 9
orphan drugs, 244–245

Oscars, recipients of, 100
Oscars Database, 321
OSHA (Occupational Safety and
    Health Administration), 182
Oxford Companion to Wine, 328

P

Pacific Film Archive, 219
package tracking, 314
PackTrack, 314
page capture utilities, 112
Papers of Thomas A. Edison, 266
paperwork reduction legislation, 59
Park Search (Worldwide), 341
Parline database, 230
Partial Immersion Language
    Programs in U.S. Schools,
    Directory of, 210
PASLMIDS (Labor Market Data)
    (Pennsylvania), 308–309
passwords, 63, 73
Patent and Trademark Office, U.S.
    patents databases, 277–278
    registered attorneys and agents,
    272
Patent Attorneys and Agents
    Registered to Practice before
    PTO, 272
Patent Office, U.S., 98
patents
    Australian, 277
    Canadian, 277
    Delphion Intellectual Property
    Network, 84–85
    DNA, 247
    esp@cenet (European Patent
    Office), 277
    European attorneys database, 272
    information on, 117–118
    Invisible Web access, 98
    United Kingdom, 278
    U.S., 277
Patents and Trademarks Depository
    Library Program, 118
Patents Databases, U.S., 277–278
PATH database, 385
pathfinders, Invisible Web, 135–137
patient information, 254–256
Pavnet (Partnership against Violence)
    Research Database, 375

Payment Systems Research Database, 172

PDF formats, 58–59, 67, 74–75

PDQ (Physician Data Query) comprehensive cancer database, 244

PDS Planetary Image Atlas, 315

Peabody awards, recipients of, 100

Peanut Literature Database, 348

peer-to-peer file sharing systems, 7

Penn World Tables, 175

Pension Benefit Guaranty Corporation (PBGC) Pension Search, 190

pension resources, 189

people, searching for, 291–300

PeopleTracker, 293

periodicals, resources, 331–332

Perseus Digital Library, 269

personal finance information resources, 190

Pesticide Database, 359

Pesticide Database (Oklahoma), 309

Pesticide Products Database (USEPA/OPP), 360

Peterson's GradChannel, 102

Peterson's Graduate School Databases, 212

Peterson's Law School Search, 212

Peterson's Lifelong Learning Resources, 212

Peterson's MBA Concentration Search, 212

pharmaceutical drugs, 256

pharmacy database, NHS, 249

Philadelphia Historical Digital Image Library (PHDIL), 266

Philanthropic Studies Index (PSI), 191–192

philanthropy information resources, 101, 190–192

philosophy information resources, 39

Photo Bank — UNESCO, 373

Photoshare, 246

physical fitness information resources, 256

physics information resources, 362

Picture Australia, 269

PIE (Policy Information Exchange) Database, Mental Health Policy, 244

pilots, certified, 295

Pinkerton, Brian, 14

planetary bodies, 315

plant names, 346

Plants Database, 348

Playbill Theatre Database, 224, 225

plays, 220

poetry, American Verse Project, 262

point and click interfaces, 18

political conflicts, KOSIMO database, 236–237

Political Database of the Americas, 237

political information resources, 236–238. See also government information resources
  American political prints, 148
  campaign financing information, 102
  Federal Election Commission, 302
  History and Politics Out Loud, 264
  registered political parties in Canada, 229
  Washington Post Poll Database, 375

Politicalinformation.Com, 42

Pollstar Concert Database, 223

pollution, air, 312

POPINFORM, 372

POPLINE (Grateful Med), 371–372

Population Estimates by Age, Sex, and Race, 371

Population Index, 371–372

Port Facilities Database, 385

Port State Information eXchange (PSIX) and, 386

PORTS (Physical Oceanographic Real-time System), 313

Post Office Locator, U.S., 335

postal codes, 101, 121–122, 235, 335. See also ZIP codes

Postal Inspection Service Office Locator, U.S., 335

Postcode Plants Database (U.K.), 348

PostScript formats, 58–59, 67, 74–75

POW/MIA Database, 300

Power Reactor Information System (PRIS), 354–355

practice guidelines, NGC, 250
precision
  the invisible Web, 96
  Invisible Web content, 142–143
  recall and, 94–95
PrePRINT Network, 361
prestige, targeted directories, 40
Price Waterhouse Coopers Money
  Tree Survey, 167–168
Prince Edward Islands Places
  Database, 336
prisons, inmate information, 305
privacy
  concerns about, 104
  guidelines, 29
Private School Locator, U.S., 211
private sector, Internet and, 12
private Web, 73
PRO-NET, 177
Prodigy, 47
product catalogs, 103
Profile (Architectural Firms
  Database), 181
ProFusion, 45, 137
Properties of Crude Oils and Oil
  Products, 358
Property Assessment Databases, 303
proprietary databases, 104, 124–125
proximity operators, 30
PsychCrawler, 42
psychoanalysis, 377
psychological journals, 377
psychologists, 296
psychology information resources,
  42, 296, 377
ptcalculator.pl, 256
PubCrawler (MEDLINE Update
  Service), 250
public company filings, 96–97
Public Diplomacy Query (PDQ)
  (U.S.), 232–233
Public Health Databases (Georgia),
  306
Public Health Image Library(PHIL),
  246
Public Library Comparison Tool, 334
Public Library Locator, 334
Public Records Office/National
  Archives Online Catalogue, 159
public records resources, 104,

  301–309, 302–303
Public School District Finance Peer
  Search, 213
public service providers (U.K.), 230
Publications of the United States
  Geological Survey, 352
PublicRadioFan.com, 314
publishers, directory (Canada),
  322–323
Publishers Weekly Bestseller Lists, 323
publishing industry, circulation data,
  179
Publist, 332
PubMed/MEDLINE, 250–251
PubSCIENCE, 361
Puget Sound Region Traffic Map, 316
Pulitzer Prize Database, 322
PWGSC, contracts awarded, 177–178

Q

Qixo, 339
Quakeline, 351
quality control
  duplicates, 28
  search engines, 33
  smarter crawlers, 128
  spam, 28
  Vortals, 44
  Web directories, 22–23, 24–25
Quaran Browser, 379
QueerAmerica, 320
queries
  Boolean operators, 6
  database material, 60–61
  keyword-based, 29–30
  metasearch engines structure, 46
query processors, 26, 30–32
question mark (?) symbol, 65, 80–81
Quicken, 60, 183
QuickFacts, state and county, 239
Quirk's Researcher Sourcebook, 189

R

RAAM-Register of Australian Archives
  and Manuscripts, 160
radio
  call sign lookup, 297
  FCC database, 182
  NPR Archive Search, 284
  PublicRadioFan.com, 314

railroad industry, by state, 181
railroad information resources, 181, 340, 387
RAMBI (Index of Articles on Jewish Studies), 379
Rand McNally Downloadable U.S. State and Thematic Maps, 338
Rand McNally U.S. Road Construction Database, 338
RAPID (European Union News), 233
Rare Disease Database, 244–245
RateNet, 190
RDF (Resource Description Framework), 129
Reading Pathfinder Database, 209
real estate information resources, 193–194, 229, 281, 303, 307, 320
Real Estate Investment Trusts (REIT) Directory, 194
Real Estate Retrieval System (FDIC), 194
Real-Time 911 Dispatches (Seattle Fire Department), 313
Real-Time Airport Status, U.S., 316
real-time data, 60–61, 66–67, 102–103
real-time information resources, 311–317
Real-Time Streamflow Water Data, USGS, 312
Realtor.Com, 194
recall
    CPSC, 169
    precision and, 94–95
recalls, products, 169, 324
ReCap Biotech Alliance Database, 179
Recent Advances in Manufacturing (RAM), 181
Recent Home Sale Purchase Prices, 194
Recent Marine Data, National Buoy Data Center, 313
recipes, 328
RECON-Regional Economic Conditions, 100, 172
Recording Industry Association of America (RIAA), 223

Records and Information Management System (RIMS), 274
Records Search: National Archives of Australia, 159–160
Recreational Opportunities on Federal Lands, 341
Red Cross Chapter Locator, 334
Red Herring Company and Persons Search, 168
redherring.com, 167, 168
Redlist (Threatened Species Database), 347
REEF Database (Marine Species Data), 362
ReefBase, 357
reference resources, 319–341
REFORGEN (forestry), 348
Refugee Caselaw Site, 282
Regional Economic Data, U.S., 172
Regional Economic Forecasts, 170
Regional Economic Information System, 170
Regional Gasoline Costs, U.S., 323
Registered Aircraft Databases, 383
Registered Identification Number Database, 181
Registry of Joint Stock Companies Database (NS), 166
REIT (Real Estate Investment Trusts) Directory, 194
relevance ranking
    calculations, 32
    definition, 21
    Invisible Web content, 142–143
    manipulation of, 112
    metasearch engines, 46
religion information resources, 378–379
Religious Centers, Directory of, 378–379
Remote Sensing Glossary, 352
reputation, directory resources, 141
resAnet, National Library of Canada, 157–158
Research Index search engine, 74
research resources, 193
Research Ship Schedules, 364
Research Ship Specifications, 364
ResearchBuzz, 110

ResearchIndex, 67, 104, 202
resources
    collection goals, 153
    customized collection of, 111, 113
    discovery of, 78–79
Restaurant Health Inspection
        Reporting System (Denver),
        308
Restaurant Inspection Search
        (Boston), 308
results
    maximum viewable, 72
    speed of, 35
results-output format, 30
Reverse Telephone and Address
        Lookup, 188
Reverse Telephone Directory, 188,
        298
RhymeZone, 327
RIAA Gold and Platinum Database,
        223
Rice Bibliography, 348
Right-to-Know Network, 357
River Statistics, U.S., 385
rivers, 385
Roberts, Larry, 2
robots, 26
Robots Exclusion Protocol, 53, 72–73,
        73, 89–90
robots.txt, 73
Roll Call U.S. Congress Directory, 234
Roller Coaster Database, 218
Rolling Stone Album Review search,
        222
Rolling Stone Cover Art Archive, 150
RRSP Calculator (Canada), 190

S

Safer (U.S. Motor-Carrier
        Information), 384
salary trends, 186–187
salary.com, 187
Sanitation Inspections of International
        Cruise Ships, 255
satellites, real-time resources,
        314–315
SavvySearch, 16
SCALEplus, Australia, 279
Schipol Airport Flight Information,
        316

Scholarly and Professional
        E-Conferences, Directory of,
        329
scholarly journals, access to, 104
Scholarly Societies Project, 321
scholarship resources, 212–213
scholarship Search (U.K.), 213
School Data (Dataquest) (California),
        309
schools. *See also* academic informa-
        tion resources; education
        information resources; higher
        education; universities
    code search, 213
    private, 211
    public, 211
    SearchEdu.Com, 42
    selection called, 102
sciBASE, 361
science information resources,
        343–368. *See also* specific sci-
        entific disciplines
Science Policy Data (U.K.), 361–362
Scientific American Frontiers Video
        Archive, 289
Scientific and Technical Information
        Network (STINET) (DOD),
        365
Scientific Research in Yellowstone
        National Park, 365
Scout Report, 109–110, 162
Search Engine Guide, 205
Search Engine Showdown, 34
search engines
    basis of, 19
    coverage issues, 34
    data-centric, 128
    directories and, 36
    dynamically generated data and,
        65–66
    early examples, 13–16
    format negotiation, 68
    functioning of, 26–36
    and Hypertext, 62–63
    indexes, 20–21, 30, 53–54
    Invisible Web and, 62–70, 74–75,
        105–109, 142–143
    issues with, 32–36
    private Web and, 73
    proprietary Web and, 73–74

relevance, 94–95
resource use, 28–29, 92–93
similarity of, 27
timeliness, 31
Search Systems Public Records
    Databases, 303
Search.Com, News Search, 286
SearchEdu.com, 42
searching. *See also* search engines
    browser agents, 50
    browsing and, 18–22
    control of input, 93–94
    coverage by indexes, 53–54
    early tools, 3–8
    metasearch engines, 16
    number of viewable results, 72
    relevance scores, 21
    speed vs. thorough results, 35
    timeline of technologies, 15
    tools, 37–54, 40–43, 95–96
    visible Web, 17–36
SearchMil.Com, 42
Seattle Municipal Archives
    Photograph Collection, 266
Seattle Public Library, Municipal
    Code Online, 280
Sector Facility Indexing Project
    (SFIP), 359
Securities and Exchange Commission
    (SEC), 48, 96–97, 164, 165
SecuritySearch.net, 202
SEDAR (Public Company Filings)
    (Canada), 97, 168
Selectline (Market Research Firm
    Database) (U.K.), 189
service marks, 84–85
SESRTCIC, 379
SESTAT, 216
Sexology Database (NISSO), 374–375
SGML (Standard Generalized Markup
    Language), 11
shadow sites, 78–79
Shaw Guides, 212
sheet music, public domain, 223
SHIPDES (Ship Descriptions), 269
Shipping Data (Global Transport
    Analyzer), 385
ships. *See also* shipwrecks
    descriptions of, 269
    maritime information, 386–387

merchant, 386
    Research Ship Schedules, 364
    sanitation inspections, 255
shipwrecks
    Australian database, 263
    California database, 263
shockwave formats, 58, 74–75
shopping centers, 193
shopping information resources, 103
sign language, American, 325
Silicon Valley Companies Database,
    168
SIMBAD Astronomical Database, 367
SIRIS (Smithsonian Institution
    Research Information
    System), 162
sleep literature, 243
Sloane's Online Encyclopedia of
    Integer Sequences, 362
Slurp, 66
Small Business Association (SBA),
    171, 177, 193
Small Business Funding, 235
Smithsonian Image Database, 162
Smithsonian Institution Online
    Collections, 162
Smithsonian Institution Research
    Information System (SIRIS),
    162
Smithsonian Museum, 150
SOAR (Searchable Online Archive of
    Recipes), 328
social sciences information
    resources, 369–379
Social Security Administration (SSA),
    236
Social Security Death Index, 294
Software Centers Directory, 365
solar radiation, 353
Solar System Live, 314
Solar System Simulator, 367
Solicitors Online (U.K.), 272
Solvents Database (SOLV-DB), 350
Source, 47
Source Available in Dow Jones
    Interactive, 322
Space Command Satellite/Space
    Catalog, U. S., 367
space information resources,
    314–315, 365–367

Space Orbit 3-D Visualization Tool, 367
spam, 28, 33, 65, 69, 106
Special Libraries Association (SLA), 286
Species and Parks: Flora and Fauna in the U.S. National Parks, 348
Species at Risk Canada, 347
SpeechBot, 65, 284
Spencer Art Reference Library, 156
spider traps, 65–66, 74–75, 131
spiders. *See* crawlers; spider traps
SPIRLIB Antarctica, 351
S*P*I*R*O (Architecture Slide Library), 147
sports resources, 338–339
SPOT (Tennessee), 309
Standard Generalized Markup Language (SGML), 11
Standard Industrial Classification Search, 181–182, 330
Stanford University, 15
State Exports Database, U.S., 196
State Hermitage Museum Digital Collection (Russia), 150–151
State Medicaid Policy Search Application, 255
State Personal Income, 170
states, quick facts, 238–239
Statistical Profiles of Canadian Communities, 239
statistics
    campus security, 273
    educational, 215–216
    energy, 354
    Federal Justice, 274
    Genderstats, 375
    government, 238–239
    injuries, 251
    Islamic countries, 379
    NCAA, 339
    Universal Postal Union (UPU), 330–331
    U.S. hospitals, 249
stock market resources
    Canadian stock charts, 182
    Dow Jones averages, 182
    EDGAR Online, 48
    historical quotes, 183

real-time, 315
real-time quotes, 60
Stock Market Valuation Calculator, 185
stock quotes, 99, 115–117, 123–124, 315
valuation calculator, 185
Stock Market Valuation Calculator, 185
Stock Quotes, Real-Time, 315
stop words, 30
Streetmap.co.uk, 337
Strong Numbers, 169
STRUQL, 132
Student Planner Learning Opportunities Databank (Canada), 209
Student Planner Occupations Databank, 209
students, cost of living, 190
subject matter, familiarity with, 95
subscriptions, 46–48, 104
Substance Abuse and Mental Health Services, 257–258
Substance Abuse Treatment Facility Locator, 253
Subway Navigator, 340
Suffragists Oral History Project, 266
sun, 365
Supplemental Environmental Project (SEP) National Database, 360
Supreme Court of Canada Judgments, 274
Supreme Court Opinions, U. S., 273–274
Switchboard.com, 97

T

targeted crawlers, 143
targeted directories, 38–43
tariff resources, 194–196
Tariff Wizard (Canada), 195
Tax Exempt Organizations, U.S., 192
taxonomy, 346
TCP/IP hardware, 17
TECH-Net (SBA), 192–193
TechCalendar, 197
Technologies for Learning Database, 215
TechTracS/TechFinder (NASA), 193

Techweb Technology Encyclopedia, 204
Telecom Acronym Database, 326
telephone numbers, 97, 121–122,
    187–188, 297, 298
television, 182, 218–219, 285
Television News Archives: Evening
    News Abstracts, 287–288
Telnet, definition, 4
10 Downing Street News Search
    (U.K.), 231
1040.com, 231
10Kwizard.Com (Public Company
    Filings), 97, 164–165
tennis, 338
TerraServer, 352–353
text, search engine biases, 35
ThemeFinder, 223–224
THERMODEX (Thermochemical
    Data), 350
TheTrip.Com, 66, 119–120
Thinker ImageBase, 151
Thinking Machines
    WAIS, 8
THOMAS, 233
Thomas Food Industry Register, 169
Thomas Register of American
    Manufacturers, 85, 168–169
Thomas Register of European
    Manufacturers, 168–169
Thompson's Dialogue, 104
Tide and Current Predictor, 363
Tiger Mapping Service, 338
timeliness
    directory resources, 141
    frequency of crawl, 71–72
    of information, 108–109
    Invisible Web resources, 92–93,
        142–143
    keeping current, 109–111
    search engine indexers, 31
    targeted directories, 40
    Web directories, 25
Times, The, Archive Search (U.K.), 288
Tobacco Control Archives, 245
tobacco industry, 243, 245
Today's House Proceedings, 313
Tokyo Stock Exchange Listed
    Company Directory, 185
toll-free hotlines, health information,
    255

Tony Awards Database, 321
Topica Newsletter and Internet List
    Directory, 329
toponyms, 335–336
Toporama Canada, 337
Topozone, 337
Toronto Stock Exchange Listed
    Company Directory, 185
TotalNews, 286
Trade Balance (by country), U.S., 196
Trade Compliance Center, U.S., Trade
    Agreements Database,
    196–197
trade reports, U.S., 195
trade resources, 194–196
Trade Show Central, 180
trade show resources, 180, 196–197
Trade Summary (regional), U.S., 196
trademarks, 84–85, 98, 118
TradePort Trade Events Calendar,
    197
Traffic Calming Library, 384
Traffic Incident Information
    (California), 316
Trail Finder, 340
Train Arrival Information, Amtrak,
    316–317
Transborder Surface Freight Data,
    385
translation resources, 325–327
Translation Services Directory, 296
translation tools, 101
Transmission Control
    Protocol/Internet Protocol
    (TCP/IP), 3
Transplant Patient Data Source,
    UNOS, 256
transportation information
    resources, 315–317, 381–387.
    See also specific mode of
    transportation
travel information resources, 212,
    255. See also specific mode of
    travel
Travel Offices Worldwide Directory,
    340–341
travel resources, 339–341
treaties, 278–282
Tree Conservation Database, 360
TRIP Database, 251

TRIS (Transportation Research Information Service), 386
TRUSTe, 129
Tsunami Database, 363
21 North Main, 121, 154
Tyburski, Genie, 109

U

UBL Ultimate Band List, 224
UnclaimedPersons.com, 303
UnCover Web, 160
Underwriters Laboratories Certification Database, 324–325
Union List of Artists Names Browser (ULAN), 140
United Kingdom
   192.Com, 187
   Commonwealth War Graves Commission, 299
   Court Service Judgments Database, 279
   Current Controlled Trials, 257
   Good Practice Database, 231
   Heritage Assets Exemption Database, 191
   Inforoute, 230
   ISA Growth Calculator, 190
   Land Registry Residential Price Report, 194
   London Theatre Guides, 224
   market research firms, 189
   MP Lookup, 235
   National Lottery Award Search, 236
   National Statistics, 372
   NHS Economic Evaluation Database, 248–249
   Online Citizen Portal, 230
   Ordinance Survey Get-a-Map, 338
   Patent Search, 278
   Postcode Finder, 335
   Prime Minister's press releases, 231
   Register of Charities, 192
   Scholarship Search, 213
   searchable TV listings, 219
United Nations. See also specific agencies
   Daily Press Briefing Search, 233
   Days, Decades, Years Database, 330
   Food and Agriculture Organization (FAO), 345
   Index to Speeches, 233–234
   Infonation, 238
   INFOTERRA, 358
   Photo Banks — UNESCO, 373
   Population Fund, 278
   Voting Records, 233
United Network for Organ Sharing (UNOS), 256
United States, national atlas, 337–338
United States Navy Directory (X.500), 300
Universal Currency Converter, 324
Universal Postal Union (UPU) Statistics, 330–331
Universal Resource Identifiers. See URLs
universities. See also specific universities
   SearchEdu.Com, 42
   selection of, 102
University of California at Los Angeles (UCLA), 2
University of Colorado, 15
University of Durham, 237
University of Michigan, 262
University of Minnesota, 5–6
University of Stirling (U.K.), 15
University of Utah, 7
University of Virginia, 170
University of Waikato, 161
University of Washington, 16
URLs
   "?" In, 65
   broken links, 25
   capitalization, 69
   cloaking, 68–69
   direct vs. indirect, 79–81
   disconnected, 72
   disconnected pages, 57
   history of, 11
   indirect, 80
   information from, 108
   search engine addition of, 28, 31
   spam, 208
   testing of, 80–81
   Web ring databases, 52

U.S. News
scholarship search, 213
U.S. News and World Report
education databases, 211
U.S.A. Counties, 371
USAID Development Experience
System, 373–374
USEPA/OPP Pesticide Products
Database, 360
users, impact on results, 33, 35
USITC Tariff and Trade DataWeb, 196
UV Index, 368

V

validity, URL information, 108
value-added search services, 43,
46–48, 47–48
Van Gogh Museum Amsterdam, 103
Vehicle Emissions Guide, U.S., 323
vehicle price guides, 324
Vehicle Recalls Online Database
Canada, 324
VELMA (Virginia), 309
Venture Capital Deal Monitor, 168
Venture Capital Firm Database, 168
Venue Center, 180
Verbix, 327
Veronica, 6–7
vertical portals (Vortals), 43–44
VerticalMatter.com, 44
Vessel Query Registration System
(Canada), 387
veterans, 299
VIA Rail Canada Timetable, 340
Victoria and Albert Museum Images
Online (U.K.), 150
video. *See also* non-text content
ALT text, 58
festivals, 219
materials, 288–289
Mathline, 208
SpeechBot, 65
Video Distributors Database, 221
Vietnam, The Virtual Wall, 300
Viola, 11
violence information resources, 375
Virtual Wall, The (Vietnam Veterans
Memorial Wall), 300
viruses, computer, 201
Visa/Plus ATM Locator, 335

visibility, invisibility and, 77–90
Visit Your Parks, 341
Visitors Bureau Directory, 196
Vital Statistics Query System
(California), 309
Voice of America Pronunciation
Guide, 327
volcanos, 353
volunteers, Web directories, 24

W

wage trends, 186–187
WAIS (Wide Area Information
Servers), 5, 8
Wang, Jerry, 15
Washington Post, 287
Washington Post Poll Database, 375
water information resources, 312–313
Municipal Water Use Database,
359
oceanography information
resources, 362–363
rivers, 385
World Lakes Database, 360
weather information resources,
367–368
data, 102–103
real-time, 60, 317
Weatherbase, 341
Weatherplanner, 341
Weaving the Web (Berners-Lee), 8–9,
11
Web crawlers. *See* crawlers
Web directories. *See* directories
Web pages. *See* Web sites
Web Rings, 51–52
Web robots, 14–16
Web sites
content maintenance, 105
credibility, 105–109
disconnected, 57
duplicate copies, 78–79
early directories, 12–13
navigation vs. content, 78–79
proprietary, 73–74
search engine coverage, 34
use of, 11
Web Trax Flight Tracking, 315
WebCASPAR, 216
webCATS, 98–99

WebCrawler, 14
WebData.com, 137
Webmasters
    blocking crawlers by, 62–70
    cloaking, 68–69
    robots exclusion, 53–54
    spider traps, 65–66
    Web ring use, 52
WebMD, 86
Webopedia, 204
WebOQL, 132
WebRings, 43
WebSQL, 132
WED—World Email Directory, 298
Weekly Checklist Catalogue
    (Canadian government),
    234
West Legal Directory, 272–273
Western History Photos, 266–267
Westfall, Richard S., 292–293
WhatsGoingOn.com, 341
Whereis Street Atlas (Australia), 337
Wherewithal, 23
Who's Who in American Art, 142
Wildland Fire Support, 357
WILMA (Washington), 309
Windows, Microsoft, 10
Wine Spectator Restaurant Database,
    328
Winefiles.Org, 328
WIPO (World Intellectual Property
    Organization) Digital Library,
    278
WISDOM (Science Policy Data)
    (U.K.), 361–362
WISQARS (Web-Based Injury
    Statistics Query and
    Reporting System), 251
WITHIN (Wisconsin), 307
Women, Work, and Gender Database,
    375
Women in Politics Bibliographic
    Database, 238
Women's Right to Maternity
    Protections Database, 282
Wordsmyth, 326
Workopolis.Com (Canada), 186
World Aircraft Accident Summary
    (WAAS), 383–384

World Bank
    Economics of Tobacco Control
        Country Report Database,
        64
    Genderstats, 375
    Global Banking Law Database, 280
    Judicial Sector Indicators,
        275–276
World Biographical Index 7, The, 293
World Brands Database (Advertising
    Age), 169
World Chambers of Commerce
    Directory, 177
World Data Sheet, 372
World Health Organization (WHO),
    Cancer Mortality Databank,
    245
World Lakes Database, 360
World Register of Large Dams, 356
World War II Poster Collection, 270
World Wide Web
    description, 1
    the Internet and, 7
    on vs. via, 60
World Wide Web Wanderer, 14
World Wide Web Worm, 15
Worldwide School Weathernet, 317
Worldwide Volcano Database, 353
W3QL, 132
wrapper induction techniques, 131
Wright Investor's Services, 100, 183
Writers Digest Guidelines Database,
    331
WWW. See World Wide Web
WWW JumpStation, 15

X

Xanadu, 10
Xerox, 10
XML (Extensible Markup Language),
    129
xrefer, 331

Y

Yahoo!
    business to business marketplace,
        44
    direct URLs, 79
    function of, 22–26
    lopsided categories, 25

My Yahoo!, 60
    origins of, 15
Yale Law School, 263
Yellowstone National Park, 365
Yet Another Hierarchical Officious
    Oracle. *See* Yahoo!
Your Cancer Risk, 246
Youth at Risk Success Stories
    Database Canada, 374

Z

Z39.50, 8
Zagat Restaurant Surveys, 328
Zapper, 49–50
ZIP Code +4 Database, U.S., 335
ZIP codes, 121–122, 172, 188–189,
    335. *See also* postal codes
Zoo and Aquarium Directory, 347

More CyberAge Books from Information Today, Inc.

The Extreme Searcher's Guide to Web Search Engines
A Handbook for the Serious Searcher, 2nd Edition

By Randolph Hock
Foreword by Reva Basch

In this completely revised and expanded version of his award-winning book, the "extreme searcher," Randolph (Ran) Hock, digs even deeper, covering all the most popular Web search tools, plus a half-dozen of the newest and most exciting search engines to come down the pike. This is a practical, user-friendly guide supported by a regularly updated Web site.

2001/250 pp/softbound/ISBN 0-910965-47-1 $24.95

International Business Information on the Web
Searcher Magazine's Guide to Sites and Strategies for Global Business Research

By Sheri R. Lanza
Edited by Barbara Quint

Here is the first ready-reference for effective worldwide business research, written by experienced international business researcher Sheri R. Lanza and edited by *Searcher* Magazine's Barbara Quint. This book helps readers identify overseas buyers, find foreign suppliers, investigate potential partners and competitors, uncover international market research and industry analysis, and much more.

2001/380 pp/softbound/ISBN 0-910965-46-3 $29.95

Millennium Intelligence

Understanding and Conducting Competitive Intelligence in the Digital Age

By Jerry P. Miller and the Business Intelligence Braintrust

With contributions from 12 of the world's leading business intelligence practitioners, here is a tremendously informative and practical look at the CI process, how it is changing, and how it can be managed effectively in the Digital Age. Loaded with case studies, tips, and techniques.

2000/276 pp/softbound/ISBN 0-910965-28-5 $29.95

Internet Prophets

The Complete Guide to Enlightened E-Business Strategies

By Mary Diffley

Since the bursting of the dot.com balloon, companies are approaching e-business with a new wariness—and rightly so, according to author and entrepreneur Mary Diffley. In *Internet Prophets*, Diffley speaks directly to the skeptics, serving up straightforward advice that will help even the most technophobic executive do more business on the Web. This readable, easy-to-use handbook is the first to detail the costs of proven e-commerce strategies, matching successful techniques with budgetary considerations for companies of all types and sizes. Unlike other books, Internet Prophets gets down to the nitty-gritty that every business-person wants to know: "What's it going to cost?" Supported by a dynamic Web site.

2001/softbound/ISBN 0-910965-55-2 $29.95

Super Searchers on Mergers & Acquisitions

The Online Research Secrets of Top
Corporate Researchers and M&A Pros

By Jan Davis Tudor
Edited by Reva Basch

The sixth title in the "Super Searchers" series is a unique resource for business owners, brokers, appraisers, entrepreneurs, and investors who use the Internet and online services to research Mergers & Acquisitions (M&A) opportunities. Leading business valuation researcher Jan Davis Tudor interviews 13 top M&A researchers, who share their secrets for finding, evaluating, and delivering critical deal-making data on companies and industries. Supported by the Super Searchers Web page.

2001/208 pp/softbound/ISBN 0-910965-48-X $24.95

Super Searchers Go to the Source

The Interviewing and Hands-On Information
Strategies of Top Primary Researchers—Online, on
the Phone, and in Person

By Risa Sacks • Edited by Reva Basch

For the most focused, current, in-depth information on any subject, nothing beats going directly to the source—to the experts. This is "Primary Research," and it's the focus of the seventh title in the "Super Searchers" series. From the boardrooms of America's top corporations, to the halls of academia, to the pressroom of *The New York Times*, Risa Sacks interviews 12 of the best primary researchers in the business. These research pros reveal their strategies for integrating online and "offline" resources, identifying experts, and getting past gatekeepers to obtain information that exists only in someone's head. Supported by the Super Searchers Web page.

2001/420 pp/softbound/ISBN 0-910965-53-6 $24.95

Super Searchers on Health & Medicine
The Online Secrets of
Top Health & Medical Researchers

By Susan M. Detwiler
Edited by Reva Basch

With human lives depending on them, skilled medical researchers rank among the best online searchers in the world. In *Super Searchers on Health & Medicine*, medical librarians, clinical researchers, health information specialists, and physicians explain how they combine traditional sources with the best of the Net to deliver just what the doctor ordered. If you use the Internet and online databases to answer important health and medical questions, these Super Searchers will help guide you around the perils and pitfalls to the best sites, sources, and techniques. Supported by the Super Searchers Web page.

2000/208 pp/softbound/ISBN 0-910965-44-7 $24.95

Super Searchers in the News
The Online Secrets of
Journalists and News Researchers

By Paula J. Hane • Edited by Reva Basch

Professional news researchers are a breed apart. The behind-the-scenes heroes of network newsrooms and daily newspapers, they work under intense deadline pressure to meet the insatiable, ever-changing research needs of reporters, editors, and journalists. Here, for the first time, 10 news researchers reveal their strategies for using the Internet and online services to get the scoop, check the facts, and nail the story. If you want to become a more effective online searcher and do fast, accurate research on a wide range of moving-target topics, don't miss *Super Searchers in the News*. Supported by the Super Searchers Web page.

2000/256 pp/softbound/ISBN 0-910965-45-5 $24.95

Super Searchers Cover the World

The Online Secrets of International Business Researchers

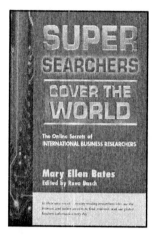

By Mary Ellen Bates
Edited by Reva Basch

The Internet has made it possible for more businesses to think internationally, and to take advantage of the expanding global economy. Through 15 interviews with leading online searchers, Mary Ellen Bates explores the challenges of reaching outside a researcher's geographic area to do effective international business research. Experts from around the world—librarians and researchers from government organizations, multi-national companies, universities, and small businesses—discuss such issues as non-native language sources, cultural biases, and the reliability of information. Supported by the Super Searchers Web page.

2001/320 pp/softbound/ISBN 0-910965-54-4 $24.95

Super Searchers on Wall Street

Top Investment Professionals Share Their Online Research Secrets

By Amelia Kassel • Edited by Reva Basch

Through her probing interviews, Amelia Kassel reveals the online secrets of 10 leading financial industry research experts. You'll learn how information professionals find and analyze market and industry data, as well as how online information is used by broker-ages, stock exchanges, investment banks, and individual investors to make critical invest-ment decisions. The Wall Street Super Searchers direct you to important sites and sources, illuminate the trends that are revolu-tionizing financial research, and help you use online research as a powerful investment strategy. Supported by the Super Searchers Web page.

2000/256 pp/softbound/ISBN 0-910965-42-0 $24.95

Electronic Democracy
Using the Internet to Transform American Politics,
2nd Edition

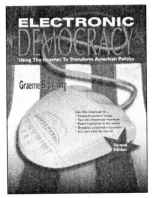

By Graeme Browning
Foreword by Adam Clayton Powell III

In this new edition of *Electronic Democracy*,
award-winning journalist and author Graeme
Browning details the colorful history of politics and the Net, describes the key Web-
based sources of political information, offers
practical techniques for influencing legislation online, and provides a fascinating, realis-
tic vision of the future.

2002/260 pp/softbound/ISBN 0-910965-41-2 $19.95

The Modem Reference
The Complete Guide to PC Communications,
4th Edition

By Michael A. Banks

Now in it's 4th edition, this popular handbook explains the concepts behind computer
data, data encoding, and transmission, providing practical advice for PC users who
want to get the most from their online operations. In his uniquely readable style, author
and techno-guru Mike Banks (*The Internet
Unplugged*) takes readers on a tour of PC
data communications technology, explaining
how modems, fax machines, computer net-
works, and the Internet work. He provides an in-depth look at how
data is communicated between computers all around the world, demys-
tifying the terminology, hardware, and software. *The Modem Reference* is
a must-read for students, professional online users, and all computer
users who want to maximize their PC fax and data communications
capabilities.

2000/306 pp/softbound/ISBN 0-910965-36-6 $29.95

Great Scouts!

CyberGuides for Subject Searching on the Web

By Nora Paul and Margot Williams
Edited by Paula Hane
Foreword by Barbara Quint

Great Scouts! is a cure for information overload. Authors Nora Paul (The Poynter Institute) and Margot Williams (*The Washington Post*) direct readers to the very best subject-specific, Web-based information resources. Thirty chapters cover specialized "CyberGuides" selected as the premier Internet sources of information on business, education, arts and entertainment, science and technology, health and medicine, politics and government, law, sports, and much more. With its expert advice and evaluations of information and link content, value, currency, stability, and usability, *Great Scouts!* takes you "beyond search engines"—and directly to the top sources of information for your topic. As a reader bonus, a Web page features links to all the sites covered in the book.

1999/320 pp/softbound/ISBN 0-910965-27-7 $24.95

Design Wise

A Guide for Evaluating the Interface Design of Information Resources

Design Wise *takes us beyond what's cool and what's hot and shows us what works and what doesn't.*

—Elizabeth Osder,
The New York Times on the Web

By Alison J. Head

Knowing how to size up user-centered interface design is becoming as important for people who choose and use information resources as for those who design them. This book introduces readers to the basics of interface design and explains why a design evaluation should be tied to the use and purchase of information resources.

1999/224 pp/softbound/ISBN 0-910965-31-5 $29.95
1999/224 pp/hardbound/ISBN 0-910965-39-0 $39.95

Internet Business Intelligence

How to Build a Big Company System
on a Small Company Budget

By David Vine

According to author David Vine, business success in the competitive, global marketplace of the 21st century will depend on a firm's ability to use information effectively—and the most successful firms will be those that harness the Internet to create and maintain a powerful information edge. In *Internet Business Intelligence*, Vine explains how any company can build a complete, low-cost, Internet-based business intelligence system that really works. If you're fed up with Internet hype and wondering "Where's the beef?," you'll appreciate this savvy, no-nonsense approach to using the Internet to solve everyday business problems and stay one step ahead of the competition.

2000/448 pp/softbound/ISBN 0-910965-35-8 $29.95

net.people

The Personalities and Passions
Behind the Web Sites

By Eric C. Steinert and Thomas E. Bleier

With the explosive growth of the Internet, people everywhere are bringing their dreams and schemes to life as Web sites. In *net.people*, get up close and personal with the creators of 36 of the world's most intriguing online ventures. For the first time, these entrepreneurs and visionaries share their personal stories and hard-won secrets of Webmastering. You'll learn how each of them launched a home page, increased site traffic, geared up for e-commerce, found financing, dealt with failure and success, built new relationships—and discovered that a Web site had changed their life forever.

2000/317 pp/softbound/ISBN 0-910965-37-4 $19.95

The Quintessential Searcher
The Wit and Wisdom of Barbara Quint

Edited by Marylaine Block

Searcher Magazine editor Barbara Quint (bq) is not only one of the world's most famous online searchers, but the most creative and controversial writer, editor, and speaker to emerge from the information industry in the last two decades. bq is a guru of librarians and database professionals the world over, and, as her readers, publishers, and "quarry" know, when it comes to barbed wit she is in a class by herself. Whether she's chastising database providers about unacceptable fees, interfaces, and updates; recounting the ills visited on the world by computer makers; or inspiring her readers to achieve greatness; her voice is consistently original and compelling. In this book, for the first time anywhere, hundreds of bq's most memorable, insightful, and politically incorrect quotations have been gathered for the enjoyment of her many fans.

2001/232 pp/softbound ISBN 1-57387-114-1 $19.95

Internet Blue Pages
The Guide to Federal Government Web Sites, 2001-2002 Edition

Edited by Laurie Andriot

Internet Blue Pages (IBP) is the leading guide to federal government information on the Web. *IBP 2001-2002* includes over 1,800 annotated agency listings, arranged in U.S. Government Manual style to help you find the information you need. Entries include agency name and URL, function or purpose of selected agencies, and links from agency home pages. With double the coverage of the previous edition, *IBP* now includes federal courts, military libraries, Department of Energy libraries, Federal Reserve banks, presidential libraries, national parks, and Social Security offices. A companion Web site features regularly updated agency links.

2000/464 pp/softbound/ISBN 0-910965-43-9 $34.95

Creating Web-Accessible Databases

Case Studies for Libraries, Museums,
and Other Non-Profits

Edited by Julie M. Still

Libraries, museums, and other not-for-profit institutions are increasingly looking for (and finding) ways to offer patrons and the public Web access to their collections. This new book from Julie Still and her expert contributors explores the unique challenges non-profit archival institutions face in leveraging the Internet and presents a dozen case studies showcasing a variety of successful projects and approaches.

**2001/200 pp/hardbound/ISBN 1-57387-104-4
$39.50**

Naked in Cyberspace

How to Find Personal Information Online

By Carole A. Lane

Now that so many types of personal records are searchable online, the bureaucratic red tape that used to protect our secrets from prying eyes has been stripped away ... and we're all naked in cyberspace. Without taking sides on the right and wrong of using online ingredients to compile a detailed dossier, *Naked in Cyberspace* tells you where to find personal information online.

**1997/544 pp/softbound/ISBN 0-910965-17-X
$29.95**